SYSTEM SOFTWARE

:: AN INTRODUCTION TO SYSTEMS PROGRAMMING ::

SYSTEM SOFTWARE

:: AN INTRODUCTION TO SYSTEMS PROGRAMMING ::

DR. IKVINDERPAL SINGH

KHANNA BOOK PUBLISHING CO. (P) LTD.
Publisher of Science, Technology and Engineering Books
4C/4344, Ansari Road, Darya Ganj, New Delhi-110002
Phone: 011-23244447-48 **Mobile:** +91-99109 09320
E-mail: contact@khannabooks.com, sales@khannapublishers.com
Website: www.khannabooks.com, www.khannapublishers.com

SYSTEM SOFTWARE

Dr. Ikvinderpal Singh

ISBN: 978-93-81068-71-7

First Edition: 2013

Reprint 2015

Published by:

KHANNA BOOK PUBLISHING CO. (P) LTD.

Head Off.: 4C/4344, Ansari Road, Darya Ganj, New Delhi-110 002

Phone: 011-23244447-48 **Fax:** 011-23244447

E-mail: contact@khannabooks.com

Website: www.khannabooks.com

Printed in India by:

India Book Printers & Binders, Delhi

Dedicated to

MY PARENTS

Preface

Welcome to the world of System Software. System Software designers and system programmers will find the text useful as a reference as well. A course on System Software is an essential part of any computer-science education. This field is undergoing rapid change, as computers are now prevalent in virtually every application, from games for children through the most sophisticated planning tools for governments and multinational firms. This book aims to present a balanced treatment of both the academic and industry sides of System Software theory and practice. It presents the fundamental concepts and basic design of each type of software in a machine-independent way. Our goal is to apprise the reader of both the beneficial and challenging aspects of System Software. The material in this book is organized in 8 chapters, as follows.

Chapter 1 is a survey of the field of machine structure at an introductory level. We first study the evolution of System Software and then the detailed study of components of System Software. It also explains the concept of language processing.

Chapter 2 covers the programming languages and language processors.

Chapter 3 describes the Assembler: Overview of assembler process, design of one pass and two pass assembler. It also explains the design of single pass assembler for IBM PC.

Chapter 4 discusses the Macro Processors: Macro definition and expansion, Concatenation of macro parameters, Generations of unique labels, Conditional macro expansion, Recursive macro expansion, and design of Macro Processors.

Chapter 5 covers the compilers: Phases of compilation process, Lexical analysis, Parsing, Storage management optimization, Incremental compilers, Cross compilers, P code compilers.

Chapter 6 navigates through the loaders and linkers: Basic loader functions, Relocation, Program linking, Linkage editors, dynamic linking, and Bootstrap loaders.

Chapter 7 is about operating systems: different tasks of an operating systems like process management, file management, memory management, I/O and device management etc.

Chapter 8 illustrates the system software tools: DBMS, text editor and interactive debugging systems.

This book is intended for students in computer engineering, computer science, and electrical engineering. The material covered in the book is suitable for a one semester course on "System Software" and a one semester course on "System Programming." Most of the material used in the book has been used in our undergraduate and postgraduate classes. In what follows, we provide a chapter-by-chapter review of the material covered in the book. In doing so, we aim at providing course instructors, students, and practicing engineers/scientists with enough information that can help them select the appropriate chapter or sequences of chapters to cover/review.

We welcome comments from all readers to improve this book as a useful guide for the community of engineers and technologists who will become knowledgeable about the potential of System Software for their use in solving the problems that challenge us each day.

DR. IKVINDERPAL SINGH

Contents

Chapter

1

Introduction

1.1 INTRODUCTION

At a top level, a computer consists of processor, memory, and I/O components, with one or more modules of each type. These components are interconnected in some fashion to achieve the main function of the computer, which is to execute programs. Thus, there are four main structural elements:

- **Processor:** Controls the operation of the computer and performs its data processing functions. When there is only one processor, it is often referred to as the **central processing unit** (CPU).
- **Main memory:** Stores data and programs. This memory is typically volatile; that is, when the computer is shut down, the contents of the memory are lost. In contrast, the contents of disk memory are retained even when the computer system is shut down. Main memory is also referred to as real memory or primary memory.
- **I/O modules:** Move data between the computer and its external environment. The external environment consists of a variety of devices, including secondary memory devices (e. g., disks), communications equipment, and terminals.
- **System bus:** Provides for communication among processors, main memory, and I/O modules.

Figure 1.1 depicts these top-

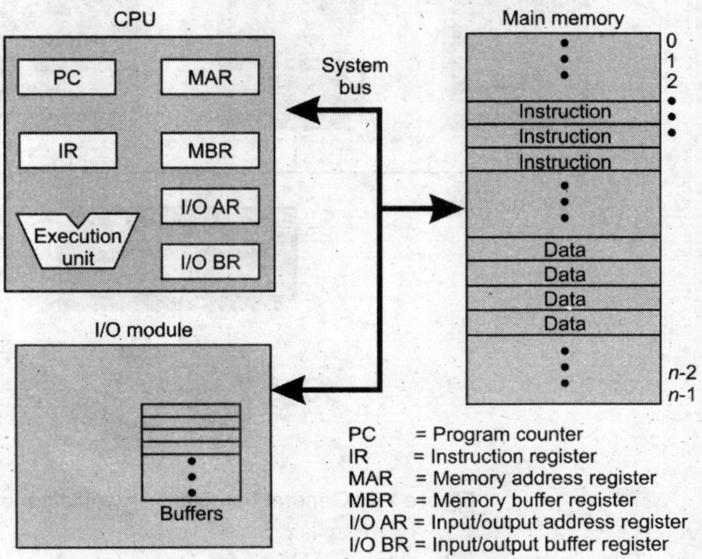

Figure 1.1: Computer Components Top-Level View

level components. One of the processor's functions is to exchange data with memory. For this purpose, it typically makes use of two internal (to the processor) registers: a memory address register (MAR), which specifies the address in memory for the next read or write; and a memory buffer register (MBR), which contains the data to be written into memory or which receives the data read from memory. Similarly, an I/O address register (I/OAR) specifies a particular I/O device. An I/O buffer register (I/OBR) is used for the exchange of data between an I/O module and the processor.

A memory module consists of a set of locations, defined by sequentially numbered addresses. Each location contains a bit pattern that can be interpreted as either an instruction or data. An I/O module transfers data from external devices to processor and memory, and vice versa. It contains internal buffers for temporarily holding data until they can be sent on.

1.2 MACHINE STRUCTURE

A modern general-purpose computer system consists of one or more CPUs and a number of device controllers connected through a common bus that provides access to shared memory (Figure 1.2). Each device controller is in charge of a specific type of device (for example, disk drives, audio devices, and video displays). The CPU and the device controllers can execute concurrently, competing for memory cycles. To ensure orderly access to the shared memory, a memory controller is provided whose function is to synchronize access to the memory.

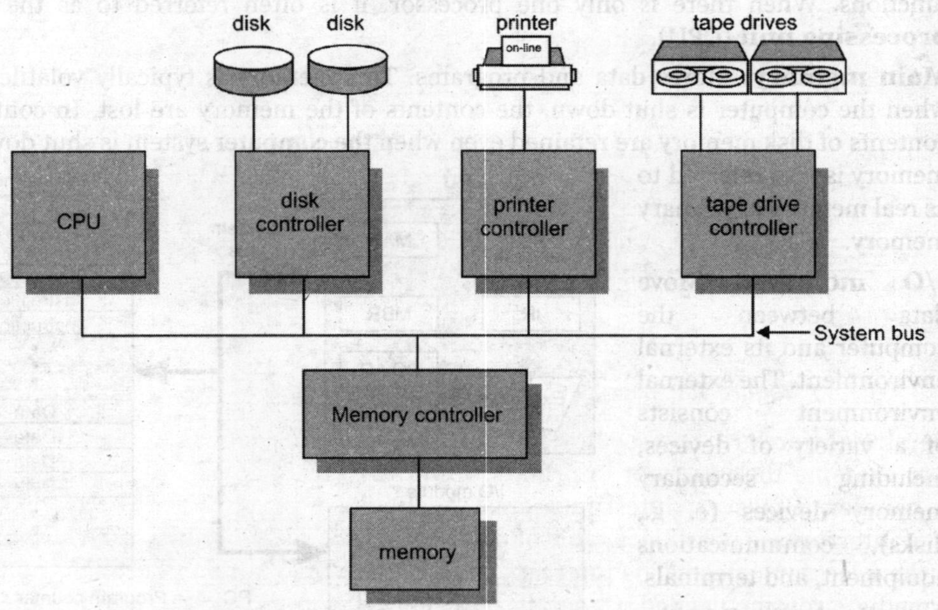

Figure 1.2: General hardware organization of a computer system

For a computer to start running—for instance, when it is powered up or rebooted—it needs to have an initial program to run. This initial program, or bootstrap program, tends to be simple.

Typically, it is stored in read-only memory (ROM) or electrically erasable programmable read-only memory (EEPROM), known by the general term firmware, within the computer hardware. It initializes all aspects of the system, from CPU registers to device controllers to memory contents. The bootstrap program must know how to load the operating system and to start executing that system. To accomplish this goal, the bootstrap program must locate and load into memory the operating- system kernel. The operating system then starts executing the first process, such as and waits for some event to occur.

The occurrence of an event is usually signaled b y an interrupt from either the hardware or the software. Hardware may trigger an interrupt at any time by sending a signal to the CPU, usually by way of the system bus. Software may trigger an interrupt by executing a special operation called a system call (also called a monitor call).

When the CPU is interrupted, it stops what it is doing and immediately transfers execution to a fixed location. The fixed location usually contains the starting address where the service routine for the interrupt is located. The interrupt service routine executes; on completion, the CPU resumes the interrupted computation. A time line of this operation is shown in Figure 1.3. Interrupts are an important part of computer architecture. Each computer design has its own interrupt mechanism, but several functions are common. The interrupt must transfer control to the appropriate interrupt service routine.

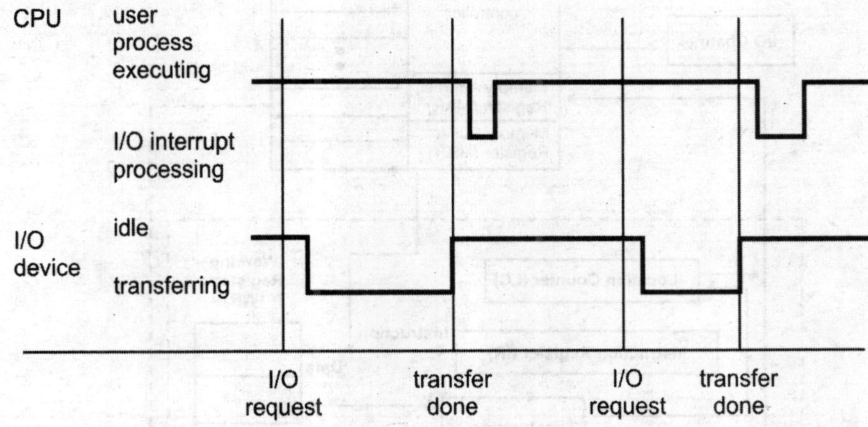

Figure 1.3: Interrupt time line for a single process doing output.

The straightforward method for handling this transfer would be to invoke a generic routine to examine the interrupt information; the routine, in turn, would call the interrupt-specific handler. However, interrupts must be handled quickly. Since only a predefined number of interrupts is possible, a table of pointers to interrupt routines can be used instead to provide the necessary speed. The interrupt routine is called indirectly through the table, with no intermediate routine needed. Generally, the table of pointers is stored in low memory (the first 100 or so locations). These locations hold the addresses of the interrupt service routines for the various devices. This array, or interrupt vector, of addresses is then indexed by a unique device number, given with the interrupt request, to provide the address of the interrupt service routine for the interrupting device. Operating systems as different as Windows and UNIX dispatch interrupts in this manner.

The interrupt architecture must also save the address of the interrupted instruction. Many old designs simply stored the interrupt address in a fixed location or in a location indexed by the device number. More recent architectures store the return address on the system stack. If the interrupt routine needs to modify the processor state—for instance, by modifying register values—it must explicitly save the current state and then restore that state before returning. After the interrupt is serviced, the saved return address is loaded into the program counter, and the interrupted computation resumes as though the interrupt had not occurred.

1.3 SIC (SIMPLIFIED INSTRUCTIONAL COMPUTER)

All the conventional modern computers are based upon the model proposed by the mathematician John von Neumann. This machine has been designed to illustrate the most commonly encountered hardware features and concepts, while avoiding most of the complex details. The following figure 1.4 shows the architecture of such a typical von Neumann machine:

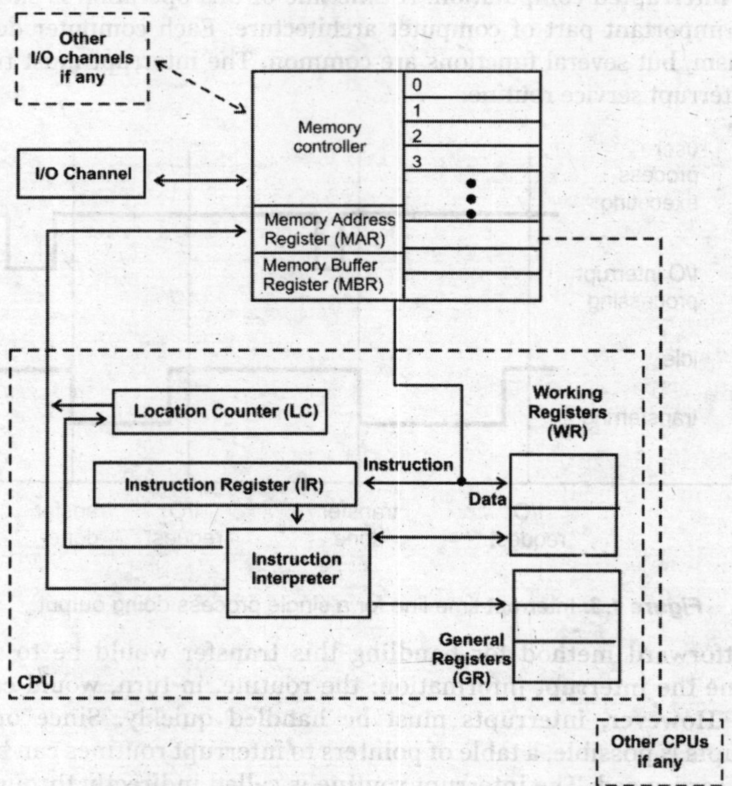

Figure 1.4: General Machine Structure

The CPU consists of an Instruction Interpreter, Instruction Register, and various other working registers. Instruction Interpreter is a hardware device that performs all the work intended by the instructions under scan. The Location Counter (LC) is the hardware device that stores the address of the instruction currently being executed. The instruction is also copied in the Instruction Register (IR). Working registers are used by IR while the general registers are used by the programmers as storage locations.

The CPU and memory communicate via Memory Address Register (MAR) and Memory Buffer Register (MBR). MAR contains the address of memory location that is to be read from or stored into. The MBR contains a copy of the contents of the memory location specified by MAR before a write or after a read operation is performed. Hence all the data between memory and CPU moves to and fro through the MBR only. The memory controller controls this transfer from a memory location to MBR and vice versa. The I/O channels are the special hardware that that execute special instructions for input and output from memory.

The general computer that we use has four registers, designated 00, 01, 10, and 11 in binary notation. The format for a basic instruction is as follows:

Operation Code	Register Number	Memory Location (addr)

Figure 1.5: Instruction Format

For example,

ADD 3, 200

This instruction would cause the data stored in memory location 200 to be added to the contents of the memory register 3. The resulting sum will reside as the new contents of the register. The following flowchart explains the sequence of hardware operations that are performed by an Instruction Interpreter to execute an instruction:

Although the specific details may vary from computer to computer, this basic flowchart remains the same for all conventional machines. SIC comes in the following two versions:

(i) the standard model

(ii) an XE version (extra equipment)

The two versions are designed to be upward compatible which means that an object program designed for the standard SIC machine will also execute properly on SIC/XE machine. The next two sections summarize the basic features of SIC and SIC/XE.

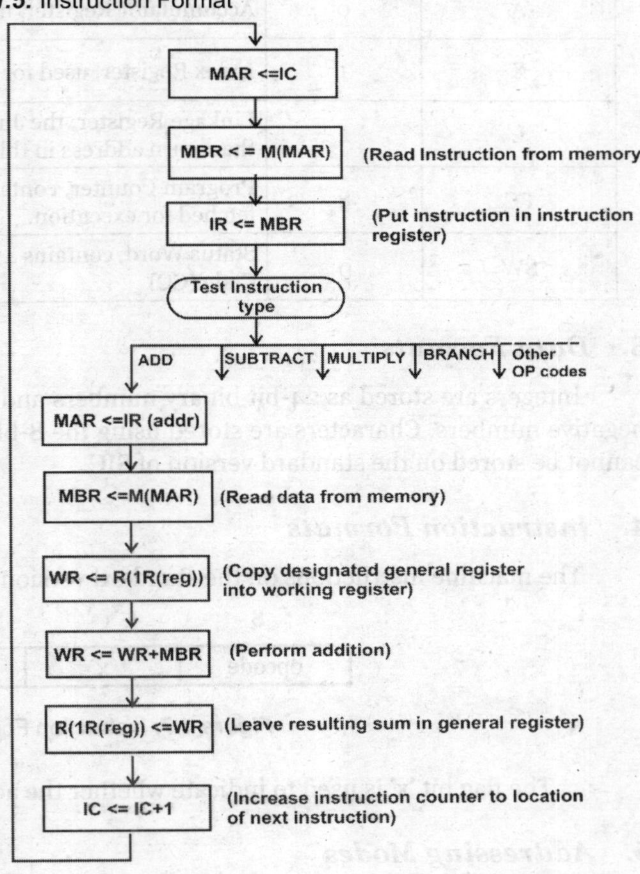

Figure 1.6: Example micro flowchart for an ADD operation

1.3.1 SIC MACHINE ARCHITECTURE

Following are the components of SIC machine architecture:

1. ***Memory***

The memory consists of 8-bit bytes, of which any 3 consecutive bytes can be accessed as a word (24 bits). All SIC addresses are byte addresses, while the words are addressed by the location of the lowest numbered byte. There are total of 32,768 (2^{15}) bytes in the computer memory.

2. ***Registers***

There are five registers, all of which have special use. Each register is 24 bits in length. The following table indicates the numbers, mnemonics, and uses of each of these registers

Mnemonic	Number	Use
A	0	Accumulator Register, used for arithmetic operations.
X	1	Index Register, used for addressing.
L	2	Linkage Register, the Jump to Subroutine (JSUB) instruction stores the return address in this register.
PC	8	Program Counter, contains the address of the next instruction to be fetched for execution.
SW	9	Status Word, contains a variety of information including a Condition Code (CC)

3. ***Data Formats***

Integers are stored as 24-bit binary numbers and 2's complement representation is used for negative numbers. Characters are stored using the 8-bit ASCII codes. The floating point numbers cannot be stored on the standard version of SIC.

4. ***Instruction Formats***

The machine instructions on the standard version of SIC have the following 24-bit format:

8	1	15
opcode	x	address

Figure 1.7: Instruction Format on SIC

The flag bit 'x' is used to indicate whether the address is a direct or an indirect address.

5. ***Addressing Modes***

There are two basic addressing modes available in SIC, which is indicated by the setting of the 'x' bit in the instruction. The following table describes how the target address is calculated from the address given in the instruction. Parenthesis is used to indicate the contents of a register or a memory location. For example (X) represents the contents of the contents of register X.

Mode	Indication	Target address calculation
Direct	x=0	TA=address
Indirect	x=1	TA=address + (X)

6. *Instruction Set*

SIC provides almost all basic set of instruction which are sufficient for performing the most simple tasks. These include instructions that load and store registers (LDA, LDX, STA, STX, etc.), as well as integer arithmetic operations (ADD, SUB, MUL, DIV). All arithmetic operations involve the register A and a word from memory, with the result being stored in the register after the operation. There is an instruction (COMP) that compares the value in register A with a memory word, and sets a condition code (CC) to indicate the result (<, =, or >). Conditional jump instructions (JLT, JEQ, JGT) can test the setting of CC, and jump accordingly. Two other instructions are provided for linking of subroutines. JSUB jumps to the subroutine, placing the return address in register L, while RSUB returns by jumping to the address contained in register L.

7. *Input and Output*

On the standard version of SIC, input and output are performed by transferring 1 byte at a time to or from the rightmost 8 bits of the register A. Each device is assigned a unique 8-bit code. There are three I/O instructions, each of which specifies the device code as an operand.

The Test Device (TD) instruction tests whether the addressed device is ready to send or receive the bytes of data. The condition code is set to indicate the result of this test. A program needing to transfer data must wait until the device is ready, and then execute a Read Data (RD) or Write Data (WD) instruction. The same sequence must be repeated for each byte of data to be read or written.

1.3.2 SIC/XE MACHINE ARCHITECTURE

Following are the components of SIC/XE machine architecture:

1. *Memory*

The memory structure for SIC/XE is same as that for SIC. Just the maximum memory available on a SIC/XE machine is 1 megabyte (2^{20} bytes). This increase leads to a change in instruction formats as well as addressing modes.

2. *Registers*

The same register set is available for SIC/XE as in SIC machine. Along with the following additional registers:

Mnemonic	Number	Use
B	3	Base Register, used for addressing.
S	4	General working register.
T	5	General working register.
F	6	Floating point accumulator.

3. *Data Formats*

SIC/XE provides the same data formats as are available in standard SIC version. In addition, there is a 48-bit floating point data type which has the following format:

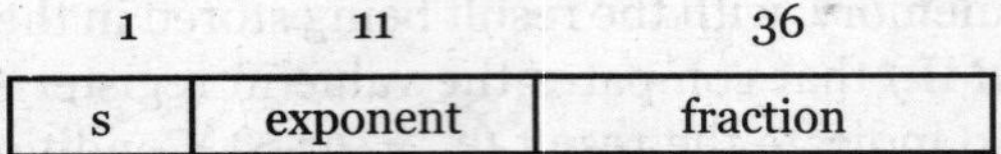

Figure 1.8: Floating-point Data Type

The fraction is interpreted as a value between 0 and 1 and the assumed binary point is immediately before the high order bit. The normalized floating point numbers have the high order bit of the fraction as 1. The exponent is interpreted as an unsigned binary number between 0 and 2047. If the exponent has the value e and the fraction has the value f, the absolute value of the number represented is as follows:

$$f*2^{(e-1024)}$$

The sign of the floating point number is indicated by the value of 's' which is 0 for positive and 1 for negative.

4. *Instruction Formats*

As the larger memory is available on SIC/XE machine, hence the addresses will no longer fit into a 15-bit field. Hence the instruction format used on the standard SIC version is no longer used. There are two options for addressing on SIC/XE machine: either use some form of relative addressing, or extend the address field to 20-bits. Both these options are included in SIC/XE machine as Format 3 and Format 4. In addition, SIC/XE also uses some instructions that do not reference the memory at all. These instructions are known as Format 1 and Format 2 instructions.

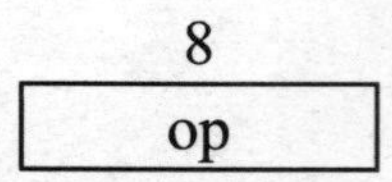

Figure 1.9: Format 1 (1 byte)

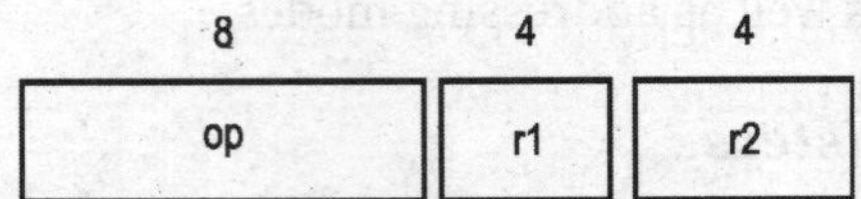

Figure 1.10: Format 2 (2 bytes)

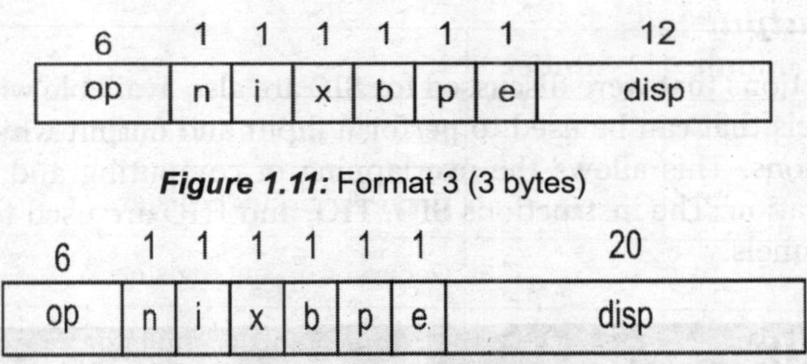

Figure 1.11: Format 3 (3 bytes)

Figure 1.12: Format 4 (4 bytes)

5. *Addressing Modes*

There are two new relative addressing modes that are available for use with instructions assembled using Format 3. They are described in the following table:

Mode	Indication	Target address calculation
Base relative	b=1, p=0	TA = (B) + disp
Program-counter relative	b=0, p=1	TA = (PC) + disp

For base relative addressing, the displacement field is interpreted as a 12-bit unsigned integer, while for program-counter relative addressing, this field is interpreted as a 12-bit signed integer, with negative values represented as 2's complement.

Any of these addressing schemes can be combined with indexed addressing- if bit 'x' is set to 1, the term (X) is added in the target address calculation.

If both b and p bits are set to 0, the disp field from Format 3 instruction is used as the target address. For a Format 4 instruction, bits b and p are mostly set to 0, and the address is used from the address field of the instruction.

Bits i and n in Formats 3 and 4 are used to specify how the target address is used. If bit i=1 and n=0, the target address itself is used as the operand value and no memory reference is performed. This is called immediate addressing. If bit i=0 and n=1, the word given at the location specified by the target address is fetched, the value contained in this word is then taken as the address of the actual operand value. This is called indirect addressing. If bits i and n are both set to 0 or both 1, the target address is taken as the location of the operand.

6. *Instruction Set*

SIC/XE provides all the instructions that are available on the standard version. In addition, there are instructions to load and store the new registers (LDB, STB, etc.) and to perform floating-point arithmetic operations (ADDF, SUBF, MULF, DIVF). There are also instructions that take operands from registers. Besides the register move (RMO) instruction, these include register-to-register arithmetic operations (ADDR, SUBR, MULR, DIVR). A special supervisor call (SVC) is also provided to generate an interrupt that can be used for communication with the operating system.

7. *Input and Output*

The I/O instructions that were discussed for SIC are also available with SIC/XE. In addition, there are I/O channels that can be used to perform input and output while the CPU is executing some other instructions. This allows the overlapping of computing and I/O, resulting in more efficient system operation. The instructions SIO, TIO, and HIO are used to start test and halt the operation of I/O channels.

1.4 SOFTWARE

Software is the language of a computer. And like human language, there are many different computer languages. Software is a general term for the various kinds of programs used to operate computers and related devices. (The term hardware describes the physical aspects of computers and related devices.) Software can be thought of as the variable part of a computer and hardware the invariable part. Software is often divided into application software (programs that do work users are directly interested in) and system software (which includes operating systems and any program that supports application software). The term middleware is sometimes used to describe programming that mediates between application and system software or between two different kinds of application software (for example, sending a remote work request from an application in a computer that has one kind of operating system to an application in a computer with a different operating system).

An additional and difficult-to-classify category of software is the utility, which is a small useful program with limited capability. Some utilities come with operating systems. Like applications, utilities tend to be separately installable and capable of being used independently from the rest of the operating system.

1.4.1 COMPUTER SOFTWARES

Computer software, or just **software**, is the collection of computer programs and related data that provide the instructions telling a computer what to do and how to do it. We can also say software refers to one or more computer programs and data held in the storage of the computer for some purposes. Program software performs the function of the program it implements, either by directly providing instructions to the computer hardware or by serving as input to another piece of software. The term was coined to contrast to the old term hardware (meaning physical devices).

"Computer software is defined as a set of programs and procedures that are intended to perform some tasks on a computer system. A software program is a set of instructions that are aimed at changing the state of computer hardware. At the lowest level software is in a form of an assembly language, a set of instructions in a machine-understandable form. At the highest level, software is in a form of high-level languages, which are compiled or interpreted into machine language code."

In contrast to hardware, software is intangible, meaning it "cannot be touched". Software is also sometimes used in a more narrow sense, meaning application software only. Sometimes the term includes data that has not traditionally been associated with computers, such as film, tapes, and records.

The seven layers of software are (top to bottom): Programs; System Utilities; Command Shell;

System Services; User Interface; Logical Level; and Hardware Level. A Graphics Engine straddles the bottom three layers. Strictly speaking, only the bottom two levels are the operating system, although even technical persons will often refer to any level other than programs as part of the operating system (and Microsoft tried to convince the Justice Department that their web browser application is actually a part of their operating system). Because this technical analysis concentrates on servers, Internet Facilities are specifically separated out from the layers.

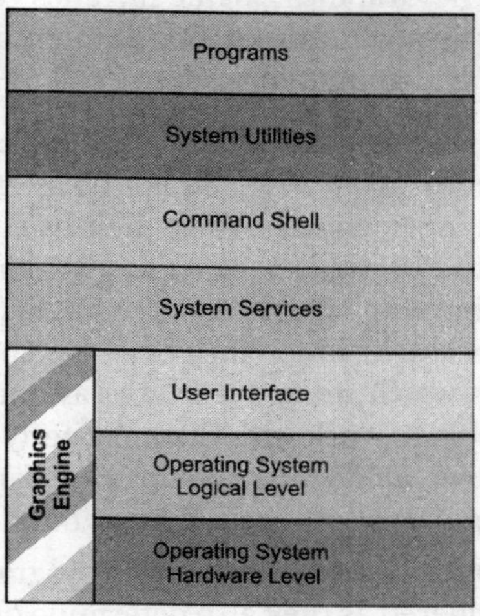

Examples

The following are examples of each category:

1. **Programs:** Examples of Programs include your word processor, spreadsheet, graphics programs, music software, games, etc.
2. **System Utilities:** Examples of System Utilities include file copy, hard drive repair, and similar items. On the Macintosh, all the Desk Accessories (calculator, key caps, etc.) and all of the Control Panels are examples of System Utilities.
3. **Command Shell:** The Command Shell on the Macintosh is the Finder and was the first commercially available graphic command shell. On Windows, the Command Shell is a poorly integrated combination of the File Manager and the Program Manager. The command line (C:\ prompt) of MS-DOS or Bourne Shell of UNIX is examples of the older style text-based command shells.
4. **System Services:** Examples of System Services are built-in data base query languages on mainframes or the QuickTime media layer of the Macintosh.
5. **User Interface:** Until the Macintosh introduced Alan Kay's (inventer of the personal computer, graphic user interfaces, object oriented programming, and software agents) ground breaking ideas on human-computer interfaces, operating systems didn't include support for user interfaces (other than simple text-based shells). The Macintosh user interface is called the Macintosh ToolBox and provides the windows, menus, alert boxes, dialog boxes, scroll bars, buttons, controls, and other user interface elements shared by almost all programs.

6. **Logical Level of Operating System:** The Logical Level of the operating system provides high level functions, such as file management, internet and networking facilities, etc.
7. **Hardware Level of Operating System:** The Hardware Level of the operating system controls the use of physical system resources, such as the memory manager, process manager, disk drivers, etc.
8. **Graphics Engine:** The Graphics Engine includes elements at all three of the lowest levels, from physically displaying things on the monitor to providing high level graphics routines such as fonts and animated sprites.

Computers are fundamental in the world in which we live as without them numerous things could not be possibly done and in this way we could not be as effective and productive as we are in certain situations and activities in which we involve their use. As every computer includes both a hardware and a software part it is important for us to also consider them both when trying to understand very well the way in which our computers function by understanding the importance of each of their components and the way in which they operate. The hardware part of the computer deals with all sorts of components which we notice every day and which are very important to be very familiar to us in order to be able to work with them properly and to realize when they need to be improved and the way in which we can do this. The software part on the other hand does not deal with such components and it is not that easily noticed by us but it is also very important.

The software part of the computer deals with all sorts of programs, applications and instructions which are also essential to be considered as they also determine our computer to function properly and can also be improved in the idea of improving the way in which we work with our computers and the quality of the results being displayed for us after all sorts of instructions might have been operated by the computer system. In this way, it might also be very useful for some computer users trying to learn the basic notions related to their computers and not only for them to be mentioned the **types of computer software** available for us to work with nowadays.

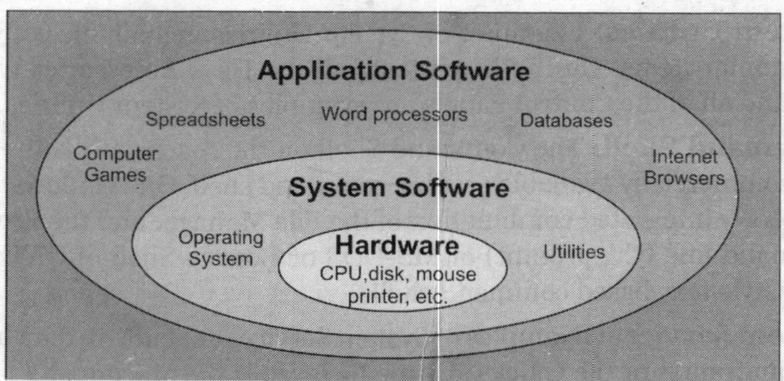

Figure 1.13: Types of Computer Software

In this respect, it can be mentioned the fact that there are three main **types of computer software**. These three **types of computer software** are the system software, the programming type of software and the application software. The system **type of computer software** refers to all sorts of device drivers, operating systems installed on our computers, utilities used in this respect, servers which are useful for us and windowing types of systems that we might decide to work with. When discussing about the programming **type of computer software** it is important to be mentioned that it deals with all sorts of tools that all computer users dealing with creating all sorts of computer programs work with. Such tools have been considered all sorts of compilers, text editors, interpreters and other similar ones. In this category of software have also been included tools such as all sorts of debuggers and linkers which might enable such programmers with their work. The third category of **computer software** which is as important as the other two **types of** software includes all sorts of applications such as video games which computer users can decide to play, databases, image editing and simulation type of software as well as numerous others **types of computer software**.

All of these three **types of computer software** are very important for us to become familiar with as we all need to benefit from using them nowadays and the best way in which we can do this is by getting a good understanding of the way in which they really function and enable us to be effective and productive in the activities in which we involve their use.

1.5 RELATIONSHIP BETWEEN HARDWARE AND SOFTWARE

Hardware in a computer system refers to the physical equipment that are directly involved in the performance of data-processing or communications functions, such as the central processing unit, peripheral devices, and memory. Software is the code and instructions that control the functioning of the hardware and direct its operation, such as Microsoft Windows and Internet browser. Without one the other would not exist.

Both hardware and software are integral components of all digital electronic devices like computers, cellular systems, satellite systems etc. These computer related terms work in a combination to make computers function. The components of computer that have physical existence and touchable are hardware while software are those programs that run on hardware. No doubt, both components have their individual identity and function-ability, but it is the fact that without any component other is useless. Therefore, to make a system operational, it is very necessary that both hardware and software support each other to run a program.

1.6 TYPES OF COMPUTER SOFTWARES

Software is only a eight letter word. Still you could talk about it for ages and you could find so much information about this vast topic that you couldn't possibly read all of it even if you spent years doing only that. There is some kind of software for almost anything in this world involving computer use.

You can find a special software to help you calculate your taxes, draw the floor plans for your future home, design your baby's clothes, operate your computer, watch movies, edit photos and what not? But all these tones of examples of software must be gathered and divided into major groups according to their main features and purposes because we don't live in a chaotic world, after all.

Well, people argue about this classification, too. Some people say there are two **major types of software** (operating systems and applications), others that there are three (system software, programming software and application software) and finally some others think there are more of them which I will enumerate later on.

1.7 SYSTEM SOFTWARE

System software helps run the computer hardware and computer system. System software is responsible for controlling, integrating, and managing the individual hardware components of a computer system so that other software and the users of the system see it as a functional unit without having to be concerned with the low-level details such as transferring data from memory to disk, or rendering text onto a display. Generally, system software consists of an operating system and some fundamental utilities such as disk formatters, file managers, display managers, text editors, user authentication (login) and management tools, and networking and device control software. System software provides the basic functions for computer usage and helps run the computer hardware and system. The examples of system software are:

- Operating systems.
- Utility programs.
- Device Drivers.
- Language Processors.

System software is responsible for managing a variety of independent hardware components, so that they can work together harmoniously. Its purpose is to unburden the application software programmer from the often complex details of the particular computer being used, including such accessories as communications devices, printers, device readers, displays and keyboards, and also to partition the computer's resources such as memory and processor time in a safe and stable manner.

1.7.1 TYPES OF PROGRAMS IN SYSTEM SOFTWARE

System software is a program that manages and supports the computer resources and operations of a computer system while it executes various tasks such as processing data and information, controlling hardware components, and allowing users to use application software. That is, systems software functions as a *bridge* between computer system hardware and the application software. System software is made up of many control programs, including the operating system, communications software and database manager. There are many kinds of computers these days. Some of them are easier to learn than others. Some of them perform better than others. These differences may come from different systems software.

1.7.1.1 THREE TYPES OF PROGRAMS

Systems software consists of three types of programs. The system management programs, system support programs, and system development programs are they. These are explained briefly.

1. System Management Programs

These are programs that manage the application software, computer hardware, and data resources of the computer system. These programs include operating systems, operating environment programs, database management programs, and telecommunications monitor programs. Among these, the most important system management programs are operating systems. The operating systems are needed to study more details. There are two reasons. First, users need to know their functions first. For the second, there are many kinds of operating systems available today.

Telecommunications monitor programs are additions of the operating systems of microcomputers. These programs provide the extra logic for the computer system to control a class of communications devices.

2. System Support Programs

These are the programs that help the operations and management of a computer system. They provide a variety of support services to let the computer hardware and other system programs run efficiently. The major system support programs are system utility programs, system performance monitor programs, and system security monitor programs (virus checking programs).

3. System Development Programs

These are programs that help users develop information system programs and prepare user programs for computer processing. These programs may analyze and design systems and program itself. The main system development programs are programming language translators, programming environment programs, computer-aided software engineering packages.

1.7.2 OBJECTIVES OF SYSTEM SOFTWARE

System software includes general programs written for a computer. It consists of pre-written programs and documentation supplied by the manufacturer along with the computer. These programs are held permanently in the machine. The primary objectives of this software are to:

(i) Enhance the efficiency of hardware utilization, and
(ii) Make computers simple to use.

The first objective is realized by that component of system software which is commonly known as operating system. System Software is a set of instruction to the machine to interpret and execute application software, for example, language translators (called compilers and interpreters), operating systems, utilities and special purpose software.

1.7.3 EVOLUTION OF SYSTEM SOFTWARE

One may think of a computer as a monster that obeys all commands. But as we get near to the technology, we come to know that they are basically machines that follow the very specific instructions in a very basic manner.

In the early days of computer technology, people had to communicate with the machine with the use of on/off switches which sent the primitive signals of 0's and 1's. As the time advanced, people wanted an interactive way for communication. For example, the instructions such as 'if a>b then print a else print b'. Present day computers need the help of system programs or system software (compilers, loaders, linkers, macro processors, operating systems) to understand such instructions.

Compilers are programs that accept people like languages and translate them into the actual machine language (0's and 1's) that is executed by the system. Loaders are system programs that prepare machine language programs for execution. Macro processors allow the use of abbreviations in the programs. While operating systems and file systems allow for flexible storage and retrieval of information.

System software consists of a variety of programs that support the operation of the computer. They allow the user to focus on an application or problem to be solved without the need to know the details of how the machine works internally. The main difference between system software and application software is machine dependency. An application program is mainly concerned with the solution of some problem, using computer as a tool. The main focus is on the development of the application, not on the computing system. System programs, on the other hand, are supposed to support the operation and use of the computer system itself, rather than any particular application. Hence they are related to the architecture of the machine on which they run.

For example, assemblers have to translate assembly language instructions into machine language, where the instruction formats, addressing modes, etc. are directly related with the computer architecture. Compilers must also generate machine language code only after taking into account the hardware characteristics of computer system. Operating systems are also directly concerned with the management of all the resources of the computer system.

On the other hand, in some aspects system software is not directly dependent upon the type of computer system being supported. For example, the general design and logic behind the working of the assembler is same on most computers. Similarly code optimization techniques followed by compilers are independent of the machine in use. The process of linking the assembled programs also does not depend upon the machine either. Hence a system program can be views as having some machine dependent features while some of the features are machine independent.

But because most system software is machine dependent, real machines should be included in the study of system programming. However, most real computers have certain characteristics that are unusual and unique; it can be quite difficult to distinguish between the fundamental and dependent features of a particular machine. To avoid this problem, the fundamental pieces of software are presented in the form of a Simplified Instructional Computer (SIC) SIC is a hypothetical computer that is carefully designed to include hardware features mostly found on real machines, leaving the unusual and irrelevant complexities. The approach provides the user with a starting point to begin the study of design of system software for a new unfamiliar computer. In this way, the central concepts of system software can be separated from the important details that are concerned with a particular machine.

Here first we go into the details of the need for development of system software, and then we present the basic architecture of our Simplified Instructional Computer (SIC). Further the various components of system software are discussed in detail. The following chapters will be giving a more detailed analysis of the above mentioned system programs.

1.7.4 SYSTEM PROGRAMMING

System programming (or **systems programming**) is the activity of programming system software. The primary distinguishing characteristic of systems programming when compared to application programming is that application programming aims to produce software which provides services to the user (e.g. word processor), whereas systems programming aims to produce software which provides services to the computer hardware (e.g. disk defragmenter). It requires a greater degree of hardware awareness.

In system programming more specifically:

- The programmer will make assumptions about the hardware and other properties of the system that the program runs on, and will often exploit those properties (for example by using an algorithm that is known to be efficient when used with specific hardware)
- Usually a low-level programming language or programming language dialect is used that:
  - can operate in resource-constrained environments
  - is very efficient and has little runtime overhead
  - has a small runtime library, or none at all
  - allows for direct and "raw" control over memory access and control flow
  - lets the programmer write parts of the program directly in assembly language
- Debugging can be difficult if it is not possible to run the program in a debugger due to resource constraints. Running the program in a simulated environment can be used to reduce this problem.

Systems programming is sufficiently different from application programming that programmers tend to specialize in one or the other.

In system programming, often limited programming facilities are available. The use of automatic garbage collection is not common and debugging is sometimes hard to do. The runtime library, if available at all, is usually far less powerful, and does less error checking. Because of those limitations, monitoring and logging are often used; operating systems may have extremely elaborated logging subsystems.

Implementing certain parts in operating system and networking requires systems programming (for example implementing Paging (Virtual Memory) or a device driver for an operating system).

1.8 COMPONENTS OF SYSTEM SOFTWARE

System software is a set of programs that control the operations of a computer and devices attached with the computer. It creates links between user and computer as well as controls the execution of application programs. System software is essential for a computer to do work, without this software no link can be created between user and computer. Following are the major components of system software's:

1.8.1 OPERATING SYSTEM

The **operating system** and **utility programs** are the two major categories of **system software**. Just as the processor is the nucleus of the computer system, the **operating system is the nucleus of all software activity.**

The operating system is the **most important program** that runs on a computer. Every general-purpose computer **must have** an operating system to run other programs. Operating systems perform basic tasks, such as

- recognizing input from the keyboard
- sending output to the display screen
- keeping track of files and directories on the disk

- controlling peripheral devices such as disk drives and printers

It is the **first program loaded into memory** when the computer is turned on and, in a sense, **brings life to the computer hardware**. Without it, you cannot use your word processing software, spreadsheet software, or any other applications.

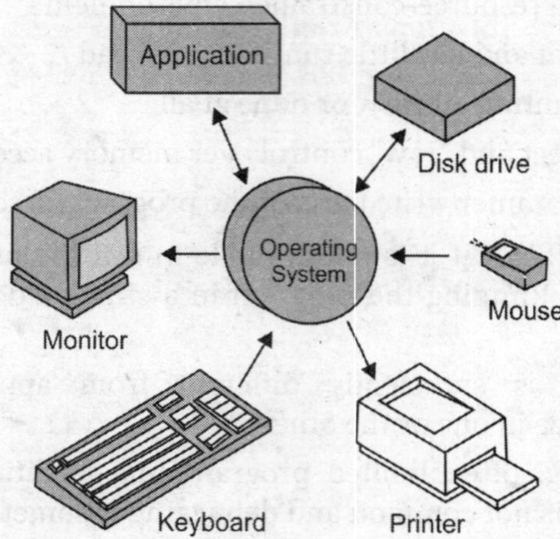

Figure 1.14: System Software- operating system

Without an operating system, you **cannot communicate** with your computer. When you give the computer a command, the operating system relays the instructions to the 'brain' of the computer, called the microprocessor or CPU. You cannot speak directly to the CPU because it only understands **machine language**. When you are working in an application software program, such as Microsoft Word, commands that you give the application are **sent through the operating system** to the CPU. Windows2000, Window 95/98/XP/vista/7, Mac OS, UNIX and DOS are all examples of operating systems.

1.8.2 UTILITY PROGRAMS

A program that performs a very specific task, usually related to managing system resources. Operating systems contain a number of utilities for managing disk drives, printers, and other devices.

Utilities differ from applications mostly in terms of size, complexity and function. For example, word processors, spreadsheet programs, and database applications are considered applications because they are large programs that perform a variety of functions not directly related to managing computer resources.

Utility programs help **manage, maintain and control computer resources**. These programs are available to help you with the day-to-day chores associated with personal computing and to keep your system running at **peak performance**.

Utilities include a variety of specialized programs that can be applied across application programs. Basic utilities include trouble-shooting and/or diagnostic program. Other utilities may include backup programs, file compression, uninstall, and antivirus programs. Device drivers are needed for every peripheral connected to the computer, from the mouse and keyboard to the printer and/or scanner. Device drivers for basic components — like the mouse and keyboard — are included in the system, while others may be supplied by the peripheral manufacturer.

1.8.2.1 SYSTEM CONTROL PROGRAMS

They provide routine service functions to other computer programs and computer users Examples are:

1. Utility Programs

System utility programs perform day-to-day tasks related to the maintenance of the computer system. They are used to support, enhance, expand and secure existing programs and data in the computer system. Utilities programs are also known as service programs. Let up consider some popular utility programs.

2. Antivirus utility

The special programs that are used to detect and remove the viruses from the computer are called anti4irus programs. A large number of anti-virus programs are available: The McAfee and Norton are examples of most popular anti-virus programs. There is no such anti-virus program available which alone can detect all types of viruses.

A good anti-virus program automatically checks for the infected files every time you insert a disk or download files and e-mails from the Internet. It is recommended that you must regularly upgrade anti-virus program in your computer. The latest versions of these programs are available on the Internet and you can upgrade your anti-virus program free of cost. You must visit the site of the manufacturer of the anti-virus (or antiviral) program and follow the procedure to upgrade anti-virus program.

Another most important thing about the anti-virus programs is that these programs not only detect and remove the viruses present inside your computer but also protect the computer from new viruses getting to the computer.

3. File Viewer

A File Viewer is a utility program that is used to view the contents of files as well as to manage files. For example, Windows operating system has the "Windows Explorer" Utility program. This program is also used to perform various operations on files.

4. File Compression

File compression program is a utility program that is used to shrink the size of file. It reduces the size of file. The compressed file takes up less space on the storage media. The compressed files are also referred to as zipped files. Usually these files have extension ZIP. A single compressed file may have large number of files or folders. Mostly, the files are compressed to send the files with e-mail or to upload the files on the Internet. Through this technique data is transferred from one location to another very easily and quickly.

When you receive or download a compressed file from the Internet then you have to uncompress the zip file. The unzip utility program is used for this purpose. When the zip tile is un-zipped, all the files and folders contained in that file are restored to their original form. The Windows XP operating system has also built-in features to compress as well as unzip files. The other popular utility programs for file compression and un-compression are PKZIP, PKUNZIP, W1NZIP, WINRAR AND POWER ARCHIVER etc.

5. Text Editors

Text editors are used to create or edit text files. They allow you to create new files, save files to disk, open files for editing and printing. For example, notepad is a text editor available in Windows operating system.

6. Backup Utility

These utilities programs help us to take backup of our important data. Backup are generally taken to retrieve data in case of any damage to the original data. The files are backed up to floppies. CDs and DVDs using these programs and when there is a need, the backup is restored in the system.

7. Data Recovery Software

Sometimes an illegal operation may result in an accidental loss of data i.e. an important file may be deleted which is still to be needed. So we need to recover this data. Many data recovery software are available to us in our operating system itself. Like in Windows operating system we have 'recycle bin'.

8. Compression Utilities

Compression utilities are used to compress large sized files so that they can be stored in a storage of low capacity. At the destination, the same utility is used to uncompress the files. On uncompressing, the original file is retrieved. WinZip is a popular compression utility used in Windows based desktop.

9. Disk Defragmenter

Disk Defragmenter utilities are used to reduce fragments created on the disks. Fragments are the small portions of unused disk space left between the used areas of disk. The disk defragmenter utilities combine the fragments to create a large unused space and rearranges fragments of files to speed up the access. Windows contains an inbuilt disk defragmenter utility.

10. Disk Scanner

This utility program is used to detect and to remove the physical as well as logical problems on the disk (hard disk or floppy disk). It also removes the unnecessary files such as swap files on the disk. The physical problem on the disk represents the bad sectors or scratches on the surface of disk. The logical problem specifies the problem in accessing data such as error in data file, error in FAT (file allocation table). The Windows operating system has built-in disk scanner called the Scandisk.

1.8.3 DEVICE DRIVER

A device driver is a computer file that allows the operating system (OS) on a computer to properly communicate with and control hardware connected to that computer. Different devices often require different drivers to function properly, though an OS will typically have default drivers installed for a number of devices to allow for minimal functionality with such devices.

"A device driver is a program that controls a particular type of device that is attached to your computer."

In order for full functionality of many devices to be utilized by the OS on a computer, however, the proper drivers typically need to be installed. A device driver for a device will usually be provided with the hardware for installation by the device manufacturer, though they can typically be downloaded and installed as well.

While there are many different specific types of drivers, a device driver in general is a file that allows the OS on a computer to properly communicate with a corresponding device. Such drivers are needed for just about any type of device on a computer, including the motherboard, universal serial bus (USB) ports, Ethernet ports, printers, network adapters, and video cards. Of course, if these devices are relatively simple, then the default drivers provided with an OS may be sufficient for the system to run properly. Oftentimes, however, a device driver will need to be installed with a new device or piece of hardware to ensure proper compatibility.

1.8.3.1 USE OF DEVICE DRIVER

A device driver simplifies programming by acting as translator between a hardware device and the applications or operating systems that use it. Programmers can write the higher-level application code independently of whatever specific hardware device.

A driver typically communicates with the device through the computer bus or communications subsystem to which the hardware connects. When a calling program invokes a routine in the driver, the driver issues commands to the device. Once the device sends data back to the driver, the driver may invoke routines in the original calling program. Drivers are hardware-dependent and operating-system-specific.

1.8.4 LANGUAGE PROCESSORS

We know that computer understands instructions in machine code, i.e. in the form of 0s and 1s. It is difficult to write computer program directly in machine code. Nowadays, the programs are written mostly in high-level languages, i.e. BASIC, C, C++, PASCAL, etc. A program written in any high-level programming language (or written in assembly language) is called the Source Program. The source code cannot be executed directly by the computer. The source program must be converted into machine code to run it on the computer. The program translated into machine code is known as Object Program. Every language has its own language processor (or translator). **Therefore, language processor is defined as:**

The special translator system software that is used to translate the program written in high-level language (or Assembly language) into machine code is called language processor or translator program.

1.8.4.1 ASSEMBLERS

Programmers in early times had to program using 0's and 1's i.e. machine language, and then execute that program. This was a very difficult task to do and required tough brainstorming sessions by programmers. It was very difficult to read and write programs in such a manner. So for the aid of programmers an interactive way was formulated in the form of mnemonics (symbols) for each machine instruction, which can be translated into the actual machine code at the time of execution. Such a mnemonic machine language is known as an assembly language. These programs need to be converted to the equivalent machine code before they can be executed by the computer. Hence system programs called assemblers were thus developed to automatically convert assembly language programs to the actual machine code.

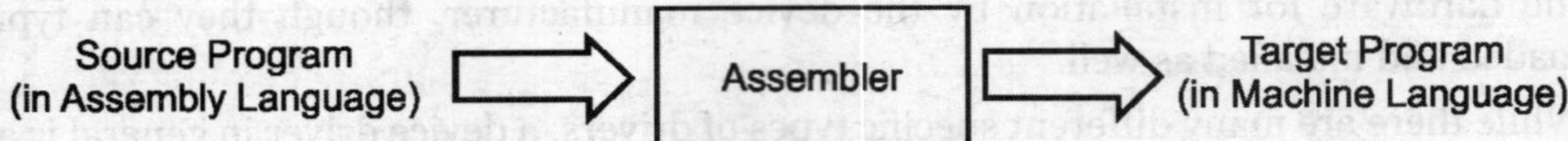

Figure 1.15: Working of Assembler

1.8.4.2 INTERPRETERS AND COMPILERS

Even after the success of assembly language, programmers were in need of easier to use and people-like language that had more functionality than currently available. The user's problems got to become more categorized into the specialized areas such as business, science, statistical etc. Hence specialized languages (like FORTRAN, COBOL, BASIC, C) were developed that allowed users to program their problems more easily and in a more independent way than assembly language. Now the need arose to convert these languages into machine language as the assembler could not do the same task due to the added functionality of the language. This task of conversion is performed by interpreters and compilers.

An **interpreter** is a system program that appears to execute a source program as if it were in machine language i.e. line by line compilation. A **compiler** is a system program that accepts a program written in any of the high level languages and coverts it to the equivalent machine code. Normally the same name (FORTRAN, COBOL, BASIC, C) is used to designate the compiler and its associated language.

Modern day programmers are now demanding more functionality from the compilers. It must be able to process the complex accessing methods for pointer variables, data structures, etc. used in languages like FORTRAN, COBOL, BASIC, and C.

1.8.5 LOADERS

After the object program is produced by assembler, it needs to be placed in memory before being executed. Loader assures that the object programs are placed in memory in an executable form.

In the basic computer system, there are two types of storage that are used:

(i) Primary Storage

(ii) Secondary Storage

The assembler mostly outputs the result i.e. object program in machine language, on the secondary storage. But the computer requires every program to be present on the primary storage prior to its execution. This is the task of loader to bring that executable object code to the primary storage so that it can be successfully executed.

One scenario that can be followed is adding the features of loaders to the assembler and making it place the object program into the main memory after conversion to the equivalent machine code. But this scenario has a major disadvantage of wasted storage as the assembler resides in the memory even when the converted machine language program is executed by the computer, and there is no need for the large assembler program to occupy the memory space.

Hence a separate loader program was required for saving memory space that could be used for storing other programs. In this scenario, an assembler produces an object program that is stored somewhere on secondary storage. This object program is bought into the memory at the time of execution by a loader. As the functionality of assembler and loader is separated in this scenario, hence the assembler need not be present in the memory at the time of execution of program. The smaller loader program alone can do the task independently, thus saving memory space.

After a while in assembly language programming, it was seen that the users and programmers were writing virtually the same code. Hence the need for ready-made programs arose which were introduced in the form of subroutines. Subroutines are the body of computer instructions designed to be used by other routines to accomplish a task. The users started to mix their code with these subroutines for better functionality and easier coding. There are two types of subroutines:

(i) Open Subroutine

(ii) Closed Subroutine

Open subroutine is the one whose code is inserted into the main program at the time of assembly. Hence if a routine is called five times, it will appear five times in the resulting object code. Closed subroutine can be stored outside the main routine and the control transfers to the subroutine when a call is made. Main program has to associate two tasks while working with closed subroutines:

(i) Transfer of data

(ii) Transfer of control

Initially, a closed subroutine had to be loaded at a specific location at the time of assembly. For example, if a user had to use a square root subroutine, he would have to write his main program so that it would transfer to the location assigned to the square root routine (SQRT). His original program and the subroutine will be assembled together. If another user wishes to use the same subroutine, he would also assemble it along with his own program, and the complete machine code would be loaded into the main memory. The figure 1.16 depicts an example of memory allocation under this inflexible loading scheme:

Note that Program 1 has 'holes' in memory. Program 2 overlays and hence destroys a part of the SQRT subroutine. This is a major disadvantage of this inflexible technique that it can overlay the parts of other subroutines that may be still be required by other programs.

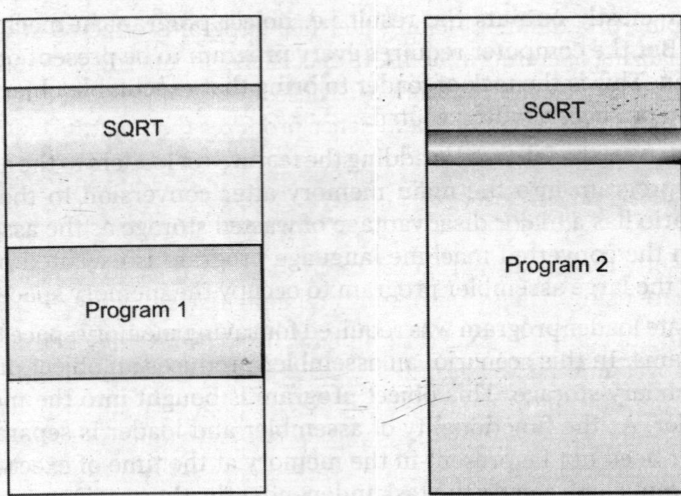

Figure 1.16: Example of memory allocation at time of absolute loading

Programmers wanted to use subroutines that referred to each other symbolically and did not want to be concerned with the address parts of the program. They expected the computer system to assign memory to their subroutines and to substitute addresses for their symbolic references.

System programmers noted that it would be more efficient if subroutines could be translated into the object form that the loader could relocate directly without any user intervention. The task of adjusting programs so that they can be placed in arbitrary memory locations is known as relocation. Relocating loaders perform the following four functions:

1. Allocation of space for programs in memory. (allocation)
2. Resolve symbolic references between objects (linking)
3. Adjust all address dependent locations to correspond to the allocated space (relocation)
4. Physically place the machine instructions and data into the memory (loading)

The various types of loaders (compile-and-go, absolute, relocating, direct-linking, dynamic-loading, and dynamic-linking etc.) differ mainly in the manner in which these four basic functions are performed.

The time required for the execution of a user program is known as execution time. The time required for translating a source program into machine code is known as assembly or compile time. Load time refers to the time required for loading and preparing the object program for execution.

1.8.6 MACROS

As another effort to make the assembly language programming easier macros were introduced. They permit programmers to define an abbreviation for a part of his program and use it in his program. The identical parts of the assembly language are called and saved as macro definition. The macro processor processes macros by substituting the appropriate definitions for the corresponding macro calls.

Along with helping programmers abbreviate their programs, macros are used as general text handlers and for specializing operating systems. In specializing operating systems, the whole operating system is written as a series of macro definitions. These are again processed by the macro processor that substitutes the appropriate definitions, and hence produces the programs for an operating system.

1.9 PROGRAMMING SOFTWARE

Programming software usually provides tools to assist a programmer in writing computer programs, and software using different programming languages in a more convenient way.

Now this is a kind of computer software which is used exclusively by computer programmers. Unless we are also programmers, we are unlikely to come across programming languages. A simple way to understand programming languages is to think of them as bricks which can be used to create applications and operating system. It deals mainly with providing tools that will assist computer programmers in their attempt to write computer programs and allow them to use different programming languages in a way that is convenient for them.

The tools include:

- compilers
- interpreters
- text editors
- debuggers
- linkers

An Integrated development environment (IDE) is a single application that attempts to manage all these functions. An Integrated development environment (IDE) merges those tools into a software bundle, and a programmer may not need to type multiple commands for compiling, interpreter, debugging, tracing, and etc., because the IDE usually has an advanced graphical user interface, or GUI.

C++, Java and Simlab are some popular programming languages. Generally Java is used for internet applications. C++ is a language of professional developers and used extensively in developing operating systems. PHP is another language used for internet applications. There is a new class of languages which are being utilized for the mobiles. These are light weight, modular languages which are used to design mobile applications.

1.10 LANGUAGE PROCESSING

Language processing was the need of the hour because of the differences in the working and thinking of a software designer and the actual working of the computer system. Any software developer thinks in terms of the application one is designing and hence the name application domain is appropriate for the same. To implement these methods on a computer system, they need to be converted in terms related to the execution domain of the system. The rules of meaning of these domains are known as semantics, while the difference between the two domains is known as the semantics gap. The figure 1.17 shows a pictorial representation of semantics gap between application and execution domains:

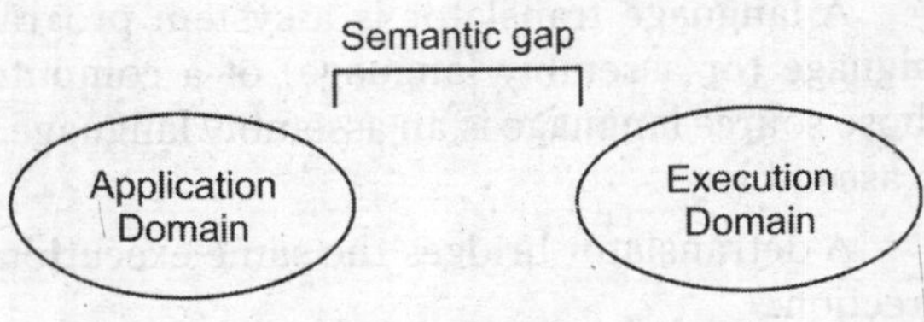

Figure 1.17: Semantic Gap

Due to semantic gap between the domains, the software designs encounter many adverse effects like prolonged development times, more efforts, and low quality of software. Software engineering looks into the details of removing such design defects through the use of methodologies and programming languages, thus the designers aim at producing good quality software.

The software engineering steps can be grouped into the following:

1. Specification, design and coding
2. Programming language implementation

Software implementation using a programming language (PL) introduces a new domain that can be known as PL domain. The semantic gap between the application domain and execution domain are bridged by these two software engineering steps. The first step bridges the gap between the application domain and the PL domain known as specification gap, while the second step bridges the gap between the PL domain and the execution domain. The gap between application and PL domains is referred to as the specification gap, and the gap between the PL and execution domains as the execution gap. The specification gap is bridged by the software development team while the execution gap is bridged by the designer of the programming language processor, like a compiler.

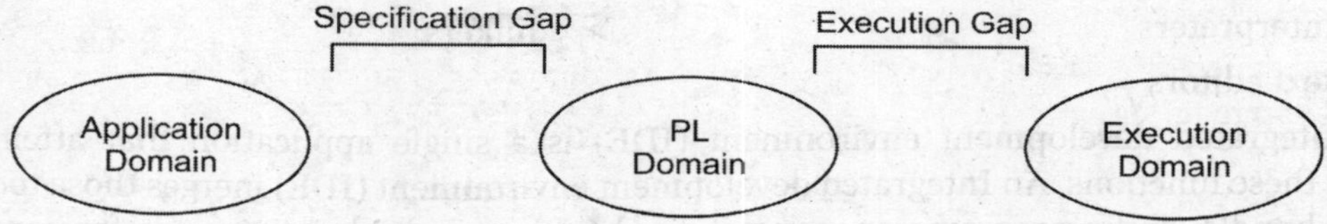

Figure 1.18: Specification and Execution Gaps

The main advantage of introduction of a PL domain is to reduce the gap to be bridged by a software designer. First he had to work upon bridging the gap between the application domain and the execution domain, which is now reduced to the PL domain only. This reduces the severity of the consequences of the semantic gap. Not only this, the language processors also provide the diagnostic capability of detecting and indicating the errors in the input from application domain. This helps in further improvement of the software.

Hence a language processor is software which bridges the gap between a specification or execution gap. We use the term language processing to describe the activity performed by a language processor and assume the diagnostic capability as an implicit part of any form of language processing. The program that forms the input to a language processor is called a source program while its output is called target program. Similarly the languages in which those programs are written are called source language and target language, respectively.

A language translator is a system program that bridges an execution gap to the machine language (or assembly language) of a computer system. An assembler is a language translator whose source language is an assembly language. A compiler is any language translator which is not an assembler.

A detranslator bridges the same execution gap as the language translator, but in the reverse direction.

1.10.1 TRANSLATORS

A translator is a system program that bridges an execution gap to the machine language (or assembly language) of a computer system. An assembler is a language translator whose source language is an assembly language. A compiler is any language translator which is not an assembler.

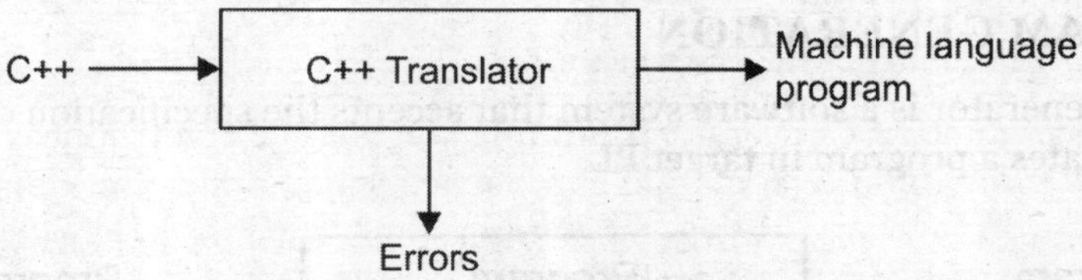

Figure 1.19: A typical C++ translator

1.10.1.1 INTERPRETERS

Interpreter is a language translator which bridges an execution gap without generating a machine language program. This leads to many similarities as well as many differences between the translators and the interpreters.

The absence of a target program leads to an absence of the output interface of interpreter. Hence the language processing activities of an interpreter cannot be separated from its program execution activities. Thus it can be said that an interpreter 'executes' a program written in a PL. In essence, the execution gap vanishes completely.

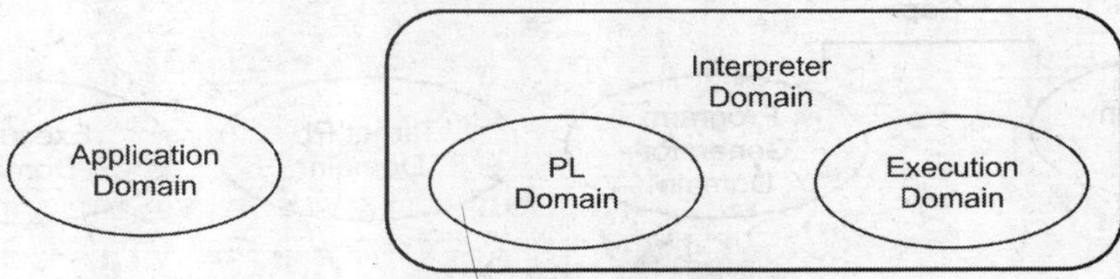

Figure 1.20: Interpreter Domain

The figure 1.20 shows the schematic representation of an interpreter where the interpreter domain includes the PL and execution domains. Hence it is clear that the specification language of PL domain is same as the specification language of the interpreter domain. Since the interpreter domain also includes the execution domain, it seems as if we have a computer which is capable of understanding the programming language itself.

1.10.2 LANGUAGE PROCESSING ACTIVITIES

The fundamental language processing activities are divided into two parts:

1. *Program Generation Activities*

These are the category of those activities which bridge the specification gap. They aim at the automatic generation of a program. The source language of such activities is a specification language of the application domain and the target language is typically a PL.

2. Program Execution Activities

These are the category of those languages which bridge the execution gap. They organize the execution of a program written in a PL on a computer system. the source language of these activities is any procedure oriented or problem oriented PL and the target language is the corresponding code in machine language.

1.10.2.1 PROGRAM GENERATION

The program generator is a software system that accepts the specification of a program to be generated and generates a program in target PL.

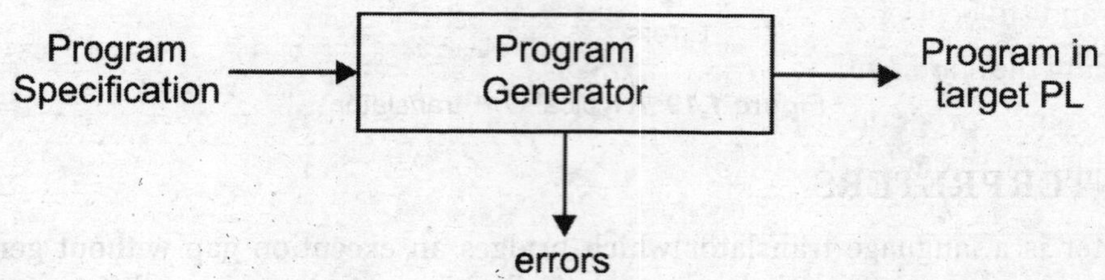

Figure 1.21: Program Generation

Hence it introduces a new domain in-between the application and PL domains, which can be known as the program generator domain.

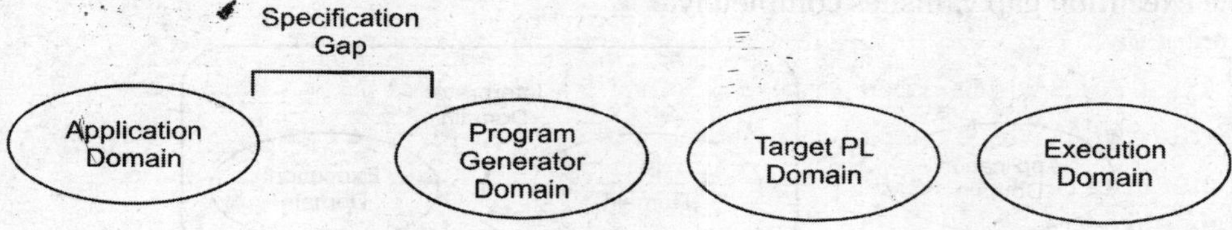

Figure 1.22: Program Generator Domain

The specification gap is now the gap between the application domain and the program generator domain. This gap is much smaller than the gap between application and target PL domain.

1.10.2.2 PROGRAM EXECUTION

Program execution can be carried out in one of the following ways:

1. Program Translation

The program translation model bridges the execution gap by translating a program written in a PL, called the source program (SP), into the equivalent program in the machine language of the computer system called target program (TP).

Any program in PL needs to be translated before it can be executed. The translated program should then be saved in a file on the hard drive. This saved program can be executed any number of times by various users. If any modifications are made to the original program, then the program must be retranslated to reflect the changes done in the final output.

2. *Program Interpretation*

The interpreter reads a source program and stores it in the memory. While interpretation, it reads each statement, determines its meaning and performs the actions which are indicated. This includes all the computational as well as the input-output actions.

A program counter (PC) indicates the statement of source program that is to be interpreted next. A certain interpretation cycle is followed by each statement of the source program, which has the following steps:

(i) Fetch the statement.

(ii) Analyze the statement to find its meaning in the form of action to be performed and the operands to be used.

(iii) Execute the statement.

Hence the source program is retained in its original form itself as no target program is generated, and it is just the analyzing of each statement which is done during the interpretation.

1.10.3 FUNDAMENTALS OF LANGUAGE PROCESSING

Language processing can be broken down into two tasks:

(i) Analysis of Source Program

(ii) Synthesis of Target Program

A specification of the source language forms the basis of source program analysis, which consists of the following three components:

(i) Lexical rules which check for the formation of valid lexical units in the source language.

(ii) Syntax rules which check for the formation of valid statements in the source language.

(iii) Semantic rules which associate meaning with the valid statements of the source language.

The analysis of the source language thus can be thought of consisting lexical, syntax and semantic analysis.

The synthesis phase is mainly concerned with the construction of target language statements which should have the same meaning as the source language statements. This mainly consists of the following two activities:

(i) Memory Allocation: Creation of data structures in the target program.

(ii) Code Generation: Generation of target code.

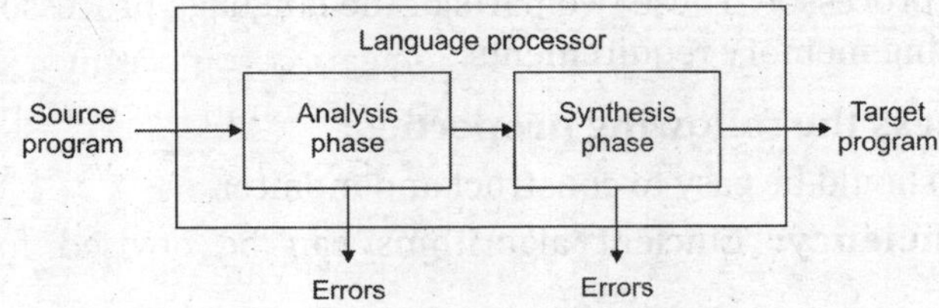

Figure 1.23: Phases of a Language Processor

It is clear from the above scenario that the language processing can be carried out on a statement-by-statement basis, i.e. the analysis of a single source language statement followed by the synthesis of the same statement. But this scenario may not be feasible due to the forward references that are encountered in source programs.

A forward reference of a program entity is a reference to the entity which precedes its definition in the program. While such a statement is encountered, the language processor does not have relevant information about the referenced entity. This is a problem in synthesis of the same statement. Such a problem of forward references can be solved by postponing the generation of target code till all the required information gets available. Hence leaving behind the statement-b-statement translation, a newer multi-pass model of language processors gets introduced in this regard.

A pass of language processor is the processing of every statement in a source program to perform a language processing function. The programs thus can be translated in a two-pass sequence as follows:

Pass I: Perform the analysis of the source program and note the relevant information required by synthesis phase.

Pass II: Perform the synthesis of target program.

In this two pass scenario, the language processor reads the source program to note down the required information in pass I. It again reads the source program for pass II while generating the target code. Now the problem that arises that the source program needs to be scanned twice, which can be avoided by the use of an intermediate representation of the source program.

An intermediate representation (IR) is an equivalent representation of the source program which reflects the effect of some analysis and synthesis tasks performed during the language processing.

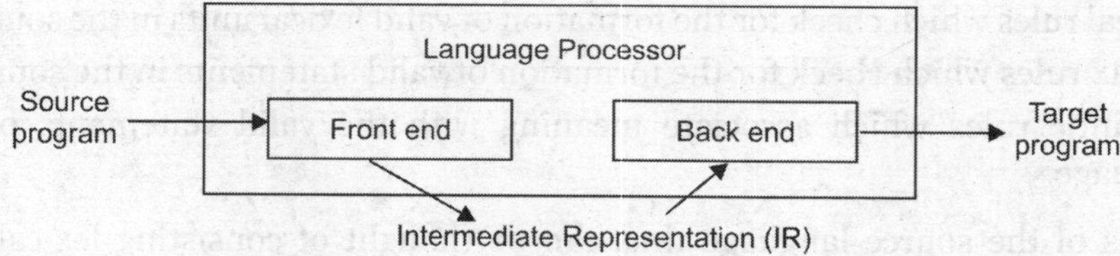

Figure 1.24: Language processing by two pass scheme.

Now the first pass performs analysis of the source program and reflects its results in the IR formed. The second pass reads and analyses the IR, instead of the source program, and performs the synthesis of the target code. This avoids the repeated processing of the source program. The first pass is concerned with the source language issues and thus called front end of the language processor. The second pass is concerned with the synthesis of the target program and hence called back end of the language processor. These two parts of the language processor need not coexist in the memory, hence reducing memory requirements.

The IR must possess the following properties:

- **Easy to use:** IR should be easy to construct and monitor.
- **Processing Efficiency:** Efficient algorithms can be devised for construction and analyzing of IR.
- **Memory Efficiency:** IR must not occupy large memory space and must be compact.

1.11 APPLICATION SOFTWARE

Application software, on the other hand, is used to accomplish specific tasks other than just running the computer system. Application software may consist of a single program, such as an image viewer; a small collection of programs (often called a software package) that work closely together to accomplish a task, such as a spreadsheet or text processing system; a larger collection (often called a software suite) of related but independent programs and packages that have a common user interface or shared data format, such as Microsoft Office, which consists of closely integrated word processor, spreadsheet, database, etc.; or a software system, such as a database management system, which is a collection of fundamental programs that may provide some service to a variety of other independent applications.

Figure 1.25: Application software

These software applications have specific purposes and are designed for a certain purpose, for example play games, listen to music, write letters, etc. Examples of such software: educational software, medical software, tax software, database, military software and a lot others. This is probably the most used type of software that is used by all the people all over the world. Not all of us use the same software applications, but the fun is the fact that you have the possibility which application to use. Besides, hey are very easy to purchase, either by buying them from specialized stores or simply downloading the free version from the internet. It all depends on your tastes and preoccupations.

System software differs from application software in several ways besides in general purpose. First, it is necessary, whereas any particular example of application software is optional. Second, it is complete in that no computer needs to have more than one type of system software on it at any given time, although some set-ups allow for multiple types of system software to be installed. Applications, on the other hand, are generally placed on a computer in large numbers. In addition, system software is independent and requires no application software to run, whereas application software cannot run in the absence of system software.

1.11.1 DIFFERENT TYPES OF APPLICATION SOFTWARE

A set of programs used to solve particular problems of user through computer is called Application software. It is also known as application package. The ready packages are also available in market on CDs for various purposes. These are used by user who does not know the computer programming. The users solve their problems by using ready packages more easily and quickly.

Some of application packages are:

1. Word processing software.
2. Spreadsheet software.

3. Database Management System software.
4. Graphics software.
5. Communication software.

1.11.1.1 WORD PROCESSING SOFTWARE

This software is used to create and to edit documents such as letters, reports, essays etc. The word processing software provides several features for document editing and formatting. In. editing process, text is entered into the document, deleted, copied or moved to another location etc. In formatting process, different formats can be applied on the text to make the document more attractive before to print on the printer. The most popular word processing software programs are: Microsoft Word, Word Perfect etc.

1.11.1.2 SPREADSHEET SOFTWARE

Spreadsheet software is used to store and process data in an electronic sheet having columns and rows. The data is entered into the cells of the sheet. The intersection of a row and a column is known as cell. Each cell is a unique address. The numbers and formulas are entered into the cells and the computer can automatically perform the calculation on numerical data in cells.

The spreadsheet software is commonly used for business application such as for performing financial calculations and recording transactions. The most popular example of spreadsheet software is Microsoft Excel etc.

1.11.1.3 DATABASE MANAGEMENT SOFTWARE

Database management software is used to create and manage databases. A database is a collection of related information or records on any subject such as records of the books in a library, information about the students of a college etc.
Database Management Software stores and manages records in databases. These records can be accessed very quickly when required. The Microsoft Access, Oracle etc. are most popular examples of Database Management Software.

1.11.1.4 PRESENTATION GRAPHICS SOFTWARE

The presentation graphic software is used to create slides for making presentations. The presentation graphic software also has pre-drawn clip art images, which can be inserted into slides and can be modified. The PowerPoint is an example of presentation graphic software.

1.11.1.5 COMMUNICATION SOFTWARE

The Communication software is used to exchange information electronically. It is most commonly used software to send and receive information on the Internet. It also allows for sending and receiving faxes directly. The computer files can also be transferred from one PC to another through this software. The Internet Explorer is an example of this software.

Application software is further divided into different subclasses for easier identification and depending on their different functions. They are:

1. **Word Processing Software:** This software enables the users to create and edit documents. The most popular examples of this type of software are MS-Word, WordPad, Notepad and some other text editors.
2. **Multimedia Software:** They allow the users to create and play audio and video media. They are capable of playing media files. Audio converters, players, burners, video encoders and decoders are some forms of multimedia software. Examples of this type of software include Real Player and Media Player.
3. **Presentation Software:** The software that is used to display information in the form of a slide show is known as presentation software. This type of software includes three functions, namely, editing that allows insertion and formatting of text, methods to include graphics in the text and a functionality of executing the slide shows. Microsoft PowerPoint is the best example of presentation software.
4. **Enterprise Software:** It deals with the needs of organization processes and data flow. The customer relationship management or the financial processes in an organization are carried out by means of enterprise software.
5. **Information Worker Software:** Individual projects within a department and individual needs of creation and management of information are handled by information worker software. Documentation tools, resource management tools and personal management systems fall under the category of this form of application software.
6. **Educational Software:** It has the capabilities of running tests and tracking progress. It also has the capabilities of collaborative software. It is often used in teaching and self-learning.
7. **Simulation Software:** Used to simulate physical or abstract systems, simulation software finds applications in both, research and entertainment. Flight simulators and scientific simulators find a place in the list of simulation software.
8. **Content Access Software:** It is used to access content without editing. The common examples of content access software are web browsers and media players.
9. **Media development software:** These types of application software are used by individuals who create and develop print, digital and electronic media that others may use. Common examples of such software applications include desktop publishing software, digital animation editors, digital audio and video composition tools and many others.
10. **Desktop Publishing Software:** Special application software is created to satisfy specific needs of an organization. In this case software engineers are hired to create such software. The cost of such software depends upon the extent of work automated through software.
11. **Web Browser Software:** With an internet connection, these types of software enable a user to visit from one web site to another by hyperlinks.

Thus we see that application software have made it possible for us users to interact with the computer systems. Application software has served as a boon in harnessing the computing power in the accomplishment of certain important individual and organizational tasks.

EXERCISES

1. What do you mean by machine structure?
2. Explain the general architecture of Simplified Instructional Computer?
3. Explain the general architecture of SIC/XE machine?
4. What is software?
5. What do you mean by computer software? Explain the types of computer software?
6. Define system software?
7. What do you mean by system programming?
8. Explain the three types of programs in system software?
9. Explain the evolution of system software?
10. Explain the various components of system software?
11. What do you mean by operating system?
12. Explain the utility software in detail?
13. What are device drivers?
14. Explain the concept of language translators?
15. Explain the concept of language processing?
16. Explain the various language processing activities?
17. What are the fundamentals of language processing?
18. What is assembler?
19. Define interpreter?
20. Define compiler?
21. Explain the role of loader?
22. Explain the concept of application software?

Chapter

2

Programming Languages

2.1 INTRODUCTION

In all over the world, language is the source of communication among human beings. Different countries/regions have different languages. Similarly, in order to communicate with the computer user also needs to have a language that should be understood by the computer. For this purpose, different languages are developed for performing different types of work on the computer.

There is only one programming language that any computer can actually understand and execute: its own native binary machine code. This is the lowest possible level of language in which it is possible to write a computer program. All other languages are said to be high level or low level according to how closely they can be said to resemble machine code.

In this context, a low-level language corresponds closely to machine code, so that a single low-level language instruction translates to a single machine-language instruction. A high-level language instruction typically translates into a series of machine-language instructions.

Low-level languages have the advantage that they can be written to take advantage of any peculiarities in the architecture of the central processing unit (CPU) which is the "brain" of any computer. Thus, a program written in a low-level language can be extremely efficient, making optimum use of both computer memory and processing time. However, to write a low-level program takes a substantial amount of time, as well as a clear understanding of the inner workings of the processor itself. Therefore, low-level programming is typically used only for very small programs, or for segments of code that are highly critical and must run as efficiently as possible.

High-level languages permit faster development of large programs. The final program as executed by the computer is not as efficient, but the savings in programmer time generally far outweigh the inefficiencies of the finished product. This is because the cost of writing a program is nearly constant for each line of code, regardless of the language. Thus, a high-level language where each line of code translates to 10 machine instructions costs only one tenth as much in program development as a low-level language where each line of code represents only a single machine instruction.

2.2 · LANGUAGE

You are aware with the term language. It is a system of communication between you and me. Some of the basic natural languages that we are familiar with are English, Hindi, and Oriya etc. These are the languages used to communicate among various categories of persons. But how you will communicate with your computer? Your computer will not understand any of these natural languages for transfer of data and instruction. So there are programming languages specially developed so that you could pass your data and instructions to the computer to do specific job. You must have heard names like FORTRAN, BASIC, and COBOL etc. These are programming languages. So instructions or programs are written in a particular language based on the type of job. As an example, for scientific application FORTRAN and C languages are used. On the other hand COBOL is used for business applications.

2.3 PROGRAMMING LANGUAGE

A language is defined as the way of communication between two persons. Therefore, computer-programming language is defined as a way of communication between user and the computer. The instructions are given to the computer to perform a specific task. These instructions are given to the computer according to the rules of programming language.

Computer programming languages are used to prepare computer programs or software. Early computer programs were prepared directly in machine language i.e. in binary code. It was very difficult to prepare program in machine code. Today, there re several programming languages, each programming language has its own rules for writing the program. Each language is also used for specific purpose. For example, FORTRAN is used for scientific purposes, COBOL for business solutions, Ada for defense applications etc.

Programming languages are divided into two types:

1. Low-level languages
2. High-level languages

2.3.1 LOW-LEVEL LANGUAGES

Low level computer languages are machine codes or close to it. Computer cannot understand instructions given in high level languages or in English. It can only understand and execute instructions given in the form of machine language i.e. language of 0 and 1. There are two types of low level languages:

- **Machine Language.**
- **Assembly Language**

While Von Neumann systems deal easily with their machine language instructions, machine language is not an easy language for programmers to write and read.

In the 1950's, assembly language was developed. Assembly language uses mnemonic codes (such as ADD for addition) that are easier to learn and remember than machine language's numeric codes. In assembly language, each instruction has a one-to-one correspondence to a machine language instruction.

Assembly languages require the use of assemblers, programs that translate assembly language into machine language. Since each processor has a unique set of machine language instructions, it also has its own assembler. This means that an assembly language program can only be written for one particular type of machine.

Machine language and assembly language are called low-level languages.

L0W-LEVEL LANGUAGES

```
00110101  01111010
10110000  10100100
1.101111  11100101
0.010100  10001001
10001001  01011010
```

```
MUA  FIELDA   FIELD3
ADD  FIELDC   TALLY
CPN  TALLY    MAX
GTR  LOOPA
MUN  PARTNO   MUMBER
BUN  LABELA
```

Assembly languages helped programmers by allowing them to think using the name of each instruction instead of its binary representation. Still, writing even a simple program in such a low-level language requires a large number of very simple instructions. This makes writing most assembly language programs into a time-consuming task.

Even though some programmers developed large libraries of pre-written routines they could call on, it didn't take away the basic problem --- the programmer still had to write a significant amount of assembly language to connect the routines together, and the program was still only suitable for one type of machine. Something better was needed...

2.3.2 HIGH-LEVEL LANGUAGES

Solving the problems of assembly language would require a new kind of computer language --- a high-level language where the programmer could state the problem to be solved in a more "natural" and machine-independent form. Such languages would allow a programmer to think in terms of how to solve a particular problem rather than having to think about how to translate the problem into a form a particular machine can understand.

FORTRAN & COBOL

FORTRAN

```
X= SQRT (( A** 2+Y)/(2.*B))
```

COBOL

```
SUBTRACT DEDUCTIONS FROM
GROSS-PAY GIVING NET-PAY.
```

For example "A = B + C" is easier to write than "MOV @A, R1; ADD @B, R1; MOV R1, @C". The first expression is more abstract, and makes fewer assumptions about the machine on which it will run.

High-level languages were developed during the mid-1950. The first such language was FORTRAN, followed by ALGOL, COBOL, and LISP. Modern high-level languages include Pascal, C, C++ (pronounced "C-plus-plus"), and Smalltalk.

These high-level languages require compilers: programs that translate the high-level source code into the machine language of a particular computer (a/k/a object code.) Each source code instruction might correspond to several machine language instructions.

HIGH-LEVEL LANGUAGES

for example...

C	C++
Pascal	COBOL
FORTRAN	FORTH
LISP	RPG

Compilers give high-level language programmers several advantages over assembly-language programmers:

- High-level languages aren't tied to any particular computer, which means that programs written on one computer could be run on another by re-compiling the source for the other machine. (Doing this successfully requires writing portable code which isolates or removes dependencies on a particular operating system.)
- Programmers who learn a particular high-level language on one system typically can use that language on another system.
- Optimizing compilers can generate code which is as efficient as the best assembly language programmers. In fact, since a compiler doesn't tire, it may generate better code overall than a talented assembly-language programmer.

2.4 MACHINE LANGUAGE

Machine code or **machine language** is a system of instructions and data executed directly by a computer's central processing unit. Machine code may be regarded as a primitive (and cumbersome) programming language or as the lowest-level representation of a compiled and/or assembled computer program. Programs in interpreted languages are **not** represented by machine code however, although their interpreter (which may be seen as a processor executing the higher level program) often is. Machine code is sometimes called **native code** when referring to platform-dependent parts of language features or libraries. Machine code should not be confused with so called **"bytecode"**, which is executed by an interpreter.

2.4.1 MACHINE CODE INSTRUCTIONS

Every processor or processor family has its own machine code instruction set. Instructions are patterns of bits that by physical design correspond to different commands to the machine. The instruction set is thus specific to a class of processors using (much) the same architecture. Successor or derivative processor designs often include all the instructions of a predecessor and may add additional instructions. Occasionally a successor design will discontinue or alter the meaning of some instruction code (typically because it is needed for new purposes), affecting code compatibility to some extent; even nearly completely compatible processors may show slightly different behavior for some instructions but this is seldom a problem. Systems may also differ in other details, such as memory arrangement, operating systems, or peripheral devices; because a program normally relies on such factors, different systems will typically not run the same machine code, even when the same type of processor is used.

A machine code instruction set may have all instructions of the same length, or it may have variable-length instructions. How the patterns are organized varies strongly with the particular architecture and often also with the type of instruction. Most instructions have one or more opcode fields which specifies the basic instruction type (such as arithmetic, logical, jump, etc) and the actual operation (such as add or compare) and other fields that may give the type of the operand(s), the addressing mode(s), the addressing offset(s) or index, or the actual value itself (such constant operands contained in an instruction are called immediates).

Machine Language is the only language that is directly understood by the computer. It does not need any translator program. We also call it machine code and it is written as strings of 1's (one) and 0's (zero). When this sequence of codes is fed to the computer, it recognizes the codes and converts it in to electrical signals needed to run it. For example, a program instruction may look like this:

1011000111101

It is not an easy language for you to learn because of its difficult to understand. It is efficient for the computer but very inefficient for programmers. It is considered to the first generation language. It is also difficult to debug the program written in this language.

A system of codes directly understandable by a computer's CPU is termed this CPU's **native** or **machine language**. Although machine code may seem similar to assembly language they are in fact two different types of languages. Assembly code consists of both binary numbers and simple words whereas machine code is composed only of the two binary digits 0 and 1. Every CPU has its own machine language, although there is considerable overlap between some. If CPU *A* understands the full language of CPU *B* it is said that *A* is compatible with *B*. CPU *B* may not be compatible with CPU *A*, as *A* may know a few codes that *B* does not.

The "words" of a machine language are called *instructions*; each of these gives a basic command to the CPU. A program is just a long list of instructions that are *executed* by a CPU. Older processors executed instructions one after the other, but newer superscalar processors are capable of executing several instructions at once. Program flow may be influenced by special *jump* instructions that transfer execution to an instruction other than the following one. Conditional jumps are taken (execution continues at another address) or not (execution continues at the next instruction) depending on some condition.

Instructions are simply a pattern of bits -- different patterns correspond to different commands to the machine. The more readable rendition of a machine language is called assembly language.

Some languages give all their instructions the same number of bits, while the instruction length differs in others. How the patterns are organized depends largely on the specific language. Common to most is the division of an instruction into *fields*, of which one or more specify the exact operation (for example "add"). Other fields may give the type of the operands, their location, or their value directly (operands contained in an instruction are called *immediate*).

It is the lowest and most elementary level of Programming language and was the first type of programming language to be developed. Machine Language is basically the only language which computer can understand. In fact, a manufacturer designs a computer to obey just one Language, its machine code, which is represented inside the computer by a String of binary digits (bits) 0 and 1. The symbol 0 stands for the absence of Electric pulse and 1 for the presence of an electric pulse. Since a computer is Capable of recognizing electric signals, therefore, it understands machine Language. For example, a program instruction may look like this:

1011000111101

It is not an easy language for you to learn because of its difficult to understand. It is efficient for the computer but very inefficient for programmers. It is considered to the first generation language.

In machine language program, the computation is based on binary numbers. All the instructions including operations, registers, data and memory locations are given in there binary equivalent. The machine directly understands this language by virtue of its circuitry design so these programs are directly executable on the computer without any translations. This makes the program execution very fast. Machine languages are also known as first generation languages.

operation part	address part

A typical low level instruction consists essentially of two parts:

1. An Operation Part:

It specifies operation to be performed by the computer, also known as Opcode.

2. An Address Part:

It specifies location of the data on which operation is to be performed.

All computers use binary digits (0s and 1s) for performing internal operations. Hence, most computers' machine language instructions consist of strings of binary numbers. For example, a typical program instruction to print a number on a printer might be

101100111111010011101100

A program to add two numbers in memory, and print the result might appear as follows:

001000000000001100111001

001100000000001000100001

011000000000001110010111O

101000111111011100101110

000000000000000000000000

Obviously, this language is not easy to use because it is difficult to read and understand, and because it is written in a number system, which we are not familiar with. However, some of the first programmers, who worked with the first few computers, actually wrote their programs in binary form as this one.

Since human programmers are more familiar with decimal number system, they prefer to write computer instructions in decimal, and leave it to the input device to convert them into binary.

In fact, without too much effort a computer can be wired so that instead of using long strings of 1s and 0s we can use the more familiar decimal numbers. With this change, the preceding program appears as follows:

10001471
14002041
30003456
50773656
50773456
00000000

This set of instruction, whether in binary or decimal, which a computer can understand directly without the help of a translating program is called machine code or machine language program. Hence, a machine language program need not necessarily be coded as strings of binary digits (1s and 0s). It can also be written using decimal digits if the computer's circuitry permits this.

Advantages of Machine Language

i) It makes fast and efficient use of the computer.

ii) It requires no translator to translate the code i.e. directly understood by the computer.

Disadvantages of Machine Language

i) All operation codes have to be remembered

ii) All memory addresses have to be remembered.

iii) It is hard to amend or find errors in a program written in the machine language

iv) These languages are machine dependent i.e. a particular machine language can be used on only one type of computer

2.5 ASSEMBLY LANGUAGE

Assembly languages are a family of low-level languages for programming computers, microprocessors, microcontrollers, and other (usually) integrated circuits. They implement a symbolic representation of the numeric machine codes and other constants needed to program a particular CPU architecture. This representation is usually defined by the hardware manufacturer, and is based on abbreviations (called mnemonics) that help the programmer remember individual instructions, registers, etc. An assembly language is thus specific to certain physical or virtual computer architecture (as opposed to most high-level languages, which are usually portable).

This is a brief introduction to assembly language. Assembly language is the most basic programming language available for any processor. With assembly language, a programmer works only with operations implemented directly on the physical CPU. Assembly language lacks high-level conveniences such as variables and functions, and it is not portable between various families of processors. Nevertheless, assembly language is the most powerful computer programming language available, and it gives programmers the insight required to write effective code in high-level languages. Learning assembly language is well worth the time and effort of every serious programmer.

2.5.1 BASICS OF ASSEMBLY LANGUAGE

Before we can explore the process of writing computer programs, we have to go back to the basics and learn exactly what a computer is and how it works. Every computer, no matter how simple or complex has at its heart exactly two things: a CPU and some memory. Together, these two things are what make it possible for your computer to run programs.

On the most basic level, a computer program is nothing more than a collection of numbers stored in memory. Different numbers tell the CPU to do different things. The CPU reads the numbers one at a time, decodes them, and does what the numbers say. For example, if the CPU reads the number 64 as part of a program, it will add 1 to the number stored in a special location called AX. If the CPU reads the number 146, it will swap the number stored in AX with the number stored in another location called BX. By combining many simple operations such these into a program, a programmer can make the computer perform many incredible things.

As an example, here are the numbers of a simple computer program: 184, 0, 184, 142, 216, 198, 6, 158, 15, 36, 205, 32. If you were to enter these numbers into your computer's memory and run them under MS-DOS, you would see a dollar sign placed in the lower right hand corner of your screen, since that is what these numbers tell the computer to do.

2.5.2 ASSEMBLY CODE INSTRUCTIONS

Assembly language or simply **assembly** is a human-readable notation for the machine language that specific computer architecture uses. Machine language, a pattern of bits encoding machine operations, is made readable by replacing the raw values with symbols called mnemonics. For example, a computer with the appropriate processor will understand this x86/IA-32 machine instruction:

10110000 01100001

For programmers, however, it is easier to remember the equivalent assembly language representation:

mov al, 0x61

which means to move the hexadecimal value 61 (97 decimal) into the processor register with the name 'al'. The mnemonic "mov" is short for "move," and a comma-separated list of arguments or parameters follows it; this is a typical assembly language statement.

Unlike in high-level languages, there is usually a 1-to-1 correspondence between simple assembly statements and machine language instructions. Transforming assembly into machine language is accomplished by an assembler, and the reverse by a disassembler.

Computer architecture has its own machine language, and therefore its own assembly language. Computers differ by the number and type of operations that they support. They may also have different sizes and numbers of registers and different representations of data types in storage. While all general-purpose computers are able to carry out essentially the same functionality, the way they do it differs, and the corresponding assembly language must reflect these differences.

In addition, multiple sets of mnemonics or assembly-language syntax may exist for a single instruction set. In these cases, the most popular one is usually that used by the manufacturer in their documentation.

It was developed to overcome some of the many inconveniences of machine language. This is another low level but a very important language in which operation codes and operands are given in the form of alphanumeric symbols instead of 0's and l's. These alphanumeric symbols will be known as mnemonic codes and can have maximum up to 5 letter combination e.g. ADD for addition, SUB for subtraction, START, LABEL etc. Because of this feature it is also known as 'Symbolic Programming Language'. This language is also very difficult and needs a lot of practice to master it because very small English support is given to this language. The language mainly helps in compiler orientations. The instructions of the Assembly language will also be converted to machine codes by language translator to be executed by the computer.

It is the first step to improve the programming structure. You should know that computer can handle numbers and letter. Therefore some combination of letters can be used to substitute for number of machine codes.

The set of symbols and letters forms the Assembly Language and a translator program is required to translate the Assembly Language to machine language. This translator program is called 'Assembler'. It is considered to be a second-generation language.

Assembly instructions are very simple, unlike high-level languages. Often they only accomplish a single operation. Functions that are more complex must be built up out of smaller ones.

The following are common types of instructions:

- **Moves:**
  - Set a register to a fixed constant value
  - Move data from a memory location to a register (a load) or move data from a register to a memory location (a store). All data must be fetched from memory before a computation may be performed. Similarly, results must be stored in memory after results have been calculated.
  - Read and write data from hardware devices and peripherals
- **Computation:**
  - Add, subtract, multiply, or divide. Typically, the values of two registers are used as parameters and results are placed in a register
  - Perform bitwise operations, taking the conjunction/disjunction (and/or) of corresponding bits in a pair of registers, or the negation (not) of each bit in a register
  - Compare two values in registers (>, < , >=, or <=)
- **Control Flow:**
  - Jump to another location in the program and execute instructions there
  - Jump (branch) to another location if a certain condition holds
  - Jump to another location, but save the location of the next instruction as a point to return to (a call)

2.5.2.1 BASIC ELEMENTS

Any Assembly language consists of 3 types of instruction statements which are used to define the program operations:

1. **Opcode mnemonics**
2. **Data sections**
3. **Assembly directives**

1. Opcode Mnemonics

Instructions (statements) in assembly language are generally very simple, unlike those in high-level languages. Generally, an opcode is a symbolic name for a single executable machine language instruction, and there is at least one opcode mnemonic defined for each machine language instruction. Each instruction typically consists of an operation or opcode plus zero or more operands. Most instructions refer to a single value, or a pair of values. Operands can be either immediate (typically one byte values, coded in the instruction itself) or the addresses of data located elsewhere in storage. This is determined by the underlying processor architecture: the assembler merely reflects how this architecture works.

2. Data Sections

There are instructions used to define data elements to hold data and variables. They define what type of data, length and alignment of data. These instructions can also define whether the data is available to outside programs (programs assembled separately) or only to the program in which the data section is defined.

3. Assembly Directives / Pseudo-Ops

Assembly Directives are instructions that are executed by the Assembler at assembly time, not by the CPU at run time. They can make the assembly of the program dependent on parameters input by the programmer, so that one program can be assembled different ways, perhaps for different applications. They also can be used to manipulate presentation of the program to make it easier for the programmer to read and maintain.

(For example, pseudo-ops would be used to reserve storage areas and optionally their initial contents.) The names of pseudo-ops often start with a dot to distinguish them from machine instructions.

Some assemblers also support pseudo-instructions, which generate two or more machine instructions.

Symbolic assemblers allow programmers to associate arbitrary names (labels or symbols) with memory locations. Usually, every constant and variable is given a name so instructions can reference those locations by name, thus promoting self-documenting code. In executable code, the name of each subroutine is associated with its entry point, so any calls to a subroutine can use its name. Inside subroutines, GOTO destinations are given labels. Some assemblers support local symbols which are lexically distinct from normal symbols (e.g., the use of "10$" as a GOTO destination).

Most assemblers provide flexible symbol management, allowing programmers to manage different namespaces, automatically calculate offsets within data structures, and assign labels that refer to literal values or the result of simple computations performed by the assembler. Labels can also be used to initialize constants and variables with relocatable addresses.

Assembly languages, like most other computer languages, allow comments to be added to assembly source code that are ignored by the assembler. Good use of comments is even more important with assembly code than with higher-level languages, as the meaning and purpose of a sequence of instructions is harder to decipher from the code itself.

Wise use of these facilities can greatly simplify the problems of coding and maintaining low-level code. Raw assembly source code as generated by compilers or disassemblers — code without any comments, meaningful symbols, or data definitions — is quite difficult to read when changes must be made.

All three classes of the assembly language statements use the same format:

[label] mnemonic [operands] [;comment]

The fields in the square brackets are optional in some statements. As a result of this format, it is a common practice to align the fields to aid readability.

Label: This is an optional field. The label field serves two distinct purposes: it is used to represent either an identifier or a constant. When a label appears in an executable instruction, it is used as a marker to identify the instruction. Then, for example, you can make the program execution jump to the labelled instruction. In this case, the label represents the memory address of the instruction. When used with certain assembler directives such as EQU, the label represents a constant.

Mnemonic: This is a required field and identifies the purpose of the statement. In certain lines of code, this field is not required. Examples include lines consisting of a comment, or a label, or a label and a comment.

Operands: Operands specify the data to be manipulated by the statement. The number of operands required depends on the specific statement or directive. For instance, executable statements may have zero, one, two, or three operands.

Comment: This is an optional field and serves the same purpose as comments in a high-level language. Comments play a more important role in assembly language, as it is a low-level language. Assembler ignores all comments. Comments begin with a semicolon (;) and extend until the end of the line. Since the readability of assembly language programs is poor, comments should be generously added to improve readability. It is good programming practice to explain the functionality of a group of statements by several lines of comments and then add brief comments to selected code lines within the group. This is the practice followed in this book.

Now let us look at some sample assembly language statements.

repeat: inc result; increment result by 1

The label repeat can be used to refer to this particular statement. The mnemonic inc indicates increment operation, which is done on the data stored in memory at result. The comment simply explains what the instruction is doing. We avoid such self-explanatory comments.

The following assembler directive defines the constant CR. The ASCII carriage return value is assigned to it by the EQU directive.

CR EQU 0DH; carriage return character

In the previous two examples, the label field has two different forms. The label in the executable instruction is followed by a colon (:) but not in the directive statement. Labels and other names can be formed from upper and lowercase letters (a to z, A to Z), digits (0 through 9), and special characters (_, %, ?, $, .,@).

A name may not begin with a digit and if a period is used, it must be the first character. For example, jump2 and repeat are valid but not go.back and 2_jump. Other characters may be used in any position. Among the special characters, the underscore character is frequently used to aid readability. Certain reserved words that have special meaning to the assembler are not allowed as names. These include mnemonics such as inc and EQU. The assembler is normally case insensitive. For example, labels repeat and REPEAT are treated the same. The assembler can be made case sensitive by using an option (e.g., the /ml option with TASM). We follow the convention that the source code is normally in lowercase except for the directive mnemonics and constants defined in the program. The fields in a statement must be separated by at least one space or tab character. If you want, you can use more spaces and tabs, but the assembler ignores them. It is good programming practice to use blank lines and spaces to improve the readability of assembly language programs.

As a result, you rarely see in this book a statement containing all four fields in a single line. In particular, we almost always write labels on a separate line unless doing so destroys the program structure. Thus, our first example statement would be written as repeat:

inc result

2.5.3 ASSEMBLER

An assembler is a program that takes basic computer instructions and converts them into a pattern of bits that the computer's processor can use to perform its basic operations. Some people call these instructions assembler language and others use the term assembly language.

Typically a modern **assembler** creates object code by translating assembly instruction mnemonics into opcodes, and by resolving symbolic names for memory locations and other entities. The use of symbolic references is a key feature of assemblers, saving tedious calculations and manual address updates after program modifications. Most assemblers also include macro facilities for performing textual substitution—e.g., to generate common short sequences of instructions to run inline, instead of in a subroutine.

Assemblers are generally simpler to write than compilers for high-level languages, and have been available since the 1950s. Modern assemblers, especially for RISC based architectures, such as MIPS, Sun SPARC, and HP PA-RISC, as well as x86(-64), optimize instruction scheduling to exploit the CPU pipeline efficiently.

There are two types of assemblers based on how many passes through the source are needed to produce the executable program. One-pass assembler goes through the source code once and assumes that all symbols will be defined before any instruction that references them. Two-pass assemblers (and multi-pass assemblers) create a table with all unresolved symbols in the first pass, and then use the 2nd pass to resolve these addresses. The advantage in one-pass assemblers is speed - which is not as important as it once was with advances in computer speed and capabilities. The advantage of the two-pass assembler is that symbols can be defined anywhere in the program source. As a result, the program can be defined in a more logical and meaningful way. This makes two-pass assembler programs easier to read and maintain.

Here's how it works:

- Most computers come with a specified set of very basic instructions that correspond to the basic machine operations that the computer can perform. For example, a "Load" instruction causes the processor to move a string of bits from a location in the processor's memory to a special holding place called a register. Assuming the processor has at least eight registers, each numbered, the following instruction would move the value (string of bits of a certain length) at memory location 3000 into the holding place called register 8:

  L 8,3000

- The programmer can write a program using a sequence of these assembler instructions.
- This sequence of assembler instructions, known as the source code or source program, is then specified to the assembler program when that program is started.
- The assembler program takes each program statement in the source program and generates a corresponding bit stream or pattern (a series of 0's and 1's of a given length).
- The output of the assembler program is called the object code or object program relative to the input source program. The sequence of 0's and 1's that constitute the object program is sometimes called machine code.
- The object program can then be run (or executed) whenever desired.

In the earliest computers, programmers actually wrote programs in machine code, but assembler languages or instruction sets were soon developed to speed up programming. Today, assembler programming is used only where very efficient control over processor operations is needed. It requires knowledge of a particular computer's instruction set, however. Historically, most programs have been written in "higher-level" languages such as COBOL, FORTRAN, PL/I, and C. These languages are easier to learn and faster to write programs with than assembler language. The program that processes the source code written in these languages is called a compiler. Like the assembler, a compiler takes higher-level language statements and reduces them to machine code.

More sophisticated high-level assemblers provide language abstractions such as:

- Advanced control structures
- High-level procedure/function declarations and invocations
- High-level abstract data types, including structures/records, unions, classes, and sets
- Sophisticated macro processing
- Object-Oriented features such as encapsulation, polymorphism, inheritance, interfaces

2.5.4 WHY ASSEMBLY LANGUAGE

Although the numbers of the above program make perfect sense to a computer, they are about as clear as mud to a human. Who would have guessed that they put a dollar sign on the screen? Clearly, entering numbers by hand is a lousy way to write a program.

It doesn't have to be this way, though. A long time ago, someone came up with the idea that computer programs could be written using words instead of numbers. A special program called an assembler would then take the programmer's words and convert them to numbers that the computer could understand. This new method, called writing a program in assembly language, saved programmers thousands of hours, since they no longer had to look up hard-to-remember numbers in the backs of programming books. The program above, written in assembly language, looks like this:

```
MOV AX, 47104
MOV DS, AX
MOV [3998], 36
INT 32
```

When an assembler reads this sample program, it converts each line of code into one CPU-level instruction. This program uses two types of instructions, MOV and INT. On Intel processors, the MOV instruction moves data around, while the INT instruction transfers processor control to the device drivers or operating system.

The program still isn't quite clear, but it is much easier to understand than it was before. The first instruction, MOV AX, 47104, tells the computer to copy the number 47104 into the location AX. The next instruction, MOV DS, AX, tells the computer to copy the number in AX into the location DS. The next instruction, MOV [3998], 36 tells the computer to put the number 36 into memory location 3998. Finally, INT 32 exits the program by returning to the operating system.

Before we go on, I would like to explain just how this program works. Inside the CPU are a number of locations, called registers, which can store a number. Some registers, such as AX, are general purpose, and don't do anything special. Other registers, such as DS, control the way the CPU works. DS just happens to be a segment register, and is used to pick which area of memory the CPU can write to. In our program, we put the number 47104 into DS, which tells the CPU to access the memory on the video card. The next thing our program does is to put the number 36 into location 3998 of the video card's memory. Since 36 is the code for the dollar sign, and 3998 is the memory location of the bottom right hand corner of the screen, a dollar sign shows up on the screen a few microseconds later. Finally, our program tells the CPU to perform what is called an interrupt. An interrupt is used to stop one program and execute another in its place. In our case, we want interrupt 32, which ends our program and goes back to MS-DOS, or whatever other program was used to start our program.

2.5.6 ASSEMBLER STRUCTURE

In assembly language code lines have two parts, the first one is the name of the instruction which is to be executed, and the second one are the parameters of the command.

For example: add ah bh

Here "add" is the command to be executed; in this case an addition, and "ah" as well as "bh" are the parameters.

For example: mov al, 25

In the above example, we are using the instruction mov; it means move the value 25 to al register.

The name of the instructions in this language is made of two, three or four letters. These instructions are also called mnemonic names or operation codes, since they represent a function the processor will perform.

Sometimes instructions are used as follows:

add al, [170]

The brackets in the second parameter indicate to us that we are going to work with the content of the memory cell number 170 and not with the 170 value; this is known as direct addressing.

2.5.7 ADVANTAGES OF ASSEMBLY LANGUAGE OVER MACHINE LANGUAGE

Following are the advantages of the assembly language:

1. Here, we use the mnemonics instead of numeric addresses because numeric values are not easy to understand and use. Assembly language programs are much **easier to understand and use** than machine language programs.
2. Use of mnemonic opcodes and symbolic names for different data locations so that the programmers need not keep track of storage locations of the data and instructions, fewer errors are made while writing programs in assembly language and those that are made are **easier to find and correct.**
3. They are easier to understand, it is **easier to locate**, correct, and modify instructions of an assembly language program than a machine language program.
4. An advantage of assembly language is that programmers need not keep track of storage locations of data and instructions while writing an assembly language program.
5. The **availability** of pseudo-instructions for instructing the system how we want the program to be assembled inside the computer's memory makes assembly language programs easily re-locatable because their location can be easily changed by suitably changing the pseudo-instruction. This is not possible easily in the machine language programming.
6. An assembly language program is **more efficient** than machine language program because there is one-to-one correspondence between the instructions of an assembly language program and its corresponding machine language program.

2.5.8 LIMITATIONS OF ASSEMBLY LANGUAGE

Following are the limitations of the assembly language:

1. Each instruction of an assembly language program is translated into exactly one machine language instructions with the help of language processor like assembler, assembly language programs are **machine dependent**. Assembly languages programs differ from computer to computer and an assembly language program can be executed only on the computer in whose assembly language program it has been written.
2. Assembly languages are machine dependent; an assembly language programmer must have **knowledge of the hardware of a particular computer** for which we write assembly language programs.

3. In assembly language, instructions are still written at the machine code level. One assembly language instruction is substituted for one machine language instruction with the help of assembler. Assembly language programs are also **time-consuming and difficult** to write when we have other high level languages.

2.5.9 MACROS IN ASSEMBLY LANGUAGE

Many assemblers support macros, programmer-defined symbols that stand for some sequence of text lines. This sequence of text lines may include a sequence of instructions, or a sequence of data storage pseudo-ops. Once a macro has been defined using the appropriate pseudo-op, its name may be used in place of a mnemonic. When the assembler processes such a statement, it replaces the statement with the text lines associated with that macro, and then processes them just as though they had appeared in the source code file all along (including, in better assemblers, expansion of any macros appearing in the replacement text).

Since macros can have 'short' names but expand to several or indeed many lines of code, they can be used to make assembly language programs appear to be much shorter (require less lines of source code from the application programmer - as with a higher level language). They can also be used to add higher levels of structure to assembly programs, optionally introduce embedded debugging code via parameters and other similar features. Many assemblers have built-in macros for system calls and other special code sequences.

Macro assemblers often allow macros to take parameters. Some assemblers include quite sophisticated macro languages, incorporating such high-level language elements as optional parameters, symbolic variables, conditionals, string manipulation, and arithmetic operations, all usable during the execution of a given macros, and allowing macros to save context or exchange information. Thus a macro might generate a large number of assembly language instructions or data definitions, based on the macro arguments. This could be used to generate record-style data structures or "unrolled" loops, for example, or could generate entire algorithms based on complex parameters. An organization using assembly language that has been heavily extended using such a macro suite can be considered to be working in a higher-level language, since such programmers are not working with a computer's lowest-level conceptual elements.

Macros were used to customize large scale software systems for specific customers in the mainframe era and were also used by customer personnel to satisfy their employers' needs by making specific versions of manufacturer operating systems; this was done, for example, by systems programmers working with IBM's Conversational Monitor System/Virtual Machine (CMS/VM) and with IBM's "real time transaction processing" add-ons, CICS, Customer Information Control System, and ACP/TPF, the airline/financial system that began in the 1970s and still runs many large Global Distribution Systems (GDS) and credit card systems today.

It was also possible to use solely the macro processing capabilities of an assembler to generate code written in completely different languages, for example, to generate a version of a program in COBOL using a pure macro assembler program containing lines of COBOL code inside assembly time operators instructing the assembler to generate arbitrary code.

This was because, as was realized in the 1970s, the concept of "macro processing" is independent of the concept of "assembly", the former being in modern terms more word processing, text processing, than generating object code. The concept of macro processing in fact appeared in and appears in the C programming language, which supports "preprocessor instructions" to set variables, and make conditional tests on their values. Note that unlike certain previous macro processors inside assemblers, the C preprocessor was not Turing-complete because it lacked the ability to either loop or "go to", the latter allowing the programmer to loop.

Despite the power of macro processing, it fell into disuse in high level languages while remaining a perennial for assemblers.

This was because many programmers were rather confused by macro parameter substitution and did not disambiguate macro processing from assembly and execution.

Macro parameter substitution is strictly by name: at macro processing time, the value of a parameter is textually substituted for its name. The most famous class of bugs resulting was the use of a parameter that itself was an expression and not a simple name when the macro writer expected a name. In the macro: foo: macro a load a*b the intention was that the caller would provide the name of a variable, and the "global" variable or constant b would be used to multiply "a". If foo is called with the parameter a-c, an unexpected macro expansion occurs.

To avoid this, users of macro processors learned to religiously parenthesize formal parameters inside macro definitions, and callers had to do the same to their "actual" parameters.

PL/I and C feature macros, but this facility was underused or dangerous when used because they can only manipulate text. On the other hand, homo-iconic languages, such as Lisp, Prolog, and Forth, retain the power of assembly language macros because they are able to manipulate their own code as data

2.5.10 ASSEMBLY FOR MICROPROCESSORS

First of all, we'll talk about the registers and then about the instructions to manipulate (change) them. The **8086** has 14 16-bit registers, all with different usage (see below). You might not understand some of the registers purposes, but be patient, I'll explain everything later.

1. SEGMENT REGISTERS

CS	Code Segment	16-bit number that points to the active code-segment
DS	Data Segment	16-bit number that points to the active data-segment
SS	Stack Segment	16-bit number that points to the active stack-segment
ES	Extra Segment	16-bit number that points to the active extra-segment

2. POINTER REGISTERS

IP	Instruction Pointer	16-bit number that points to the offset of the next instruction
SP	Stack Pointer	16-bit number that points to the offset that the stack is using
BP	Base Pointer	used to pass data to and from the stack

3. GENERAL-PURPOSE REGISTERS

AX	Accumulator Register	mostly used for calculations and for input/output
BX	Base Register	Only register that can be used as an index
CX	Count Register	register used for the loop instruction
DX	Data Register	input/output and used by multiply and divide

4. INDEX REGISTERS

SI	Source Index	used by string operations as source
DI	Destination Index	used by string operations as destination

(The general purpose registers can be "split". You have the AH and the AL register for example. AH contains the high byte of AX and AL contains the low byte. You also have: BH, BL, CH, CL, DL, DH so if e.g. DX contains the value 1234h DH would be 12h and DL would be 34h).

And a 16-bit FLAG Register. All "flags" (see below) are stored here. The FLAGS Register consists of 9 status bits. These bits are also called flags, because they can either be **SET (1)** or **NOT SET (0)**. All these flags have a name and purpose.

5. FLAGS REGISTER

Abr.	Name	bit nº	Description
OF	Overflow Flag	11	indicates an overflow when set
DF	Direction Flag	10	used for string operations to check direction
IF	Interrupt Flag	9	if set, interrupt are enabled, else disabled
TF	Trap Flag	8	if set, CPU can work in single step mode
SF	Sign Flag	7	if set, resulting number of calculation is negative
ZF	Zero Flag	6	if set, resulting number of calculation is zero
AF	Auxiliary Carry	4	some sort of second carry flag
PF	Parity Flag	2	indicates even or odd parity
CF	Carry Flag	0	contains the left-most bit after calculations

TEST IT!

If you want to see all these register and flags, you can go to DOS and then start "debug" (just type debug) when you're in debug, just type "r" and you'll see all the registers and some abbreviations for the flags. Type 'q' to quit again. We won't use debug to program in this tutorial, we'll use a real assembler. I use TASM 3.2, but MASM or any other assembler works just fine too.

2.5.11 MEMORY SEGMENTATION

Now I've to explain something about the way the **8086** uses memory (actually about how DOS uses memory). Since the databus of the **8086** is 16-bits, it can move and store 16-bits (1 word=2 bytes) at a time. If the processor stores a "word" (16-bits) it stores the bytes in reverse order in the memory. It looks like this:

1234h (word) → memory 34h (byte) 12h (byte)

So if the memory looks like this: 78h 56h and you get a word from memory you'll get the value 5678h. (Note, I use the "h" after a number to indicate it's hexadecimal) However, if you just get a byte from memory it goes this way: memory 78h 56h -----> first byte you get 78h.

Now let's talk about segments. The **8086** divides its memory into segments. Segments are (standard in DOS) 64 KB big and have a number. These numbers are stored in the segment registers (see above). Three main segments are the code, data and stack segment. Segments overlap each other almost completely. If you start debug again and type "d" you can see some addresses at the left of the screen. The format is like this: 4576:0100. That's a memory address. The first number is the segment number and the second number is the offset within the segment. So FFFF: FFF0 means: Segment FFFFh and FFF0h bytes from the beginning of the segment.

As I said before, segments overlap. The address 0000:0010 is EXACTLY the same address as 0001:0000. That means that segment begin at paragraph boundaries. (A paragraph=16 bytes, so the segment starts at an address divisible by 16) Now you can start calculating REAL addresses in memory. An example: 0000:0010 means: segment 0000h offset 10h now we multiply the segment number with 16 and add the offset.

Note that the offset 10h means the value 16 in decimal: *(0 * 16 = 0 + 16 = 16)* this is the linear address.

Next, the other addresses 0001:0000: *(16 * 1 = 16 + 0 = 16)*. Same linear address! Like I told you. These are some basic things you need to know when you want to program in Assembly. Learn the registers and flags by heart and try to understand the segmentation of memory.

2.6 HIGH LEVEL LANGUAGES

High level computer languages give formats close to English language and the purpose of developing high level languages is to enable people to write programs easily and in their own native language environment (English). High-level languages are basically symbolic languages that use English words and/or mathematical symbols rather than mnemonic codes. Each instruction in the high level language is translated into many machine language instructions thus showing one-to-many translation.

All high level language are procedure-oriented language and are intended to be machine independent. Programs are written in statements akin to English language, a great advantage over mnemonics of assembly languages require languages use mnemonics of assembly language. That is, the high level languages use natural language like structures. These languages require translators (compilers and interpreters) for execution. The programs written in a high level language can be ported on any computer that is why known they are known as machine independent. The early high-level language comes in third generation of languages, COBOL, BASIC, APL, etc.

These languages enable the programmer to write instruction using English words and familiar mathematical symbols which makes it easier than technical details of the computer. It makes the programs more readable too.

2.6.1 WHY HIGHER-LEVEL LANGUAGES?

Though machine language is the most efficient programming language in terms of execution, it has various drawbacks. Programming in machine language is tedious and error-prone. The use of numeric codes to represent instructions is difficult and makes programming a complex, arduous task. This complexity results in programs that are difficult to read and debug.

In addition to being tedious, machine language requires the programmer to keep track of where individual bits of data are stored in the computer's memory. Inserting new instructions or changing the address of one bit of data affects the correctness of the program and the subsequent memory addresses used in the rest of the program. Machine language programs are very long since each instruction only accomplishes a small task. For example, to multiple two numbers could require more than 10 instructions in machine language. These drawbacks make programming in machine language slow and far from cost effective. To combat these and other difficulties, other languages were developed. Higher-level programming languages allow the programmer to concentrate more fully on the problem, not how the computer software and hardware interact to solve the problem. These programs are designed for ease and reliability, while machine language is designed for efficient execution.

With the advent of higher-level languages most programmers have very little use for machine language to write programs. However, programmers still need to understand machine language. For programmers responsible for maintaining machine language code and creating assemblers, knowledge of machine language is essential. Additionally, there are still tasks best accomplished using machine languages.

2.6.2 CHARACTERISTICS OF HIGH-LEVEL LANGUAGES

In terms of technology, high-level languages are not better than the low-level versions. Rather the computing techniques used in high-level languages are simpler than those applied in low-level programming languages. The term high-level indicates greater degree of abstraction from the so-called computer languages. Unlike low-level programming languages, the high-level languages never come with opcodes. Among the other common features of high-level languages, object-oriented features, string handling schedules and modes for input or outputs of files are worth mentioning.

2.6.3 FUNCTIONS OF HIGH-LEVEL LANGUAGES

The main function of a high-level language is to simplify the use of programming systems to the users. The high-level languages break up the complicated chains of commands into simpler parts. For an efficient computer programming, the codes must be developed in low-level languages. However to make the best possible use of those codes, high-level languages are required.

Over the passage of time, the architectures of computers are becoming more complicated than before. Today's microprocessors require cutting-edge techniques to run the computer systems efficiently. Here comes the role of high-level languages. These programming languages are capable of designing cods that perfectly suit the requirements of modern computing.

High-level languages operate through different models of programming. Interpreted and compiled are the two programming languages used in the intermediate steps. Intermediate representations and machine code generation are some other steps involved in the operation of high-level languages.

2.6.4 ADVANTAGES OF HIGH-LEVEL LANGUAGES

There are several advantages of high-level programming languages. The most important advantages are:

1. Easy to Learn

The high-level languages are very easy to learn than low-level languages. The statements written for the program are similar to English like statements.

2. Easy to Understand

The program written is high-level language by one programmer can easily be understood by another because the program instructions are similar to the English Language.

3. Easy to Write Program

In high-level language, a new program can easily be written in a very short time. The larger and complicated software can be developed in few days or months.

4. Easy to Detect and Remove Errors

The errors in a program can be easily detected and removed. Mostly the errors are occurred during the compilation of new program.

5. Built-in Library Functions

Each high-level language provides a large number of built-in functions or procedures that can be used to perform specific tasks during designing of news programs. In this way, a large amount of time of programmer is saved.

6. Machine Independence

Program written in high-level language is machine independent. It means that a program written on one type of computer can be executed on another type of computer.

2.6.5 DISADVANTAGES OF HIGH-LEVEL LANGUAGES

Two main disadvantages of high-level languages are:

1. High cost

A high-level language has to be translated into the machine language by a translator and thus a price in computer time is paid.

2. Lower efficiency

The object code generated by a translator might be inefficient Compared to an equivalent assembly language program

3. Less flexibility

High-level languages are less flexible than assembly languages because they do not normally have instructions or mechanism to control a computer's CPU, memory, and registers. An assembly language provides the programmers access to hardware components easily.

2.7 COMPARISON OF MACHINE, ASSEMBLY AND HIGH LEVEL LANGUAGE

Assembly languages are close to a one to one correspondence between symbolic instructions and executable machine codes. Assembly languages also include directives to the assembler, directives to the linker, directives for organizing data space, and macros. Macros can be used to combine several assembly language instructions into a high level language-like construct (as well as other purposes). There are cases where a symbolic instruction is translated into more than one machine instruction. But in general, symbolic assembly language instructions correspond to individual executable machine instructions.

High level languages are abstract. Typically a single high level instruction is translated into several (sometimes dozens or in rare cases even hundreds) executable machine language instructions. Some early high level languages had a close correspondence between high level instructions and machine language instructions. For example, most of the early COBOL instructions translated into a very obvious and small set of machine instructions. The trend over time has been for high level languages to increase in abstraction. Modern object oriented programming languages are highly abstract (although, interestingly, some key object oriented programming constructs do translate into a very compact set of machine instructions).

Assembly language is much harder to program than high level languages. The programmer must pay attention to far more detail and must have an intimate knowledge of the processor in use. But high quality hand crafted assembly language programs can run much faster and use much less memory and other resources than a similar program written in a high level language. Speed increases of two to 20 times faster are fairly common, and increases of hundreds of times faster are occasionally possible. Assembly language programming also gives direct access to key machine features essential for implementing certain kinds of low level routines, such as an operating system kernel or microkernel, device drivers, and machine control.

High level programming languages are much easier for less skilled programmers to work in and for semi-technical managers to supervise. And high level languages allow faster development times than work in assembly language, even with highly skilled programmers. Development time increases of 10 to 100 times faster are fairly common. Programs written in high level languages (especially object oriented programming languages) are much easier and less expensive to maintain than similar programs written in assembly language (and for a successful software project, the vast majority of the work and expense is in maintenance, not initial development).

Difference between machine level language and assembly level language and high level language

Machine language	Assembly language	High level language
1. It is a language in which program are written as string of binary 1's or 0's.	1. Assembly language is a language in which program are written as symbolic codes called mnemonics	1. High level language program are written in the form of English statements
2. Computer directly understood the machine language program written in 0 and 1.	2. Assembly level program are not directly understood by computer.	2. High level language program are also bit directly understood by computer.
3. There is no need of translator for machine level program.	3. Assembler is translator used to convert assembly level language to machine level language.	3. Compiler or interpreter is requires to convert high level program to machine level program.
4. Program written in machine level language are executed very fast by the computer.	4. Assembly level program are executed slowly as compared to machine level program.	4. High level program are also executed slowly because they have to be converted into low level before execution.
5. Machine level program are not portable programs they are machine dependent.	5. Assembly level program are also machine dependent.	5. High level language program are portable i.e. they are machine independent.
6. Program is not easy to modify.	6. Program is comparatively easy to modify.	6. Program is very easy to modify.
7. It is difficult to write program in machine level language programmer has to memory the instruction set of a machine.	7. It is easy to with program in assembly level language as compare to machine level language.	7. It is very easy to write program in high level language.
8. Debugging is difficult in machine level language.	8. Debugging is easy to compared to machine level language.	8. Debugging is very easy in high level language.
9. Large number of errors occurs in machine level program.	9. Less number of errors occurs.	9. Chances of error very less in high level language.
10. Addressing is handled by the programmer him self.	10. Addressing is handled by the assembler. Programmer has no worry about address of instruction.	10. Addressing is handled by the compiler programmer has no worry about address of instruction.
11. Machine level language program are very lengthy.	11. Assembly level language program are small as compare to machine level language.	11. High level language program are very small in size.
12. It is difficult to relocate machine level program.	12. Assembly level program are easily relocatable.	12. High level program can be easily relocated by compiler.
13. Knowledge of hardware is required to write program in machine level language.	13. Knowledge of hardware is still required for assembly level language.	13. No knowledge of hardware is required for high level language.

2.8 LANGUAGE PROCESSORS

We know that computer understands instructions in machine code, i.e. in the form of 0s and 1s. It is difficult to write computer program directly in machine code. Nowadays, the programs are written mostly in high-level languages, i.e. BASIC, C, PASCAL, etc. A program written in any high-level programming language (or written in assembly language) is called the **Source Program**.

The **source code** cannot be executed directly by the computer. The source program must be converted into machine code to run it on the computer. The program translated into machine code is known as **Object Program.**

Every language has its own language processor (or translator). Therefore, language processor is defined as:

The special translator system software that is used to translate the program written in high-level language (or Assembly language) into machine code is called language processor or translator program.

The language processors or translators are divided into three types:

1. **Compilers**
2. **Interpreters**
3. **Assemblers**

These are programs which translate computer programs from high-level languages such as Pascal, C++, Java or JavaScript into the raw 1s and 0s which the computer can understand, but the human programmers cannot:

You write this

```
sum = 0;
for (x = 3; x < 5; x++)
  {count << "x is" << x;
     count << end1;
     sum +=x;
     a *= b/2;
```

The computer translates it ... into this, which it can run

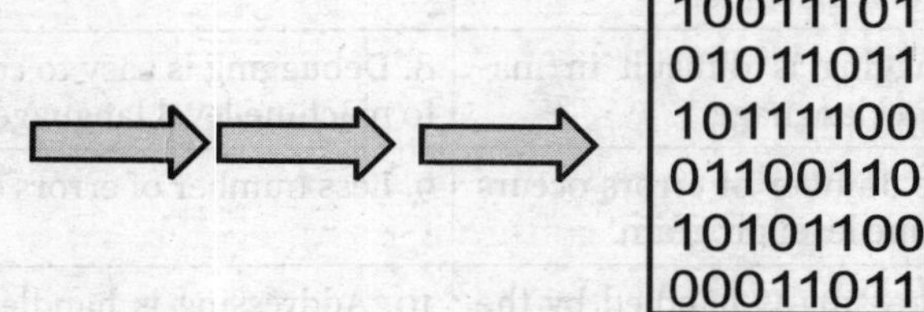

2.8.1 COMPILER

The language processor that translates the complete source program as a whole in machine code before execution is called compiler. The C and C++ compilers are best examples of compilers.

It is a program translator that translates the instruction of a higher level language to machine language. It is called compiler because it compiles machine language instructions for every program instructions of higher level language. Thus compiler is a program translator like assembler but more sophisticated. It scans the entire program first and then translates it into machine code.

Source code

Program written in a particular programming language in its original form is called source code (program). The word source differentiates code from various other forms that it can have (for example, object code and executable code). To execute the program, however, the programmer must translate it into machine language. The compiler translates the source code into a form called object code. Source code is the only format that s readable by humans. When we purchase programs, we usually receive them in their machine-language format. This means that we can execute them directly, but cannot read or modify them.

Object code

Object code is the code produced by a compiler. Object code is often the same as or similar to a computer's machine language. The final step in producing an executable program is to transform the object code into machine languages, if it is not already in this form. A program called linker does this job.

The programs written by the programmer in higher level language is called source program. After this program is converted to machine languages by the compiler it is called object program.

Higher Level Language → (Compile) → Program → Machine Language Program

A compiler can translate only those source programs, which have been written, in that language for which the compiler is meant for. For example FORTRAN compiler will not compile source code written in COBOL language.

Object program generated by compiler is machine dependent. It means programs compiled for one type of machine will not run in another type. Therefore every type of machine must have its personal compiler for a particular language. Machine independence is achieved by using one higher level language in different machines.

2.8.1.1 COMPILING PROCESS

Compiling is a process of transforming a program written in a high-level programming language from source code into object code. Programmers write programs in a form called source code. Source code must go through several steps before it becomes an executable program. The first step is to pass the source code through a compiler, which translates the high-level language instructions in the source code follow its syntax rules. If not it will inform the programmer where rules have been violated.

The final step in producing an executable program –after the compiler has produced object code – is to pass the object code through a linker. The linker combines molecules (different program segments) and gives real values to all symbolic addresses (memory locations), thereby producing machine code.

2.8.1.2 COMPILED LANGUAGES

The most conventional kind of language is a compiled language. Compiled languages get translated into runnable files of binary machine code by a special program called (logically enough) a compiler. Once the binary has been generated, you can run it directly without looking at the source code again. (Most software is delivered as compiled binaries made from code you don't see.)

Compiled languages tend to give excellent performance and have the most complete access to the OS, but also to be difficult to program in.

C, the language in which UNIX itself is written, is by far the most important of these (with its variant C++). FORTRAN is another compiled language still used among engineers and scientists but years older and much more primitive. In the UNIX world no other compiled languages are in mainstream use. Outside it, COBOL is very widely used for financial and business software.

There used to be many other compiler languages, but most of them have either gone extinct or are strictly research tools. If you are a new UNIX developer using a compiled language, it is overwhelmingly likely to be C or C++.

2.8.2 INTERPRETER

An interpreter is another type of program translator used for translating higher level language into machine language. It takes one statement of higher level languages, translate it into machine language and immediately execute it. Translation and execution are carried out for each statement. It differs from compiler, which translate the entire source program into machine code and does involve in its execution.

You write the program using a text editor or something similar, and then instruct the interpreter to run the program. It takes the program, one line at a time, and translates each line before running it: It translates the first line and runs it, then translates the second line and runs it etc. The interpreter has no "memory" for the translated lines, so if it comes across lines of the program within a loop, it must translate them afresh every time that particular line runs.

The advantage of interpreter compared to compiler is its fast response to changes in source program. It eliminates the need for a separate compilation after changes to each program. Interpreters are easy to write and do not require large memory in computer.

The main disadvantages of Interpreter are:

- **It is a time consuming process of translating and executing statements** one by one.
- **Each time** the program is run, the source code is translated and executed have a translator program (Interpreter) permanently in your computer.

2.8.2.1 INTERPRETING PROCESS

An interpreting process translates high-level instructions into an intermediate form, which it then executes. Interpreter analyzes and executes each line of source code in succession, without looking at the entire program; the advantage of interpreters is that they can execute a program immediately. Compilers require some time before an executable program emerges. However, programs produced by compilers run much faster than the same programs executed by an interpreter.

Compiled programs generally run faster than interpreted programs. The advantage of an interpreter, however, is that it does not need to get through the compilation stage during which machine instructions are generated. This process can be time-consuming if the program is long. The interpreter, on the other hand, can immediately execute high-level programs. For this reason, interpreters are sometimes used during the development of a program, when a programmer wants to add small sections at a time and test them quickly.

2.8.2.2 INTERPRETED LANGUAGES

An interpreted language depends on an interpreter program that reads the source code and translates it on the fly into computations and system calls. The source has to be re-interpreted (and the interpreter present) each time the code is executed.

Interpreted languages tend to be slower than compiled languages, and often have limited access to the underlying operating system and hardware. On the other hand, they tend to be easier to program and more forgiving of coding errors than compiled languages.

Many Unix utilities, including the shell and bc(1) and sed(1) and awk(1), are effectively small interpreted languages. BASICs are usually interpreted. So is Tcl. Historically, the most important interpretive language has been LISP (a major improvement over most of its successors). Today, UNIX shells and the Lisp that lives inside the Emacs editor are probably the most important pure interpreted languages.

2.8.3 COMPILER VERSUS INTERPRETER

An interpreter translates some form of source code into a target representation that it can immediately execute and evaluate. The structure of the interpreter is similar to that of a compiler, but the amount of time it takes to produce the executable representation will vary as will the amount of optimization. The following diagram shows one representation of the differences.

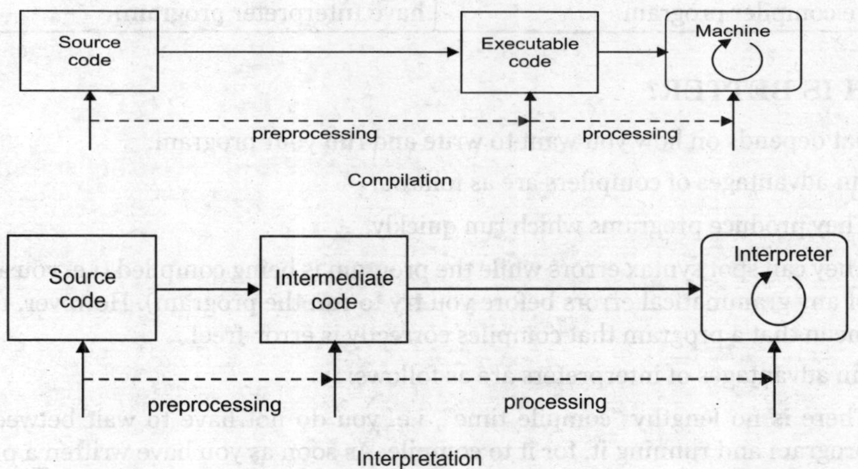

Compiler characteristics:

- spends a lot of time analyzing and processing the program
- the resulting executable is some form of machine- specific binary code
- the computer hardware interprets (executes) the resulting code
- program execution is fast

Interpreter characteristics:

- relatively little time is spent analyzing and processing the program
- the resulting code is some sort of intermediate code
- the resulting code is interpreted by another program
- program execution is relatively slow

The above characteristics are typical. There are well-known cases that are somewhere in between, such as Java with it's JVM.

The main difference between compiler and interpreter is

Compiler	Interpreter
1) It translates source code into object codes as a whole.	1) It translates the statements of the source code one by one and execute immediately.
2) It creates an object file.	2) It does not create an object file.
3) Program execution is very fast.	3) Program execution is slow.
4) Translator program is not required to translate the program each time you want to run the program.	4) Translator program is required to translate the program each time you want to run the program.
5) It does not make easier to correct the mistakes in the source code.	5) It makes easier to correct the mistakes in the source code.
6) Most of the high-level programming languages have compiler program.	6) A few high-level programming languages have Interpreter program.

SO WHICH IS BETTER?

Well, that depends on how you want to write and run your program.

The main advantages of compilers are as follows:

- They produce programs which run quickly.
- They can spot syntax errors while the program is being compiled (i.e. you are informed of any grammatical errors before you try to run the program). However, this does not mean that a program that compiles correctly is error-free!

The main advantages of interpreters are as follows:

- There is no lengthy "compile time", i.e. you do not have to wait between writing a program and running it, for it to compile. As soon as you have written a program, you can run it.
- They tend to be more "portable", which means that they will run on a greater variety of machines. This is because each machine can have its own interpreter for that language. For instance, the version of the BASIC interpreter for the PDP series computers is different from the QBasic program for personal computers, as they run on different pieces of hardware, but programs written in BASIC are identical from the user's point of view.

Some computer systems try to get the best of both worlds. For instance, when I was at Durham, we programmed in Pascal on the old PDP/11 machines. Running a Pascal program on those machines was a two-stage process. Firstly, we ran a compiler program (called pc) which compiled the program to a low-level version, and spotted any grammatical errors in the process. We then ran an interpreter program which took the output of pc and ran it. The fact that pc produced something that didn't have to run directly as machine code made the program more portable. Different versions of the low-level interpreter could be written for different machines in the PDP range, each taking as its input the same output from pc.

Considerations

There are a number of other points which we need to consider:

- Because the interpreter must be loaded into memory, there is less space available during execution; a compiler is only loaded into memory during compilation stage, and so only the machine code is resident in memory during run-time;
- Once we have a compiled file, we can re-run it any time we want to without having to use the compiler each time; With any interpreted language, however, we would have to re-interpret the program each time we wanted to run it;
- Machine code programs run more quickly than interpreted programs;
- However, it is often quicker and easier to make changes with an interpreted program than a compiled one, and as such development time may be reduced.

2.8.4 LINKERS AND LOADERS

Linkers and loaders are utilities that function in the execution, or running, of programs. A linker, which can also be called a link editor or a binder, is a program that combines object modules together to form a program that can then be executed. Modules are parts of programs. Until modules are combined, or linked, the program will not function. An individual module can contain one or several routines, and so can be linked with other modules to support programs of differing functionality.

A link editor is a program that takes one or more objects generated by a compiler and combines them into a single executable program. Link editors are commonly known as linkers. The compiler automatically invokes the linker as the last step in compiling a program. The linker inserts code (or maps in shared libraries) to resolve program library references, and/or combines object modules into an executable image suitable for loading into memory.

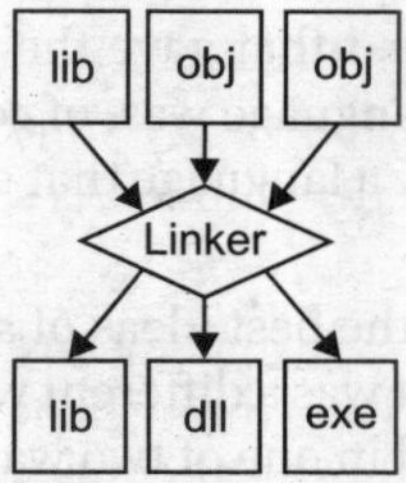

Figure 2.1: An illustration of the linking process. Object files and static libraries are assembled into a new library or executable.

A linker performs an important function. Without it, programs would have to be written completely. The presence of the linker allows a large program to be broken into small, more manageable pieces. In addition to the combining function, a linker can replace a so-called symbolic address with a real address. Even a program consisting entirely of one module may need to be linked, if address replacement is done.

Static linking is the result of the linker copying all library routines used in the program into the executable image. This may require more disk space and memory than dynamic linking, but is both faster and more portable, since it does not require the presence of the library on the system where it is run.

Dynamic linking is accomplished by placing the name of a sharable library in the executable image. Actual linking with the library routines does not occur until the image is run, when both the executable and the library are placed in memory. An advantage of dynamic linking is that multiple programs can share a single copy of the library.

A loader is a utility of an operating system. It copies programs from a storage device to a computer's main memory, where the program can then be executed. Like linkers, loaders can also replace virtual addresses with real addresses. Most loaders function without user involvement. They are invisible to the user, but are a recognizable utility to the operating system.

2.9 OBJECT-ORIENTED PROGRAMMING

Object-oriented programming (OOP) is a currently popular and powerful programming technique. The three main characteristics of OOP are encapsulation, inheritance, and polymorphism. Encapsulation is a form of information hiding or abstraction. Inheritance has to do with writing reusable code. Polymorphism refers to a way that a single name can have multiple meanings in the context of inheritance. Having made those statements, we must admit that they will hold little meaning for readers who have not heard of OOP before. However, we will describe all these terms in detail later in this chapter.

OOP is a powerful way to approach the job of programming. Programming methodologies have changed dramatically since the invention of the computer, primarily to accommodate the increasing complexity of programs. For example, when computers were first invented, programming was done by toggling in the binary machine instructions using the computer's front panel. As long as programs were just a few hundred instructions long, this approach worked. As programs grew, assembly language was invented so that a programmer could deal with larger, increasingly complex programs, using symbolic representations of the machine instructions. As programs continued to grow, high-level languages were introduced that gave the programmer more tools with which to handle complexity. The first widespread language was, of course, FORTRAN. Although FORTRAN was a very impressive first step, it is hardly a language that encourages clear, easy to understanding programs.

Object-oriented programming took the best ideas of structured programming and combined them with several new concepts. The result was a different way of organizing a program. In the most general sense, a program can be organized in one of two ways: around its code (what is happening) or around its data (who is being affected). Using only structured programming techniques, programs are typically organized around code. This approach can be thought of as "code acting on data." For example, a program written in a structured language such as C is defined by its functions, any of which may operate on any type of data used by the program. Object-oriented programs work the other way around. They are organized around data, with the key principle being "data controlling access to code." In an object-oriented language, you define the data and the routines that are permitted to act on that data. Thus, a data type defines precisely what sort of operations can be applied to that data.

2.10 LANGUAGE CHARACTERISTICS

The following language characteristics are used in the Programming languages. They are defined below, along with an explanation of what each characteristic contributes to software development. Although these characteristics are not entirely independent, they are the characteristics of common interest to most decision makers. The value assigned to each characteristic is a number between 0 and 10, where 0 means the language support for this characteristic is extremely poor or non-existent and 10 means the language support for this characteristic is extremely good or as good as it could possibly be.

It should be emphasized that the ratings given to the characteristics from this appendix are an indication of the extent of language support for the characteristics. Actual programs written in a particular language will vary widely with respect to these characteristics, depending on both the support provided by the language and the skill and discipline of the programmers.

Clarity of source code: The extent to which inherent language features support source code that is readable and understandable and that clearly reflects the underlying logical structure of the program.

Most of the life cycle cost of a software system (usually between 60% and 80%) will come during the time after its initial development has been completed. This includes all efforts to change the software, whether it is to fix problems or to add new capabilities. Regardless of the purpose, changing the software implies that a significant cost will be associated with understanding the program and its structure, since this is a necessary first step before any changes can be made. Although it is always possible to use techniques to make a program easier to understand, language support for source code clarity can facilitate this process considerably. Note that clarity is a readability issue, not necessarily an ease of use issue. It is not unusual for languages with good readability to be somewhat more verbose than less readable languages.

Complexity management (architecture support): The extent to which inherent language features support the management of system complexity, in terms of addressing issues of data, algorithm, interface, and architectural complexity.

The more complex a system becomes, the more important that its complexity be managed. Waiting until a system gets large enough to manifest complexity before preparing to manage that complexity does not work well. Properly structuring a system from the beginning, as well as using appropriate supporting tools, is essential. However, complexity management is always difficult, and it is very helpful if the language can facilitate this goal.

Concurrency support: The extent to which inherent language features support the construction of code with multiple threads of control (also known as parallel processing).

For many types of applications, multiple threads of control are very useful or even necessary. This is particularly true of real-time systems and those running on hardware with multiple processors. Concurrency is rarely directly supported by a language, and, in fact, the philosophy of some languages is that it should be a separate issue for the operating system to deal with. However, language support can make concurrent processing more straightforward and understandable, and it can also provide the programmer with more control over how it is implemented.

Distributed system support: The extent to which inherent language features support the construction of code to be distributed across multiple platforms on a network.

It is becoming more and more common for the software components of systems, particularly very large software systems, to be distributed across multiple platforms on a network. In this networked configuration, each platform performs some portion of the system processes, communicating with the other platforms to accomplish the overall system functions. This makes sense for various reasons, with performance right at the top of the list. However, distribution creates many new problems, not the least of which is that the multiple platforms are generally heterogeneous (different hardware and/or operating systems). The problems of distribution can be dealt with by tools rather than language (see the software engineering factor Tool support for interoperability requirements). However, some newer languages also address the issues of distribution.

Maintainability: The extent to which inherent language features support the construction of code that can be readily modified to satisfy new requirements or to correct deficiencies.

Support for code clarity has already been mentioned above as one type of support for maintainability. Maintainability is actually facilitated by many of the language characteristics—those which make it easier to understand and then change the software. The structure of the code also has a significant impact on how easy code is to change. The technique of encapsulating units and limiting their access through well-defined interfaces greatly facilitates maintainability. Hence, language features which facilitate encapsulation can be very beneficial.

Mixed language support: The extent to which inherent language features support interfacing to other languages.

This should not be confused with the complementary product support that provides calling interfaces (called bindings) for specific languages. Mixed language support, from the perspective of the language, means the provision of specific capabilities to interface with other languages. This type of support can have a significant impact on the reliability of the data that is exchanged between languages. Without specific language support, no checking may be done on the form, or even the existence, of data exchanged on a call between units of different languages, and the potential for unreliability is high. Specific language support can provide the expected reliability.

Object-oriented programming support: The extent to which inherent language features support the construction of object-oriented code.

There is general agreement that object-oriented programming support means specific language support for the creation of code with encapsulated classes and objects, inheritance, and polymorphism. This form of programming is associated with software that has good maintainability characteristics because of the encapsulation of classes and objects. It also facilitates the creation of reusable software because it encourages well-structured software with well-defined interfaces, and it encourages extending existing abstractions. There are two different ways a language can provide object-oriented programming support. Some languages are strictly object-oriented and do not support any other form of programming. Other languages provide object-oriented capabilities along with more conventional programming capabilities, and the programmer determines whether or not the language is used to create object-oriented software. For this language characteristic, the specific mechanism for providing the capability is not the issue, the extent of support is.

Portability: The extent to which inherent language features support the transfer of a program from one hardware and/or software platform to another.

To make software readily portable, it must be written using non-system-dependent constructs except where system dependencies are encapsulated. The system dependent parts, if any, must be reaccomplished for the new platform, but if those parts of the software are encapsulated, a relatively small amount of new code is required to run the software on the new platform. Language support for portability can come from support for encapsulation, and it can also come from support for expressing constructs in a non-system-dependent manner. Language standardization has a significant impact on portability because non-standard language constructs can only be ported to systems that support the same non-standard constructs—for example, if both systems have compilers from the same vendor. In some circles, the issue of existing compatible support products, including compilers, on many different platforms is considered in the concept of portability. Note that a language's portability characteristics can be severely compromised by poor programming practices.

Real-time support: The extent to which inherent language features support the construction of real-time systems.

Real-time systems have mandatory time constraints, and often space constraints, that must be met. These will usually tax both the software and the hardware of the system, and system performance predictability becomes an important issue. Language can support real-time systems in two ways. A language can provide specific constructs for specifying the time and space constraints of a system. It can also support streamlined ways to express program instructions. For example, real-time systems often have unique requirements in areas such as device control and interrupt handling, and a language can support managing these in a straightforward, predictable manner. Since many real-time systems are concurrent systems, real-time support and concurrency support are closely related.

Reliability: The extent to which inherent language features support the construction of components that can be expected to perform their intended functions in a satisfactory manner throughout the expected lifetime of the product.

Reliability is concerned with making a system failure free, and thus is concerned with all possible errors. System reliability is most suspects when software is being stressed to its capacity limits or when it is interfacing with resources outside the system, particularly when receiving input from such resources. One way that interfacing with outside resources occurs is when users operate the system. Reliability problems often surface when novices use the system, because they can provide unexpected input that was not tested. Interfacing with outside resources also occurs when the system is interfacing with devices or other software systems. Language can provide support for this potential reliability problem through consistency checking of data exchanged. Language can provide support for robustness with features facilitating the construction of independent (encapsulated) components which do not communicate with other parts of the software except through well-defined interfaces. Language may also provide support for reliability by supporting explicit mechanisms for dealing with problems that are detected when the system is in operation (exception handling). Note that poor reliability in a safety-critical portion of the software also becomes a safety issue.

Reusability: The extent to which inherent language features support the adaptation of code for use in another application.

Code is reusable when it is independent of other code except for communication through well-defined interfaces. This type of construction can occur at many levels. It is very common, for example, to reuse common data structures, such as stacks, queues, and trees. When these have been defined with common operations on the structures, these abstract data types are easy to reuse. When reusing larger portions of code, the biggest issue for reusability is whether the interfaces defined for the code to be reused are compatible with the interfaces defined for the system being created. This is significantly facilitated by the definition of software architecture for the domain of the system under construction. If those defining the components to be reused are aware of the architecture definition, then they can follow the standard interfaces defined in the architecture to ensure the code is reusable for other systems using the same architecture. Reuse at any level can be facilitated by language features that make it easy to write independent (encapsulated) modules with well-defined interfaces.

Safety: The extent to which inherent language features support the construction of safety-critical systems, yielding systems that are fault-tolerant, fail-safe, or robust in the face of systemic failures.

Safety is related to reliability, but it is a great deal more. The more reliable a system is, the more it does what is expected. A system is safe if it protects against physical danger to people, as well as against loss or damage to other physical resources, such as equipment. This implies that the system must always do what is expected and be able to recover from any situation that might lead to a mishap or actual system hazard. Thus, safety tries to ensure that any failures that do occur result in minor consequences, and even potentially dangerous failures are handled in a fail-safe fashion. Language can facilitate this through such features as a rigorous computational model, built-in consistency checking, and exception handling.

Standardization: The extent to which the language definition has been formally standardized (by recognized bodies such as ANSI and ISO) and the extent to which it can be reasonably expected that this standard will be followed in a language translator.

Most popular languages are standardized through at least ANSI and ISO, but an important issue here is that the language definition that is supported by a compiler product may not be that which is standardized. Most languages have evolved in a manner that has produced a proliferation of different dialects before the language was standardized, and the result has been that most compiler products support non-standard features from these dialects in addition to the standard language. Some of these products also support a mode that enforces the use of only the standard language constructs, but programmer discipline is still required to use this mode.

Support for modern engineering methods: The extent to which inherent language features support the expression of source code that enforces good software engineering principles.

Support for modern software engineering methods is support that encourages the use of good engineering practices and discourages poor practices. Hence, support for code clarity, encapsulation, and all forms of consistency checking are language features that provide this support. Also, support for complexity management and construction of large systems and subsystems support software engineering tenets.

2.11 WHY PROGRAMMING?

You may already have used software, perhaps for word processing or spreadsheets, to solve problems. Perhaps now you are curious to learn how programmers write software. A program is a set of step-by-step instructions that directs the computer to do the tasks you want it to do and produce the results you want.

There are at least three good reasons for learning programming:

- Programming helps you understand computers. The computer is only a tool. If you learn how to write simple programs, you will gain more knowledge about how a computer works.
- Writing a few simple programs increases your confidence level. Many people find great personal satisfaction in creating a set of instructions that solve a problem.
- Learning programming lets you find out quickly whether you like programming and whether you have the analytical turn of mind programmers need. Even if you decide that programming is not for you, understanding the process certainly will increase your appreciation of what programmers and computers can do.

A set of rules that provides a way of telling a computer what operations to perform is called a programming language. There is not, however, just one programming language; there are many. In this chapter you will learn about controlling a computer through the process of programming. You may even discover that you might want to become a programmer.

An important point before we proceed: You will not be a programmer when you finish reading this chapter or even when you finish reading the final chapter. Programming proficiency takes practice and training beyond the scope of this book. However, you will become acquainted with how programmers develop solutions to a variety of problems.

2.12 WHAT PROGRAMMERS DO

In general, the programmer's job is to convert problem solutions into instructions for the computer. That is, the programmer prepares the instructions of a computer program and runs those instructions on the computer, tests the program to see if it is working properly, and makes corrections to the program. The programmer also writes a report on the program. These activities are all done for the purpose of helping a user fill a need, such as paying employees, billing customers, or admitting students to college.

The programming activities just described could be done, perhaps, as solo activities, but a programmer typically interacts with a variety of people. For example, if a program is part of a system of several programs, the programmer coordinates with other programmers to make sure that the programs fit together well. If you were a programmer, you might also have coordination meetings with users, managers, systems analysts, and with peers who evaluate your work-just as you evaluate theirs.

Let us turn to the programming process.

2.13 THE PROGRAMMING PROCESS

Developing a program involves steps similar to any problem-solving task. There are five main ingredients in the programming process:

1. Defining the problem
2. Planning the solution
3. Coding the program
4. Testing the program
5. Documenting the program

Let us discuss each of these in turn.

1. Defining the Problem

Suppose that, as a programmer, you are contacted because your services are needed. You meet with users from the client organization to analyze the problem, or you meet with a systems analyst who outlines the project. Specifically, the task of defining the problem consists of identifying what it is you know (input-given data), and what it is you want to obtain (output-the result). Eventually, you produce a written agreement that, among other things, specifies the kind of input, processing, and output required. This is not a simple process.

2. Planning the Solution

Two common ways of planning the solution to a problem are to draw a flowchart and to write pseudocode, or possibly both. Essentially, a flowchart is a pictorial representation of a step-by-step solution to a problem. It consists of arrows representing the direction the program takes and boxes and other symbols representing actions. It is a map of what your program is going to do and how it is going to do it. The American National Standards Institute (ANSI) has developed a standard set of flowchart symbols. Figure 2.2 shows the symbols and how they might be used in a simple flowchart of a common everyday act-preparing a letter for mailing.

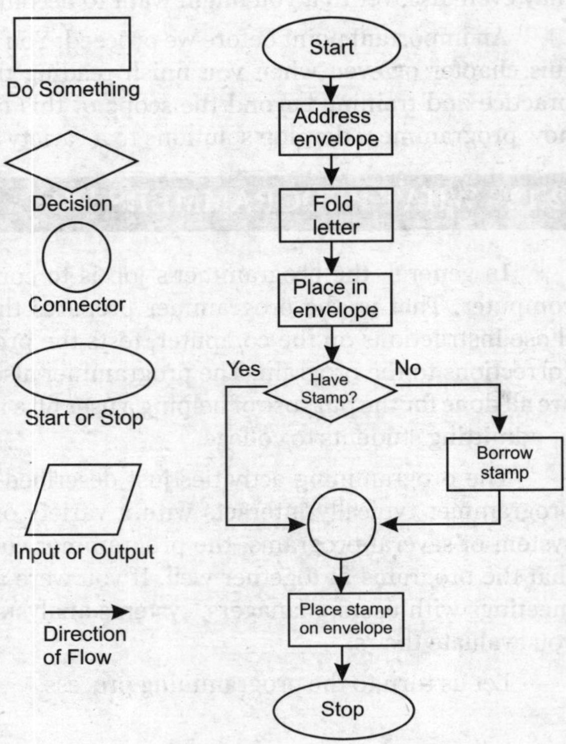

Figure 2.2: Programming Process

Pseudocode is an English-like non-standard language that lets you state your solution with more precision than you can in plain English but with less precision than is required when using a formal programming language. Pseudocode permits you to focus on the program logic without having to be concerned just yet about the precise syntax of a particular programming language. However, pseudocode is not executable on the computer. We will illustrate these later in this chapter, when we focus on language examples.

3. Coding the Program

As the programmer, your next step is to code the program-that is, to express your solution in a programming language. You will translate the logic from the flowchart or pseudocode-or some other tool-to a programming language. As we have already noted, a programming language is a set of rules that provides a way of instructing the computer what operations to perform. There are many programming languages: BASIC, COBOL, Pascal, FORTRAN, and C are some examples. You may find yourself working with one or more of these. We will discuss the different types of languages in detail later in this chapter.

Although programming languages operate grammatically, somewhat like the English language, they are much more precise. To get your program to work, you have to follow exactly the rules-the syntax-of the language you are using. Of course, using the language correctly is no guarantee that your program will work, any more than speaking grammatically correct English means you know what you are talking about. The point is that correct use of the language is the required first step. Then your coded program must be keyed, probably using a terminal or personal computer, in a form the computer can understand.

One more note here: Programmers usually use a text editor, which is somewhat like a word processing program, to create a file that contains the program. However, as a beginner, you will probably want to write your program code on paper first.

4. Testing the Program

Some experts insist that a well-designed program can be written correctly the first time. In fact, they assert that there are mathematical ways to prove that a program is correct. However, the imperfections of the world are still with us, so most programmers get used to the idea that their newly written programs probably have a few errors. This is a bit discouraging at first, since programmers tend to be precise, careful, detail-oriented people who take pride in their work. Still, there are many opportunities to introduce mistakes into programs, and you, just as those who have gone before you, will probably find several of them.

Eventually, after coding the program, you must prepare to test it on the computer. This step involves these phases:

- **Desk-checking:** This phase, similar to proofreading, is sometimes avoided by the programmer who is looking for a shortcut and is eager to run the program on the computer once it is written. However, with careful desk-checking you may discover several errors and possibly save yourself time in the long run. In desk-checking you simply sit down and mentally trace, or check, the logic of the program to attempt to ensure that it is error-free and workable. Many organizations take this phase a step further with a walkthrough, a process in which a group of programmers-your peers-review your program and offer suggestions in a collegial way.

- **Translating:** A translator is a program that (1) checks the syntax of your program to make sure the programming language was used correctly, giving you all the syntaxerror messages, called diagnostics, and (2) then translates your program into a form the computer can understand. A by-product of the process is that the translator tells you if you have improperly used the programming language in some way. These types of mistakes are called syntax errors. The translator produces descriptive error messages. For instance, if in FORTRAN you mistakenly write N=2 *(I+J))-which has two closing parentheses instead of one-you will get a message that says, "UNMATCHED PARENTHESES." (Different translators may provide different wording for error messages.) Programs are most commonly translated by a compiler. A compiler translates your entire program at one time. The translation involves your original program, called a source module, which is transformed by a compiler into an object module. Prewritten programs from a system library may be added during the link/load phase, which results in a load module. The load module can then be executed by the computer.

- **Debugging:** A term used extensively in programming, debugging means detecting, locating, and correcting bugs (mistakes), usually by running the program. These bugs are logic errors, such as telling a computer to repeat an operation but not telling it how to stop repeating. In this phase you run the program using test data that you devise. You must plan the test data carefully to make sure you test every part of the program.

5. Documenting the Program

Documenting is an ongoing, necessary process, although, as many programmers are, you may be eager to pursue more exciting computer-centered activities. Documentation is a written detailed description of the programming cycle and specific facts about the program. Typical program documentation materials include the origin and nature of the problem, a brief narrative description of the program, logic tools such as flowcharts and pseudocode, data-record descriptions, program listings, and testing results. Comments in the program itself are also considered an essential part of documentation. Many programmers document as they code. In a broader sense, program documentation can be part of the documentation for an entire system.

The wise programmer continues to document the program throughout its design, development, and testing. Documentation is needed to supplement human memory and to help organize program planning. Also, documentation is critical to communicate with others who have an interest in the program, especially other programmers who may be part of a programming team. And, since turnover is high in the computer industry, written documentation is needed so that those who come after you can make any necessary modifications in the program or track down any errors that you missed.

EXERCISES

1. What do you mean by language?
2. What do you mean by programming language?
3. Explain the types of programming languages?
4. What do you mean machine language?
5. Explain the advantages and disadvantages of machine language?
6. What do you mean by assembly language?

7. Explain the basic elements of assembly language?
8. Explain the concept of assembler in detail?
9. Explain the structure of assembler?
10. What are the advantages of assembly over machine language?
11. What are the limitations of assembly language?
12. Explain the role of macros in assembly language?
13. Why we use high level languages?
14. What are the advantages and disadvantages of high level languages?
15. Distinguish between machine, assembly and high level languages?
16. Explain the concept of compiler in detail?
17. What do you mean by interpreter?
18. Distinguish between compiler and interpreter?
19. Explain the concept of linkers and loaders?
20. What do you mean by OOPs?
21. Explain the concept of programming?
22. Explain the concept of programming process?

Chapter 3

Assemblers

3.1 INTRODUCTION

An assembler is a program that converts a program in assembly language to the equivalent code in machine language, along with information for loader. This chapter focuses mainly on procedures for producing machine language, but the assembler must also produce other information for the loader to use. For example, the externally defined symbols must be noted and passed on to the loader. The assembler is not aware of the addresses of these symbols, and hence it is the task of the loader to locate them, load them into the memory and prepare them for execution by placing their values in the calling program. Loaders are discussed in detail in the following chapters.

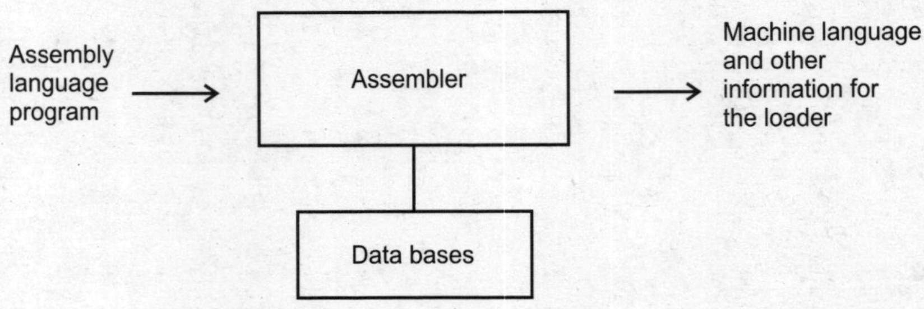

Figure 3.1: Function of Assembler

This chapter deals with the production of machine language from the given assembly language. We first discuss a simple assembly language and then the detailed design of the assembler is discussed.

3.2 HOW THE OPERATING SYSTEM HANDLES YOUR PROGRAM

Once you have coded and punched your program, it must be processed by the assembler and the linkage editor or loader before it can be executed.

3.2.1 ASSEMBLER

The assembler translates your source module into an object module, the machine language equivalent of the source module. The object module, however', is not ready for execution; it must first be processed by the linkage editor or loader.

3.2.2 LINKAGE EDITOR

The linkage editor prepares your program for execution. The output of the linkage editor is called a load module and can be executed by the computer. The linkage editor can combine your program with other object modules and load modules to produce a single load module. The linkage editor stores your program in a load module library, a collection of data sets on a direct-access device. These load modules can be read into the computer and given control. The load module library may be either permanent, so that you can execute your program in later jobs, or temporary, so that the program is deleted at the end of your job.

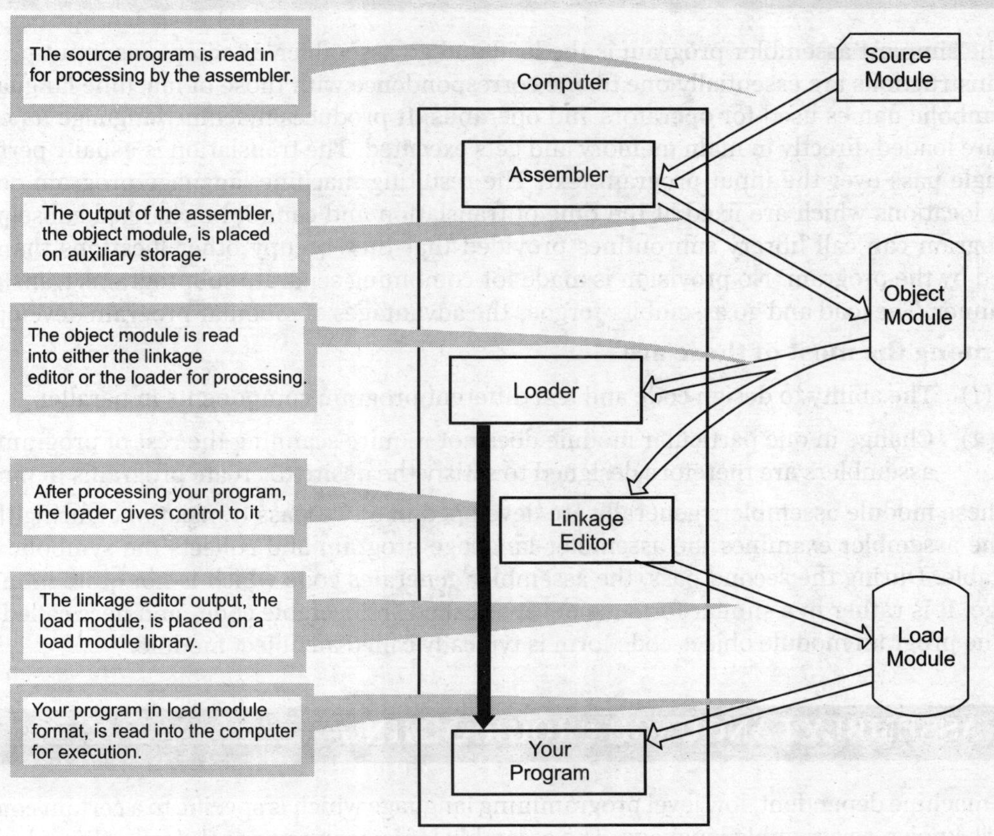

Figure 3.2: How the Operating System handles your Program

3.2.3 EXECUTION OF YOUR PROGRAM

Once you have included your program in a permanent load module library, you can execute it any number of times without assembly and linkage editing. However, if you need to change your program, you must assemble and linkage edits it again. Therefore, you should not store your program in a permanent load module library until it has been tested properly. To save time during test runs, you can use a program that combines the basic functions of the linkage editor with the execution of your program. That program is the loader.

3.2.4 LOADER

The loader performs most of the functions of the linkage editor; in addition, it loads your program into the computer and passes control to your program. The loader cannot, however, include your program in a load module library. For a full description of the linkage editor and loader, refer to chapter loaders and linkage editors.

3.3 LOAD AND GO ASSEMBLER

The simplest assembler program is the load and go assembler. It accepts as input programs whose instructions are essentially one to one correspondence with those of machine language but with symbolic names used for operators and operands. It produces machine language **as** outputs which are loaded directly in main memory and gets executed. The translation is usually performed in a single pass over the input program text. The resulting machine language program occupies storage locations which are fixed at the time of translation and cannot be changed subsequently. The program can call library subroutines provided that they occupy other locations than those required by the program. No provision is made for combining separate subprograms translated in this manner. The load and go assembler forgoes the advantages of modular program development.

Among the most of these are

(1) The ability to design code and test different program components in parallel.

(2) Change in one particular module does not require scanning the rest of program. Most assemblers are therefore designed to satisfy the desire to create programs in modules.

These module assemblers generally are developed in a two-pass translation. During the first **pass** the assembler examines the assembler-language program and collects the symbolic names into a table. During the second pass, the assembler generates code which is not quite in machine language. It is rather in a similar form, sometimes called "relocatable code" and here called object code. The program module object-code form is typically called an object module.

3.4 ASSEMBLY LANGUAGE PROGRAMMING

A machine dependent, low level programming language which is specific to a certain computer system is known as assembly language. The assembly language provides the following advantages over the machine languages:

1. **Mnemonic Operation Codes:** The programmer writes mnemonics e.g. STORE instead of the bit configuration 010100 for the store instruction. Use of such opcodes eliminates the need to memorize numeric operation codes. It also enables the assembler with the helpful diagnostics, e.g. the indication of misspelt operation codes.
2. **Symbolic Operands:** Data as well as instructions are symbolic, not absolute. These symbolic names can then be used as operands in assembly language statements. The assembler performs the task of binding these names with actual memory locations. The programmer does not have to know the details of these bindings which are performed by the assembler.
3. **Data Declarations:** Data can be declared in a variety of forms, including the decimal notation. The programmer has no worry of manually converting them into their internal machine representation.

3.4.1 ASSEMBLY LANGUAGE STATEMENT FORMAT

An assembly language statement has the following format:

[Label] <Opcode> <operand1 specification> [, <operand2 specification> ..]

where [ ] indicates an optional field in the format. The Label field is used as a symbolic name for the memory words generated for the statement. The general syntax for <operand specification> is as follows:

<symbolic name> [+displacement] [(<index register>)]

Hence the possible operand forms can be SUM, SUM+10, SUM (4), and SUM+10(4). The first operand refers to the memory word which is labeled as SUM. The second operand refers to a word which is 10 words ahead of the memory word to which the name SUM is associated. Hence the value 10 is the offset or displacement from SUM. The third operand refers to indexing with register 4, and the actual address is calculated after adding the contents of the register 4 with the address of label SUM. The last operand is the combination of the previous two specifications.

3.4.2 SAMPLE ASSEMBLY LANGUAGE PROGRAM

Here we present a sample assembly language, and the techniques used to design simple assembly language programs. In this language, each statement has two operands from which the first one is always a register from AREG, BREG, CREG and DREG. The second operand is always a memory word having the format as specified above. Following is a list of mnemonic opcodes that can be used in the instructions of our assembly language:

Machine Opcode	Mnemonic Opcode	Description
00	STOP	Stops execution
01	ADD	Adds the first operand with second and leaves the result in first operand

02	SUB	Subtracts the second operand from first and leaves the result in first operand
03	MULT	Multiplies the operands and leaves the result in first operand
04	MOVER	Transfers the contents of second operand into the first operand i.e. transfer from memory to the register
05	MOVEM	Transfers the contents of first operand into the second operand i.e. transfer from the register to memory
06	COMP	Sets the condition code which is further used by BC mnemonic
07	BC	Branches to the specified location if condition code is true
08	DIV	Divides the first operand with the second and leaves the result in first operand
09	READ	Writes data to memory, the register need not be specified for this instruction
10	PRINT	Reads from memory and prints the contents, the register need not be specified for this instruction

The MOVE instruction is used for coping the contents from register to memory and vice versa. The MOVER instruction uses the first operand as the source operand and the second as the target, while the MOVEM does the reverse. All the arithmetic operations are performed in registers, and set the condition code. A comparison instruction sets the condition code which can then be tested by Branch on Condition (BC) instruction. BC statement can be written in the following format:

BC <condition code specification>, <memory address>

This statement transfers control to the address specified in <memory address> if the value of condition code matches the <condition code specification>. The <condition code specification> can be any character string with obvious meaning as GT, EQ, LT etc.

The figure 3.3 shows the sample machine code instruction format:

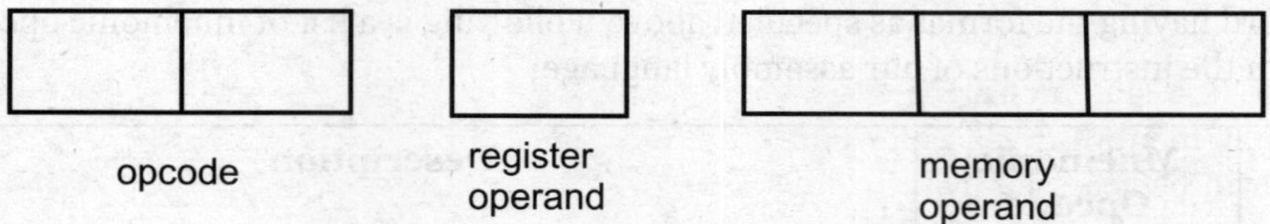

Figure 3.3: Machine Instruction Format

	START	101				
	READ	N	101)	09	0	111
	MOVER	BREG, ONE	102)	04	2	113
	MOVEM	BREG, TERM	103)	05	2	114
AGAIN	MULT	BREG, TERM	104)	03	2	114
	ADD	CREG, ONE	105)	01	3	113
	COMP	CREG, N	106)	06	3	111
	BC	LE, AGAIN	107)	07	2	104
	MOVEM	BREG, RESULT	108)	05	2	112
	PRINT	RESULT	109)	10	0	112
	STOP		110)	00	0	000
N	DS	1	111)			
RESULT	DS	1	112)			
ONE	DC	'1'	113)	00	0	001
TERM	DS	1	114)			
	END		115)			

Figure 3.4: A sample assembly language code and equivalent machine code

3.4.3 TYPES OF STATEMENTS

An assembly language program contains three kinds of statements:

1. Imperative Statements

An imperative statement is an action that needs to be performed during the execution of the assembled program. Each such statement translates to a single machine instruction. These are also known as machine-op instructions as they specify the operation to be performed by the machine.

2. Declaration Statements

The declaration statements follow the syntax as shown:

```
[Label]    DS    <constant>
[Label]    DC    '<value>'
```

The DS (declare storage) statement declares a name for the specific memory area. For example:

```
A    DS    1
B    DS    30
```

Here the first statement reserves a memory area of 1 word and associates a name A with it. The second statement reserves a block of 30 words and associates a name B with it. The first word of this block can be accessed by the name B and the consecutive words can be accessed by using suitable offsets as B+1, B+2,...,B+29.

The DC (declare constant) statement declares the memory words that contain constants. For example:

```
ONE    DC    '1'
```

This statement associates a name ONE with the memory word which contains the value '1'. The programmer can declare the constants in any of the formats as decimal, hexadecimal, binary etc. It is the job of the assembler to convert them to appropriate format required by the machine.

Literals

The DC (declare constant) statement actually does not really implement constants, but it just initializes memory words to given values, which are not protected by the assembler and can be changed by moving a new value to the same place.

The constants can only be applied in assembly language program by means of literals. A literal is an operand with the syntax ='<value>'. It differs somewhat from actual constant because its value cannot be specified in the assembly program. It helps to ensure that this value never gets changed during the execution of the program. Here are presented two scenarios that add the contents of AREG with the value 5.

```
ADD AREG, ='5'          ADD AREG, FIVE
                        ---     ---
                        FIVE    DC      '5'
```

Both the scenarios have the same effect. The first scenario uses a literal while the second scenario has the same effect with the use of DC statement. The difference is only that if the second scenario results in a change of value at location specified by FIVE anywhere in the assembly program, then the result would be incorrect, while the literal cannot be modified in any way by the assembly program. The value of the literal is protected by the fact that the name and address of this word is not known to the assembly language programmer.

3. Assembler Directives

Assembler directives are the instructions for the assembler to perform certain actions during the assembly of the program. They are also known as pseudo-op instructions and specify an operation for the assembler. For example:

```
START       <constant>
```

This statement indicates the assembler that the first word of the generated target program should reside at the memory location specified by the value in <constant>.

```
END    [<operand specification>]
```

This statement indicates the end of the source program. The optional <operand specification> field indicates the address of the instruction from where the execution of the assembled program should begin. If left blank, the execution starts from the first instruction by default.

```
USING       BEGIN, CREG
```

If the assembler has to compute the displacement field of instructions automatically, it should know what register is used as the base register and what that register contains. It is specified by the USING instruction. As the above instruction indicates CREG as the base register and the contents of the register are given by the instruction labeled BEGIN.

3.5 DESIGN OF ASSEMBLER

The fundamental translation model that was described in previous chapter is followed for the design of the assembler here. A four step approach is used for developing a design specification for an assembler:

1. Identify the information necessary for assembling the program.
2. Determine a suitable data structure for storage of information.
3. Determine the processing that is necessary for obtaining and maintaining the information.
4. Determine the processing necessary for performing the task of assembly.

The synthesis phase of the assembler requires sufficient information from the analysis phase. Hence we would first consider the information requirements of the synthesis phase and then we consider how to make that information available through the analysis phase or synthesis phase.

3.5.1 SYNTHESIS PHASE

Let there be any assembly language statement like:

MOVEM CREG, TERM

To convert this assembly language statement to the corresponding machine language, the following information should be made available:

1. Machine operation code that corresponds to the mnemonic MOVEM.
2. Address of the memory word where TERM is stored.

The first item of information does not depend on the source program, but merely depends upon the assembly language that is being used. Hence the synthesis phase can determine this information for itself. The second item of information depends entirely on the source program; hence it must be made available by the analysis phase.

From the above discussion, we know that we require the following data structures for the proper functioning of the synthesis phase:

1. Symbol Table
2. Mnemonics Table

Symbol table is a table having primarily two entries- name and address. The table is built by the analysis phase. The mnemonics table also has two primary entries- mnemonic and opcode. These tables are searched with symbol name and mnemonic as keys to obtain the equivalent machine instruction for the source assembly language program.

3.5.2 ANALYSIS PHASE

The primary function that is performed by the analysis phase is building of the symbol table. Hence it must determine the associated addresses for all the labels used in the assembly language program. Some addresses can be determined directly, while some have to be inferred. Consider the sample program given in the previous section. To determine the address for the label N, the analysis phase needs to fix the addresses of all the program elements preceding that statement. This function is known as memory allocation.

Location counter (LC) is used to implement this function of memory allocation. The LC always points to the next memory word in the target program. At the beginning, LC is initialized to the value specified in START statement. Whenever a label is encountered in the assembly language by the analysis phase, the name of the label is entered as a new entry in the symbol table, and the corresponding contents are added as the address part of the information. Then the analysis phase finds out the number of memory words required for the statement and updates the contents of LC accordingly. This enables the LC to point to the next instruction in the target program, even when the instructions have varying lengths and DC/DS statements have reserved different amounts of memory for the corresponding labels. To update the contents of LC, the analysis phase needs to know the lengths of each instruction. For this purpose, the mnemonics table can be extended to include another field length, to know the lengths of various instructions. This updating of LC contents after processing each instruction is known as LC processing.

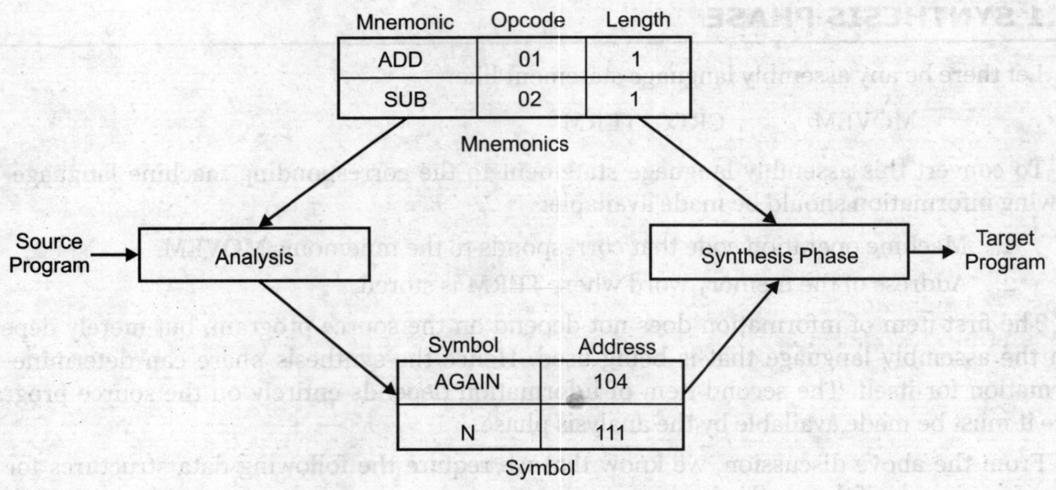

Figure 3.5: Data Structures for Assembler

The figure 3.5 illustrates the data structures that are needed for the process of assembly of a source program in assembly language into a target program in machine language. The mnemonics table is a fixed predefined table present along with the assembly language in use. The symbol table is constructed during the analysis phase by the process of memory allocation discussed above and used by the synthesis phase. According to the above discussion, the tasks to be performed by analysis and synthesis phase are categorized below:

Steps for Analysis Phase:

1. Separate the label, mnemonic opcode and operand fields of an assembly language statement.

2. If the statement contains a label, enter the name of label and the contents of LC as a new entry in symbol table.
3. Check for presence of the mnemonic in the mnemonics table, hence its validity.
4. Perform LC processing by updating the contents of LC after considering the length of the instruction under scan.

Steps for Synthesis Phase:

1. Obtain the machine opcode for the mnemonic from the mnemonics table.
2. Obtain the address of memory operand from the symbol table.
3. Convert the assembly language statement to the equivalent machine language by combining the information obtained in above two steps of synthesis phase.

3.6 PASS STRUCTURE OF ASSEMBLERS

One pass of assembler equals a complete scan of the source program, or its equivalent representation (IR) as discussed in the previous chapter for language processors. There are two basic pass structures available for assemblers which are discussed as follows:

3.6.1 TWO PASS TRANSLATION

Forward references are handled in an easy manner by two pass translation scheme. LC processing is performed in the first pass and symbol table is constructed. The second pass uses this symbol table to synthesize the target program. Hence the first pass performs the analysis of the source program and the second pass performs the synthesis of the target program. An Intermediate Representation (IR) is constructed by the first pass and used by the second pass. This representation consists of two main components- data structures (symbol table) and a processed form of source program (intermediate code (IC)).

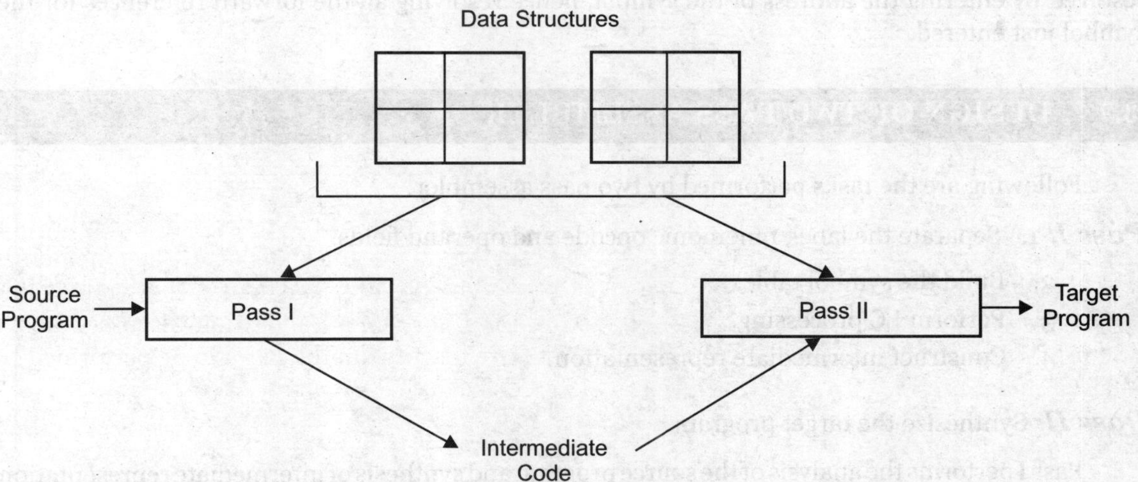

Figure 3.6: Two Pass Assembly Scheme

3.6.2 SINGLE PASS TRANSLATION

In single pass translation, the LC processing and symbol table construction is done as in two pass translation. The problem of forward references occurs in single pass translation when a symbol is encountered whose memory location is not yet known to the assembly language program. Such problem is handled by the process of backpatching. While processing of statements is done, if a symbol with a forward reference is encountered, it is initially left blank. The address of the forward referenced symbol is filled when the definition is encountered. For example, consider the statement:

MOVEM CREG, TERM

This statement can only be partially synthesized as the symbol TERM is a forward reference and its address is not known at the instant. Hence just the mnemonic opcode MOVEM is converted to the equivalent machine code and the location for the symbol TERM is left blank. The need for inserting the address of TERM in the instruction has to be illustrated to the assembler in some manner. It is done by adding an entry to the Table of Incomplete Instructions (TII). The table contains two fields- instruction address and symbol, which defines the list of incomplete instruction along with the symbols whose addresses need to be filled up later. Suppose the instruction above has the LC contents as 101, then the TII entry will correspond to the value (101, TERM), which signifies that the instruction at 101 needs to fill up the address of the symbol TERM.

When the END statement is processed in the assembly program, the symbol table would be complete with the addresses of all the symbols that were encountered in the program, and the TII will contain a list of all the incomplete instructions having some forward reference. The assembler can now start processing one entry at a time from TII for completion. For example, the entry (101, TERM) is processed by obtaining the address for the symbol TERM and inserting it in the operand field of the instruction at the location 101 where the actual instruction resides.

Another scheme can be followed for processing the entries in TII where the table is searched every time a symbol is entered into the symbol table. TII is searched for containing any entry that contains a forward reference to the symbol just added to symbol table. If found, the TII entry is resolved by entering the address of the symbol, hence resolving all the forward references for the symbol just entered.

3.7 DESIGN OF TWO PASS ASSEMBLER

Following are the tasks performed by two pass assembler:

Pass I: 1. Separate the label, mnemonic opcode and operand fields.

2. Build the symbol table.
3. Perform LC processing.
4. Construct intermediate representation.

Pass II: Synthesize the target program.

Pass I performs the analysis of the source program and synthesis of intermediate representation while Pass II processes the intermediate representation to synthesize the target program.

3.7.1 STATEMENT OF THE PROBLEM

The assembly process is divided into two passes or sequential scans over the input. Associated with each pass are the following assembler modules:

Pass I: Purpose- define symbols and literals

1. Determine the length of machine instructions (MOTGET1)
2. Keep track of Location Counter (LC)
3. Remember values of symbols until Pass II (STSTO)
4. Process some pseudo ops (POTGET1)
5. Remember literals (LITSTO)

Pass II: Purpose- generate object program

1. Look for the value of symbols (STGET)
2. Generate instructions (MOTGET2)
3. Generate data (for DS, DC, and literals)
4. Process pseudo ops (POTGET2)

The figures 3.7 and 3.8 outline the basic steps involved in Pass I and Pass II of the assembler. The databases which are used and a more detailed algorithm are presented in the next sections.

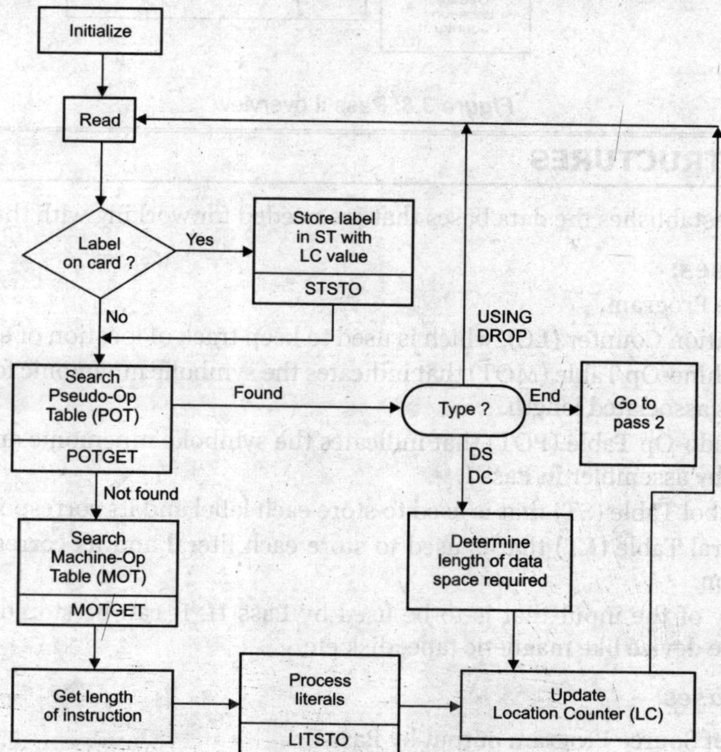

Figure 3.7: Pass I overview

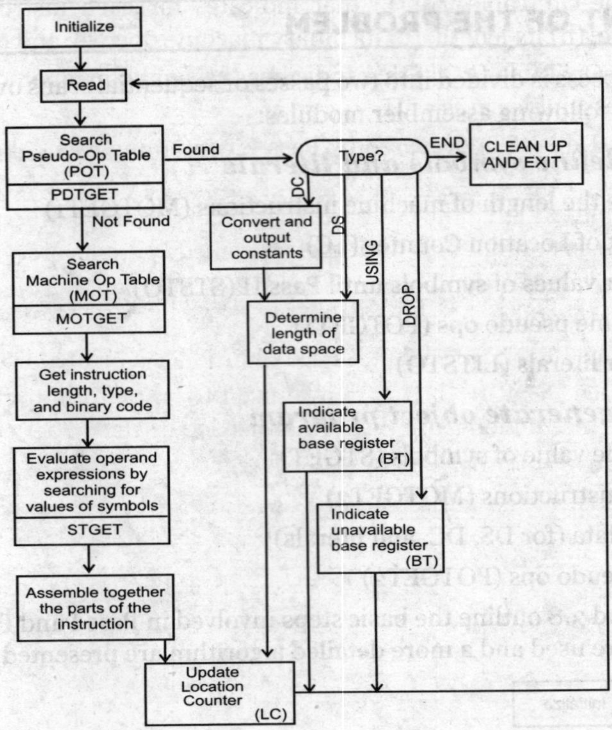

Figure 3.8: Pass II overview

3.7.2 DATA STRUCTURES

This section establishes the data bases that are needed for working with the assembler.

Pass I data bases:

1. Source Program.
2. A Location Counter (LC), which is used to keep track of location of each instruction.
3. A Machine-Op Table (MOT) that indicates the symbolic mnemonic for each instruction and its associated length.
4. A Pseudo-Op Table (POT) that indicates the symbolic mnemonic and the action to be taken by assembler in Pass I.
5. A Symbol Table (ST) that is used to store each label and its corresponding location.
6. A Literal Table (LT) that is used to store each literal and its corresponding assigned location.
7. A copy of the input that is to be used by Pass II. It can be stored in any secondary storage device like magnetic tape, disk etc.

Pass II data bases:

1. Copy of Source Program output by Pass I.
2. Location Counter (LC).

3. A Machine-Op Table (MOT) that indicates for each instruction: (a) the symbolic mnemonic, (b) its length, (c) its binary machine opcode, and (d) its format.
4. A Pseudo-Op Table (POT) that indicates the symbolic mnemonic and the action to be taken by assembler in Pass II.
5. A Symbol Table (ST) prepared by Pass I, containing each label and its corresponding location.
6. A Base Table (BT) that indicates which registers are currently specified as base registers by USING pseudo-ops and what their specified contents are.
7. A workspace INST, that is used to hold each instruction as its various parts are being assembled together.
8. A workspace PRINTLINE that is used to produce a printed listing.
9. A workspace PUNCH CARD, that is used to prior to outputting for converting the assembled instructions into the format needed by the loader.
10. An output copy of program as needed by the loader.

The figure 3.9 illustrates the interrelation of some of the data bases and the two passes of assembler.

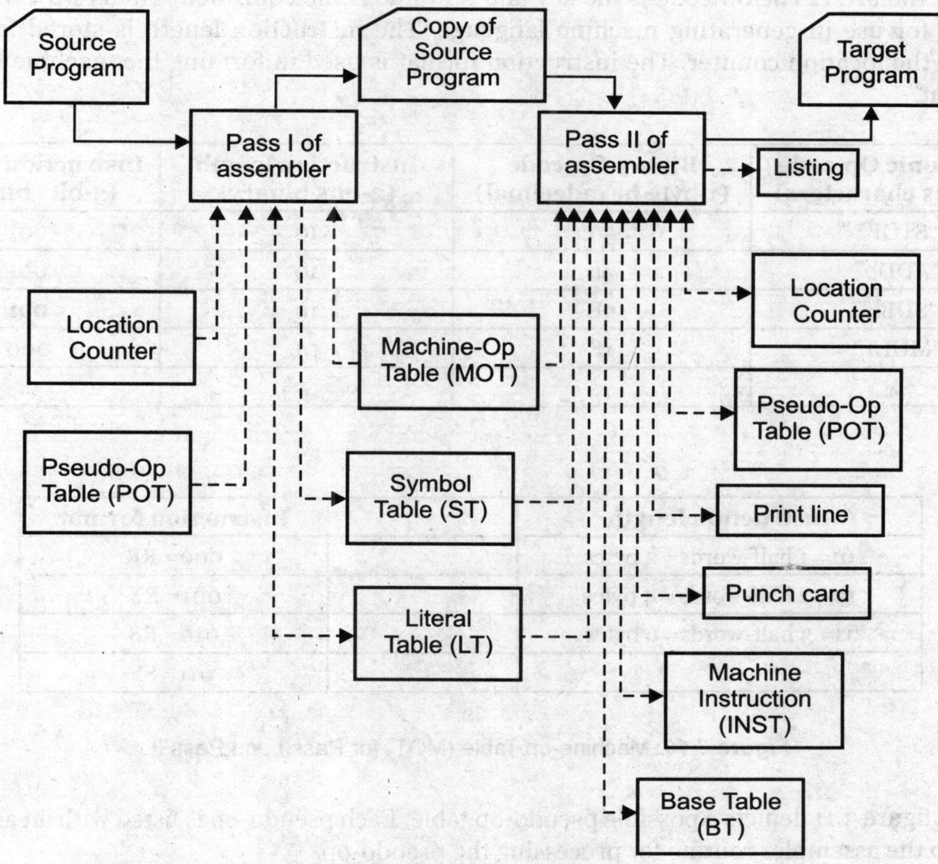

Figure 3.9: Use of databases by assembler

3.7.3 FORMAT OF DATA BASES

The next step in our design procedure is to specify the format and content of each of the databases. Pass II requires Machine Operation Table (MOT) containing name, length, binary code, and format while Pass I requires only name and length. We could use two separate tables with different formats and contents or use the same table for both the passes. The same is true for Pseudo Operation table (POT). By generalizing the table formats, we could combine MOT and POT into one table. For our design of databases, we would use a single MOT but two separate POTs.

Once the information in each table is decided, the format of each entry must be decided. For example, in what format are symbols to be stored (left justified, padded with spaces, ASCII etc.) and what coding conventions are used. The Extended Binary Coded Decimal Interchange Code (EBCDIC) is the standard IBM 360 coding scheme for representing characters as eight-bit bytes. The character 'A' for instance is represented in EBCDIC as 11000001 binary (C1 in hexadecimal).

The MOT and POT are examples of fixed tables. The contents of these tables are not filled in or altered during the process of assembly. The figure 3.10 depicts the possible content and format of the MOT. The op-code is the key and its value is the equivalent binary op-code, which is stored for use in generating machine language. The instruction length is stored for use in updating the location counter. The instruction format is used in forming the machine language equivalent.

Mnemonic Op-code (4-bytes characters)	Binary Op-code (1-byte hexadecimal)	Instruction length (2-bits binary)	Instruction format (3-bits binary)
"STOP"	5A	10	001
"ADDb"	4a	10	001
"SUBb"	5E	10	001
"MULT"	1E	01	000
...	...	...	...

Codes:

Instruction length		Instruction format
01= 1 half-words= 2 bytes		000= RR
10= 2 half-words= 4 bytes		001= RX
11= 3 half-words= 6 bytes		010= RS
		011= SI

Figure 3.10: Machine-op Table (MOT) for Pass I and Pass II

The figure 3.11 depicts a possible pseudo-op table. Each pseudo-op is listed with an associated pointer to the assembler routine for processing the pseudo-op.

Pseudo-op (5 bytes character)	Address of routine to process pseudo-op (3 bytes = 24 bit address)
"DROPb"	P1DROP
"ENDbb"	P1END
"EQUbb"	P1EQU
"START"	P1START
"USING"	P1USING
...	...

Note: The second column has been made to contain the labels of routines in Pass I, the table will actually contain the physical addresses.

Figure 3.11: Pseudo-op Table (POT) for Pass I (similar for Pass II)

The Symbol Table and Literal Table include for each entry not only the name and assembly-time value fields but also a length field and a relative-location indicator. The length field indicates the length (in bytes) of the instruction to which the symbol is attached.

Symbol (8-bytes characters)	Value (4-bytes hexadecimal)	Length (1-byte hexadecimal)	Relocation (1-byte character)
"JOHNbbbb"	0000	01	"R"
"FOURbbbb"	0000	04	"R"
"FIVEbbbb"	0010	04	"R"
"TEMPbbbb"	0014	04	"R"

Figure 3.12: Symbol Table (ST) for Pass I and Pass II

The relative-location indicator tells the assembler whether the value of the symbol is absolute (does not change if the program is moved in the memory), or relative to the base of the program. The assembler can use a simple technique to decide into which category a symbol falls. If the symbol is defined by equivalence with a constant (e.g. 6) or an absolute symbol, then the symbol is absolute. Otherwise, it is a relative symbol. The relative-location field in the symbol will have an "R" in it if the symbol is relative, or an "A" if the symbol is absolute.

The figure 3.13 depicts a possible base table that is used by the assembler to generate the proper base table reference in machine instructions and to compute the correct offsets. The assembler must generate an address for every symbolic reference in the program. The symbol table contains the address of the symbol relative to the beginning of the program. While generating an address, the assembler may use the base register table to choose a base register that will contain a value closest to the symbolic reference. The address is then formulated. Base register number = the base register containing a value closest to the symbolic reference. Offset = value of symbol in the symbol table – contents of base register.

	Availability Indicator (1-byte character)	Designated Relative Address Contents of base register (3-bytes = 24-bit address hexadecimal)
1	"N"	-
2	"N"	-
:	:	:
14	"N"	-
15	"Y"	00 00 00

***Codes* Availability:**

Y register specified in USING pseudo-op

N register never specified in USING pseudo-op or made unavailable by DROP pseudo-op

Figure 3.13: Base Table for Pass II

The following example illustrates the use of the variable tables (symbol table, literal table, base table) and demonstrates the motivation for algorithms presented in the next sections. The specific function of this program is irrelevant and we are only concerned with the assembly of process associated.

Statement No.			
1	PRGRM2	START	0
2		USING	*,15
3		LA	15, SETUP
4		SR	TOTAL, TOTAL
5	AC	EQU	2
6	INDEX	EQU	3
7	TOTAL	EQU	4
8	DATABASE	EQU	13
9	SETUP	EQU	*
10		USING	SETUP, 15
11		L	DATABASE, =A(DATA1)
12		USING	DATAAREA, DATABASE
13		SR	INDEX, INDEX
14	LOOP	L	AC, DATA1(INDEX)
15		AR	TOTAL, AC
16		A	AC, =F'4'
17		ST	AC, SAVE(INDEX)
18		A	INDEX, =F'4'
19		C	INDEX, =F'8000'
20		BNE	LOOP
21		LR	1, TOTAL
22		BR	14
23		LTORG	
24	SAVE	DS	2000F
25	DATAAREA	EQU	*
26	DATA1	DC	F'25, 26, 97, 101, ...' [2000 numbers]
27		END	

Figure 3.14: Sample Assembly Source Program

The symbols and literals can be defined as the purpose of Pass I of an assembler, by means of symbol and literal tables as shown below:

Symbol	Value	Length	Relocation
PRGRM2	0	1	R
AC	2	1	A
INDEX	3	1	A
TOTAL	4	1	A
DATABASE	13	1	A
SETUP	6	1	R
LOOP	12	4	R
SAVE	64	4	R
DATAAREA	8064	1	R
DATA1	8064	4	R

Figure 3.15: Symbol Table

Symbol	Value	Length	Relocation
A (DATA1)	48	4	R
F '5'	52	4	R
F '4'	56	4	R
F '8000'	60	4	R

Figure 3.16: Literal Table

As depicted in the flowchart of Pass I of assembler, the program is scanned keeping a location counter. For each symbol in the label field, an entry is made in the symbol table. For the symbol PRGRM2 its value is its relative location, and its length is 1.

The location counter is updated after noting that the LA instruction is four bytes long and SR is two. Continuing in the same manner, it is found that the next five symbols are defined by pseudo-op EQU. These symbols are entered into the symbol table and the associated values given in the arguments fields are also entered. The location counter is further updated noting that the L instruction is four bytes and SR is two. Thus the location counter has the value 12 when the LOOP is encountered. Therefore, LOOP is entered into the symbol table with the value 12. It is relocatable variable and hence R. Its length is four bytes. All other symbols are also entered in the same manner.

In the same pass, all the literals are also recognized and entered into a literal table. The first literal is encountered in the statement 11 and its value is the address of the location that will contain the literal. Since this is the first literal, it will have the first address of the literal area. The LTORG pseudo-op in statement 23 forces the literal table to be placed there, where the location counter is updated to the next double word boundary which equals 48. Thus the value of '=A(DATA1)' is its address, 48. Similarly, the value of the literal F'5' is the next location in the literal table, 52 and so on.

After the symbol table and literal table are completed, Pass II may be initiated, whose purpose is to evaluate arguments and generate machine code. To generate proper address in an instruction, the base register needs to be specified. To compute the offset, the contents of base register need to be known. The assembler does not know the execution time of the base register, but it does know the value relative to the start of the program. Therefore, the assembler enters as contents its relative value. The value is used to compute the offset. Processing the USING opcodes produces the base table as shown below:

1) After statement 2:

base	contents
15	0

2. After statement 10:

base	contents
15	6

3) After statement 12:

base	contents
13	8064
15	6

Figure 3.17: Base Table (showing only base registers in use)

For each instruction in Pass II, the equivalent machine code is generated as shown below:

Corresponding Statement No.	Location	Instruction	
3	0	LA	15, 6 (0,15)
4	4	SR	4, 4
11	6	L	13, 42 (0,15)
13	10	SR	3, 3
14	12	L	2, 0 (3,13)
15	16	AR	4, 2
16	18	A	2, 46 (0,15)
17	22	ST	2, 58 (3,15)
18	26	A	3, 50 (0,15)
19	30	C	3, 54 (0,15)
20	34	BC	7, 6 (0,15)
21	38	LR	1, 4
22	40	BCR	15, 14
23	48	8064	
	52	X'000000005'	
	56	X'000000004'	
	60	8000	
24	64	:	
	:	:	
25	8064	X'00000019'	
		:	
		:	

Figure 3.18: Generated machine code

For example, for conversion of statement 3 the following steps are followed:

1. Look up of value SETUP in symbol table (which is 6).
2. Look up value of op-code in machine-op table (binary-opcode for LA).
3. Formulate address in this manner:
   a) Determine base register by picking up the register that has content closest to the value of SETUP (register 15)
   b) Offset = value of symbol – content of base register = 6-0 = 6
   c) Formulate the address: offset (index register, base register) = 6 (0,15)
4. Average output code in appropriate formula.

In the similar manner, the other instructions are interpreted and converted to the equivalent machine code.

3.7.4 ALGORITHM

The flowcharts described in the following sections depict the task of Pass I and Pass II in more detail by representing a simplification of the operands performed in a complex assembler.

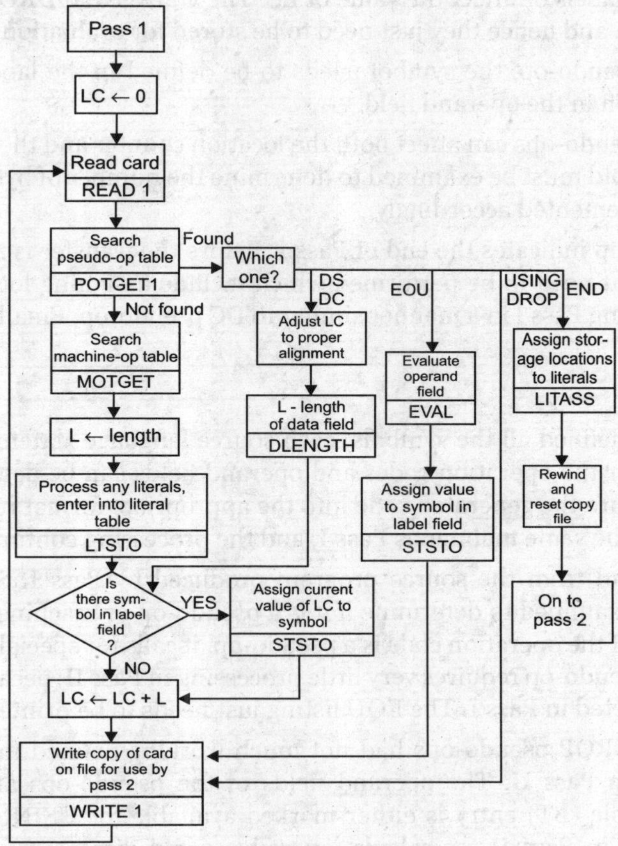

Figure 3.19: Detailed Pass I flowchart

Pass I

The main purpose of Pass I is to assign a location to each instruction and data defining pseudo-instruction, and thus to define the values for symbols appearing in the label fields of the source program. Initially, the Location Counter (LC) is set to the first location in the program, relative address 0. Then a source program statement is read. The operation-field is examined to decide if it is a pseudo-op or machine-op. If the field is not found in the Pseudo-Op Table (POT), then it is searched in Machine-Op Table (MOT) to find a match. The matched POT/MOT entry specifies the length of the instruction. The operand field is then scanned for the presence of a literal. If a new literal is found, it is entered into Literal Table (LT) for later processing. The label field of the source statement is then examined for the presence of a symbol. If there is a label, the symbol is saved in Symbol Table (ST) along with the current value of the LC. Finally the current value of the LC is incremented by the length of the instruction and a copy of source program is saved for use by Pass II and the above sequence is repeated for the next instruction.

The above loop is just a small portion of working in Pass I although it is the most important function. The largest sections of Pass I and Pass II are devoted to the special processing needed for the pseudo-operations. Here we consider what needs to be done to process a pseudo-op. The simplest procedure occurs for USING and DROP pseudo-ops. Pass I is only concerned with the pseudo-ops that define labels or affect the value of LC. The USING and DROP operations do none of the defined functions, and hence they just need to be stored for evaluation by Pass II.

In case of EQU pseudo-op, the symbol needs to be defined in the label field. This requires evaluating the expression in the operand field.

The DC and DS pseudo-ops can affect both the location counter and the definition of symbols in Pass I. the operand field must be examined to determine the number of bytes needed for storage and the value of LC incremented accordingly.

The END pseudo-op indicates the end of Pass I. Before the transfer is made to Pass II, there are some operations that need to be performed which include assigning locations to literals that have been collected during Pass I in a manner similar to DC pseudo-op. Finally the transfer is made to Pass II.

Pass II

After Pass I have defined all the symbols, each source language statement can be processed again, and the values for the operation codes and operand fields can be determined. In addition, Pass II must also structure the generated code into the appropriate format required by the loader. The LC is initialized in the same manner as Pass I, and the processing continues as follows.

A statement is read from the source program produced by Pass I. Similar to Pass I, the operation code field is examined to determine if it is a pseudo-op or machine-op by first searching in POT and then MOT. If the operation code is a pseudo-op, it calls for special processing by Pass II as in Pass I. The EQU pseudo-op requires very little processing in Pass II, because symbol definition has already been completed in Pass I. The EQU listing just needs to be printed in the target code.

The USING and DROP pseudo-ops had not much working defined for Pass I, and require additional processing in Pass II. The operand fields of the pseudo-ops are evaluated and the corresponding Base Table (BT) entry is either marked available for USING and unavailable for DROP. The BT is used in Pass II for calculation of base and displacement fields for machine instructions with storage operands.

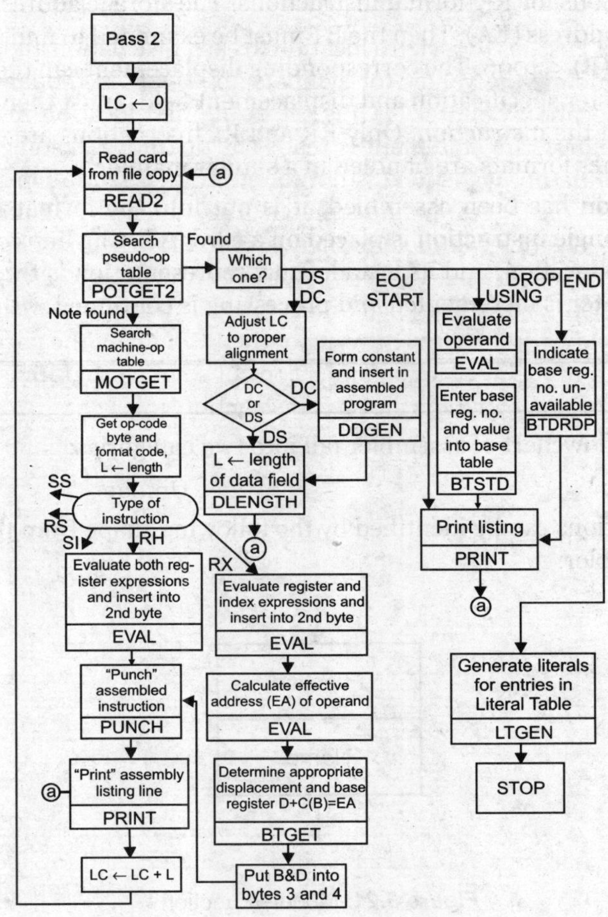

Figure 3.20: Detailed Pass II flowchart

The DC and DS pseudo-ops are processed mainly in Pass I, while Pass II just generates the actual code for the statements. Depending upon the data values specified, this task may involve various conversions (e.g. floating point to binary representation) and symbol evaluations (e.g. address constants).

The END pseudo-op indicates the end of source program and terminates the process of assembly. Various tasks such as generating of code for literals from Literal Table (LT) must be performed before ending the process completely.

If the operation code is not found in the POT, then it is searched in MOT for a match. The matching MOT entry defines the length, binary op-code and the format of the instruction. The operand fields of different format instructions require somewhat different processing.

For the RR- format instructions, each of the two register specification fields is evaluated. The two fields are inserted into their respective four-bit fields in the second byte of the RR-instruction. For RX-format instruction, the register and index fields are evaluated and processed in the same way as the register specifications for RR-format instructions. The storage address operand is evaluated to generate an effective address (EA). Then the BT must be examined to find a suitable base register (B) such that D = EA – c(B) < 4096. The corresponding displacement can then be determined from this value. The base register specification and displacement fields must then be assembled into the third and fourth bytes of the instruction. Only RR and Rx instructions are explicitly shown in the above flowchart. The other formats are handled in a similar manner.

After the instruction has been assembled, it is put into the format needed by the loader. Typically, more than a single instruction is placed on a card. A listing line containing a copy of the source card, its assigned location, and its hexadecimal representation is then printed for the user. Finally the location counter is incremented and processing is continued with the next card.

3.7.5 MODULES

Modules from the flowchart of assembler fall into two categories:

1. Multi-use
2. Unique

The modules/functions can be identified by the following shape from the flowcharts of Pass I and Pass II of the assembler.

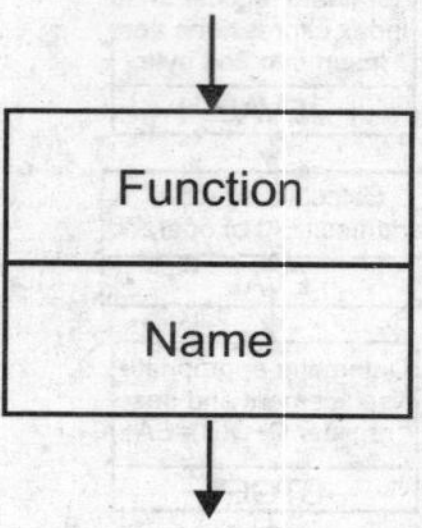

Figure 3.21: Module/Function

Following is a list of modules that are present in Pass I and Pass II of the assembler:

Pass I:

1.	**READ1:**	Reads the next assembly language statement.
2.	**POTGET1:**	Searches the Pass I Pseudo-Op Table (POT) for a match with the operation field of the current statement.
3.	**MOTGET1:**	Searches the Machine-Op Table (MOT) for a match with the operation of the current statement.
4.	**STSTO:**	Stores the name of label and its associated address into the Symbol Table (ST). If the name already exists in the table, it returns an error indicating multiply-defined symbol.
5.	**LITSTO:**	Stores a literal into Literal Table (LT), while checking for the literals to be unique.
6.	**WRITE1:**	Writes a copy of assembly source program on a storage device for use by Pass II.
7.	**DLENGTH:**	Scans an operand field of DC or DS statement and determines the amount of storage required.

8.	EVAL:	Evaluates an arithmetic expression consisting of constants and symbols.
9.	STGET:	Searches the Symbol Table (ST) for a match with the corresponding symbol.
10.	LITASS:	Assigns a storage location to each of the literal in the Literal Table (LT).

Pass II:

1.	READ2:	Reads the assembly language statements from the copy of file stored by Pass I.
2.	POTGET2:	Performs similar function as POTGET1.
3.	MOTGET2:	Performs similar function as MOTGET1.
4.	EVAL:	Evaluates expressions as in Pass I.
5.	PUNCH:	Converts the generated statements to card format, i.e. print line number along with the statements generated.
6.	PRINT:	Converts the generated code to character format.
7.	DCGEN:	Processes the fields of the DC statements to generate the object code.
8.	DLENGTH:	Performs similar function as in Pass I.
9.	BTSTO:	Inserts data into appropriate entry of Base Table (BT).
10.	BTDROP:	Inserts unavailable indicator into appropriate entry of Base Table (BT).
11.	BTGET:	Converts the effective address into base and displacement by searching the Base Table (BT) for available base registers.
12.	LTGET:	Generates code for literals.

These functions can be implemented in the design of the assembler as external subroutines, or as internal subroutines, or as sections of Pass I and Pass II programs as required by the programmer. In any way, the ability to treat functions as an independent unit makes it much easier to design the structure of assembler and each of its respective parts. Hence, rather than viewing whole of assembler as a single program, one can view it as a coordinated collection of routines which are individually smaller in size and complexity.

3.8 SINGLE PASS ASSEMBLER FOR IBM PC

The single pass assembler for Intel 8088 processor used for IBM PC. The problem of forward references is handled in the design procedure with the use of segment based addressing.

3.8.1 ARCHITECTURE OF INTEL 8088

The Intel 8088 microprocessor has the capability to support 8 and 16 bit arithmetic, as well as special instructions for string manipulation are also included in it. The Central Processing Unit contains the following:

1. Data Registers (AX, BX, CX, and DX)
2. Index Registers (SI and DI)
3. Stack Pointers (BP and SP)
4. Segment Registers (Code, Stack, Data and Extra)

AH	AL	AX
BH	BL	BX
CH	CL	CX
DH	DL	DX

BP
SP

SI
DI

Code
Stack
Data
Extra

Figure 3.22: Data, Base, Index and Segment Registers

Each register is 16 bits in size, and split into upper and lower parts of 8 bits each, which can be used individually for 8-bit arithmetic or combined for 16-bit arithmetic. The architecture also supports stacks for storing of subroutines and interrupt return addresses, their parameters and other data. The Index Registers, SI and DI, are used for indexing the source and destination addresses in instructions manipulating strings. They are also provided with auto-increment and auto-decrement functions. Two Stack Pointers, SP and BP, are provided for addressing the stack. SP points into stack implicitly and is used by the architecture to store subroutines and interrupt return address. BP is used by the programmers in any desired manner. Push and Pop operations are also provided on this register.

The 8088 implements 24 addressing modes which are summarized in the table below:

Addressing Mode	Example	Description
Immediate	MOV DATA1, 44H	Data = 44H
Register	MOV DATA1, CX	CX contains the data
Direct	MOV DATA1, [1234H]	Data Displacement = 1234H
Register Direct	MOV DATA1, [DX]	Data Displacement = (DX)
Register Indirect	MOV DATA1, CS : [DX]	Segment override: Segment Base = (CS) Data Displacement = (DX)

Based	MOV DATA1, 12H [DX]	Data Displacement = 12H+(DX)
Indexed	MOV DATA1, 34H [SI]	Data Displacement = 34H+(SI)
Based and Indexed	MOV DATA1, 22H [SI] [DX]	Data Displacement = 22H+(SI)+DX

In the immediate addressing mode, the instruction itself contains the data that is to be manipulated, which can be 8-bits or 16-bits in length. In the direct addressing mode, the instruction contains a 16-bit value which is the displacement from the segment base contained in a segment register. In the indexed mode, contents of the index register as indicated in the instruction are added to the 8-bit or 16-bit displacement contained in the instruction. The result is taken to be the displacement from the segment base of the data segment. In the based mode, contents of the base register are added to the displacement. The result is taken to be the displacement from data segment base unless BP is specified, in which case it is taken the displacement from the stack segment base. The based and indexed with displacement mode combines the effect of based and indexed mode.

3.8.2 ARITHMETIC INSTRUCTIONS

For arithmetic to take place, the operands can be in one of the four 16-bit registers, or in a memory location designated by one of the 24 addressing modes. The following three instruction formats are supported by 8088 processor:

Register/Memory to Register

opcode d w	mod reg r/m

Immediate to Register/Memory

opcode d w	mod op r/m	data	data

Immediate to Accumulator

opcode w	data	data

Figure 3.23: Instruction Formats

The mod and r/m fields specify the first operand that can be in a register or in memory. The reg field describes the second operand which is always a register. The instruction opcode indicates which instruction format is applicable. The direction field (d) indicates which operand is the destination operand in the instruction. If d=0, the register/memory operand is the destination, else the register operand indicated by reg is the destination. The width field (w) indicates whether the 8-bit arithmetic or 16-bit arithmetic is to be used.

3.8.3 CONTROL TRANSFER INSTRUCTIONS

Two types of control transfer instructions are supported in 8088 microprocessor:

1. Calls, jumps and returns
2. Iteration control instructions

The calls, jumps and returns can occur within the same segment, or can also jump the segment boundaries. Intra-segment transfers are assembled using a self-relative displacement in the range of -128 to 127. The longer form of intra-segment transfer uses a 16 bit logical address within the segment. Inter-segment transfers indicate a new segment base and an offset. Their execution is expensive since the code segment register has to be modified. Control transfers can be both direct and indirect. Their instruction formats are illustrated below:

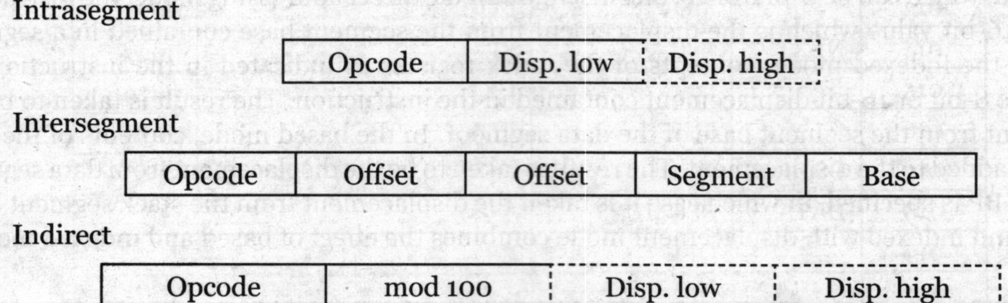

Figure 3.24: Formats of Control Transfer Instructions

3.8.4 STATEMENT FORMAT

The format of an assembly language statement for 8088 microprocessor is as follows:

[Label:]	opcode	operand(s)	;	comment string

The label field is optional. In the operand field, the operands are separated by commas. If parenthesis is included in the operand field, it represents the words 'contents of'. Base and index registers specifications, as also direct addresses specified as numeric offsets from the segment base are enclosed in parenthesis.

3.8.5 PROBLEMS OF SINGLE PASS ASSEMBLY

A single pass assembler for Intel 8088 has the problem of forward references and in error reporting. The forward reference problem is aggravated by the nature of the 8088 architecture. There are two aspects of this problem which are illustrated through the following problem:

Sr. No.		Statement		Offset
001	CODE	SEGMENT		
002		ASSUME	CS:CODE, DS:DATA	
003		MOV	AX, DATA	0000
004		MOV	DS, AX	0003
005		MOV	CX, LENGTH STRNG	0005
006		MOV	COUNT, 0000	0008
007		MOV	SI, OFFSET STRNG	0011

008		ASSUME	ES:DATA, DS:NOTHING	
009		MOV	AX, DATA	0014
010		MOV	ES, AX	0017
011	COMP:	CMP	[SI], 'A'	0019
012		JNE	NEXT	0022
013		MOV	COUNT, 1	0024
014	NEXT:	INC	SI	0027
015		DEC	CX	0029
016		JNE	COMP	0030
017	CODE	ENDS		
018	DATA	SEGMENT		
019		ORG	1	
020	COUNT	DB	?	
021	STRNG	DW	50 DUP (?)	0001
022	DATA	ENDS		0002
023		END		

3.8.6 FORWARD REFERENCES

A symbol may be forward referenced in a variety of ways. When used as a data operand in a statement, the assembly of the statement is straightforward. An entry can be made in Table of Incomplete Instructions (TII), which would identify the bytes in code where the address of the referenced symbol should be entered. When the symbol's actual definition is encountered, this entry would be analyzed to complete the instruction.

However, the use of a symbolic name as a destination in a branch statement gives rise to a peculiar problem. Some of the opcodes like JMP can give rise to instructions of different formats and different lengths depending on whether the jump is near or far, i.e. whether the destination symbol is 128 bytes away from the JMP instruction. But this can be known only sometime later in the assembly process. This problem is solved by assembling such instructions with a 16-bit logical address unless the programmer indicates a short displacement, e.g. JMP SHORT LOOP. The program in the above example also contains the forward branch instruction JNE NEXT. However, the problem does not arise here as the opcode JNE indicates that the instruction should be in a self-relative format.

3.8.7 SEGMENT REGISTERS

An ASSUME statement indicates that a segment register contains the base address of a segment. The assembler represents this information by a pair of the form (segment register, segment name). This information can be stored in a Segment Register Table (SRTAB). SRTAB is updated every time an ASSUME statement is encountered. For processing a reference to a symbol symb in an assembly language statement, the assembler accesses the symbol table entry of symb and finds (seg_{symb}, $offset_{symb}$) where seg_{symb} is the name of the symbol containing the definition of symb. It uses the information in SRTAB to find the register which contains seg_{symb}. Let it be register r. It now synthesizes the pair (r, $offset_{symb}$). This pair is put in the address field of target instruction.

However, this strategy would not work while assembling forward references. Consider the statements 6 and 13 in the above table which make forward references to COUNT. When the definition of COUNT is encountered in statement 20, information concerning these forward references can be found in TII. The first reference was made in the statement 6 when DS was the segment register containing the segment base of DATA. However, SRTAB presently contains the pair (ES, DATA) as a result of statement 8. A similar problem may arise while assembling forward references contained in branch instructions. The following provisions are made to handle this problem:

1. A new SRTAB is created while processing an ASSUME statement. This SRTAB differs from the previous SRTAB only in the entries for the segment registers named in the ASSUME statement. Since many SRTAB's exist at any time, an array named SRTAB_ARRAY is used to store SRTAB's. This array is indexed using a counter srtab_no.
2. Instead of TII, a Forward Reference Table (FRT) is used. Each entry of FRT contains the following entries:
   (a) Address of the instruction whose operand contains the forward reference.
   (b) Symbol to which forward reference is made.
   (c) Type of reference made (e.g. T: analytic operator TYPE, D: data address, S: self relative address, L: length, F: offset, etc.).
   (d) Number of the SRTAB to be used for assembling the reference.

3.8.8 DESIGN OF THE ASSEMBLER

Here is presented an algorithm for Intel 8088 assembler. LC processing in this algorithm differs from LC processing in the first pass of two pass assembler in one significant way. In Intel 8088, the unit for memory allocation is byte; however certain entities require their starting byte to be aligned on specific boundaries in the address space. Such alignment requirements may force some bytes to be left unused during memory allocation. Hence while processing DB statements and imperatives; assembler first aligns LC on the requisite boundary. This process is known as LC alignment. Allocation of memory for a statement and entering its label in the symbol table is performed after LC alignment.

1. code_area_address = address of code_area;

   srtab_no = 1;

   LC = 0;

   stmt_no = 1;

   SYMTAB_segment_entry = 0;

   Clear ERRTAB, SRTAB_ARRAY.
2. While next statement is not an END statement
   (a) Clear machine_code_buffer.

(b) If label is present then

this_label = symbol in label field;

(c) If an EQU statement

(i) this_address = value of operand expression;

(ii) Make an entry for this_label in SYMTAB with

offset = this_address;

Defined = 'yes';

owner_segment = owner_segment of operand symbol;

source_stmt_# = stmt_no;

(iii) Enter stmt_no in the CTR list of the label in the operand field.

(iv) Process forward references to this_label;

(v) size = 0;

(d) If an ASSUME statement

(i) Copy the SRTAB in SRTAB_ARRAY [srtab_no] into SRTAB_ARRAY [srtab_no+1];

(ii) srtab_no = srtab_no+1;

(iii) this_register = register mentioned in the statement.

(iv) this_segment = entry number of SYMTAB entry of the segment appearing in operand field.

(v) Make the entry (this_register, this_segment) in SRTAB_ARRAY [srtab_no].

(vi) size = 0;

(e) If a SEGMENT statement

(i) Make an entry for this_label in SYMTAB.

(ii) Set segment name? = true;

(iii) SYMATB_segment_entry = entry no. in SYMTAB;

(iv) LC = 0;

(v) size = 0;

(f) If an ENDS statement then

SYMTAB_segement_entry = 0;

(g) If a declaration statement

(i) Align LC according to the specification in the operand field.

(ii) Assemble the constants, if any, in the machine_code_buffer.

(iii) size = size of memory area required;

(h) If an imperative statement

(i) If operand is a symbol symb then

enter stmt_no in CRT list of symb.

(ii) If the operand symbol is already defined then

Check its alignment and addressability,

Generate address specification (segment register, offset) for the symbol using its SYMTAB entry and SYMTAB_ARRAY [srtab_no].

Make an entry for symbol in SYMTAB.

Defined = 'no';

Enter (srtab_no, LC, usage code, stmt_no) in FRT.

(iii) Assemble instruction in machine_code_buffer.

(iv) size = size of the instruction;

(i) If size != 0 then

(i) If label is present then

Make an entry for this_label in SYMTAB.

owner_segment = SYMTAB_segment_entry;

Defined = 'yes';

offset = LC;

source_stmt_# = stmt_no;

(ii) Move contents of machine_code_buffer to the address code_area_address;

(iii) code_area_address = code_area_address + size;

(iv) Process forward references to the symbol. Check for alignment and addressability errors. Enter errors in ERRTAB.

(v) List the statement with errors contained in ERRTAB.

(vi) Clear ERRTAB.

3. (Processing of END statement)

(a) Report undefined symbols from SYMTAB.

(b) Produce cross reference listing.

(c) Write code_area into output file.

The numbers in parenthesis indicate the number of bytes required for a field. The Mnemonics Table (MOT) is a hash organized and contains the following fields: mnemonic opcode, machine opcode, alignment/format info, and routine id. The routine id field of an entry specifies the routine which processes that opcode. Alignment/format info is specific to a given routine. For example, the code of '00H' for routine R2 implies that only one instruction format, that with self-relative displacement, is supported. 'FFH' for the same routine implies that all formats are supported; hence the routine must decide which opcode to use. The symbol table (SYMTAB) is also hash organized and contains all relevant information about symbols defined and used in the source program. The contents of some important fields are as follows: The owner segment field indicates id of the segment in which a symbol is defined. It contains the SYMTAB entry # of the segment name. For a non-EQU symbol the type field indicates the alignment information. For an EQU symbol, type field indicates whether the symbol is to be given a numeric value or a textual value. The owner segment and offset fields are used to accommodate the value.

The data structures for the assembler are illustrated in the figure 3.25:

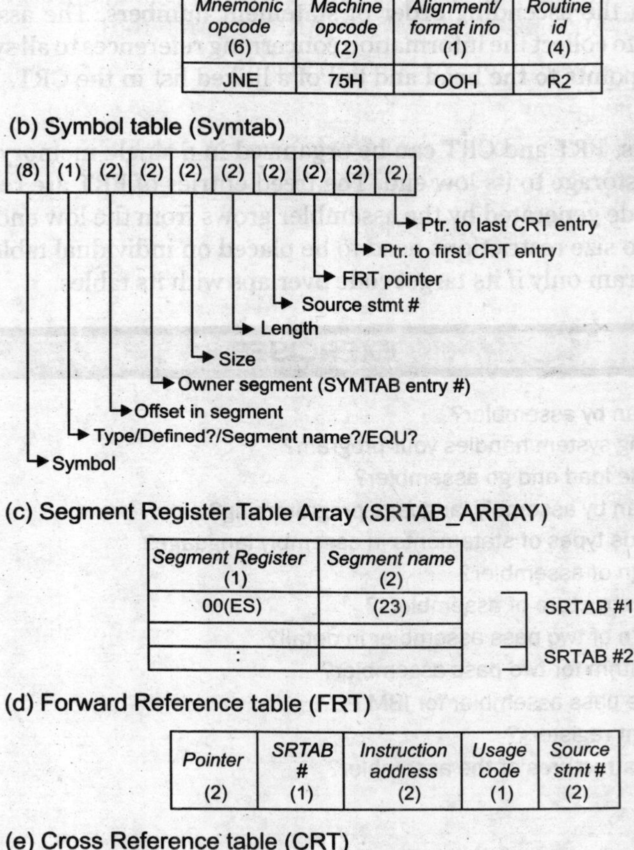

Mnemonic opcode (6)	*Machine opcode* (2)	*Alignment/ format info* (1)	*Routine id* (4)
JNE	75H	OOH	R2

(b) Symbol table (Symtab)

(c) Segment Register Table Array (SRTAB_ARRAY)

Segment Register (1)	*Segment name* (2)	
00(ES)	(23)	SRTAB #1
:		SRTAB #2

(d) Forward Reference table (FRT)

Pointer (2)	*SRTAB #* (1)	*Instruction address* (2)	*Usage code* (1)	*Source stmt #* (2)

(e) Cross Reference table (CRT)

Pointer (2)	*Source stmt #* (2)

Figure 3.25: Data structures of the assembler

An SRTAB can contain up to four entries, one for each register. The current SRTAB exists in the last entry of SRTAB_ARRAY. SRTAB's are accessed by their entry numbers in SRTAB_ARRAY.

3.8.8.1 FORWARD REFERENCES

Information concerning forward references to a symbol is organized in the form of a linked list. Thus the forward reference table (FRT) contains a set of linked lists. The FRT pointer field of a SYMTAB entry points to the head of this list. Since ordering of FRT entries is not important, new entries are added at the beginning of the list. Each FRT entry contains SRTAB # to be used to assemble the forward reference. It also contains the instruction address and a usage code indicating where and how the reference is to be assembled. When the definition of a symbol is encountered, its forward references are processed, and the forward references list is discarded. This minimizes the size of FRT at any time.

3.8.8.2 CROSS REFERENCES

A cross reference directory is a report produced by the assembler which lists all the references to a symbol sorted in the ascending order of statement numbers. The assembler uses the cross reference table (CRT) to collect the information concerning references to all symbols in the program. Each SYMTAB entry points to the head and tail of a linked list in the CRT. New entries are added at the end of the list.

Being linked lists, FRT and CRT can be organized in a single memory area. The tables grow from the high end of storage to its low end. The freed entries of FRT are reused by maintaining a free list. The target code generated by the assembler grows from the low end to the high end of the storage. As a result, no size restrictions need to be placed on individual tables. The assembler fails to handle source program only if its target code overlaps with its tables.

EXERCISES

1. What do you mean by assembler?
2. How the operating system handles your program?
3. Explain the simple load and go assembler?
4. What do you mean by assembly language programming?
5. Explain the various types of statements in assembly language?
6. Explain the design of assembler?
7. Explain the pass structure of assemblers?
8. Explain the design of two pass assembler in detail?
9. Explain the algorithm for two pass assembler?
10. Explain the single pass assembler for IBM PC?
11. What are segment registers?
12. Explain the data structures of the assembler?

Chapter

4

Macro Processors

4.1 INTRODUCTION

There are situations when certain blocks of code are needed to repeat many times in the course of a program. The code may be a set of instruction(s) to save or exchange a set of registers, or code to set up linkages, or to perform some arithmetic operations. In such situations, programmers find the macro facility as a helpful tool. Macro instructions (or simply macros) are single-line abbreviations for a group of instructions. The programmer defines a single instruction to represent a block of code. For every occurrence of this one-line macro, the macro processor substitutes the entire block of code.

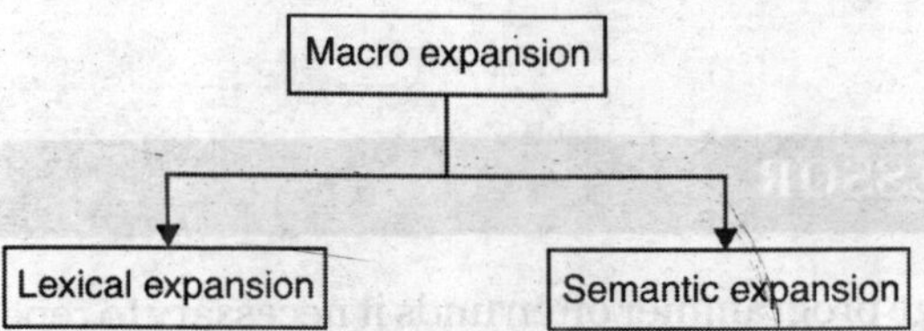

Figure 4.1: Macro Expansion

A macro is thus a unit of specification for program generation through expansion. A macro consists of a name, a set of formal parameters and a body of code. The use of a macro name with a set of actual parameters is replaced by some code from its body. This process of replacing the instruction with actual code is known as macro expansion. Two kinds of expansions are described as follows:

1. **Lexical Expansion:** Lexical expansion is the replacement of a character string by another character string during program generation. It is mainly employed for replacement of the occurrences of formal parameters by actual parameters.
2. **Semantic Expansion:** Semantic expansion is the generation of instructions tailored to the requirements of a specific usage. It is characterized by the fact that different uses of a macro can lead to codes which differ in number, sequence and opcodes of instructions.

By the use of macros, an assembly language programmer can tailor his own higher level facility in a convenient manner, at no cost in control over the structure of his program. One can achieve the ease in coding of high level languages without losing the basic advantage of assembly language programming. Macro instructions are considered an extension of the basic assembler language, and the macro processor is thus known to be an extension of the basic assembler algorithm.

The macros and subroutines can be differentiated by one fundamental aspect. The use of a macro name in the mnemonic field leads to the expansion, while the use of a subroutine name in the instruction leads to its execution. Thus the programs using macros and subroutines differ significantly in terms of program size and execution efficiency.

Macro is a unit of specification for program generation through expansion. A macro represents a commonly used group of statements in the source pro ramming language. The macro processor replaces each macro instruction with the corresponding group of source language statements. This is called expanding of macros.

Macro instructions allow the programmer to write a shorthand version of a program, and leave the mechanical details to be handled by the macro processor.

For example, suppose that it is necessary to save the contents of all registers before calling a subprogram. On SIC/XE, this would require a sequence of seven instructions (STA, STB, etc.).

Using a macro instruction, the programmer could simply write one statement like SAVEREGS. This macro instruction would be expanded into the seven assembler language instructions needed to save the register contents.

The most common use of macro processors is in assembler language programming. However, macro processors can also be used with high-level programming languages, operating system command languages, etc.

4.2 MACRO PROCESSOR

The assembly language programmer often finds it necessary to repeat some statements or block of code several times in a program. The block may consist of code to swap sets of registers, do some arithmetic operations. In this situation the programmer find a macro instruction facility useful. Macro instructions (often called macros) are single line abbreviations for group of instructions. In employing a macro, the programmer essentially defines a single instruction to represent a block of code. For every occurrence of this one-line macro instruction in his program, the macro processing assembler substitute the entire block.

In this section we will discuss an assembler macro facility and its implementation within an assembler.

4.2.1 MACRO DEFINITION AND USAGE

In this section we will present one more example to highlight salient aspects of macro-processor. The example is very similar to Intel's 8 bit microprocessor assembly language instruction.

Example:

MACRO INCRMT LOAD ADD STORE ENDM	 &A, &B &A &B &A	 Macro definition
——— ——— ———		
INCRMT ENDM	X,Y	LOAD X Macro ADD Y expansion STORE X Macro Program

Figure 4.2: Macro Program

A macro definition is placed at the start of a program, enclosed between the statements MACRO and ENDM. A MACRO statement indicates that a macro definition starts, while the statement ENDM indicates the end of a macro definition. Thus, a group of statements starting with MACRO and ending with ENDM constitutes one macro definition unit. If many macros are to be defined in a program, as many definition modules will exist at the start of the program. Each definition module contains a new operation and defines it to consist of a sequence of assembly language statements. In example above, INCRMT is defined to be the name of the LOAD-ADD-STORE instruction sequence.

The operation defined by a macro can be used by writing the macro name in the mnemonic field and its operands in the operand field of an assembly statement Appearance of a macro name in the mnemonic field amounts to a call on the macro. The assembler replaces such a statement by the statement sequence comprising the macro. This is known **as** macro expansion.

In example

INCRMT X, Y

is shown to lead to insertion of the assembly statements

LOAD X

ADD **Y**

STORE **X**

in its place. All macro calls in a program **are** expanded in this fashion.

4.2.2 MACRO INSTRUCTIONS

In the simplest of form, the macro is known to be an abbreviation for a sequence of operations. Consider the following example:

:

ADD AREG, DATA

ADD BREG, DATA

ADD CREG, DATA

:

:

ADD AREG, DATA

ADD BREG, DATA

ADD CREG, DATA

:

:

DATA DC '5'

:

:

Example:

In the above program, the following sequence of instructions occurs twice.

ADD AREG, DATA

ADD BREG, DATA

ADD CREG, DATA

The use of macros permits us to use a name for this sequence and to use this name in the place of repeated code.

4.2.3 MACRO DEFINITION

A macro definition is enclosed within a macro header and a macro end statement. Macros are typically defined at the start of an assemble language program. A macro definition consists of following parts:

1. A macro prototype statement (Macro Name)

This statement declares the name of the macro and the names and kinds of its parameters. The syntax for this statement is as follows:

<macro name> [<formal parameter spec> [,..]]

The <macro name> appears in the mnemonic field of an assembly language statement. The <formal parameter spec> has the following syntax:

&<parameter name> [<parameter kind>]

2. One or more model statements

A model statement is a statement from which an assembly language statement may be generated during macro expansion.

3. Macro preprocessor statements

A preprocessor statement performs auxiliary functions during macro expansion.

A macro definition has the following form:

MACRO ← Start of definition

<macro name> ← Name of macro

---------- ← Sequence to be abbreviated

MEND ← End of definition

The MACRO pseudo-op is the first line of the definition and identifies the next line as macro instruction name. Following the name is the sequence of instructions being abbreviated. These are the statements which comprise the macro instruction. The definition is terminated by MEND pseudo-op.

Once the macro is defined at the start of the assembly language program, the use of macro name as an operation mnemonic in the rest of the program is equivalent to the use of corresponding instruction sequence. The previous example can be re-written using a macro named ADDER to repeat the sequence.

	Source Code		Expanded Code

	MACRO
	ADDER
	ADD AREG, DATA
	ADD BREG, DATA
	ADD CREG, DATA
	MEND
	:
	:
	ADDER
	:
	:
	ADDER
	:
	:
			:
			:
			:
			ADD AREG, DATA
			ADD BREG, DATA
			ADD CREG, DATA
			:
			:
			ADD AREG, DATA
			ADD BREG, DATA

DATA	DC '5' : :		ADD CREG, DATA : :
		DATA	DC '5' : :

In the above example, the macro processor replaces each macro call with the lines:

ADD AREG, DATA
ADD BREG, DATA
ADD CREG, DATA

This process of replacement of macro call by the actual statements is known as macro expansion. The occurrence in the source program of the macro name, as an operation mnemonic to be expanded is called the macro call. The macro definition itself does not appear in the expanded source code. The definition is saved by the macro processor.

4.2.4 SCHEMATICS FOR MACRO-EXPANSION

In the last section, we touched upon the fundamental aspects of macro expansion. From the discussion, it appears that the process of macro expansion is similar to language translation. The source program containing macro definitions and calls is translated into an assembly language program without any macro definitions or calls. This program form can now be handed over to a conventional assembler as to obtain the target languages form of the program.

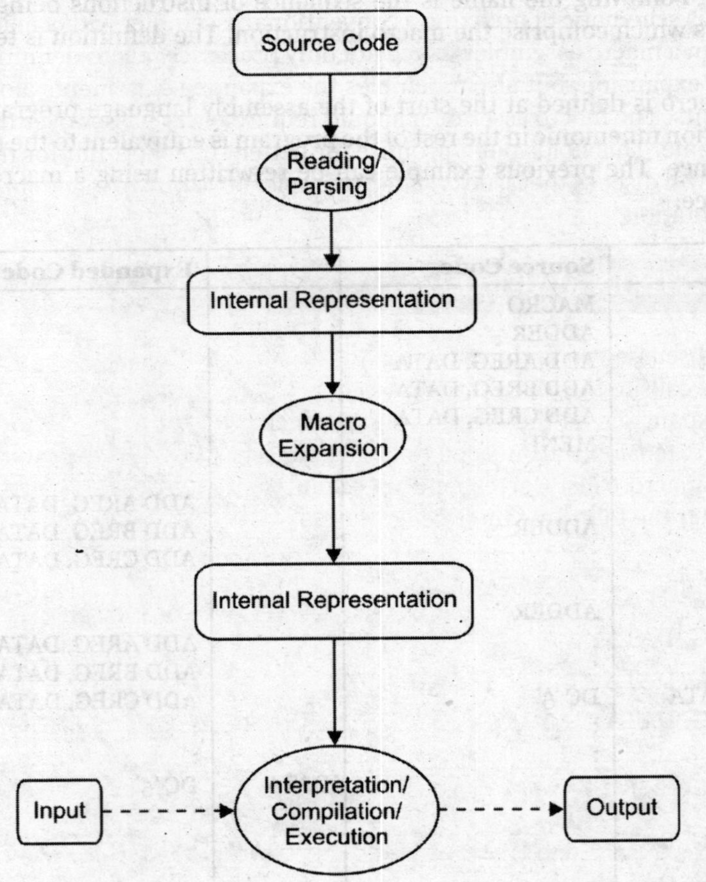

Figure 4.3: Schematic for macro expansion

In such a schematic (Figure 4.4), the process of macro expansion is completely segregated from the process of assembly program. The translator which performs macro expansion in this manner is called a macro pre-processor. The advantage of this scheme is that any existing conventional assembler can be enhanced in this manner to incorporate macro processing. It would reduce the programming cost involved in making a macro facility available to prograrnmer using a computer system. The disadvantage is that this scheme is probably not very efficient because of the time spent in generating assembly language staternents and processing them again for the purpose of translation to the target language.

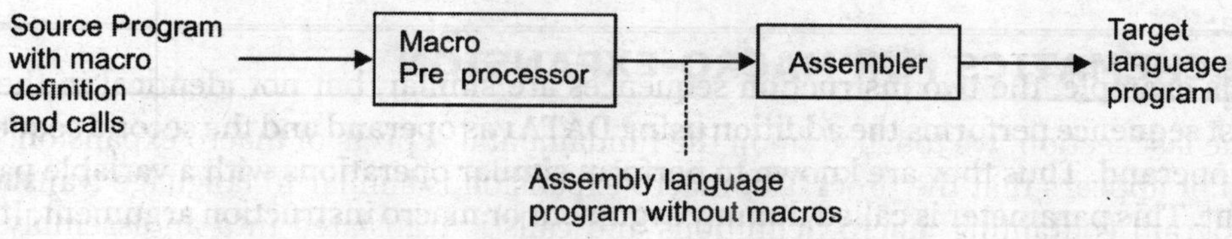

Figure 4.4: A pre-processor based scheme for macro assembly

As against this schematic of prefixing a conventional assembler with a macro pre-processor, it is possible to design a macro assembler which not only processes macro definitions and macro calls for the purpose of expansion, but also assembles the expanded statements along with the original assembly staternents. The macro assembler should require fewer passes over the program than the pre-processor scheme. This holds out a promise for better efficiency. But for the sake of simplicity in this section, we will discuss the issues related to implementation of macro pre- processor instead of actual implementation.

4.3 ARGUMENTS IN MACROS

The macros discussed so far have the capability of inserting blocks of instructions in place of macro calls. All the calls to the macro are replaced by the same block of code. There is no flexibility in this model of expansion, as there is no way in which a macro call can modify the instructions that replace it. An extension thus needed to be introduced, which came in the form of arguments, or parameters, in macro calls. Corresponding dummy arguments will thus appear in the macro definitions. Consider the following modified example:

```
:
:
ADD AREG, DATA1
ADD BREG, DATA1
ADD CREG, DATA1
:
:
ADD AREG, DATA2
ADD BREG, DATA2
ADD CREG, DATA2
:
:
DATA1 DC '5'
DATA2 DC '15'
:
:
```

Example:

In this example, the two instruction sequences are similar, but not identical in the manner that the first sequence performs the addition using DATA1 as operand and the second sequence uses DATA2 as operand. Thus they are known to perform similar operations with a variable parameter, or argument. This parameter is called dummy argument or macro instruction argument. It needs to be specified on the macro name line and distinguished by the ampersand (&) as the first character. The program in Example 2 can be modified using macros in this manner:

Source Code		Expanded Code	
	MACRO		
	ADDER2 &ARG		
	ADD AREG, &ARG		
	ADD BREG, &ARG		
	ADD CREG, &ARG		
	MEND		:
	:		:
	:		ADD AREG, DATA1
	ADDER2 DATA1		ADD BREG, DATA1
	:		ADD CREG, DATA1
	:		:
	ADDER2 DATA2		:
	:		ADD AREG, DATA2
	:		ADD BREG, DATA2
DATA1	DC '5'		ADD CREG, DATA2
DATA2	DC '15'		:
	:		
	:	DATA1	DC '5'
		DATA2	DC '15'
			:
			:

Hence the operands DATA1 and DATA2 are passed as arguments to the macro named ADDER2, using the symbol &ARG. More than one argument can also be supplied in a macro call. Each argument must correspond to a dummy argument on macro name line of the macro definition. When a macro call is processed, the actual arguments are replaced for the respective dummy arguments in the macro definitions. Here in the above example &ARG was the dummy argument used to specify the position of the argument in the sequence of instructions, while DATA1 and DATA2 were the actual arguments.

Consider another example:

```
        :
        :
LOOP1   ADD AREG, DATA1
        ADD BREG, DATA2
        ADD CREG, DATA3
        :
```

```
            :
LOOP2 ADD AREG, DATA3
      ADD BREG, DATA2
      ADD CREG, DATA1
            :
            :
DATA1 DC '5'
DATA2 DC '15'
DATA3 DC '25'
            :
            :
```

Example:

In this example, the operands supplied are more than one, as well as the labels used for the sequence of statements is also different. In such cases, label arguments can also be used:

Source Code		Expanded Code	

&LAB
&LAB
	MACRO
	ADDER3 &ARG1, &ARG2, &ARG3
	ADD AREG, &ARG1
	ADD BREG, &ARG2
	ADD CREG, &ARG3
	MEND
	:
	:
			:
			:

LOOP1	ADDER3 DATA1, DATA2, DATA3
	:
	:
		LOOP1	ADD AREG, DATA1
			ADD BREG, DATA2
			ADD CREG, DATA3
			:
			:

LOOP2	ADDER3 DATA3, DATA2, DATA1
	:
	:
		LOOP2	ADD AREG, DATA3
			ADD BREG, DATA2
			ADD CREG, DATA1
			:

DATA1 DATA2 DATA3	DC '5' DC '15' DC '25' : :	DATA1 DATA2 DATA3	DC '5' DC '15' DC '25' : :

In this example, four arguments are specified including a label argument. Label arguments are treated in the same manner as dummy arguments. They just differ in their location in the macro definition. Arguments used as labels within a macro need not appear in the label field of the call, and arguments appearing in the label field of the call may be used as operands within the macro instruction code. These are convenient but not essential feature to enhance the similarity between macro instructions and ordinary assembly language statements. The previous example can thus be encoded without using label arguments in a way shown below:

Source Code		Expanded Code	
	MACRO		
	ADDER4 &ARG1, &ARG2, &ARG3, &LAB		
&LAB	ADD AREG, &ARG1		
	ADD BREG, &ARG2		
	ADD CREG, &ARG3		:
	MEND		:
	:	LOOP1	ADD AREG, DATA1
	:		ADD BREG, DATA2
	ADDER4 DATA1, DATA2, DATA3, LOOP1		ADD CREG, DATA3
	:		:
	:		:
	ADDER4 DATA3, DATA2, DATA1, LOOP2	LOOP2	ADD AREG, DATA3
	:		ADD BREG, DATA2
	:		ADD CREG, DATA1
DATA1	DC '5'		:
DATA2	DC '15'		:
DATA3	DC '25'	DATA1	DC '5'
	:	DATA2	DC '15'
	:	DATA3	DC '25'
			:
			:

There are generally two ways of passing arguments to a macro call. The first way, called positional arguments is illustrated till now in example, where the actual arguments are matched with dummy arguments according to the order in which they appear. Thus in a macro call 'ADDER A, B, C' A, B, and C replace the first, second, and third dummy arguments.

Another way is to use keyword arguments, in which dummy arguments can be referenced by name as well as by position. Referring to the last example, we could use keyword arguments in the form:

ADDER4 &ARG1=A, &ARG2=B, & ARG3=C, &LAB=LOOP1

or,

ADDER4 &ARG1=C, &ARG2=B, & ARG3=A, &LAB=LOOP2

Such a technique is useful when a macro has arguments that are not always needed, and any arguments not supplied are presumed blank by the macro processor.

4.4 CONCATENATION OF MACRO PARAMETERS

Most macros also have the facility of concatenating the parameters with other character strings. For example, a assembly language program having a series of variables named by symbols XA1, XA2, XA3, etc. and another series named by XB1, XB2, XB3, etc. If similar instructions have to be processed for both the series of variables, the programmer may need to incorporate that processing in the form of a macro. The parameter to such a macro could specify the series of variables to be operated upon i.e. A, B, etc. The macro processor would use this parameter to construct the symbols required in the expansion of macro.

Let the parameter to this macro be named &ID. Then the body of macro definition would have instructions like this:

ADD AREG, X&ID1

In this instruction, the parameter &ID is concatenated after the character string X and before the character string 1. Analyzing this statement closely, we know that the beginning of the macro parameter can clearly be identified with the symbol '&' however the end is not marked properly. Thus the operand in the statement can represent the character string X followed by &ID as well as &ID1. This problem can be solved by deducing the meaning for the specified parameter, but there may be a situation when the definition contains &ID and &ID1 both as parameters. Such a situation would be unavoidably ambiguous.

Some macro processors solve this problem by providing a special concatenation operator. In some languages, character '→' is used as the operator in the form:

ADD AREG, X&ID→1

Now the end of the parameter is clearly identified by the symbol '→'. The macro processor deletes all the occurrences of the concatenation operator as soon it substitutes the parameters, so that the character '→' does not appear in the macro expansion.

The following example shows the use of concatenation operator in detail:

Source Code	Expanded Code

MACRO
SUMS &ID
ADD AREG, X&IDà1
ADD BREG, X&IDà2
ADD CREG, X&IDà3
MEND
:
:
SUMS A
:
:
SUMS PI
:
:
	
	:
	:
	ADD AREG, XA1
	ADD BREG, XA2
	ADD CREG, XA3
	:
	:
	ADD AREG, XPI1
	ADD BREG, XPI2
	ADD CREG, XPI3
	:
	:

4.5 GENERATION OF UNIQUE LABELS

It is generally not possible for the body of macro instructions to contain labels of usual kind. This leads to the use of relative addressing at the source statement level. For example, we have a macro definition which is called twice with different parameters. If the macro definition has a label in the body of statements and the macro is called twice in the program, then the label would also be defined twice- one for each invocation of the macro. This duplicate definition would prevent the correct assembly of the expanded program.

The following statement illustrates one technique for generating unique labels within a macro expansion. Here is presented the definition of a macro. The labels begin with the special character '$'.

	MACRO
	READBUFF &A, &B, &C
	ADD AREG, &A
$LOOP	ADD BREG, &B
	ADD CREG, &C
	MOVEM CREG, &B
$EXIT	PRINT CREG
	MEND

For the macro call such as this:

READBUFF DATA1, DATA2, DATA3

The macro expansion would result in the code as given below:

	ADD AREG, DATA1
$AALOOP	ADD BREG, DATA2
	ADD CREG, DATA3
	MOVEM CREG, DATA2
$AAEXIT	PRINT CREG

Each symbol beginning with '$' has been modified by replacing $ with $AA. More generally, the character $ will be replaced by $xx, where xx is two character alphanumeric counter of the number of macro instructions expanded. For the first macro expansion in a program, xx will have the value AA. For succeeding macro expansions, xx will be set to AB, AC, etc. Hence if only alphabetic and numeric counters are allowed in xx, the resulting two-character counter would provide as many as 1296 macro expansions in a single program. This results in the generation of unique labels for each expansion of a macro instruction.

4.6 CONDITIONAL MACRO EXPANSION

In all of the previous examples of macro statements, each call of a particular macro was expanded into the same sequence of statements. These statements could be varied by the substitutions of the parameters, but the actual form of the statements, and the order in which they appeared, were unchanged. Most macro processors, however, can also modify the sequence of statements generated for a macro expansion, depending upon the arguments supplied in the macro call. Such a capability adds to the great power and flexibility of macros.

The term conditional assembly is often used for such kind of assembling of statements. However, there are applications of macro processors that are not related to assemblers or assembly language programming. Hence, we use the term conditional macro expansion.

AIF and AGO pseudo-ops are used to permit conditional reordering of the sequence of macro expansion. This allows conditional selection of the machine instructions that appear in the expansion of macro call. Consider the following example:

```
        :
        :
LOOP1 ADD AREG, DATA1
      ADD BREG, DATA2
      ADD CREG, DATA3
        :
        :
LOOP2 ADD AREG, DATA3
      ADD BREG, DATA2
        :
        :
LOOP3 ADD AREG, DATA1
        :
        :
DATA1 DC '5'
DATA2 DC '15'
DATA3 DC '25'
        :
        :
```

Example:

In this example, the operands, labels, as well as the number of instructions differ for each sequence of instructions. Hence the use of AIF pseudo-op can be made in this manner:

Labels starting with a period (.) are known as macro labels. They do not appear in the output of the expanded code. The statement AIF (&COUNT EQ 3).FINI are macro preprocessor statements which tell the macro processor to skip to the statement labeled .FINI if the parameter corresponding to &COUNT is 3. Otherwise, the macro processor continues with the statement following AIF pseudo-op.

AIF is a conditional branch pseudo-op, which performs an arithmetic test and branches only if the tested condition is true. A similar pseudo-op AGO is an unconditional branch pseudo-op, which makes the macro processor to branch to the specified location as a 'go to' statement. It specifies a label appearing on some other statement in the macro definition and the processing continues with the indicated instruction. Both these statements are directives to the macro processor and do not appear in the expanded code.

Source Code		Expanded Code	
	MACRO		
&ARG0	ADDC &COUNT, &ARG1,		
&ARG0	&ARG2, &ARG3		
	ADD AREG, &ARG1		
	AIF (&COUNT EQ 1).FINI		
	ADD BREG, &ARG2		
	AIF (&COUNT EQ 2).FINI		
.FINI	ADD CREG, &ARG3		:
	MEND		:
	:	LOOP1	ADD AREG, DATA1
LOOP1	:		ADD BREG, DATA2
	ADDC 3, DATA1, DATA2,		ADD CREG, DATA3
	DATA3		:
LOOP2	:		:
	:	LOOP2	ADD AREG, DATA3
	ADDC 2, DATA3, DATA2		ADD BREG, DATA2
LOOP3	:		:
	:		:
	ADDC 1, DATA1	LOOP3	ADD AREG, DATA1
DATA1	:		:
DATA2	:		:
DATA3	DC ‘5’	DATA1	DC ‘5’
	DC ‘15’	DATA2	DC ‘15’
	DC ‘25’	DATA3	DC ‘25’
	:		:
	:		:

4.6.1 IF-ELSE STRUCTURE

When an IF statement is encountered during the expansion of a macro, the specified Boolean expression is evaluated.

If the value of this expression TRUE,

The macro processor continues to process lines from the DEFTAB until it encounters the ELSE or ENDIF statement.

- If an ELSE is found, macro processor skips lines in DEFTAB until the next ENDIF.
- Once it reaches ENDIF, it resumes expanding the macro in the usual way.

If the value of the expression is FALSE,

- The macro processor skips ahead in DEFTAB until it encounters next ELSE or ENDIF statement.
- The macro processor then resumes normal macro expansion.

The macro-time IF-ELSE-ENDIF structure provides a mechanism for either generating (once) or skipping selected statements in the macro body. There is another construct WHILE statement which specifies that the loop until the next ENDW statement, are to be generated repeatedly as long as a particular condition is true. The testing of this condition, and the looping are done during the macro is under expansion. The example shown below shows the usage of Macro-Time Looping statement.

4.6.2 WHILE-ENDW STRUCTURE

When an WHILE statement is encountered during the expansion of a macro, the specified Boolean expression is evaluated.

TRUE

The macro processor continues to process lines from DEFTAB until it encounters the next ENDW statement.

When ENDW is encountered, the macro processor returns to the preceding WHILE, re-evaluates the Boolean expression, and takes action based on the new value.

FALSE

The macro processor skips ahead in DEFTAB until it finds the next ENDW statement and then resumes normal macro expansion.

4.7 NESTED MACROS (RECURSIVE MACRO EXPANSION)

Till now we have dealt with the macros which have statements like a simple assembly language program. However, a statement in a macro may constitute a call on another macro. Such calls are known as nested macro calls. Since macro calls are abbreviations for a sequence of instructions, hence it seems alright that those abbreviations should also be available within other macro definitions. The macro containing the nested call is referred to as outer macro and the macro which is called is known as inner macro. Expansion of such calls follows the last-in-first-out (LIFO) rule, i.e. expansion of the latest macro call is completed first. Consider the following example:

```
MACRO
ADD1 &ARG
ADD AREG, &ARG
ADD BREG, &ARG
ADD CREG, &ARG
MEND
MACRO
ADDS &ARG1, &ARG2, &ARG3
ADD1 &ARG1
ADD1 &ARG2
ADD1 &ARG3
MEND
:
:
```

```
        ADDS DATA1, DATA2, DATA3
            :
            :
DATA1 DC '5'
DATA2 DC '15'
DATA3 DC '25'
            :
            :
```

Example:

Here within the definition of macro ADDS are three calls to a previously defined macro named ADD1. The use of macro ADD1 has shortened the length of the macro ADDS and thus made it easily understood. Such macros need to be expanded on multiple levels as shown below:

<table>
<tr><th>Source Code</th><th>Expanded Code (Level 1)</th><th>Expanded Code (Level 2)</th></tr>
<tr><td>MACRO
ADD1 &ARG
ADD AREG, &ARG
ADD BREG, &ARG
ADD CREG, &ARG
MEND
MACRO
ADDS &ARG1, &ARG2, &ARG3
ADD1 &ARG1
ADD1 &ARG2
ADD1 &ARG3
MEND
:
:
ADDS DATA1, DATA2, DATA3
:
:
DATA1 DC '5'
DATA2 DC '15'
DATA3 DC '25'
:
:</td><td>:
:
ADD1 DATA1
ADD1 DATA2
ADD1 DATA3
:
:
DATA1 DC '5'
DATA2 DC '15'
DATA3 DC '25'
:
:</td><td>:
:
ADD AREG DATA1
ADD BREG, DATA1
ADD CREG, DATA1
ADD AREG, DATA2
ADD BREG, DATA2
ADD CREG, DATA2
ADD AREG, DATA3
ADD BREG, DATA3
ADD CREG, DATA3
:
:
DATA1 DC '5'
DATA2 DC '15'
DATA3 DC '25'
:
:</td></tr>
</table>

Nested macros can involve more than two levels, if there are calls to more than a single macro within a macro. For example, if there was another macro which was called within the macro ADD1, then our above example would have 3 levels of expansion.

AIF and AGO pseudo-ops may also permit a macro to call itself, so long as it does not create an infinite loop.

4.8 MACROS DEFINING MACROS

If a call to a macro is permitted inside a macro definition, hence a definition of another macro within a macro is also permitted as a valid syntax in assembly language programming. That is, a single macro instruction can be used to simplify the process of defining a group of similar macros.

The inner macro definition is actually not defined (i.e. callable) until the outer macro is called. This is due to the method by which these definitions are implemented. For example, programmer may want to define a group of macros for subroutine calls with some standardized calling sequence. The following example defines a macro instruction DEFINE; which when called with the name of a subroutine defines a macro with the same name as the subroutine. The individual macros thus generated have the names of their associated subroutines.

```
MACRO
DEFINE &SUB                Macro name DEFINE
MACRO
&SUB &Y                    Dummy macro name
CNOP 0, 4                  Align boundary
BAL 1,*+8                  Set register 1 to parameter list pointer
DC A (&Y)                  Parameter list pointer
LOAD 15, =V (&SUB)         Address of subroutine
BALR 14, 15                Transfer control to subroutine
MEND                       End of inner macro
MEND                       End of macro DEFINE
```

Example:

The programmer can then call this macro with the following macro call:

DEFINE SQRT

This statement defines a new macro named ABC. The statement thus expands into a new macro definition which the programmer can call with another name as:

SQRT ABC

This statement will generate the following sequence:

```
BAL 1,*+8
DC A(ABC)
LOAD 15, =V(SQRT)
BALR 14, 15
```

4.9 ADVANCED MACRO FACILITIES

Advanced macro facilities aim at providing support for semantic expansion. These facilities can be grouped into:

1. Facilities for alteration of flow of control during expansion.
2. Expansion time variables.
3. Attributes of parameters.

This section describes some of these advanced facilities and illustrates their use in performing conditional expansion of statements and in writing expansion time loops.

4.9.1 ALTERATION OF FLOW OF CONTROL DURING EXPANSION

Two features are provided to facilitate the alteration of flow of control during expansion:

1. Expansion time sequencing symbols.
2. Expansion time statements AIF, AGO and ANOP.

A sequencing symbol (SS) has the following syntax:

<ordinary string>

An SS is defined by putting it in the label field of a statement in the body of macro. It is used as an operand in an AIF or AGO statement to designate the destination of an expansion time control transfer. It does not appear in the expanded form of a model statement.

An AIF statement has the following syntax:

AIF (<expression>) <sequencing symbol>

The <expression> here is a relational expression involving ordinary strings, formal parameters, and their attributes, and expansion time variables. If the relational expression evaluates to true, expansion time control is transferred to the statement containing <sequencing symbol> in its label field. An AGO statement has the syntax:

AGO <sequencing symbol>

Such a statement unconditionally transfers expansion time control to the statement containing <sequencing symbol> in its label field. An ANOP statement has the following syntax:

<sequencing symbol> ANOP

It simple defines the sequencing symbol.

4.9.2 EXPANSION TIME VARIABLES

Expansion time variables (EV's) are variables which can only be used during the expansion of macro calls. A local EV is created for use only during a particular macro call, while a global EV exists across all macro calls situated in a program and can be used in any macro which has a declaration for it. Local and global EV's are created through the declaration statements with the following syntax:

LCL <EV specification> [,<EV specification> ..]

GBL <EV specification> [,<EV specification> ..]

The <EV specification> has the syntax &<EV name>, where <EV name> is any ordinary string. Values of EV's can be manipulated with the preprocessor statement SET. A SET statement is written as:

<EV specification> SET <SET-expression>

Here <EV specification> appears in the label field and SET the mnemonic field. A SET statement assigns the value of <SET-expression> to the EV specified in <EV specification>. The value of an EV can be used in any field of body of program, and in the expression of an AIF statement.

	MACRO
	CONSTANTS
	LCL &A
&A	SET 1
	DB &A
&A	SET &A+1
	DB &A
	MEND

The call for this macro results in the creation of a local EV named A. The first SET statement assigns the value '1' to it. The first DB statement thus declares a byte constant '1'. The second SET statement assigns the value '2' to A and the second DB statement declares a constant '2'.

4.9.3 ATTRIBUTES OF FORMAL PARAMETERS

An attribute is written using the syntax:

<attribute name>'<formal parameter spec>

It represents the information about the value of the formal parameter i.e. about the corresponding actual parameter. The type, length and size attributes have the name T, L and S.

	MACRO
	DCONST &A
	AIF (L'&A EQ 1) .NEXT
	:
.NEXT	:
	MEND

As in the example above, the expansion time control is transferred to the statement having .NEXT in its label field only if the actual parameter corresponding to the formal parameter A has the length of '1'.

4.10 DESIGN OF A MACRO PROCESSOR

The macro processor is a system program that accepts an assembly program containing definitions and calls to macros and translates it into an assembly program which does not contain any macro definitions or calls. This assembly program without macro calls and definitions can then be fed to the general assembler for corresponding conversion to the equivalent machine code. The figure 4.5 shows a general scenario that is followed by macro processors:

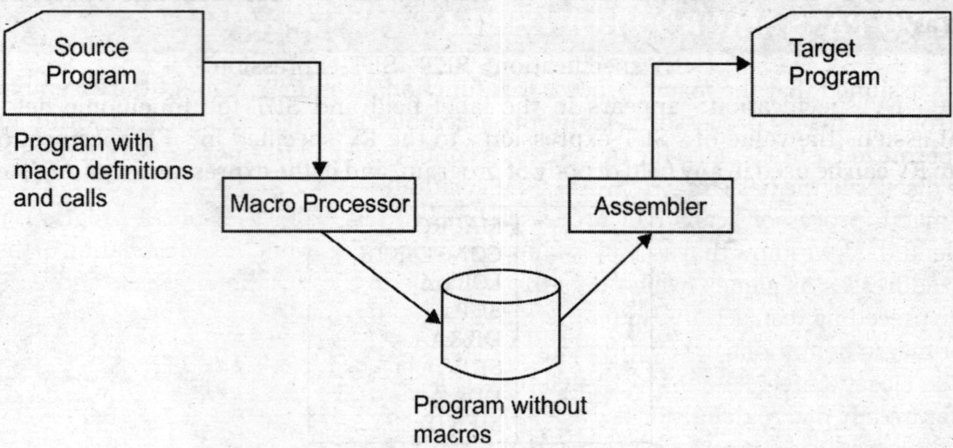

Figure 4.5: A schematic of a Macro Processor

Hence we can say that the main task of macro processor is to separate the macro expansion from the process of program assembly. This process is considered economical because there is no need to design a new assembler, and the existing one can be made to use. However, it is not as efficient as a macro-assembler, which performs the task of macro expansion as well as assembly.

4.10.1 BASIC TASKS OF MACRO PROCESSOR

There are four basic tasks that are performed by a macro processor:

1. **Recognize Macro Definitions:** A macro processor should be able to recognize the macro definitions from the MACRO and MEND pseudo-ops. This is a complex task when macro definitions occur within macros. When nested macros are encountered, the macro processor must recognize them and correctly match the last MEND with the first MACRO instruction.
2. **Save the Definitions:** The macro processor must store these definitions, because they may be needed while expansion of macros.
3. **Recognize Calls to Macros:** The processor must recognize the macro calls that appear in the assembly program. This enables the macro names to be used as operation mnemonics.
4. **Expand Calls and Substitute Arguments:** For every macro call, the macro processor must substitute actual arguments for dummy arguments in the definition of the macro. Hence the resulting code is substituted for the macro call and any additional macro calls in the resultant code, if any, are again expanded.

In summary, the macro processor should recognize and process macro definitions and macro calls. Here we present the macro processor that uses two passes for the task and then a single pass macro processor is discussed in the next section.

4.11 TWO PASS MACRO PROCESSOR

It is assumed that the macro processor is functionally independent of the assembler and the output from the macro processor is fed to the assembler later. The macro calls within macros are not yet permitted as they make the design more complex. Hence we postpone that discussion until we have discussed the basic macro processor algorithm.

A macro processor scans and processes lines of text from the source program, just as an assembler did. As we know that assembly language programs permit the interrelation of instructions by their addresses or names, which must be available to the assembler. These addresses depend upon the preceding instructions, upon their addresses, and possibly upon their contents too. If we consider macro definitions to constitute integrals entities, we may say that the macros instructions are not so closely interrelated. Macro definitions refer to nothing outside themselves, and macro calls refer to only macro definitions.

The macro processor we design has two passes, which individually scan the source program as the two pass assembler did. First pass searches for the macro definitions and the second searches for macro calls. Just as the assembler could not process the forward references to symbols before their definition is encountered, similarly the macro processor cannot expand a macro call before the corresponding definition of the macro is encountered and saved. Thus two passes are needed over the input source program, one for handling the definitions and the second for handling the calls. Pass I of the macro processor save the macro definitions in a Macro Definition Table (MDT) and saves a copy of input source program excluding the macro definitions for input to the Pass II. Pass I also creates a Macro Name Table (MNT) along with MDT, which is not a necessary task to perform but it facilitates the searching for macro names. Then Pass II examines the operation mnemonic of every instruction and replaces each encountered macro name with the appropriate macro definitions.

4.11.1 DATA STRUCTURES

The following data bases are used by the two passes of the macro processor:

Pass I:

1. The Source Program.
2. A Macro Definition Table (MDT) that is used to store the definitions of macros.
3. A Macro Name Table (MNT) that is used to store the names of all the macros which are present in the program.
4. The Macro Definition Table Counter (MDTC) that is used to indicate the next available entry in the MDT.
5. The Macro Name Table Counter (MNTC) that is used to indicate the next available entry in the MNT.
6. The Argument List Array (ALA) that is used to substitute index markers for dummy arguments before storing a macro definition.

7. A copy of the input that is to be used by Pass II. It can be stored in any secondary storage device like magnetic tape, disk etc.

Pass II:

1. Copy of Source Program output by Pass I.
2. The Macro Definition Table (MDT) that was created by Pass I.
3. The Macro Name Table (MNT) that was created by Pass I.
4. The Macro Definition Table Pointer (MDTP) that is used to indicate the next line of the text to be used during macro expansion.
5. The Argument List Array (ALA) that is used to substitute macro call arguments for the index markers in the macro definitions.
6. An output copy of program as needed by the assembler.

4.11.2 FORMAT OF DATA BASES

Here we present a basic introduction to the data bases used in macro processor. We limit our discussion to the data bases with nontrivial format only, which include the Macro Definition Table (MDT), the Macro Name Table (MNT), and the Argument List Array (ALA).

4.11.2.1 MACRO DEFINITION TABLE

MDT is a table of instructions from the source program, where the width matches the actual width of the instructions. If the source program has 80-bytes per instruction, this table also saves the entries with 80-byte width. Each line of the macro definition after MACRO pseudo-op is stored in this table till the MEND pseudo-op. MACRO keyword is not stored in the MDT, as there is no need to do so. The MEND keyword needs to be stored to mark the end of the macro. The macro name is also stored as such for facilitating argument replacements. Here is presented the MDT for the macro named ADDER3 specified in previous example:

	80-bytes per entry		
Index	**Instructions**		
:	:		
:	:		
15	&LAB	ADDER3	&ARG1, &ARG2, &ARG3
16	#0	ADD	AREG, #1
17		ADD	BREG, #2
18		ADD	CREG, #3
19		MEND	
:	:		
:	:		

Figure 4.6: Macro Definition Table

4.11.2.2 MACRO NAME TABLE

MNT is a table that performs a similar function as assembler's Machine-Op Table (MOT) and Pseudo-Op Table (POT). Each entry in MNT has a macro name and a corresponding pointer to the entry in MDT which points to the beginning of the macro definition. The MNT entry for the ADDER3 macro discussed above can be as follows:

	8-bytes	**4-bytes**
Index	Name	MDT index
:	:	:
3	"ADDER3bb"	15
:	:	:

Figure 4.7: Macro Name Table

4.11.2.3 ARGUMENT LIST ARRAY

ALA is used in Pass I as well as Pass II, but for almost reverse functions. During Pass I, dummy arguments from macro definition are replaced with positional indicators when the definition is stored. The nth dummy argument is represented in the body of the macro by the index marker symbol # where #n is the symbol reserved for use of macro processor. These symbols are used in sync with the argument list prepared before expansion of a macro call. The symbolic dummy arguments are retained on the macro name instruction to enable the macro processor to handle argument replacement by name rather than position. The list is used while expanding the particular macro call. For the MDT described above, the macro processor would expand the resulting ALA as follows:

8-bytes per entry	
Index	Argument
0	"LOOP1bbb"
1	"DATA1bbb"
2	"DATA2bbb"
3	"DATA3bbb"

Figure 4.8: Argument List Array

4.11.3 ALGORITHM

The figures 4.9 and 4.10 present the flowcharts for Pass I and Pass II of the macro processor. Both algorithms make a line-by-line scan over their input.

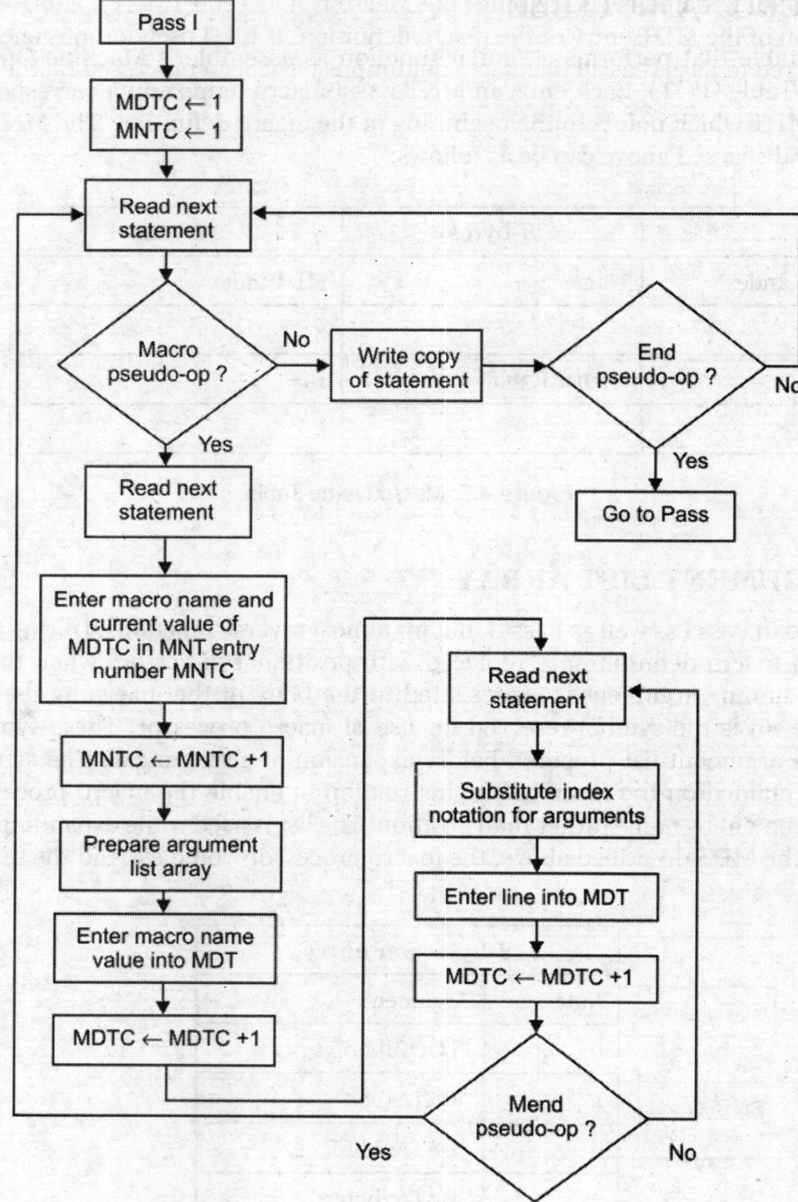

Figure 4.9: Pass I of Macro Processor

Pass I

Macro Definition:

The algorithm for Pass I read each input line and checks for the presence of MACRO pseudo-op. If the presence of the MACRO pseudo-op is encountered, the macro definition in the next instructions is saved in the Macro Definition Table (MDT). The first line of the macro definition is the macro name line. The corresponding name is entered into the Macro Name Table (MNT), along with a pointer to the first location of the MDT entry of the macro definition. If END pseudo-op is encountered, the control is transferred to Pass II as all the macro definitions have been processed till then.

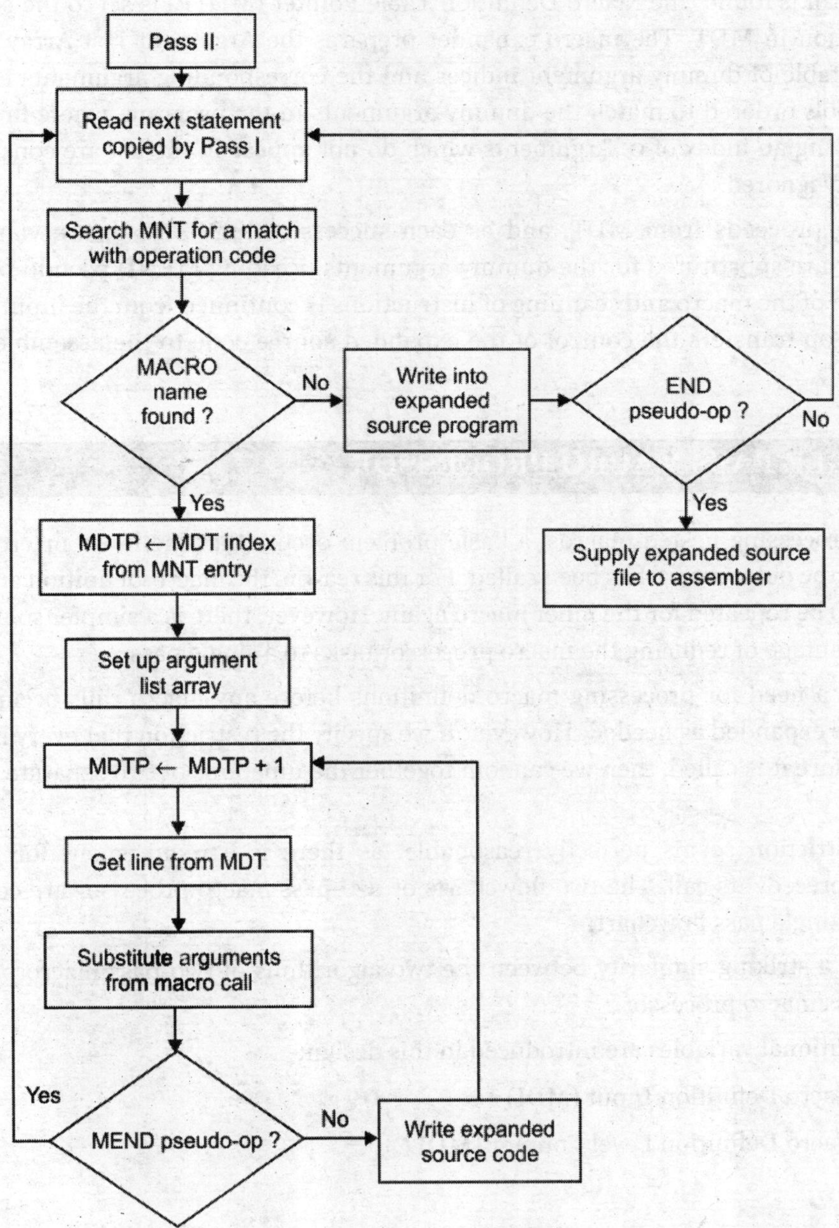

Figure 4.10: Pass II of Macro Processor

Pass II
Macro Calls and Expansions:

The Pass II of macro processor starts by testing each mnemonic code for presence in MNT. Whenever a call is found, the Macro Definition Table Pointer (MDTP) is set to the corresponding macro definition in MDT. The macro expander prepares the Argument List Array (ALA) which consists of a table of dummy argument indices and the corresponding arguments to call. This is a list of symbols ordered to match the dummy arguments in the program, where first is the label argument having an index of 0. Arguments which do not appear in the list are considered empty and are simply ignored.

Reading proceeds from MDT, and as each successive line is read, the values from the argument list are substituted for the dummy arguments. Reading MEND pseudo-op terminates the expansion of the macro and scanning of instructions is continued from the input file. Reading END pseudo-op transfers the control of the expanded source code to the assembler for further conversion.

4.12 SINGLE PASS MACRO PROCESSOR

While processing nested macros, a basic problem occurs that the inner macro can only be defined when the outer macro has been called. For this reason, the macro-definition and macro-call passes need to be repeated for the inner macro again. However, there is a simpler solution that has an added advantage of reducing the macro processor tasks to a single pass.

There is a need for processing macro definitions before any macro calls occur, so that the macros can be expanded as needed. However, if we specify the restriction that every macro should be defined before it is called, then we can join together the functions of two separate passes into a single pass.

This restriction seems perfectly reasonable, as there is a requirement for every macro definition to precede its call. The two flowcharts of two-pass macro processor are combined into the following single pass flowchart:

There is a striking similarity between the two algorithms of two-pass macro processor and this single pass macro processor.

Two additional variables are introduced in this design:

1. Macro Definition Input (MDI)
2. Macro Definition Level Counter (MDLC)

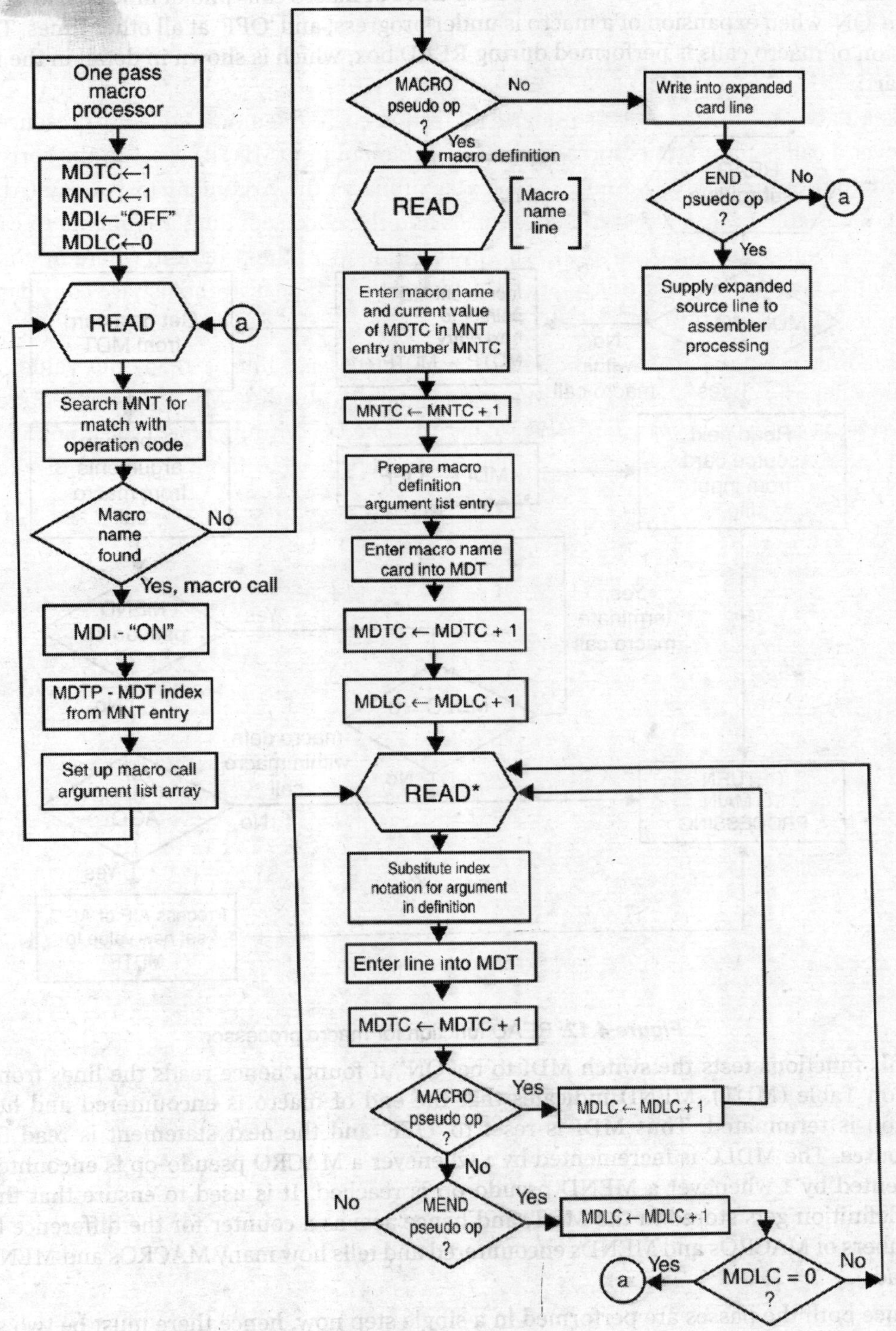

Figure 4.11: Single-Pass Macro Processor

These are switches which are used to keep track of macro calls and definitions. MDI is turned to value 'ON' when expansion of a macro is under progress, and 'OFF' at all other times. The actual expansion of macro calls is performed during READ box, which is shown in detail in the following flowchart:

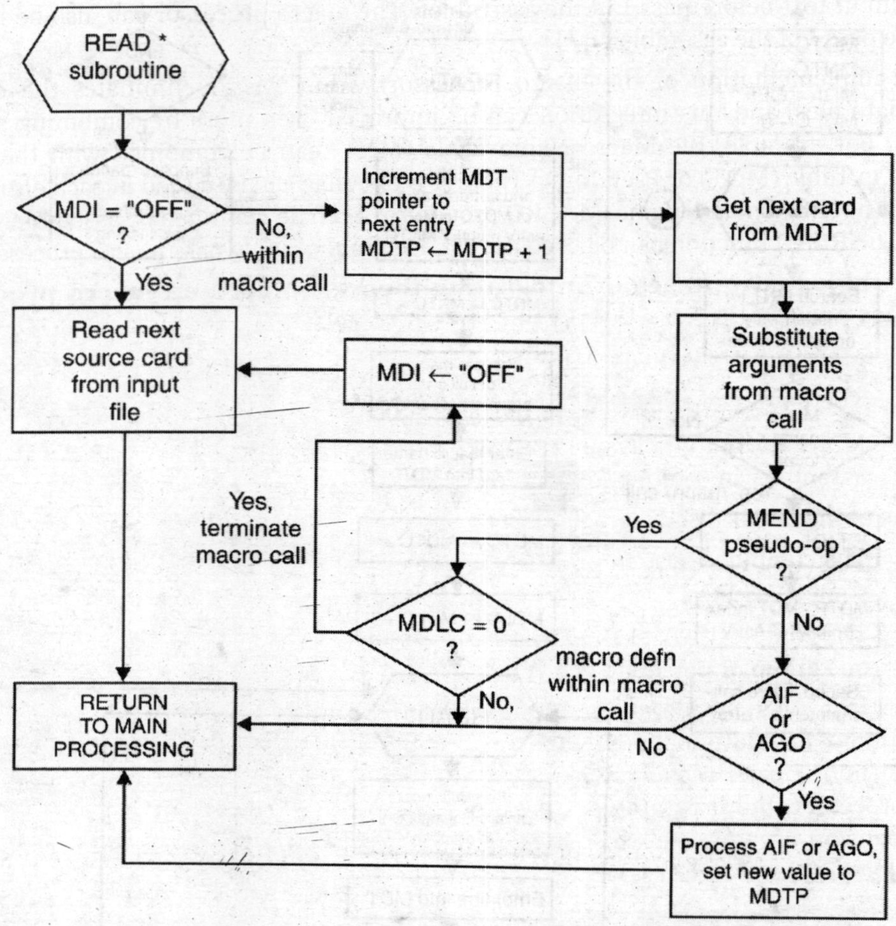

Figure 4.12: READ function for macro processor

This functions tests the switch MDI to be 'ON', if found, hence reads the lines from Macro Definition Table (MDT). MEND indicates that the end of macro is encountered and hence the expansion is terminated. Thus MDI is reset to 'OFF' and the next statement is read from the input source. The MDLC is incremented by 1 whenever a MACRO pseudo-op is encountered and decremented by 1 whenever a MEND pseudo-op is reached. It is used to ensure that the entire macro definition gets stored in the MDT, and hence acts as a counter for the difference between the numbers of MACROs and MENDs encountered and tells how many MACROs and MENDs have been read.

Since both the passes are performed in a single step now, hence there must be two separate Argument List Arrays, one for macro definitions and another for macro call expansions.

4.13 IMPLEMENTATION WITHIN AN ASSEMBLER

The macro processor can be added as a pre-processor to an assembler, making a complete pass over the input text before pass I of the assembler. The macro processor can also be implemented within the pass I of the assembler.

The implementation of the macro processor within Pass I eliminates the over-head of intermediate files, and this integration can be improved even more by combining some similar functions. For example, the Macro Name Table (MNT) can be combined with the assembler's Machine-Op Table (MOT) or Pseudo-Op Table (POT). A flag can be added in each entry to indicate whether or not it is a macro name. MACRO pseudo-op's can be identified by assembler's pseudo-op handler. The READ function can be used as that used in the single pass macro processor.

The major advantages of integrating the assembler and macro processor into single pass are:

1. Many functions do not have to be implemented twice.
2. There is lesser overhead of intermediate files during processing.
3. More flexibility is available to the programmer as he can use all the features of the assembler in conjunction with the macros.

Some of the major disadvantages of such an approach are:

1. The combined system program may be a very large program to fit into the memory of some machines.
2. The complexity of such a program increases considerably, which can be too much for one group or person to coordinate.

Other from the considerations of implementing the macro facility in the assembler is the consideration of an additional pass. Many macro processors have a "prepass" which performs the function of noting certain characteristics of the source program, such as data types. With such a macro processor, the programmer may use even more additional features such as conditional macro expansion pseudo-ops, which expand the macro conditionally only after checking certain characteristics of the program.

4.14 IMPLEMENTATION EXAMPLES

Here we present some examples of actual macro processors. All the characteristics are not covered in detail, but the focus is just on unusual and interesting characteristics. The first example is of a macro facility that is a part of the ANSI C pre-processor. The second example is a general-purpose macro processor that is not associated with any particular language.

4.14.1 ANSI C MACRO LANGUAGE

In ANSI C language, definitions and calls are handled by a preprocessor. This preprocessor is generally not integrated with the rest of the compiler. Its operation is similar to the macro processor discussed in our earlier sections. The following are two simple examples of ANSI C macro definitions:

```
#define NULL 0
#define EOF (-1)
```

After these definitions appear in any program, every occurrence of NULL will be replaced by 0, and every occurrence of EOF will be replaced by (-1). It is also possible to use macros in this form to make limited changes in the syntax of the language. For example, after defining the macro:

```
#define EQ = =
```

a programmer could write statements like:

```
while (I EQ 10)
```

The macro processor would convert it into:

```
while (I = = 10)
```

which is a corrects syntax in C language. This could help in avoiding the common C error of writing = in place of = =. The macros in ANSI C can also be defined with parameters. **Consider the following example:**

```
#define ABC(X,Y) (X>Y ? X-Y: Y-X)
```

Here a macro named ABC is defined, which has two parameters named X and Y. The body of macro makes use of conditional operator available in C language. If the condition X>Y is true, the value of this expression is first alternative specified, i.e. X-Y. Otherwise, if the condition is false, the value of the expression is second alternative, i.e. Y-X.

Call to such a macro consists of the name of the macro followed by a parenthesized list of parameters separated by commas. When the macro needs to be expanded, each occurrence of a macro parameter is replaced by the corresponding argument. For example,

```
ABC (M+1, N+2)
```

would be converted by the macro processor to the following:

```
(M+1> N+2? M+1- N+2: N+2- M+1)
```

There is much similarity between the macro call and a function call, as a function ABC can also be made to perform the same function as the macro defined above. However, the use of macro much more efficient because of the amount of computation required to compute the absolute difference is quite small and much less than the overhead of calling a function. The macros can also be used with different data types. For example, the same above macro ABC can be called as:

```
ABC (I, 5.149)
or
ABC ('C', 'D')
```

Because C macros are handled by a preprocessor, it is the task of the programmer to be careful while writing the macro definitions with parameters. The macro processor simply makes the substitutions, without considering the syntax of the C language. For example, the above macro if invoked in the following manner:

```
ABC (13+2, 10-8)
```

would result in the expanded code as:

(13+2>10-8? 13+2-10-8: 10-8-13+2)

which would not produce the intended result. In ANSI C, the parameter substitutions are not performed within quoted strings. For example, consider the following definition:

#define DISPLAY(EXPR) printf("EXPR= %d\n",EXPR)

The macro invocation for the above macro can be in the form:

DISPLAY(I+J-1)

would be expanded into:

printf("EXPR= %d\n", I+J-1)

To avoid this problem, ANSI C provides special "stringzing" operator #. When the name of the macro parameter is preceded by #, the argument substitution is performed in the usual way. After the substitution, however, the resulting string is enclosed in quotes. For example, if a programmer defines:

#define DISPLAY(EXPR) printf(#EXPR "=%d\n", EXPR)

The invocation in the form:

#define DISPLAY(I+J-1)

would result in the expanded code of the form:

printf("I+J-1" "=%d\n", EXPR)

Macros may also contain definitions or invocations of other macros. After a macro is expanded, the macro processor rescans the text that has been generated to look for more macro definitions or invocations. For example, the call:

DISPLAY(ABC(3,5))

would be expanded into

printf("ABC(3,5)" "=%d\n", ABC(3,5))

After a rescan of the statement, the macro ABC is also expanded in the form:

printf("ABC(3,5)" "=%d\n", (3>5 ? 3-5 : 5-3))

4.14.2 THE ELENA MACRO PROCESSOR

ELENA was developed as a research tool, not as a commercial software product. However, the same design and implementation techniques could be used in developing other general purpose macro processors.

Macro definitions in ELENA are composed of a header and a body. However, the header is not required to have any special form. It consists of a sequence of keywords and parameter markers %. The only restriction is that at least the first two tokens in macro header must be a keyword, not a parameter marker. A macro invocation is a sequence of tokens that matches the macro header. For example, a macro with the header:

%1 = %2 + %3

could be invoked as

ALPHA = BETA + GAMMA

and a macro with the header

ADD %1 TO %2

can be invoked as

ADD 100 TO 30

The ELENA macro processor uses a macro definition table that is similar to the one discussed earlier. However, the process of matching a macro invocation with a macro header is more complicated, as there is no single token that constitutes the macro 'name'. Instead, the macro is identified by the sequence of keywords that appear in its header. Consider the following example of two macro headers:

ADD %1 TO %2

ADD %1 TO THE FIRST ELEMENT OF %2

Furthermore it is not even clear from a macro invocation statement that which symbols are to be taken as keywords and which are parameters. A sequence of tokens as

DISPLAY TABLE

could be an invocation to the macro with header

DISPLAY %1

or

%1 TABLE

ELENA deals with this problem by constructing an index of all the macro headers according to the keywords in the first two tokens of the header. Potential macro invocations are compared against all headers with the keywords that match at least one of their first two tokens. For example the sequence:

A SUM B, C

would be compared against all macro headers in which the first token is A or the second token is SUM. During this process, it is possible that a sequence of tokens could match more than one macro header. For example the sequence:

A = B + C

might match both of the headers:

%1 = %2 + %3

and

%1 = %2 + 1

In such situations, ELENA selects the header with the fewest parameters. If there are two or more matching headers with the same number of parameters, the most recently defined macro is selected.

EXERCISES

1. Define macro?
2. What do you mean by macro processor?
3. What are the usages of macro definition?
4. Explain the simple macro instruction?
5. What do you mean by macro expansion?
6. Explain the different parts of macro definition?
7. Explain the schematic for macro expansion?
8. How can you pass arguments in macros?
9. Explain the concatenation of macro parameters?
10. Explain the generation of unique labels?
11. Explain the concept of conditional macro expansion?
12. Explain the recursive macro expansion in detail?
13. Explain the concept of nested macros?
14. Explain the different advanced macro facilities?
15. Explain the design of macro processor?
16. Describe the two pass macro processor?
17. Describe the single pass macro processor?
18. Explain the implementation examples of macro processors?

Chapter

5

Compilers

5.1 INTRODUCTION

In order to reduce the complexity of designing and building computers, nearly all of these are made to execute relatively simple commands (but do so very quickly). A program for a computer must be built by combining these very simple commands into a program in what is called machine language. Since this is a tedious and error prone process most programming is, instead, done using a high-level programming language. This language can be very different from the machine language that the computer can execute, so some means of bridging the gap is required. This is where the compiler comes in.

A compiler is a system program that reads a program written in any high-level language and converts it into the equivalent program in assembly or machine language. As an important part of this translation process, the compiler also reports to the users the presence or absence of errors in the source program.

In **earlier days**, a person used to write programs in binary form i.e. each instruction was available in binary form. It was difficult for a programmer to remember the instruction sets in binary form. The difficulty was aggravated when the programmer had to do programming on some other machine, as he had to learn the machine architecture and instruction set of that machine. Thus binary coding was dependent upon machine architecture and remembering the instruction sets in binary form was even more difficult. The portability from one machine to another was difficult task in those days. So far, we had found the English version of binary equivalent and it was called assembly language coding, which is converted by assembler to binary form called machine language.

After the development of assembly language, programmers were still facing difficulties because of its dependence on machine architecture like the machine language. The system software developers further thought to move the programmers another level above, so that they are not concerned with the machine architecture of their instruction set while writing programs. This level was called high-level language, and the software developed to convert the high level language into assembly language was called compiler.

Figure 5.1: Compiler

So the complete diagram is as follows:

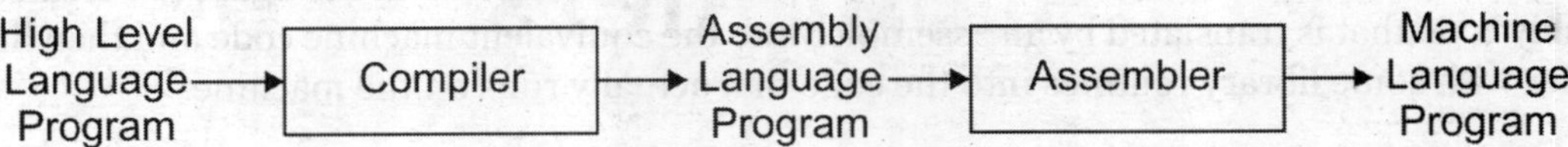

Figure 5.2: Compiler and Assembler

Now-a-days, a compiler consists of all the things, i.e. compiler, linker, loader and assembler. But when we say compiler in this chapter, we mean compiler only. Thus compiler is a system program that accepts a program written in one language and converts it into equivalent program in another language.

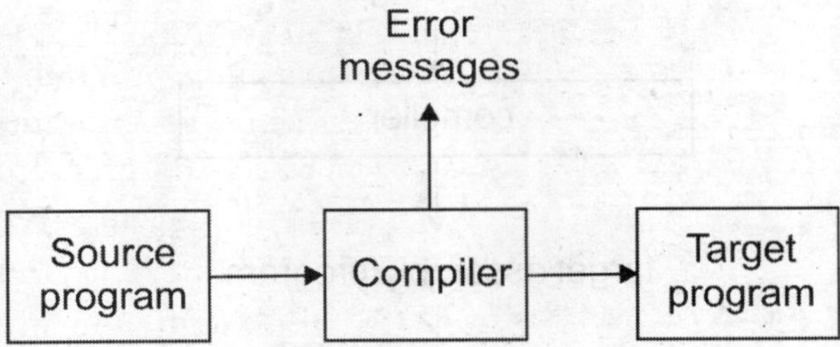

Figure 5.3: A general Compiler

A compiler bridges the semantic gap between a PL domain and an execution domain. Two aspects of compilation process are:

1. Generate code to implement the meaning of a source program in the execution domain.
2. Provide errors for violations of PL semantics in the source program.

At a first glance, the variety of compilers may appear overwhelming. There are thousands of source languages, ranging from traditional programming languages to specialized languages that have arisen in virtually every area of computer application. Target languages have an equally varied form. A target language may be any other programming language, or the machine language of any computer between a microprocessor and a supercomputer.

Compilers are sometimes classified as single-pass, multi-pass, load-and-go, debugging, or optimizing, depending upon how they have been constructed or on what function they are supposed to perform. Despite this complexity, the basic tasks that a compiler must perform remain essentially the same. By understanding these tasks, one can construct compilers for a variety of source languages and target machines using the same basic techniques.

There are two parts to compilation: analysis and synthesis. The analysis part breaks up the source program into constituent pieces and creates an intermediate representation of the source program. The synthesis part constructs the desired target program from the intermediate representation. Of the two parts, synthesis requires the most specialized techniques.

In addition to a compiler, several other programs may also be required to create an executable target program. A source program may be divided into modules stored in separate files. The task of collecting the source program is sometimes entrusted to a distinct program, known as a preprocessor. The preprocessor may also expand shorthand, called macros, into source language statements.

The figure 5.4 shows a typical 'compilation'. The target program created by the compiler may require further processing before it can run. The compiler shown in the figure 5.4 creates the assembly code that is translated by an assembler into the equivalent machine code and then linked together with some library routines into the code that actually runs on the machine.

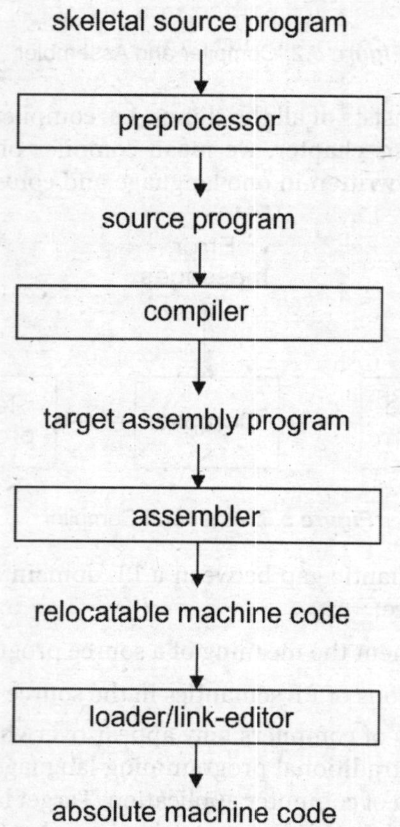

Figure 5.4: A language processing system

5.2 COMPILER

A compiler translates (or compiles) a program written in a high-level programming language that is suitable for human programmers into the low-level machine language that is required by computers. During this process, the compiler will also attempt to spot and report obvious programmer mistakes.

Using a high-level language for programming has a large impact on how fast programs can be developed. The main reasons for this are:

- Compared to machine language, the notation used by programming languages is closer to the way humans think about problems.
- The compiler can spot some obvious programming mistakes.
- Programs written in a high-level language tend to be shorter than equivalent programs written in machine language.

Another advantage of using a high-level level language is that the same program can be compiled to many different machine languages and, hence, be brought to run on many different machines.

On the other hand, programs that are written in a high-level language and automatically translated to machine language may run somewhat slower than programs that are hand-coded in machine language. Hence, some time-critical programs are still written partly in machine language. A good compiler will, however, be able to get very close to the speed of hand-written machine code when translating well structured programs.

5.3 PHASES OF COMPILATION PROCESS

A compiler operates in phases, each of which transforms the source program from one representation to another. A typical decomposition of the compiler is depicted in the figure 5.5. In practice, some of the phases may be grouped together and intermediate representations between the grouped phases need not be explicitly constructed.

The first three phases form the bulk of the analysis portion of a compiler. Two other activities, symbol table management and error handling, are shown interacting with the six phases of lexical analysis, syntax analysis, semantic analysis, intermediate code generation, code optimization, and code generation. Informally, the symbol table manager and error handler are also referred to as phases.

5.3.1 SYMBOL TABLE

An essential feature of the compiler is to record the identifiers used in the source program and collect information about various attributes of each identifier. These attributes may provide information about the storage allocated for an identifier, its type, its scope and in case of procedure name, such things as the number and types of its arguments, the method of passing each argument, and the returned, if any.

A symbol table is a table that binds names to information. A symbol table is a data structure containing a record for each identifier, with fields for the attributes of the identifier. The data structures allow the user to find the record for each identifier quickly and to store or retrieve data from that record quickly.

When an identifier in the source program is detected by the lexical analyzer, the identifier is entered into the symbol table. However, all the information about an identifier is not available with the lexical analyzer alone, but the remaining phases enter that information and then use this information in various ways.

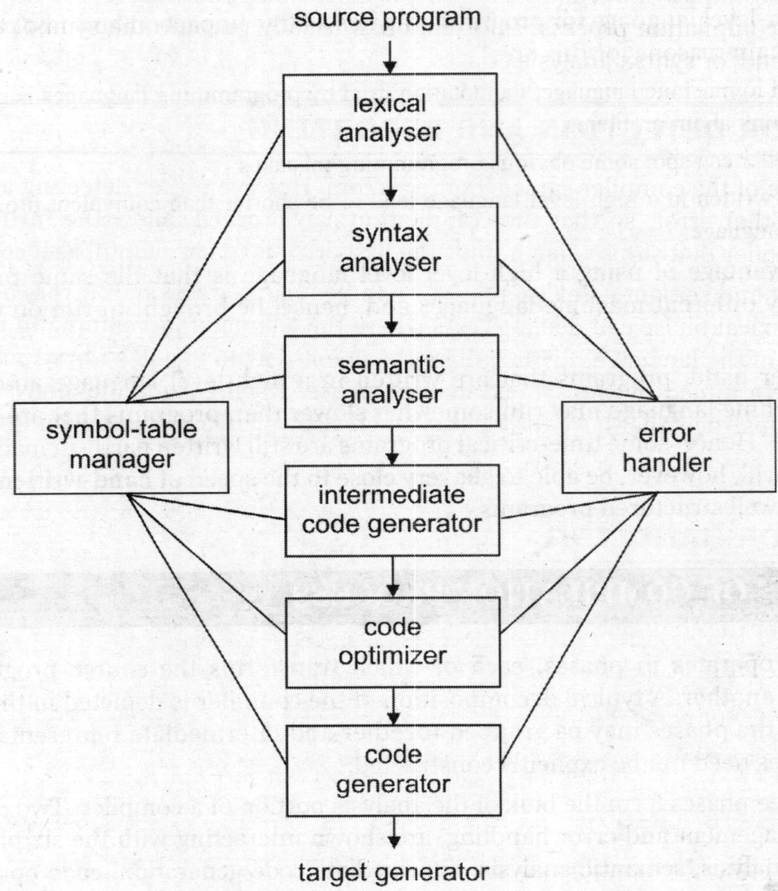

Figure 5.5: Phases of a Compiler

5.3.1.1 SYMBOL TABLE MANAGEMENT

A symbol table is a data structure containing all the identifiers (i.e. names of variables, procedures etc.) of a source program together with all the attributes of each identifier.

For variables, typical attributes include:

- its type,
- how much memory it occupies,
- its scope

For procedures and functions, typical attributes include:

- the number and type of each argument (if any),
- the method of passing each argument, and
- the type of value returned (if any)

The purpose of the symbol table is to provide quick and uniform access to identifier attributes throughout the compilation process. Information is usually put into the symbol table during the lexical analysis and/or syntax analysis phases.

5.3.2 ERROR DETECTION AND REPORTING

Each phase of the compiler can encounter errors. However, after detecting an error, a phase must deal with that error, so that the compilation can proceed, allow the further errors to be detected. A compiler that stops when it finds the first error is not as helpful as it could be.

The syntax and semantic analysis phases handle a large fraction of errors detectable by the compiler. The lexical phase can detect errors where the characters remaining in the input do not form any token of the language. Errors where the token stream violates the structure rules of the language are determined by the syntax analysis phase. During semantic analysis, the compiler tries to detect constructs that have the right syntactical structure but no meaning to the operation involved.

5.3.3 ERROR HANDLING

Each of the six phases (but mainly the analysis phases) of a compiler can encounter errors. On detecting an error the compiler must:

- report the error in a helpful way,
- correct the error if possible, and
- continue processing (if possible) after the error to look for further errors

5.3.3.1 TYPES OF ERROR

Errors are either syntactic or semantic:

1. **Syntax errors** are errors in the program text; they may be either lexical or grammatical:
   (a) A **lexical error** is a mistake in a lexeme, for examples, typing tehn instead of then, or missing off one of the quotes in a literal.
   (b) A **grammatical error** is a one that violates the (grammatical) rules of the language, for example if x = 7 y: = 4 (missing then).
2. **Semantic errors** are mistakes concerning the meaning of a program construct; they may be either type errors, logical errors or run-time errors:
   (a) **Type errors** occur when an operator is applied to an argument of the wrong type, or to the wrong number of arguments.
   (b) **Logical errors** occur when a badly conceived program is executed, for example: while x = y do ... when x and y initially have the same value and the body of loop need not change the value of either x or y.
   (c) **Run-time errors** are errors that can be detected only when the program is executed, for example:

   var x: real; readln(x); writeln(1/x)

which would produce a run time error if the user input 0.

Syntax errors must be detected by a compiler and at least reported to the user (in a helpful way). If possible, the compiler should make the appropriate correction(s). Semantic errors are much harder and sometimes impossible for a computer to detect.

5.4 ANALYSIS OF THE SOURCE PROGRAM

In compiling, analysis consists of three phases:

1. **Linear Analysis,** in which the stream of characters making up the source program are read from left-to-right and grouped into tokens that are sequences of characters having a collective meaning.
2. **Syntax Analysis,** in which characters or tokens are grouped hierarchically into nested collections of collective meaning.
3. **Semantic Analysis,** in which certain checks are performed to ensure that the components of a program fit together meaningfully.

5.4.1 LEXICAL ANALYSIS

The word "lexical" in the traditional sense means "pertaining to words". In terms of programming languages, words are objects like variable names, numbers, keywords etc. Such words are traditionally called tokens.

A lexical analyzer or lexer for short, will as its input take a string of individual letters and divide this string into tokens. Additionally, it will filter out whatever separates the tokens (the so-called white-space), i.e., lay-out characters (spaces, newlines etc.) and comments.

The main purpose of lexical analysis is to make life easier for the subsequent syntax analysis phase. In theory, the work that is done during lexical analysis can be made an integral part of syntax analysis, and in simple systems this is indeed often done. However, there are reasons for keeping the phases separate:

- **Efficiency:** A lexer may do the simple parts of the work faster than the more general parser can. Furthermore, the size of a system that is split in two may be smaller than a combined system. This may seem paradoxical but, as we shall see, there is a non-linear factor involved which may make a separated system smaller than a combined system.
- **Modularity:** The syntactical description of the language need not be cluttered with small lexical details such as white-space and comments.
- **Tradition:** Languages are often designed with separate lexical and syntactical phases in mind, and the standard documents of such languages typically separate lexical and syntactical elements of the languages.

It is usually not terribly difficult to write a lexer by hand: You first read past initial white-space, and then you, in sequence, test to see if the next token is a keyword, a number, a variable or whatnot. However, this is not a very good way of handling the problem: You may read the same part of the input repeatedly while testing each possible token and in some cases it may not be clear where the next token ends. Furthermore, a handwritten lexer may be complex and difficult to maintain. Hence, lexers are normally constructed by lexer generators, which transform human-readable specifications of tokens and white-space into efficient programs.

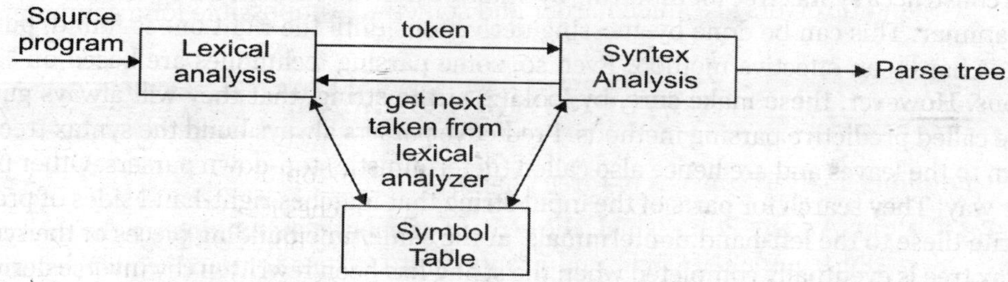

Figure 5.6: Interaction between the first two phases

In compiler, linear analysis is called **lexical analysis** or scanning. For example, in lexical analysis the characters in the following as2signment statement:

sum = addend + augend * 10

The statement above gets grouped into the following tokens:

1. The identifier 'sum'.
2. The assignment symbol '='.
3. The identifier 'addend'.
4. The plus sign '+'.
5. The identifier 'augend'.
6. The multiplication sign '*'.
7. The number 10.

The blanks that merely separate the characters of these tokens would normally be eliminated during lexical analysis.

5.4.2 SYNTAX ANALYSIS

Where lexical analysis splits the input into tokens, the purpose of syntax analysis (also known as parsing) is to recombine these tokens. Not back into a list of characters, but into something that reflects the structure of the text. This "something" is typically a data structure called the syntax tree of the text. As the name indicates, this is a tree structure. The leaves of this tree are the tokens found by the lexical analysis, and if the leaves are read from left to right, the sequence is the same as in the input text. Hence, what are important in the syntax tree is how these leaves are combined to form the structure of the tree and how the interior nodes of the tree are labelled.

In addition to finding the structure of the input text, the syntax analysis must also reject invalid texts by reporting syntax errors. As syntax analysis is less local in nature than lexical analysis, more advanced methods are required. We, however, use the same basic strategy: A notation suitable for human understanding is transformed into a machine-like low-level notation suitable for efficient execution. This process is called parser generation.

The syntax analysis phase of a compiler will take a string of tokens produced by the lexer, and from this construct a syntax tree for the string by finding a derivation of the string from the start symbol of the grammar. This can be done by guessing derivations until the right one is found, but random guessing is hardly an effective method. Even so, some parsing techniques are based on "guessing" derivations. However, these make sure, by looking at the string, that they will always guess right. These are called predictive parsing methods. Predictive parsers always build the syntax tree from the root down to the leaves and are hence also called (deterministic) top-down parsers. Other parsers go the other way: They search for parts of the input string that matches right-hand sides of productions and rewrite these to the left-hand nonterminals, at the same time building pieces of the syntax tree. The syntax tree is eventually completed when the string has been rewritten (by inverse derivation) to the start symbol. Also here, we wish to make sure that we always pick the "right" rewrites, so we get deterministic parsing. Such methods are called bottom-up parsing methods.

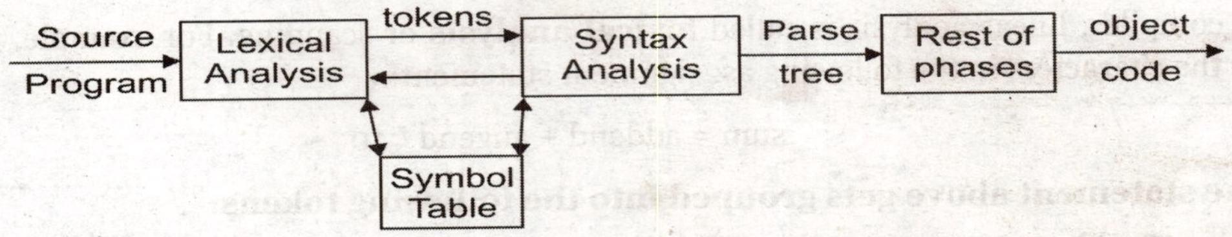

Figure 5.7: Process of Parsing

Hierarchical analysis is called syntax analysis or parsing. It involves grouping together the tokens of the source program into grammatical phrases that are used by the compiler to synthesize output. Usually the grammatical phases of the source program are represented by means of a parse tree such as the one shown below:

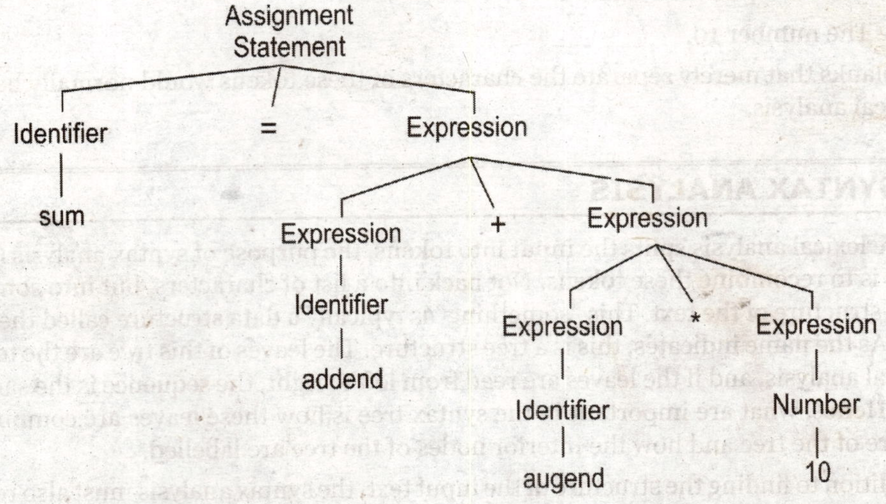

Figure 5.8: Parse Tree for sum = addend + augend * 10

The hierarchical structure of a program is usually expressed by recursive rules. For example, we have the following rules as a part of definition of expressions:

1. Any identifier is an expression
2. Any number is an expression
3. If $expression_1$ and $expression_2$ are expressions, then so are
   (i) $expression_1$ + $expression_2$
   (ii) $expression_1$ * $expression_2$
   (iii) ($expression_1$)

Here, rules (1) and (2) are basic non-recursive rules, while rule (3) defines expressions in terms of operators applied to other expressions. Thus, by rule (1), 'addend' and 'augend' are expressions. By rule (2), 10 is expression. By rule (3), we can determine first that 'augend * 10' is an expression, and finally that 'addend + augend * 10' is an expression.

5.4.3 SEMANTIC ANALYSIS

A semantic analyzer takes its input from the syntax analysis phase in the form of a parse tree and a symbol table. Its purpose is to determine if the input has a well-defined meaning; in practice semantic analyzers are mainly concerned with type checking and type coercion based on type rules.

The **semantic analysis** phase checks the source program for semantic errors and gathers type information for the subsequent code-generation phase. It uses the hierarchical structure determined by the syntax analysis phase to identify the operators and operands of expressions and statements. An important component of semantic analysis is type checking, where the compiler checks that each operator has operands that are permitted by the source language specification.

Typical type rules for expressions and assignments are:

Expression Type Rules

Let exp be an expression.

(a) If exp is a constant then exp is well-typed and its type is the type of the constant.

(b) If exp is a variable then exp is well-typed and its type is the type of the variable.

(c) If exp is an operator applied to further subexpressions such that:

o the operator is applied to the correct number of subexpressions,

o each subexpression is well-typed and

o each subexpression is of an appropriate type,

then exp is well-typed and its type is the result type of the operator.

Assignment Type Rules

Let var be a variable of type T1 and let exp be a well-typed expression of type T2. If (a) T1 = T2 and (b) T1 is an assignable type then var assign exp is a well-typed assignment.

For example, consider the following code fragment:

intvar: = intvar + realarray

where intvar is stored in the symbol table as being an integer variable, and realarray as an array or reals. In Pascal this assignment is syntactically correct, but semantically incorrect since + is only defined on numbers, whereas its second argument is an array. The semantic analyzer checks for such type errors using the parse tree, the symbol table and type rules.

5.4.4 INTERMEDIATE CODE GENERATION

The final goal of a compiler is to get programs written in a high-level language to run on a computer. This means that, eventually, the program will have to be expressed as machine code which can run on the computer. This does not mean that we need to translate directly from the high-level abstract syntax to machine code. Many compilers use a medium-level language as a stepping-stone between the high-level language and the very low-level machine code. Such stepping-stone languages are called intermediate code.

Apart from structuring the compiler into smaller jobs, using an intermediate language has other advantages:

- If the compiler needs to generate code for several different machine-architectures, only one translation to intermediate code is needed. Only the translation from intermediate code to machine language (i.e., the back-end) needs to be written in several versions.
- If several high-level languages need to be compiled, only the translation to intermediate code need to be written for each language. They can all share the back-end, i.e., the translation from intermediate code to machine code.
- Instead of translating the intermediate language to machine code, it can be interpreted by a small program written in machine code or a language for which a compiler or interpreter already exists.

The advantage of using an intermediate language is most obvious if many languages are to be compiled to many machines. If translation is done directly, the number of compilers is equal to the product of the number of languages and the number of machines. If a common intermediate language is used, one front-end (i.e., compiler to intermediate code) is needed for every language and one back-end (interpreter or code generator) is needed for each machine, making the total number of front-end and back-ends equal to the sum of the number of languages and the number of machines.

If an interpreter for an intermediate language is written in a language for which there already exist implementations for the target machines, the same interpreter can be interpreted or compiled for each machine. This way, there is no need to write a separate back-end for each machine.

The advantages of this approach are:

- No actual back-end needs to be written for each new machine, as long as the machine i equipped with an interpreter or compiler for the implementation language of the interpreter for the intermediate language.
- A compiled program can be distributed in a single intermediate form for all machines, as opposed to shipping separate binaries for each machine.
- The intermediate form may be more compact than machine code. This saves space both in distribution and on the machine that executes the programs (though the latter is somewhat offset by requiring the interpreter to be kept in memory during execution).

The disadvantage is speed: Interpreting the intermediate form will in most cases be a lot slower than executing translated code directly. Nevertheless, the approach has seen some success, e.g., with Java.

After syntax and semantic analysis, some compilers generate an explicit intermediate representation of the source program. This representation can be thought of as a program for an abstract machine. This intermediate representation should have two important properties:

- It should be easy to produce.
- It should be easy to translate into target program.

The intermediate representation can have a variety of forms. One of the forms is called "three-address code". This is like the assembly language for a machine in which every memory location can act like a register. Three-address code consists of a sequence of instructions, each of which has at most three operands. The above example might appear in three-address code as:

```
temp1 = intoreal(10)
temp2 = augend * temp1
temp3 = addend + temp2
sum = temp3
```

This intermediate form has several properties. First, each three-address instruction has at most one operator in addition to assignment. Thus, when generating these instructions, the compiler has to decide on the order in which operations are to be done. Second, the compiler must generate a temporary name to hold the values computed by each instruction. Third, some three-address instructions may also have fewer than three operands.

In general, these representations must do more than just computing expression, they must also handle flow-of-control constructs and procedure calls.

5.4.5 CODE OPTIMIZATION

An optimizer attempts to improve the time and space requirements of a program. There are many ways in which code can be optimized, but most are expensive in terms of time and space to implement.

Common optimizations include:

- removing redundant identifiers,
- removing unreachable sections of code,
- identifying common subexpressions,
- unfolding loops and
- eliminating procedures

Optimizations can be done by a compiler in three places: In the source code (i.e., on the abstract syntax), in the intermediate code, and in the machine code. Some optimizations can be specific to the source language or the machine language, but it makes sense to perform optimizations mainly in the intermediate language, as the optimizations hence can be shared among all compilers that use the same intermediate language. Also, the intermediate language is typically simpler than both the source language and the machine language, making the effort of doing optimizations smaller.

Optimizing compilers have a wide array of optimizations that they can employ, but we will mention only a few and just hint at how they can be implemented.

The code **optimization phase** makes an attempt to improve the intermediate code, so that the faster running machine code is produced. Some optimizations are minor. For example, a natural algorithm generated the intermediate code in the above addend example, using an instruction for each operator in the tree representation after semantic analysis. Even though there is a better way to perform the same calculation, using two instructions as:

temp1 = augend * 10

sum = addend + temp1

There is nothing wrong with this simple algorithm, since the problem can be fixed during the code-optimization phase. That is, the compiler can deduce that the conversion of 10 from integer to real can be done once and for all at compile time, so into real operation is eliminated. Furthermore, temp3 is used only once, to transmit its value to sum. It thus becomes safe to substitute sum for temp3, whereupon the last statement is not needed.

There is great variation in the amount of code optimization different compilers perform. In those that do the most, called "optimizing compilers", a significant fraction of the time of the compiler is spent on this phase. However, there are simple optimizations that significantly improve the running time of the target program without slowing down the compilation too much.

5.4.6 CODE GENERATION

The final phase of the compiler is to generate code for a specific machine. In this phase we consider:

- memory management,
- register assignment and
- machine-specific optimization

The output from this phase is usually assembly language or relocatable machine code.

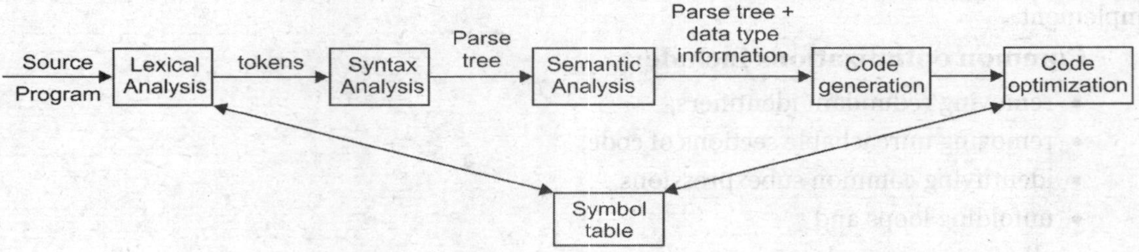

Figure 5.9: Code Generation phase

The **code generation** is used to generate the target code, consisting normally of relocatable machine code or assembly code. Memory locations are selected for each of the variables used by the program. Then, the intermediate instructions are each translated into a sequence of machine instructions that perform the same task. A crucial aspect is the assignment of variables to registers.

For example, using register 1 and 2, the translation of the above code might become:

```
MOVF augend, R2
MULF #10.0, R2
MOVF addend, R1
ADDF R2, R1
MOVF R1, sum
```

The first and second operands of each instruction specify a source and destination, respectively. The F in each instruction signifies that each instruction deals with the floating point numbers. The above code moves the contents of address augend into register 2, and then multiplies it with the real-constant 10.0. The # signifies that 10.0 are to be treated as a constant. The third instruction moves addend to register 1, and adds to it the value previously computed in register 2. Finally, the value in register 1 is moved into the address of sum, so the code implements the specified assignment.

5.5 LEXICAL ANALYSIS

A lexical analyzer or scanner is a program that groups sequences of characters into lexemes, and outputs (to the syntax analyzer) a sequence of tokens. Here:

- Tokens are symbolic names for the entities that make up the text of the program; e.g. if for the keyword if, and id for any identifier. These make up the output of the lexical analyzer.
- A pattern is a rule that specifies when a sequence of characters from the input constitutes a token.
- A lexeme is a sequence of characters from the input that match a pattern (and hence constitute an instance of a token).

The action of grouping the source program into proper syntactic classes is known as lexical analysis. An example source program in PL/I language is taken as:

```
WCM:    PROCEDURE ( RATE , START , FINISH )
        DECLARE ( COST , RATE , START , FINISH ) FIXED BINARY ( 31 ) STATIC ;
        COST = RATE * ( START – FINISH ) + 2 * RATE * ( START – FINISH - 100 ) ;
        RETURN ( COST ) ;
END;
```

The program is scanned and separated as shown below:

```
WCM:    PROCEDURE (RATE , START , FINISH)
        DECLARE (COST, RATE, START, FINISH) FIXED BINARY (31) STATIC;
        COST = RATE *(START – FINISH) + 2 RATE  (START – FINISH - 100);
RETURN (COST);
END;
```

where each underlined element denotes a token of the program. The operational details of this pass involve simple string processing techniques. The source program is scanned sequentially. The basic elements or tokens are delineated by blanks, operators, and special symbols and thereby recognized as identifiers, literals, or terminal symbols.

The basic elements are placed into tables. As other phases recognize the use and meaning of the elements, further information is also entered into these tables (e.g. data type, precision, length, etc.).

Other phases of the compiler use the attributes of each basic element and thus should have access to the information stored by earlier phases. Either all the information about each element is passed to other phases, or typically, the source string itself is converted into a string of "uniform symbols". Uniform symbols are strings of fixed length and consist of the syntactic class and a pointer to the table entry of the associated basic element. The figure 5.10 shows uniform symbols generated for the above example program:

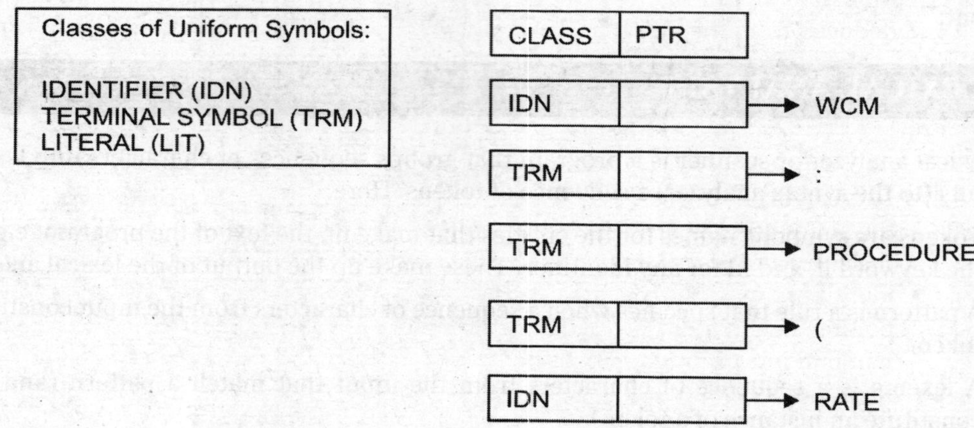

Figure 5.10: Uniform Symbols

Because the uniform symbols are of fixed size, converting to them makes the later phases of the compiler simpler. Also, testing for equality is now reduced to just a comparison of syntactic classes and pointers rather than comparing long character strings.

This lexical analyzing can be done in a one continuous pass through the program and creating an intermediate form of the program consisting of chain or table of tokens. Alternatively, some schemes reduce the size of the token table by only parsing tokens as necessary, and discarding those that are no longer needed. Current compilers implement both these approaches. Either method will discover and note the lexical errors (e.g. invalid characters and improper identifiers). The lexical phase also discards comments since they have no effect on the processing of the program.

Hence the three tasks of a lexical phase are as follows:

1. To parse the source program into the basic elements or tokens of the language.
2. To build a literal table and an identifier table.
3. To build a uniform symbol table.

These tasks involve the manipulation of the following five data bases:

1. **Source Program** is the original form of the program and appears to the compiler as a string of characters.
2. **Terminal Table** is a permanent data base that has an entry for each terminal symbol (e.g. arithmetic operators, keywords, non-alphanumeric symbols, etc.). Each entry consists of the terminal symbol, an indication of its classification, and its precedence.

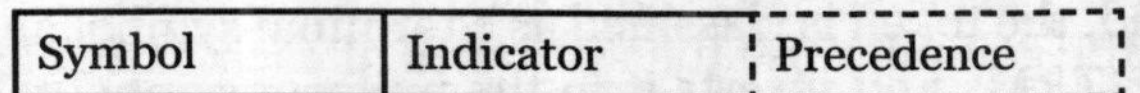

Figure 5.11: Terminal Table Entry

3. **Literal Table** is created by lexical analysis to describe all the literals that are used in the source program. There exists one entry for each literal, consisting of a value, a number of attributes, and an address denoting the location of the literal at execution time, and all other information. The attributes, such as data type or precision, can be deduced from the literal itself and filled in by lexical analysis.

Literal	Base	Scale	Precision	Other information	Address

Figure 5.12: Literal Table Entry

4. **Identifier Table** is created by lexical analysis to describe all the identifiers used in the source program. There exists one entry for each identifier. Lexical analysis creates the entry and places the name of the identifier into that entry. Since in many languages identifiers may be from 1 to 31 symbols long, the lexical analysis phase may enter a pointer in the identifier table for the efficiency of storage. The pointer points to the name in a table of names. Later phases fill in the data attributes and address of each identifier as required.

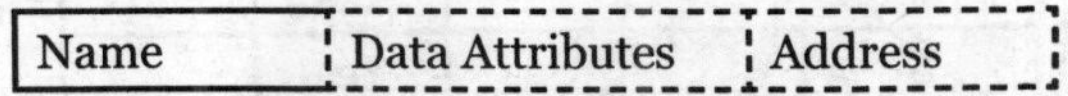

Figure 5.13: Identifier Table Entry

5. **Uniform Symbol Table** is created by lexical analysis to represent the program as a string of tokens rather than of individual characters. Each uniform symbol contains the identification of the table of which the token is a member and its index within that table.

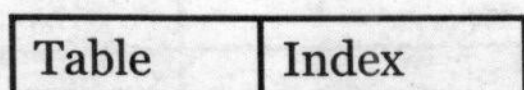

Figure 5.14: Uniform Symbol Table Entry

5.5.1 ALGORITHM

The first task of the lexical analysis is to scan the input character string and divide it into tokens. The second task is to make the appropriate entries in the tables. A token is a substring of the input string that represents a basic entity of the language. There are many ways of implementing these phases. One way is described here.

The input string is separated into tokens by break characters. Break characters are denoted by the contents of a special field in the terminal table. Source program is read, and the characters are tested to see if they are break characters. Consecutive non-break characters are accumulated into tokens. Strings that occur between break characters are the tokens, as are non-blank break characters. Blanks may serve as break characters but are otherwise ignored.

Lexical analysis should recognize three types of tokens: terminal symbols, identifiers, and literals. It checks all the tokens by first comparing them with the entries in the terminal table. Whenever a match is found, the token is classified as a terminal symbol and lexical analysis creates a uniform symbol of type 'TRM', and inserts it in the uniform symbol table. If the token is not a terminal symbol, lexical analysis proceeds to classify it as a possible identifier or a literal. Those tokens that satisfy the lexical rules for forming identifiers are classified as 'possible identifiers'. In our programming language, these are the alphabetic characters and contain up to 30 or more alphanumeric characters and underscores. If a token does not fit into one of these categories, then an error message is flagged.

After a token is classified as a 'possible identifier', the identifier table is examined for a match. If this particular token is not in the table, a new entry is made. Since the only attribute that is known about this identifier is its name, hence that is all the information that is entered till now. The remaining information is detected and added by the later phases of the compiler. The figure 5.15 displays all the tables entries that are created after the lexical analysis is competed on the sample program provided above.

Sr. No.	Symbol	Break	Other
1	:	Yes	
2	;	Yes	
3	(	Yes	
4	)	Yes	
5	.	Yes	
6		Yes	
7	PROCEDURE	No	
8	DECLARE	No	
9	RETURN	No	
10	END	No	
11	+		
12	–		
etc.			

Terminal Table

Class	Index	Tokens
IDN	1	WCM
TRM	1	:
TRM	7	PROCEDURE

TRM	3	(
IDN	2	RATE
TRM	5	.
IDN	3	START
TRM	5	,
IDN	4	FINISH
TRM	4	)
TRM	2	;
TRM	8	DECLARE
TRM	3	(
IDN	5	COST
TRM	5	,
IDN	2	RATE
etc.		

Uniform Symbol Table

S.No.	Name	Attributes
1	WCM	
2	RATE	
3	START	Filled in by later phases
4	FINISH	
5	COST	

Identifier Table

Literal	Base	Scale	Precision	Other	Address
31	DECIMAL	FIXED	2		
2	DECIMAL	FIXED	1		
100	DECIMAL	FIXED	3		

Literal Table

Figure 5.15: Lexical Phase- terminal, identifier, uniform symbol tables

Numbers, quoted string characters and other self-defining data are classified as literals. After a token has been classified as such, the literal table is examined. If a literal is not yet there, a new table entry is made. In contrast to the identifiers, lexical analysis can determine the attributes and the internal representation of the literal by looking at the characters that represent it. Thus each new entry made in the literal table consists of the literal and all its attributes. Regardless of whether or not a new entry is made, a uniform symbol of type 'LIT' is created and put into the uniform symbol table.

The lexical analysis may make one complete pass over the source code and produce the entire uniform symbol table. Another scheme can be to call the lexical phase only when the syntax phase needs the next token.

5.6 PARSING

Once the program has been broken down into tokens or uniform symbols, the compiler must:

- recognize the phrases (Syntactic Construction); each phase is a semantic entity and is a string of tokens that has an associated meaning, and
- interpret the meaning of the constructions

The first of these two steps is concerned with recognizing and thus separating the basic syntactical constructs in the source program. This process is known as syntax analysis. The input to this phase is the source program as separated by the lexical analysis phase.

Syntax analysis also notes syntactic errors and assures some sort of recovery so that the compiler continues to work even after further errors are analyzed in the input. The compiler thus continues to look for other compilation errors. Some compilers even guess what the programmer wanted to do and correct the syntax accordingly.

Once the syntax of the statement has been ascertained, the second step is to interpret the meaning (semantics) with the sentences. Associated with each syntactic construction is a defined meaning, which may be in the form of actual code or in the intermediate form of the construction.

There are many ways of recognizing the basic constructs and interpreting their meaning. We will use rules (reductions) which specify the syntax form of the source language. These reductions define the basic syntax constructions and appropriate compiler routine (action routine) to be executed whenever a construction is specified. The action routine interprets the meaning of the constructions and generates either code or the intermediate form of the construction.

The function of syntax phase is to recognize the major constructs of the language and to call the appropriate action routine that will generate the intermediate form or matrix for these constructs. The syntax phase will be presented as an interpreter for general rules and reductions that define the major constructs of the language and the appropriate action to be taken for each construct.

Following are the databases that are manipulated during syntax analysis phase:

1. **Uniform Symbol Table** is created by lexical analysis phase and contains the source program in the form of uniform symbols. It is used by the syntax and interpretation phases as the source of the input to the stack. Each symbol from the table enters the stack only once.

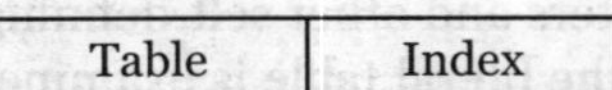

Table	Index

Figure 5.16: Uniform Symbol Table Entry

2. **Stack** is the collection of uniform symbols that is currently being worked on by the syntax analysis and interpretation phases. Additions to or deletions from the stack are made by the phases that use it. The stack is organized on a Last-In-First-Out (LIFO) basis. **'Top**

of Stack' refers to the most recent entry and **'Bottom of Stack'** to the oldest entry. The stack may be incorporated into the uniform symbol table and vice versa.

3. **Reductions** are the syntax rules of the source language which are contained in a reduction table. The syntax analysis phase is an interpreter driven by the reductions. The general form of the rule or reduction is:

   label: Old Top of Stack/ Action Routines/ New Top of Stack/ Next Reduction

The following conventions are used in the scheme:

(i) Label as an optional field.

(ii) Old Top of Stack to be compared to the top of stack.

- **(a)** Blank or null denotes always a match regardless of what is on the stack.
- **(b)** Nonblank denotes one or more items from the following categories:
  - <syntactic type> such as identifier or literal when it matches any uniform symbol of this type.
  - <any> when it matches a uniform symbol of any type.
  - Symbolic representation of a keyword, such as "PROCEDURE" or "IF" or ":" when it matches only the uniform symbol for this keyword.

(iii) Action Routines to be called if Old Top of Stack matches op of Stack.

- **(a)** Blank or null denotes no action to be taken.
- **(b)** Name of action routine(s) denotes the action routine that needs to be executed.

(iv) New Top of Stack describes the changes to be made to the Top of Stack after action routines are executed.

- **(a)** Blank or null denotes no change.
- **(b)** " denotes deletion of Top of Stack.
- **(c)** Syntactic tape, keyword, or stack item denotes the deletion of Old Top of Stack and replacement with this item.
- **(d)** * denotes the fetching of next uniform symbol from uniform symbol table and put it as Top of Stack.

(v) Next Reduction signifies the sequence that needs to be followed after this reduction is completed.

- **(a)** Blank or null to denote the next sequential reduction.
- **(b)** n to interpret the reduction specified at location 'n'.

5.6.1 ALGORITHM

The algorithm for syntax analysis or parsing phase is as follows:

1. Reductions are tested for a match between Old Top of Stack field and the actual Top of Stack, until a match is found.
2. When a match is found, the action routine specified in the action field is executed in the order from left to right.
3. When the control returns to the syntax analyzer, it modifies the Top of Stack to agree with the New Top of Stack field.
4. Step 1 is repeated starting with the reduction specified in the next reduction step.

5.6.2 INTERMEDIATE FORM

Once the syntactic construction is determined properly, the compiler can generate the object code for each construction. Typically, the compiler creates an intermediate form of the source program. The intermediate form provides the following basic advantages:

- it facilitates the optimization of the object code, and
- it allows a logical separation between the machine-independent phases (lexical, syntax, interpretation) and machine-dependent phases (code generation and assembly)

Using an intermediate form raises two important questions. One question is about the form of the representation that is to be created, and the second about the rules for converting source code into that form. The form depends upon the syntactic construction i.e. arithmetic, non-arithmetic, or non-executable statements.

5.6.2.1 ARITHMETIC STATEMENTS

Parse tree is an intermediate form used for arithmetic statements. The basic rules for converting an arithmetic statement into a parse tree are:

1. Any variable forms a terminal node of the tree.
2. Every operator forms a binary tree whose left branch is the tree for operand 1 and whose right branch is the tree for operand 2.

As an example, the following statement from our sample program would result in the parse tree of the figure 5.17:

COST=RATE*(START-FINISH)+2*RATE(START-FINISH-100);

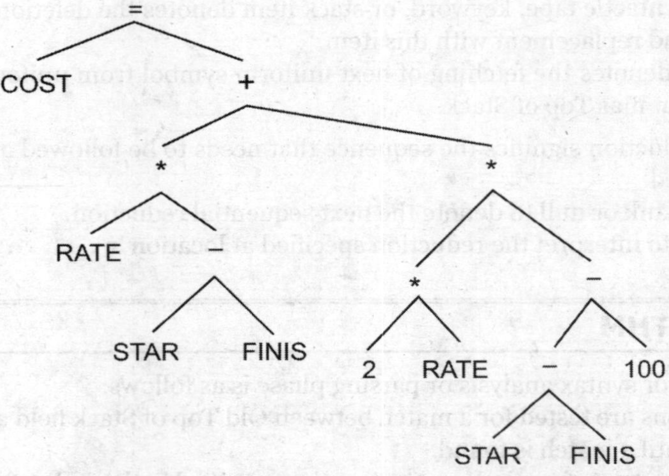

Figure 5.17: Parse Tree

Although this approach makes it easy for the programmers to visualize the structure of the statement, it is not a practical method for the compilers. The compiler may thus use an intermediate form of a linear representation of the parse tree known as a matrix. A matrix lists the operations of a program sequentially in the order they would be executed. Each matrix entry has one operator and two operands.

The operands are uniform symbols denoting either the variables, literals, or other matrix entries M_i, where i denote the matrix entry number. The matrix that would be generated for the above statement is depicted in the figure 5.18:

Matrix Line No.	Operator	Operand 1	Operand 2
1	-	START	FINISH
2	*	RATE	M1
3	*	2	RATE
4	-	START	FINISH
5	-	M4	100
6	*	M3	M5
7	+	M2	M6
8	=	COST	M7

Figure 5.18: Matrix for Arithmetic Statements

The parse tree in the figure 5.17 and the following matrix are the equivalent representations of the assignment statement. The programmer can form the tree of such a statement using rules of elementary algebra.

5.6.2.2 NON-ARITHMETIC STATEMENTS

The problem of creating an accurate intermediate representation for non-arithmetic executable statements is similar to that of arithmetic statements. The statements DO, IF, GOTO etc. can all be replaced by a sequential ordering of individual matrix entries. The operators in the matrix are defined in the later phases of the compiler so that proper code can be produced.

Source		Operator	Operand 1	Operand 2
RETURN(COST);	→	Return	COST	
END;	→	End		

Figure 5.19: Matrix for Non-Arithmetic Statements

5.6.2.3 NON-EXECUTABLE STATEMENTS

There is no intermediate form for the non-executable statements which are informative statements for the compiler about referencing or allocation of variables and their associated storage. Instead such information is entered into tables, to be used by other parts of the compiler. For example, for the DECLARE statement in our example the interpretation phase would note the data type, precision, and storage class in the identifier table for each of the variables COST, RATE, START, and FINISH.

According to the language semantics, some storage allocation and data definition are delayed until execution time, certain tables are used by the object program as well as by the compiler. Therefore, some declarative information is passed on to the object program to be used at the execution time.

The interpretation phase, as it is sometimes called, is typically a collection of routines that are called when a construct is recognized in the syntactic phase. The purpose of these routines is to create the intermediate form of the source program and add the required information to the identifier table.

The separation of the syntactic phase from the interpretation phase is a logical division. The former phase recognizes syntactic constructs while the later interprets the associated meaning into the matrix or identifier table.

Following databases are involved in this phase:

1. **Uniform Symbol Table** is used as specified in the previous phases.
2. **Stack** contains the tokens currently being parsed by the syntax and interpretation phases.
3. **Identifier Table** is initialized by lexical analysis phase to completely describe all the identifiers used in the source program. The lexical phase had entered the identifier in the name field. The interpretation phase enters the remaining attributes. The storage allocation phase will enter the address. This information is used in the later phases for assignment of storage and for generating the proper code for accessing storage associated with these entries. Most attributes may be determined during the parsing of the declaration statement.
4. **Matrix** is the primary intermediate form of the program. There are two reasons for creating a matrix: (1) it allows the first four phases of the compiler to be machine independent, and (2) it allows the machine independent optimization to occur before the code generation phase. A simple form of a matrix entry consists of a triplet where the first element is a uniform symbol denoting the terminal symbol or operator and the other two elements are uniform symbols denoting the arguments. The code generation phase will be driven by this matrix and will produce the appropriate object code. There may be entries present for chaining of entries that can be utilized by the optimization phase to add or delete entries.

Operator	Operand 1	Operand 2	
Uniform Symbol	Uniform Symbol	Uniform Symbol	Chaining

Figure 5.20: Matrix Entry

Matrix operands are uniform symbols of the type IDN, LIT, or TRM, and a fourth form MTX. A uniform symbol

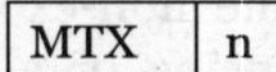

denotes the result of the nth matrix entry and points to the corresponding entry in the temporary storage area of the identifier table line.

5. **Temporary Storage Table** contains all the information about the associated values of MTX symbols, i.e. the attributes of the temporary computations resulting from matrix lines, such as data type, precision, source statement in which it is used, etc. This information is used in storage assignment and in generating code for accessing.

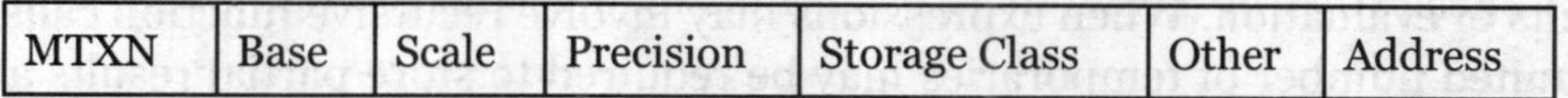

MTXN	Base	Scale	Precision	Storage Class	Other	Address

Figure 5.21: Temporary Storage Table

5.6.3 ALGORITHM

There is no single algorithm for this phase since it is a collection of individual action routines that accomplish specific tasks. In particular these routines:

1. Steps to be performed for any additional parsing, which permits routines to add symbols or delete them from the stack as necessary.
2. Create new entries in the matrix or add data attributes to the identifier table. In the former case, the routines must be able to determine the proper operator and operands and insert them into the matrix. In the latter case, they must decide exactly what attributes have been declared and put them into the identifier table. In both the cases, the complexity of the action routine will depend upon how much has been done by reductions and vice versa.

5.7 STORAGE MANAGEMENT

At some point of time, we must reserve the proper amounts of storage required by our program. Following is a list of all the major program and data elements that require storage during program execution:

1. **Code segment for translated user programs**
   A major block of storage in any system must be allocated to store the code segments representing the translated form of user programs, regardless of whether programs are hardware or software interpreted. In the former case, the programs will be blocks of executable machine code while in the latter case, in some intermediate form.
2. **System run-time programs**
   Another substantial block of storage during execution must be allocated to system programs that support the execution of user programs. They may range from simple library routines to software interpreters or translators present during execution. Also included are the routines that control run-time storage management.
3. **User-defined data structures and constants**
   Space for user data must also be allocated. This includes mainly data structures declared in or created by user programs, although constants used in programs must also be stored.
4. **Subprogram return points**
   Internally generated sequence control information, such as subprogram return points, or event notices for scheduled subprograms must be allocated storage. Storage of these data may require single locations, a central stack, or other run-time storage structure.

5. **Referencing environments**
   Storage of referencing environments during execution may require substantial space.
6. **Temporaries in expression evaluation**
   Expression evaluation requires use of system-defined temporary storage for intermediate results of evaluation. When expressions may involve recursive function calls, a potentially unlimited number of temporaries may be required to store partial results at each level of recursion.
7. **Temporaries in parameter transmission**
   When a subprogram is called, a list of actual parameters must be evaluated and the resulting values stored in temporary storage until evaluation of the entire list is completed. Where evaluation of one parameter may require evaluation of evaluation of recursive function calls, a potentially unlimited amount of storage may be required, as in expression evaluation.
8. **Input-output buffers**
   The input and output operations work through buffers which serve as temporary storage areas where data are stored between the time of actual physical transfer of the data to and from external storage and the program initiated input and output operations.
9. **Miscellaneous system data**
   In almost every language implementation, storage is required for system data: tables, status information for input output, and various miscellaneous pieces of information.

Besides data and program elements requiring storage, it is instructive also to consider various operations that may require storage to be allocated. The major operations are:

1. **Subprogram call and return operations**
   The allocation of storage for a subprogram activation record, the local referencing environment, and other data on call of a subprogram is often major operation requiring storage allocation. The execution of a subprogram return operation usually requires freeing of the storage allocated during the call.
2. **Data structure creation and destruction operations**
   If the language provides operations that allow new data structures to be crated at arbitrary points during program execution, then these operations ordinarily require storage allocation that is separate from that allocated on subprogram entry. The language may also provide an explicit destruction operator which may require that storage to be freed.
3. **Component insertion and deletion operations**
   If the language provides operations that insert and delete components of data structures, storage allocation and freeing may be required to implement these operations.

While these operations require explicit storage management, many other operations require some hidden storage management to take place. Much of this storage management activity involves the allocation and freeing of temporary storage for housekeeping purposes (e.g. during expression evaluation and parameter transmission).

In our above example, the DCL statement gives us the proper information:

DECLARE	(	COST	,	RATE	,	START	,	FINISH	)	FIXED	BINARY	(	31	)	STATIC	;

The storage allocation routine scans the identifier table and assigns a location to each value. In the case of fixed binary numbers of 32 bits, it will assign the first value to the relative location 0, the second to location 4, and so on. The absolute address of these values is unknown until load time. The storage management phase must also assume that 4 words of 31 bits and 1 sign bit are allocates at load time. The compiler uses these relative assigned addresses in the later phases for proper accessing.

Similarly, storage assigned for the temporary locations that will contain intermediate results of the matrix (e.g. M1, M2, M3, etc.).

COST	S	
RATE	I	
START	G	
FINISH	N	
Bits:	0	31

For a simple language like FORTRAN, the entry in the table is looked, its base, scale and precision are found and proper amount of storage is reserved for it. However, in languages like PL/I only STATIC storage can be assigned this way. There are other types of storage like AUTOMATIC, CONTROLLED, and BASED that need other techniques for storage. Information about each variable is included in the object program and is thus available at execution time.

Further the compilers generate, for statements such as PROCEDURE, BEGIN, and ALLOCATE the proper object code to reserve the necessary storage for these variables. In a similar way, END, RETURN, and FREE statements must generate object code to free this dynamic storage for other use. This requires that the three statements have associated entries in the matrix that will in turn cause the proper code to be generated.

Accessing this type of storage is difficult. Typically, the compiler doesn't even know whether or not it will be allocated, much less the location at which it is to be allocated. References to this type of data may be made relative to registers that can be updated at execution time to point at the dynamically allocated data.

The purpose of this phase if to:

1. Assign storage to all variables referenced in the source program.
2. Assign storage to all temporary locations that are necessary for intermediate results i.e. the results of matrix lines. These storage references were reserved by the interpretation phase and did not appear in the source code.
3. Assign storage to literals.
4. Ensure that the storage is allocated and appropriate locations are initialized.

To do this, it must insert information for the next phase into the identifier table, the literal table, and the matrix. Hence the databases that are manipulated by this phase are shown as below:

1. **Identifier Table** which is created by lexical analysis phase and furnished with all the attribute entries by the interpretation phase. Storage assignment designates locations to all the identifiers that denote data. The next two phases use this information to generate accesses to the identifiers.

Name	Base	Scale	Precision	Storage Class	Array Bounds	Structure info	Initial Value	Address

Figure 5.22: Identifier Table Entry

2. **Temporary Storage Table** is created by interpretation phase to describe the temporary results of computations in the matrix. This table may be implemented as a part of the identifier table since much of the information is of the same format. All the storage of this type is implemented as automatic, e.g. it is not physically allocated until the procedure is activated. This is satisfactory since no other procedure ever references it, nor is the space needed unless the procedure that contains the storage is activated.

Mi	Base	Scale	Precision	Automatic	Other	Address

Figure 5.23: Temporary Storage Entry

3. **Literal Table** is created by the earlier phases but the literal addresses are assigned by storage assignment phase and an entry is placed in the matrix to denote that code generation phase should allocate this storage.
4. **Matrix** is used to hold the entries to ensure that code generation phase creates enough storage for identifiers, temporary storage, and literals. It also ensures that proper ones are initialized.

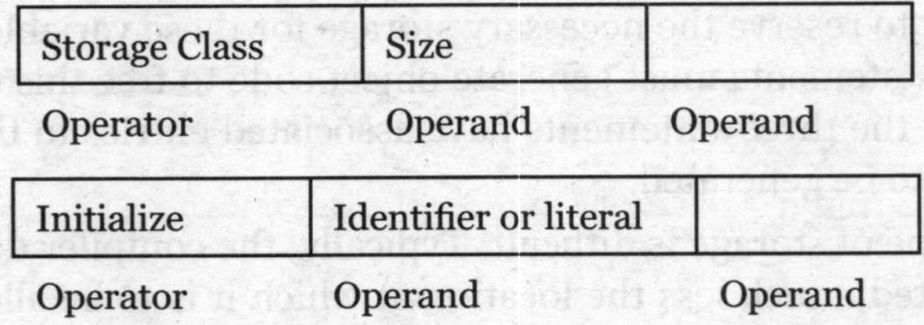

Storage Class	Size	
Operator	Operand	Operand

Initialize	Identifier or literal	
Operator	Operand	Operand

Figure 5.24: Matrix entries by storage allocation

5.7.1 ALGORITHM

Here we first provide a consideration to the format we wish storage to appear in at the execution time to allow efficient accessing. On a 360-type machine, with base and index registers, it is particularly desirable to lay out the user's storage in continuous blocks, with a register pointing to the beginning of each block.

This requires storage assignment to calculate only the offsets for all static storage. The code generation phase will use these offsets to generate the address used in the instructions and generate appropriate code that will load a register with a pointer to the appropriate storage block at the execution time and before that storage is accessed.

The storage allocation phase first scans through the identifier table, assigning locations to each entry with a storage class of static. It uses a location counter, initialized at zero, to keep track of how much storage it has assigned. Whenever it finds a static variable in the scan, the storage allocation phase does the following:

1. Updates the location counter with any necessary boundary alignment.
2. Assigns the current value of the location counter to the address field of the variable.
3. Calculates the length of the storage needed by the variable.
4. Updates the location counter be adding this length to it.

Once the relative addresses are assigned to all the identifiers requiring STATIC storage locations, this phase creates a matrix entry as:

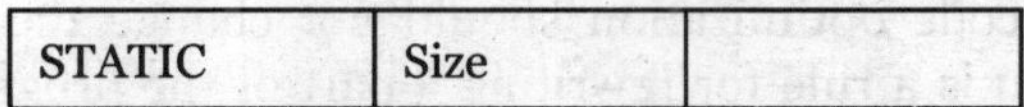

This allows code generation to generate proper amount of storage. For each variable that requires initialization, the storage allocation phase generates a matrix entry:

Initialize	Variable	

This tells code generation to put into the proper storage location the initial value that the action routines saved in the identifier table.

A similar scan of the identifier table is made for automatic storage and controlled storage. The scan enters relative locations for each entry. An 'automatic' entry and a 'controlled' entry are also made in the matrix. Code generation uses the relative location entry to generate the address part of instructions. No storage is generated at compile time for automatic or controlled. However, the matrix entry automatic does cause code to be generated that allocates this storage at execution time i.e. when the generated code is executed, it allocates automatic storage.

The literal table is similarly scanned and locations are assigned to each literal, and a matrix entry is made.

LIT	Size	

Code generation generates storage for all literals in the static area and initializes the storage with the values of the literals.

Temporary storage is handled in somewhat different manner, since each source statement may reuse the temporary storage of the previous source statement. A computation is made of the amount of temporary storage that is required for each source statement. The statement requiring the greatest amount of temporary storage determines the amount that will be required for the entire program. A matrix entry is made of the form:

AUTOMATIC	Size	

This enables the code generation phase to generate code to create the proper amount of storage. Temporary storage is automatic since it is only referenced by the source program and only needed while the source program is active.

5.8 CODE OPTIMIZATION

Code optimization aims at improving the execution efficiency of a program. It is an optional phase of a compiler, not every intermediate code needs to be optimized means some intermediate codes are already optimized. Optimization is achieved in the following two ways:

1. Redundancies in a program are eliminated.
2. Computation in a program is rearranged or rewritten to make it execute efficiently.

It is required that code optimization should not change the meaning of a program. An optimizing transformation is a rule for rewriting a part of the program to improve its execution efficiency without affecting its meaning. Optimizing transformations are classified into local and global transformations depending on whether they are applied over small segments consisting of a few source statements, or over large segments consisting of loops and function bodies. The reason for this distinction is due to the difference in their costs and benefits of optimizing transformations.

1. **Compile-time evaluation**

   Execution efficiency can be improved by performing certain actions specified in a program during compilation itself, this reduces execution time. For example, 'a=3.14157/2' can be replaced by 'a=1.570785' thus eliminating division operation.

   The process of executing the source code at compile time, whose operand values are known before runtime, is called folding.

2. **Eliminating redundant operations**

   The ith operation in a basic law is redundant if there exists an earlier identical operation j, and if none of the variables upon which the operations depend, is changed by any other operation. This is very important as we cannot say two triples having same arguments are same if the value of arguments has changed in their intermediate step.

5.9 CODE GENERATION

Once the tables and matrix of supporting information has been created, the compiler may now generate the corresponding object code. One scheme if to have a table (code production table) defining each type of matrix operation with the associated object code. The code generation phase would scan the matrix and generate, for each entry, the code defined in the table using the operands of the matrix entries to further specialize the code. This process is depicted in the figure 5.25:

-	L	1, &OPERAND1
	S	1, &OPERAND2
	ST	1,M&N
*	L	1, &OPERAND1
	M	0, &OPERAND2
	ST	1,M&N
+	L	1, &OPERAND1
	A	1, &OPERAND2
	ST	1,M&N
=	L	1, &OPERAND1
	ST	1, &OPERAND2

Figure 5.25: Code Definitions: productions for -, *, +, =

One way to view this scheme is that the operators in the matrix are taken as macro calls, operands as arguments, and the production table is taken as macro definitions.

Three questions arise after this scenario is considered:

1. Is it a good idea to generate code directly from the matrix?
2. Is the best use of machine available at the disposal made?
3. Can the machine code be generated directly?

The first two of these are issues of optimization. The first refers to the optimality of the matrix as an intermediate form (machine-independent) and the second to the optimality of the actual machine code (machine dependent). A compiler resolves the issues raised in question 1 before those raised in question 2, since if the compiler eliminates the redundant code of question 1, it will not waste time trying to improve the eliminated code in question 2.

The purpose of code generation phase is to produce the appropriate code. The code generation phase has the matrix as input. It uses code productions (macro definitions) which define the operators that may appear in the matrix to produce the code. It also references the identifier tables and literal tables in order to generate proper address and code conversions.

The following databases are manipulated during this phase:

1. Matrix entries have their operator defined in the code pattern data base. Code generation examines each entry and looks up the code to be generated in the code patterns. The operator of each entry serves as a macro with the operands as arguments.
2. Identifier Table and Literal Table both are used to determine the data type and locations of the variables so that proper accessing code with the correct address is generated. If there are mixed up data type expressions, code generation must generate proper code for conversions.
3. Code Productions are the permanent data base defining all possible matrix operations.

5.9.1 ALGORITHM

The code generation process is implemented in a way analogous to that used for macro processor. The operation field of each matrix line is treated as a 'macro-call' and the matrix operands on the line are used as 'macro arguments'.

5.9.2 MACHINE INDEPENDENT OPTIMIZATION

The issue raised by question 1 of previous section provides an example of one type of machine independent optimization problem. Operationally, when a sub-expression occurs in the same statement more than once, we can delete all duplicate matrix entries and modify all references to the deleted entries so that they refer to the remaining copy of that sub-expression.

Other machine independent optimization steps are:

1. Compile time computation of operations, both of whose operands are constants.
2. Movement of computations involving non-varying operands out of loops.
3. Use of the properties of Boolean expressions to minimize their computations.

Machine independent optimization of the matrix should occur before we use the matrix as a basis for code generation. Such a process is called optimization phase and is logically separated from code generation.

5.9.3 MACHINE DEPENDENT OPTIMIZATION

The problems raised by question 2 of the previous section can be illustrated by comparing two possible versions of the code that can be generated from an optimized matrix:

OPTIMIZED MATRIX				FIRST TRY		IMPROVED CODE		
1	-	START	FINISH	L SST	1, START 1, FINISH 1, M1	L S	1, START 1, FINISH	M1 → R1
2	*	RATE	M1	L M ST	1, RATE 0, M1 1, M2	L MR	3, RATE 2, 1	M2 → R3
3	*	2	RATE	L M ST	1, = F '2' 0, RATE 1, M3	L M	5, = F '2' 4, RATE	M3 → R5
4								
5	-	M1	100	L S ST	1, M1 1, = F 100 1, M5	S	1, = F '100'	M5 → R1
6	*	M3	M5	L M ST	1, M3 0, M5 1, M6	LR MR	7,5 6,1	M6 → R7
7	+	M2	M6	L A ST	1, M2 1, M6 1, M7	AR	3, 7	M7 → R3
8	=	M7	COST	L ST	1, M7 1,COST	ST	3, COST	

Figure 5.26: Machine dependent optimized code

The figure 5.26 depicts the matrix that is optimized by eliminating all the common sub-expressions. Next to each matrix entry is the code generated using the operators. The third column is even better code in that is uses less storage and is faster due to more appropriate mix of instructions. The following two techniques were used in getting this better version of code:

1. A better use of temporary storage was made by employing as many of 360's 16 registers as we could and by not storing the intermediate results unless necessary. This reduces the number of loads and stores from 14 to 5.

2. Shorter and faster 360 instructions were used whenever possible.

The above example of machine-dependent optimization has reduced both the memory space needed for the program and execution time of the object program. Machine dependent optimization is typically done while generating code.

The figure 5.27 depicts a matrix for the source statement A=B+C+D. The center column is the code generated using the simple definitions of + and = given in the previous section.

Matrix			Original Code			Better Code		
+	B	C	1) 2) 3)	L A ST	1,B 1,C 1,M1	1) 2)	L A	1,B 1,C
+	M1	D	4) 5) 6)	L A ST	1,M1 1,D 1,M2	3)	A	1,D
=	A	M2	7) 8)	L ST	1,M2 1,A	4)	ST	1,A

Figure 5.27: Code for statement A=B+C+D

Here we discuss some methods of achieving the better code contained in the third column. There are two types of optimizations involved. First, if a value is already contained in a register, there is no need to reload. This allows eliminating L1, M1 and L1, M2 references. Second, careful consideration of the matrix generation process shows that a matrix temporary, Mi is used once at most. Therefore, if the value of Mi is left in the register, there is no need to store that value. This allows the elimination of ST1, M1 and ST1, M2 instructions.

There are three possible ways to perform this code generation optimization:

1. during matrix optimization,
2. during code generation, or
3. during a post-pass assembly code is generated

The matrix, even when optimized, is still intended to be a machine-independent representation of the source program. If the register usage is optimized in the matrix, it becomes machine dependent. Using a post-generation optimization has many shortcomings. For example, a 100-lone matrix would generate about 400-line assembly code. Whereas we might fit the entire matrix in the memory, it would be necessary to write out and then reread the assembly code to eliminate the unnecessary code, which is a time consuming process. The best solution is to eliminate unnecessary instructions before they are generated.

The following algorithm eliminates the unnecessary load (L) and store (ST) instructions for the '+' operation.

There are two main points about the algorithm which should be noted. First if an operand Mi is already in the register, it is not reloaded. Second, the responsibility for storing the matrix temporary is left to the next matrix line code generation since it is the only line that knows whether the previous temporary will be needed immediately.

Rather than writing a separate assembler subroutine for the code generation of each operator, a code pattern language is used to represent the appropriate algorithm. For the code pattern '+', the code pattern of the figure 5.28 can be employed. Standard macro language conventions are used in this pattern for simplicity.

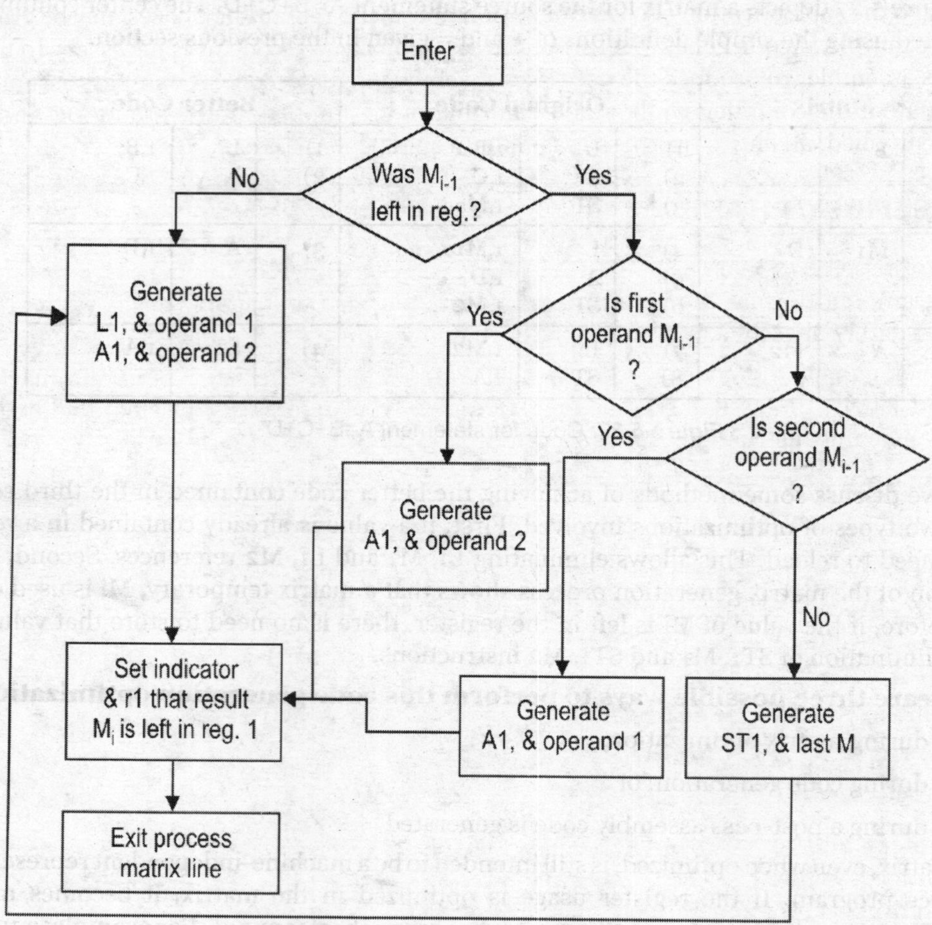

Figure 5.28: Code generation language for '+' operator with optimized register usage

5.10 PRACTICAL CONSIDERATIONS

This section discusses some of the problems that must be handled by the code generation phase. In many ways, code generation may be the most complex phase of a compiler.

One of the most difficult tasks for the compiler writer is to produce efficient code pattern definitions for every possible matrix operator, including non-numerical operators such as PROC-BGN, RTN and many others. Further, for numeric matrix operators, such as "+ A B", it is necessary to handle data conversion if A and B are not identical data types or not compatible with the "+" operator.

These problems can be handled by sufficiently powerful and flexible conditional code pattern definitions. But, in order to obtain the power and flexibility needed as well as increased speed and efficiency required in compilation, a specialized code generation process and code pattern language is often used instead of a general purpose macro processor.

According to the sophistication of code generation phase, the remaining phases may be greatly simplified. For example, if code generation produces assembly source code, it is necessary to use a one or two-pass assembler to produce the necessary machine language code. A one-pass assembler would be adequate if the compiler symbol table information is supplied intact. If only DC and DS statements are supplied, an entire two-pass assembler would be necessary.

5.10.1 ASSEMBLY PHASE

The task of assembly phase is to resolve label references in the object program, format the object program, and format the appropriate information for the loader. These are the tasks performed by assembly phase if a lot of work has been done in the code generation phase already.

At the other end, if the code generation phase has simply generated symbolic machine instructions and labels, the assembly phase must resolve label references, calculate addresses, generate binary machine instructions, and generate storage as well as convert literals.

Following data bases are manipulated during assembly phase:

1. Identifier Table is used to enter the value of all the labels into the identifier table.
2. Literal Table entries are all initialized to all the corresponding literal locations.
3. Object code is the output of the code generation phase, and assembly phase converts it into corresponding machine instructions.

Most high-speed high-performance compilers attempt to eliminate the assembly phase entirely by producing machine language directly as output from the code generation phase.

5.11 INTERPRETERS

An interpreter is another way of implementing a programming language. Interpretation shares many aspects with compiling. Lexing, parsing and type-checking are in an interpreter done just as in a compiler. But instead of generating code from the syntax tree, the syntax tree is processed directly to evaluate expressions and execute statements, and so on. An interpreter may need to process the same piece of the syntax tree (for example, the body of a loop) many times and, hence; interpretation is typically slower than executing a compiled program. But writing an interpreter is often simpler than writing a compiler and the interpreter is easier to move to a different machine, so for applications where speed is not of essence, interpreters are often used.

An interpreter processes a source program written in any high-level language, just as a compiler does. The main difference is that the interpreter executes a version of source program directly, instead of translating it into machine code.

An interpreter usually performs lexical and a syntactic analysis function, like those described for a compiler, and then translates the source program into an internal form. Many different internal forms can be used. It is also possible to use the original source program itself as the internal form, however, it is generally much more efficient to perform some preprocessing of the program before execution.

After translating the source program into an internal form, the interpreter executes the operations specified by the program. During this phase, an interpreter can be said as a set of subroutines. The execution of these subroutines is driven by the internal form of the program.

The process of translating a source program into some internal form is faster and simpler than compiling it into machine code. However, execution of the translated program by an interpreter is much slower than the execution of the machine code produced by a compiler. Thus an interpreter would not normally be used if speed of execution is important. If the speed of translation is of primary concern, and execution of translated program will be short, then an interpreter may be a good choice.

The real advantage of an interpreter over a compiler, however, is in the debugging facilities that can easily be provided. The symbol table, source line numbers, and other information from the source program are usually retained by the interpreter. During execution, these can be used to produce symbolic dumps of data values, traces of program execution related to the source statements, etc. Thus interpreters are especially attractive in an educational environment where the emphasis is on learning and program testing.

Compilation and interpretation may be combined to implement a programming language: The compiler may produce intermediate-level code which is then interpreted rather than compiled to machine code. In some systems, there may even be parts of a program that are compiled to machine code, some parts that are compiled to intermediate code, which is interpreted at runtime while other parts may be kept as a syntax tree and interpreted directly.

Each choice is a compromise between speed and space: Compiled code tends to be bigger than intermediate code, which tends to be bigger than syntax, but each step of translation improves running speed.

Using an interpreter is also useful during program development, where it is more important to be able to test a program modification quickly rather than run the program efficiently. And since interpreters do less work on the program before execution starts, they are able to start running the program more quickly. Furthermore, since an interpreter works on a representation that is closer to the source code than is compiled code, error messages can be more precise and informative.

Most programming languages can be either compiled or interpreted successfully. However, some languages are particularly well suited to the use of an interpreter. As we have seen, compilers usually generate calls to library routines to perform functions such as I/O and complex conversion operations. For some languages, such as SNOBOL and APL, a large part of the compiled program would consist of calls to such routines. In such cases, an interpreter might be preferred because of its speed of translation. Most of the execution time for the translated program would be consumed by the standard library routines. These routines would be the same, regardless of whether an interpreter or a compiler was used.

Certain languages also have features that lend themselves naturally to interpretation. For example, in some languages the type of a variable can change during the execution of a program. Other languages use dynamic scoping instead of a more usual static scoping. With dynamic scoping, the variables that can be referred to by a function or a subroutine are determined by the sequence of calls made during execution, not be nesting of blocks in the source program. It would be very difficult to compile such languages efficiently and allow for dynamic changes in the types of variables and the scope of names. These features can be more easily handled by an interpreter, which provides delayed binding of symbolic variable names to data types and locations.

5.12 INCREMENTAL COMPILERS

Conventional compilers and interpreters represent the extreme ends of the spectrum of software processors in the sense that compilers concentrate on execution efficiency of a program at the cost of compilation overheads, while the interpreters eliminate compilation overheads at the price of slower execution of programs. While this makes interpreters the ideal choice for program development, there is clearly a break-even point beyond which compilation would have an edge over interpretation. This situation can be quite confusing for a programmer, since even if he is armed with the quantitative figures of compilation, execution and interpretation times, it is not particularly easy for him to determine when to stop using an interpreter. A way out of this difficulty is to determine precisely what necessitates recompilation of the entire program for every modification made to the program. If this requirement can somehow be eliminated, it may be possible to limit recompilation to only those statements which are modified. Since the program is compiled, execution efficiency would also be high. Such a software processor can be used through all the phases of program testing up to, and possibly including, production runs on the program.

The primary difficulty faced by a conventional compiler in recompiling only the modified program statements is two-fold. First is the lack of program context in which to compile a modified statement, i.e. the information regarding program variables, their attributes and allocations, and other program statements, their labels, the structure of the program, etc. When a program was first being compiled, all this information was available in some compiler tables. However, this information would cease to exist at the end of compilation. Even is provision was made to retain this information, a second difficulty would be regarding placement of the code generated for a modified statement. When the original program was compiled, codes for all statements were generated in their textual order to form the target program. When a statement is modified, it will be necessary that the code for the new form of the statement should replace the original code. If the new code is smaller than the original code, gaps will be created in the target program. On the other hand, if the new code is larger, it will not fit into the available area. The same situation will arise when a new statement is inserted into the program.

An incremental compiler has the capability to compile arbitrary sections of the source program in increments of one or more statements (whether new statements or modifications of existing ones) in such a manner that the program comprising these program sections can execute properly. It overcomes the difficulties of a conventional compiler in this regard as follows: Provision is made to save and recall all compilation tables at the end and start of any compilation activity. The compilation and execution environment is designed to consist of two separate storage spaces. The incremental compiler, along with its routines forms the compiler space. The source program, which may be retained so that a listing can be produced whenever required, the generated code and all the compiler tables built for program, form the problem program space.

Since the coded program statements are not necessarily in their textual order, a table called the Program Structure Table (PST) is provided to facilitate sequencing of control during program execution. Each PST entry contains a pointer to the machine code for that statement and PST entry # for the next statement in textual order. During execution, this information is used to visit the target code in the proper textual order.

When a source statement is modified, the code generated for its new form is placed in some free storage area. The code pointer field of its PST entry is changed to point at the start of the new code. The old code for the statement is now automatically defunct since control can never reach it during execution. The area occupied by it may simply remain unused, or may be reclaimed by using some garbage collection or storage compaction scheme.

When a new statement is introduced, it is compiled in a similar manner. A new PST entry is created for it, with a pointer to the code. The PST entry is now linked up with other PST entries using the NEXT statement field, to represent the textual order of statements in the program. Due to this arrangement, source statements need never be presented for compilation in their actual textual order.

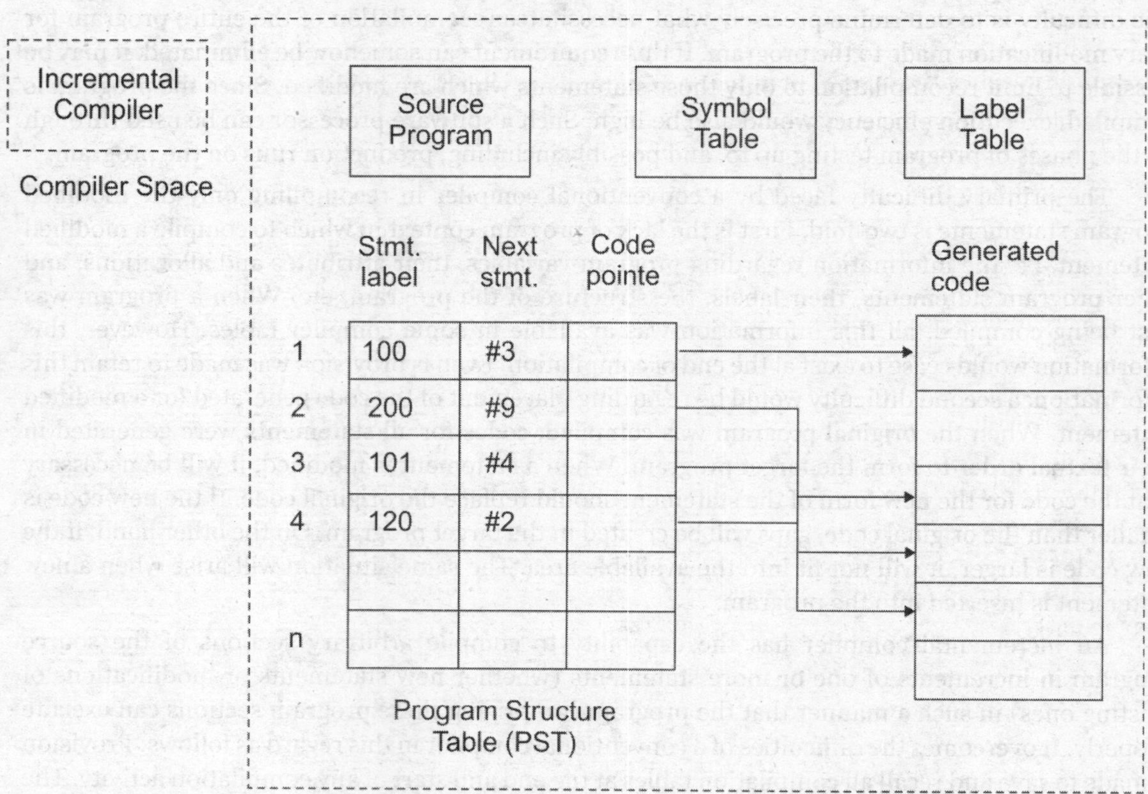

Figure 5.29: Environment for an Incremental Compiler

5.12.1 TEST/DEBUG FACILITIES

During program testing and debugging, a facility for program execution and display of data values at selected program points is of invaluable help. Most computer systems provide debug monitors to support such services. However, most of these monitors have to work at the machine code level simply because source program information is generally not available during program execution. Thus, if the value of a data item is to be dumped at a particular point in the program, the data and instruction addresses will have to be specified at the machine code level. An interpreter, or rather a pure interpreter, can provide these facilities at the source program level because source information is available through program interpretation. The same advantage carries over to the incremental compilation as well. This makes program testing and debugging much more meaningful. Let us consider the debugging facilities supported by many BASIC systems and see how they can be incorporated into an incremental compiler.

The debug package consists of a passive value dumping facility and an active status enquiry facility. The passive facility is provided by the statement:

DUMP AT <label> <list of variables>

This statement is given to the system at before execution begins. Every time program execution reaches the labeled statement, values of the variables are dumped out before execution of the statement.

The interactive facility is activated by issuing the statement:

STOP ON <label>

This statement is issued to the system before program execution begins. During execution, a conversation is initiated with the programmer terminal just prior to executing the labeled statement. The user can now issue the command:

SET <variable name> = <expression>

This would assign the value of the right hand side expression to the named variable. Obviously both DISPLAY and SET would have to be interpreted during the conversation. At the end of interaction, the programmer would issue the RUN command to start execution of the program all over again, or the RESUME command to continue execution from the point of interruption.

Incorporation of test/debug facilities in the incremental compilation environment is made particularly easy by the following two factors:

- The symbol table for the program is available during execution. Hence, variable names used in the commands can be readily looked up in the symbol table so as to access their locations for obtaining or depositing values.
- Program execution is controlled by an Execution Control Routine (ECR) which steps through the entries of PST to organize execution of statements in their textual order.

When the programmer gives a STOP ON or DUMP AT command, a flag can be set in the relevant PST entry. The ECR can be made to test this flag before arranging execution of the code for that statement. If the flag is set, it can initiate a conversation or organize some dumping before executing the code. In this manner, hardly any additional provision is required to support test/debug facilities. The figure 5.30 illustrates a schematic for the compilation, execution, and test/debug modes of an incremental compiler.

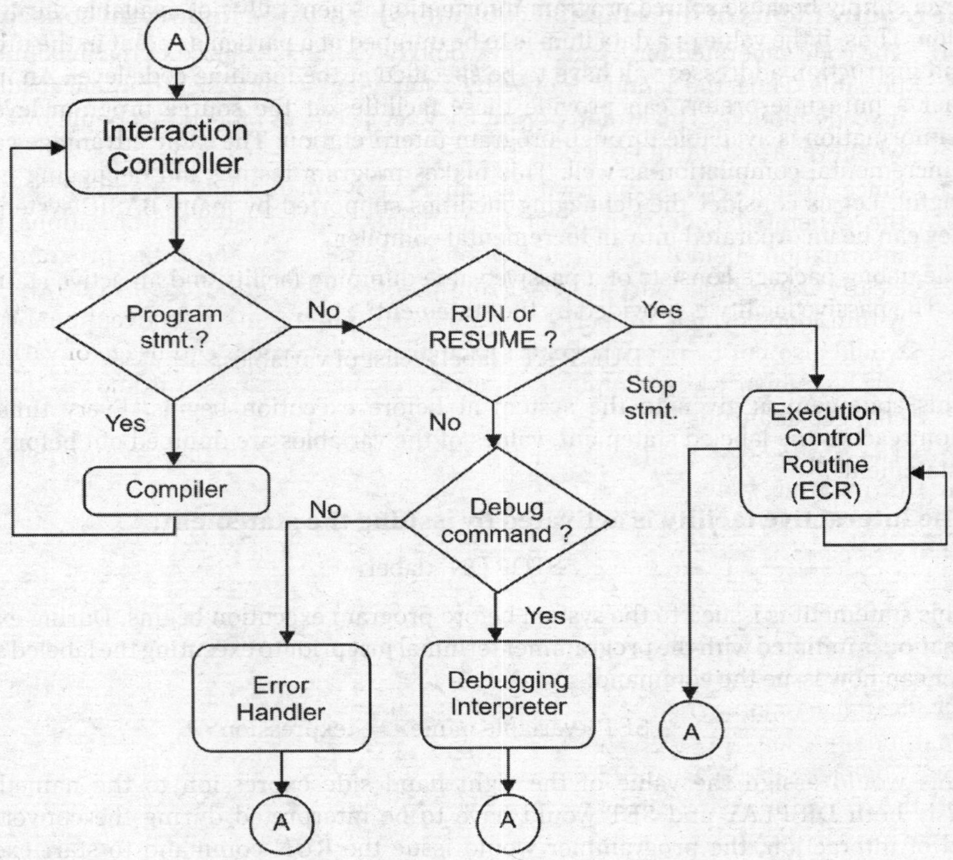

Figure 5.30: Incremental Compiler in compilation, execution and test/debug modes

5.12.2 IMPORTANT ISSUES IN INCREMENTAL COMPILATION

The incremental nature of compilation and the table-driven nature of program execution necessitate certain basic changes in the approach of compilation. Since the ECR arranges for the execution of a statement as a unit, it is necessary for each statement to be compiled as an independent module, returning control to ECR at the end of its execution. Since modules are replaced when a statement is modified, they have to be functionally independent of each other. Transfers of control, etc. must therefore be implemented with the help of ECR. Further, each statement has to be compiled as and when presented, much of the contextual information used by a conventional compiler will not be available. For example, while compiling an array reference, the array dimension information may not be known, because the dimension statement may not have been processed yet. As far as possible, the code should be generated so as to be independent of the actual array bounds. This will permit the code to remain unchanged even if the array dimensions are changed subsequently.

The requirements of incremental compilers have three important consequences:

1. The code generated for a statement would have to be localized to the maximum extent possible. Thus, the actions implied by a statement would be entirely encapsulated into its code module. This would permit easy replacement of a code module by a new one whenever a statement is modified.
2. Since no conceptual information can be presumed while compiling a statement, the generated code would not be optimal. Sophisticated optimizations requiring information about data item definitions and usage over the entire program would be clearly impossible. Further, even routine ones like optimization of array references within loops, which are performed by most non-optimizing conventional compilers, would also not be possible because the loop demarcation and usage of variables may not be known while compiling an array reference, and even if known, they may be changed at any instant.
3. The strategy of indicating 'global' errors, which arise due to interdependencies of program statements with one another, may also have to change. Due to lack of contextual information, all errors of this kind may not be detectable using the same strategies as used by conventional compilers.

5.12.3 PROBLEM AREAS IN INCREMENTAL COMPILATION

The advantage of an incremental compiler over a conventional compiler lies in the fact that a marginal modification does not require complete recompilation of a program. Such software processors would be appealing to the programmer if modifications in the program are easy to make and also, from the system's viewpoint, if the recompilation cost can be kept low. **Thus, two considerations influencing the efficiency of incremental compilation are:**

(i) Ease of program modification.
(ii) Extent of recompilation.

Both these considerations happen to be language dependent. In BASIC, program modification is made easy by the fact that each statement bears a unique line number, and cannot exceed one source line. Identification of a statement which needs modification is thus easy from the programmer as well as system viewpoints. If a language like PL/I, ALGOL, or PASCAL is required to be incrementally compiled, elaborate text processing means would have to be incorporated into the system for the purpose of program statement identification and modification. The costs would thus be raised on both the sides, reducing the appeal of incremental compilation.

The recompilation needs are directly dictated by the language specification, i.e. by the control structures of the language. Recompilation cost can be kept at a low level in case of type-less or single-type languages e.g. BASIC, which do not support block structures. If a program in such a language is modified, recompilation is restricted to the recompilation of the modified statement alone. In the case of typed data item usage, a single modification would require recompilation of several other statements, Additional provision would have to be added to keep track of various statements referring to a particular data item, or all the statements within the scope of a data item may be recompiled. This selective or exhaustive recompilation increases the complexity or the recompilation needs in the programming constructs. However, considering the increasing programmer costs and shift in the emphasis towards the total cost effectiveness of computing, it can be argued that given large multi-access computer systems, incremental compilation is worthwhile, provided statement identification (for the purpose of modification) is easy.

5.13 CROSS-COMPILING

Cross-compiling is a relatively new thing if you compare it to the history of computers and software. In the early years of computing cross-compiling was not really needed as the software was written for a specific machine and purpose. Using the same code again and again was not so much of a thing. After realization of the facts that some processors have a lot more computing power than others and we most certainly want to use the same code in many machines and for various purposes, it was easy to see that "in many cases compiling the application on some different machine would take a lot less time than compiling it on a machine where it is to be used". The basic idea of cross-compiling is to use some processor (HOST) to compile software for some other processor (TARGET) that uses different architecture. This means that the machine on which you are compiling the software cannot natively run the software it compiles. The software is compiled for another processor. This is one of the first challenges of cross-compiling. Many build environments want to run some programs during the compiling process which then of course crash the build process. To avoid the challenges of cross-compiling some people prefer compiling natively. Anyhow in many cases this is very slow and for that reason cannot be even considered as an option.

5.13.1 CROSS COMPILERS

A cross compiler is a compiler capable of creating executable code for a platform other than the one on which the cross compiler is currently running. Such a tool is handy when you want to compile code for a platform that you don't have access to, or because it is convenient to do so, or it is impossible to compile on that platform (as is the case with embedded systems, on which various kinds of microcontrollers run with a minimal amount of memory for their own purpose).

The fundamental use of a cross compiler is to separate the build environment from the target environment. This is useful in a number of situations:

- **Embedded computers, where a device has extremely limited resources:** For example, a microwave oven will have an extremely small computer merely able to read its touchpad and door sensor, provide output to a digital display and speaker, and to control the machinery for cooking food. This computer will not be powerful enough to run a compiler, a file system, or a development environment.
- **Compiling for multiple machines:** For example, a company may wish to support several different versions of an operating system or to support several different operating systems. By using a cross compiler, a single build environment can be maintained that would build for each of these targets.
- **Compiling on a server farm:** Similar to compiling for multiple machines, a complicated build that involves many compile operations can be executed across any machine that is free regardless of its brand or current version of any operating system.
- **Bootstrapping to a new platform:** When developing software for a new platform or the

emulator of the future platform, one uses a cross compiler to compile necessary tools such as the operating system and a native compiler.

Use of virtual machines (such as Java's JVM) ameliorates some of the problems for which cross compilers were developed. The virtual machine method allows the same compiler output to be used by both the host and the target system.

5.13.2 ROLE OF CROSS COMPILERS

Cross compilers are devices that are capable of manufacturing executable code that can be run on a platform that is currently not the resident platform for the compiler. The utilization of a cross compiler is common when there is a need to make use of multiple platforms in order to handle computing functions. This will include embedded systems where each embedded computer within the system has a smaller amount of resources. The use of a cross compiler makes it possible to overcome this lack of resources by creating an interrelated execution between various components on the system.

One excellent example of the use of a cross compiler is when microcontrollers are in use within a system. Generally, a microcontroller does not contain a great deal of memory. By using a cross compiler to handle the creation and issue of execution of commands, less of the resources for the microcontroller are tied up in administrative orders, and can be directed toward performing the task ordered by the cross compiler.

The cross compiler can help to create a working network between different types of machines, or even different versions of an operating system. In this application, a company could use both older and more recent versions of an operating system to access a common network, even if the workstations in the office featured a wide range of desktop computers of varying age and capacity. The use of a cross compiler makes it possible to gather all these varied elements into a cohesive build environment that will allow each of the stations to access essential files and data that resides on the common server.

Use of the cross compiler goes back to the early days of the development of Windows and the gradual decline in the use of DOS by many end users. Today, the cross compiler remains a common means of maximizing the efficiency of several components. However, virtual machines such as Java's JVM are capable of handling at last a portion of the functions that once were only possible with the use of a cross compiler.

5.13.3 CANADIAN CROSS

The **Canadian Cross** is a technique for building cross compilers for other machines. Given three machines A, B, and C, one uses machine A (e.g. running Windows XP on an IA-32 processor) to build a cross compiler that runs on machine B (e.g. running Mac OS X on an x86-64 processor) to create executables for machine C (e.g. running Android on an ARM processor). When using the Canadian Cross with GCC, there may be four compilers involved:

- The proprietary (describes goods which are made and sent out by a particular company whose name is on the product) native Compiler for machine A (1) (e.g. compiler from Microsoft Visual Studio) is used to build the gcc native compiler for machine A (2).

- The gcc native compiler for machine A (2) is used to build the gcc cross compiler from machine A to machine B (3)
- The gcc cross compiler from machine A to machine B (3) is used to build the gcc cross compiler from machine B to machine C (4)

The end-result cross compiler (4) will not be able to run on your build machine A; instead you would use it on machine B to compile an application into executable code that would then be copied to machine C and executed on machine C.

For instance, NetBSD provides a POSIX Unix shell script named build.sh which will first build its own toolchain with the host's compiler; this, in turn, will be used to build the cross-compiler which will be used to build the whole system.

The term **Canadian Cross** came about because at the time that these issues were under discussion, Canada had three national political parties.

5.13.4 TIME LINE OF EARLY CROSS COMPILERS

1979 – ALGOL 68C generated ZCODE, this added on porting the compiler and other ALGOL 68 applications to alternate platforms. To compile the ALGOL 68C compiler required about 120kB of memory. With Z80 its 64kB memory is too small to actually compile the compiler. So for the Z80 the compiler itself had to be cross compiled from the larger CAP capability computer or an IBM 370 mainframe.

5.13.5 GCC AND CROSS COMPILATION

GCC, a free software collection of compilers, can be set up to cross compile. It supports many platforms and languages.

GCC requires that a compiled copy of binutils be available for each targeted platform. Especially important is the GNU Assembler. Therefore, binutils first has to be compiled correctly with the switch --target=some-target sent to the configure script. GCC also has to be configured with the same --target option. GCC can then be run normally provided that the tools, which binutils creates, are available in the path, which can be done using the following (on UNIX-like operating systems with bash):

```
PATH=/path/to/binutils/bin:${PATH} make
```

Cross compiling GCC requires that a portion of the target platform's C standard library be available on the host platform. At least the crt0, ... components of the library must be available. You may choose to compile the full C library, but that can be too large for many platforms. The alternative is to use newlib, which is a small C library containing only the most essential components required to compile C source code. To configure GCC with newlib, use the switch --with-newlib.

The GNU autotools packages (i.e. autoconf, automake, and libtool) use the notion of a build platform, a host platform, and a target platform. The build platform is where the compiler is actually compiled. In most cases, build should be left undefined (it will default from host). The host platform is where the output artefacts from the compiler will be executed. The target platform is used when cross compiling cross compilers, it represents what type of object code the package itself will produce; otherwise the target platform setting is irrelevant. For example, consider cross-compiling a video game that will run on a Dreamcast. The machine where the game is compiled is the host platform while the Dreamcast is the target platform.

Another method that is popularly used by embedded Linux developers is to use GCC compilers with Scratchbox or the newer scratchbox2. These tools create a "chrooted" sandbox where you can build up your tools, libc, and libraries without having to set extra paths. It also has facilities for tricking the runtime into thinking it is on (for example) an ARM CPU so things like configure scripts will run. The downside to Scratchbox is that it is slower and most of your tools that are on the host must be moved into Scratchbox to function.

5.13.6 MANX AZTEC C CROSS COMPILERS

Manx Software Systems, of Shrewsbury, New Jersey, produced C compilers beginning in the 1980s targeted at professional developers for a variety of platforms up to and including PCs and Macs.

Manx's Aztec C programming language was available for a variety of platforms including MS DOS, Apple II DOS 3.3 and ProDOS, Commodore 64, Macintosh 68XXX and Amiga.

From the 1980s and continuing throughout the 1990s until Manx Software Systems disappeared, the MS DOS version of Aztec C was offered both as a native mode compiler or as a cross compiler for other platforms with different processors including the Commodore 64 and Apple II. Internet distributions still exist for Aztec C including their MS DOS based cross compilers. They are still in use today.

Manx's Aztec C86, their native mode 8086 MS DOS compiler, was also a cross compiler. Although it did not compile code for a different processor like their Aztec C65 6502 cross compilers for the Commodore 64 and Apple II, it created binary executables for then-legacy operating systems for the 16 bit 8086 family of processors.

When the IBM PC was first introduced it was available with a choice of operating systems, CP/M 86 and PC DOS being two of them. Aztec C86 was provided with link libraries for generating code for both IBM PC operating systems. Throughout the 1980s later versions of Aztec C86 (3.xx, 4.xx and 5.xx) added support for MS DOS "transitory" versions 1 and 2 and which were less robust than the "baseline" MS DOS version 3 and later which Aztec C86 targeted until its demise.

Finally, Aztec C86 provided C language developers with the ability to produce ROM-able "HEX" code which could then be transferred using a ROM Burner directly to an 8086 based processor. Paravirtualization may be more common today but the practice of creating low-level ROM code was more common per-capita during those years when device driver development was often done by application programmers for individual applications, and new devices amounted to a cottage industry. It was not uncommon for application programmers to interface directly with hardware without support from the manufacturer. This practice was similar to Embedded Systems Development today.

Thomas Fenwick and James Goodnow II were the two principal developers of Aztec-C. Fenwick later became notable as the author of the Microsoft Windows CE Kernel or NK ("New Kernel") as it was then called.

5.14 P-CODE COMPILERS

In computer programming, a **p-code machine**, or **precompiled code machine** is a virtual machine designed to execute **p-code** (the assembly language of a hypothetical CPU). This term is applied both generically to all such machines (such as the Java Virtual Machine and MATLAB precompiled code), and to specific implementations, the most famous being the p-Machine of the Pascal-P system, particularly in its UCSD Pascal incarnation.

Although the concept was first implemented circa 1966 (as O-code for BCPL), the term p-code first appeared in the early 1970s. Two early compilers generating p-code were the Pascal-P compiler in 1973, by Nori, Ammann, Jensen, Hageli, and Jacobi, and the Pascal-S compiler in 1975, by Niklaus Wirth.

Programs that have been translated to p-code are interpreted by a software program that emulates the behavior of the hypothetical CPU. If there is sufficient commercial interest, a hardware implementation of the CPU specification may be built (e.g., the Pascal MicroEngine).

5.14.1 WHY P-CODE?

Compared to direct translation into native machine code, a two-stage approach involving translation into p-code and execution by an interpreter or just-in-time compiler offers several advantages.

- **Portability:** It is much easier to write a small p-code interpreter for a new machine than it is to modify a compiler to generate native code for the same machine.
- **Simple implementation:** Generating machine code is one of the more complicated parts of writing a compiler. By comparison, generating p-code is much easier. This makes it useful for getting a compiler up and running quickly.
- **Compact size:** Since p-code is based on an ideal virtual machine, a p-code program is often much smaller than the same program translated to machine code.
- **Debugging:** When the p-code is interpreted, the interpreter can apply additional runtime checks that are difficult to implement with native code.

5.14.2 WHY NOT P-CODE?

One of the significant disadvantages of p-code is execution speed, which can sometimes be remedied through the use of a JIT compiler.

5.14.3 WORKING OF P-CODE COMPILERS

P-code compilers (also called bytecode compilers) are very similar in concept to interpreters. In both cases, the source program is analyzed and converted into an intermediate form, which is then executed interpretively. With a P-code compiler, however, this intermediate form is the machine language for a hypothetical computer, often called a pseudo-machine or P-machine. The process of using such a P-code compiler is illustrated in the figure 5.31:

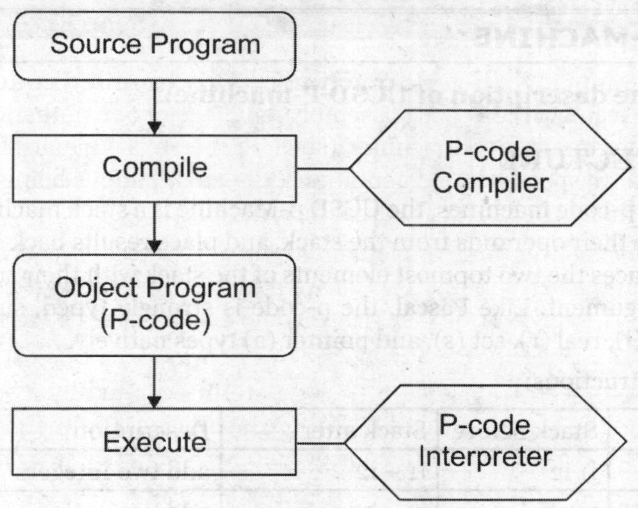

Figure 5.31: Translation and execution using a P-code Compiler

The source program is compiled, with the resulting object program being in P-code. This P-code program is then read and executed, under the control of a P-code interpreter.

The main advantage of this approach is portability of software. It is not necessary for the compiler to generate different code for different computers, because the P-code object programs can be executed on any machine that has a P-code interpreter. Even the compiler itself can be transported if it is written in the language that it compiles. To accomplish this, the source version of the compiler is compiled into P-code. This P-code can then be interpreted on any other computer. In this way, a P-code compiler can be used without modification on a wide variety of systems if a P-code interpreter is written back for each different machine. Although writing such an interpreter is not a trivial task, it is certainly easier than writing a new compiler for each different machine. The same approach can also be used to transport other types of system software without rewriting.

The design of a P-machine and the corresponding P-code is often related to the requirements of the language being compiled. For example, the P-code for a Pascal compiler might include single P-instructions that perform array-subscript calculations, handle the details of procedure entry and exit, and perform elementary operations on sets. This simplifies the code-generation process, leading to a smaller and more efficient compiler. In addition, the P-code object program is often much smaller than a corresponding machine code would be. This is particularly useful on machines with severely limited memory size.

Obviously, the interpretive execution of a P-code program may be much slower than the execution of the equivalent machine code. Depending upon the environment, however, this may not be a problem. Many P-code compilers are designed for a single user running on a dedicated microcomputer system. In that case, speed of execution may be relatively insignificant because the limited factor in system performance may be response time and think time of the user. If the execution speed is important, some P-code compilers support the use of machine language subroutines. By rewriting a small number of commonly used routines in machine language rather than P-code, it is often possible to achieve substantial improvements in performance. Of course, this approach sacrifices some of the portability associated with the use of P-code compilers.

5.14.4 UCSD P-MACHINE

Following is the description of UCSD P-machine:

5.14.4.1 ARCHITECTURE

Like many other p-code machines, the UCSD p-Machine is a stack machine, which means that most instructions take their operands from the stack, and place results back on the stack. Thus, the "add" instruction replaces the two topmost elements of the stack with their sum. A few instructions take an immediate argument. Like Pascal, the p-code is strongly typed, supporting boolean (b), character (c), integer (i), real (r), set (s), and pointer (a) types natively.

Some simple instructions:

Insn.	Stack before	Stack after	Description
adi	i1 i2	i1 + i2	add two integers
adr	r1 r2	r1 + r2	add two reals
dvi	i1 i2	i1/i2	integer division
inn	i1s1b1	set membership	b1=whether i1 is a member of s1
1dci i1		i1	load integer constant
mov	a1 a2		move
not	b1	~b1	boolean negation

5.14.4.2 ENVIRONMENT

Unlike other stack-based environments (such as Forth and the Java Virtual Machine) the p-System has only one stack shared by procedure stack frames (providing return address, etc.) and the arguments to local instructions. Three of the machines register point into the stack (which grows upwards):

- SP points to the top of the stack (the stack pointer).
- MP marks the beginning of the active stack frame (the frame pointer).
- EP points to the highest stack location used in the current procedure (the execution pointer?).

Also present is a constant area, and, below that, the heap growing down towards the stack. The NP register points to the top (lowest used address) of the heap. When EP gets greater than NP, the machine's memory is exhausted.

The fifth register, PC, points at the current instruction in the code area.

5.14.4.3 CALLING CONVENTIONS

Stack frames look like this:

EP ->

local stack

SP -> ...

locals

...

parameters

...

return address (previous PC)

previous EP

dynamic link (previous MP)

static link (MP of surrounding procedure)

MP → function return value

The procedure calling sequence works as follows: The call is introduced with mst *n* where *n* specifies the difference in nesting levels (remember that Pascal supports nested procedures). This instruction will mark the stack, i.e. reserve the first five cells of the above stack frame, and initialise previous EP, dynamic, and static link. The caller then computes and pushes any parameters for the procedure, and then issues cup *n, p*

to call a user procedure (n being the number of parameters, p the procedure's address). This will save the PC in the return address cell, and set the procedure's address as the new PC.

User procedures begin with the two instructions

ent 1, i

ent 2, j

The first sets SP to MP + i, the second sets EP to SP + j. So i essentially specifies the space reserved for locals (plus the number of parameters plus 5), and j gives the number of entries needed locally for the stack. Memory exhaustion is checked at this point.

Returning to the caller is accomplished via

retC

with C giving the return type (i, r, c, b, a as above, and p for no return value). The return value has to be stored in the appropriate cell previously. On all types except p, returning will leave this value on the stack.

Instead of calling a user procedure (cup), standard procedure q can be called with

csp q

These standard procedures are Pascal procedures like readln() ("csp rln"), sin() ("csp sin"), etc. Peculiarly eof() is a p-Code instruction instead.

EXERCISES

1. What do you mean by compiler?
2. Explain the various phases of compilation process?
3. Explain the concept of symbol table?
4. Explain the concept of error handling?
5. What do you mean by lexical analysis?
6. What do you mean by syntax analysis?

7. Explain the concept of semantic analysis?
8. What do you mean by intermediate code generation?
9. Explain the concept of code generation and optimization?
10. Describe the concept of lexical analysis?
11. Describe the concept of parsing?
12. Explain the concept of storage management?
13. Explain the concept of code generation in detail?
14. What are interpreters?
15. Describe the concept of incremental compilers?
16. Explain the problem areas of incremental compilation?
17. What do you mean by cross compiling?
18. Explain the role of cross compilers?
19. Explain the examples of cross compilers?
20. What do you mean by P code compilers?
21. Explain the working of P code compilers?
22. Describe the concept of UCSD P-machine?

Chapter

6

Loaders and Linkage Editors

6.1 INTRODUCTION

In this chapter we will understand the concept of linking and loading. As discussed earlier the source program is converted to object program by assembler. The loader is a program which takes this object program, prepares it for execution, and loads this executable code of the source into memory for execution. Loader is utility program which takes object code as input prepares it for execution and loads the executable code into the memory. Thus loader is actually responsible for initiating the execution process.

The loader is responsible for the activities such as allocation, linking, relocation and loading:

1. It allocates the space for program in the memory, by calculating the size of the program. This activity is called allocation.
2. It resolves the symbolic references (code/data) between the object modules by assigning all the user subroutine and library subroutine addresses. This activity is called linking.
3. There are some address dependent locations in the program, such address constants must be adjusted according to allocated space; such activity done by loader is called relocation.
4. Finally it places all the machine instructions and data of corresponding programs and subroutines into the memory. Thus program now becomes ready for execution, this activity is called loading.

Based on the various functionalities of loader, there are various types of loaders:

1) **"compile and go" loader:** in this type of loader, the instruction is read line by line, its machine code is obtained and it is directly put in the main memory at some known address. That means the assembler runs in one part of memory and the assembled machine instructions and data is directly put into their assigned memory locations. After completion of assembly process, assign starting address of the program to the location counter. The typical example is WATFOR-77; it's a FORTRAN compiler which uses such "load and go" scheme. This loading scheme is also called as "assemble and go".

Advantages

- This scheme is simple to implement. Because assembler is placed at one part of the memory and loader simply loads assembled machine instructions into the memory.

Disadvantages

- In this scheme some portion of memory is occupied by assembler which is simply wastage of memory. As this scheme is combination of assembler and loader activities, this combination program occupies large block of memory.
- There is no production of .obj file; the source code is directly converted to executable form. Hence even though there is no modification in the source program it needs to be assembled and executed each time, which then becomes a time consuming activity.
- It cannot handle multiple source programs or multiple programs written in different languages. This is because assembler can translate one source language to other target language.
- For a programmer it is very difficult to make an orderly modulator program and also it becomes difficult to maintain such program, and the "compile and go" loader cannot handle such programs.
- The execution time will be more in this scheme as every time program is assembled and then executed.

2) **General Loader Scheme:** In this loader scheme, the source program is converted to object program by some translator (assembler). The loader accepts these object modules and puts machine instruction and data in an executable form at their assigned memory. The loader occupies some portion of main memory.

Advantages

- The program need not be retranslated each time while running it. This is because initially when source program gets executed an object program gets generated. Of program is not modified, and then loader can make use of this object program to convert it to executable form.
- There is no wastage of memory, because assembler is not placed in the memory, instead of it, loader occupies some portion of the memory. And size of loader is smaller than assembler, so more memory is available to the user.
- It is possible to write source program with multiple programs and multiple languages, because the source programs are first converted to object programs always, and loader accepts these object modules to convert it to executable form.

3) **Absolute Loader:** Absolute loader is a kind of loader in which relocated object files are created, loader accepts these files and places them at specified locations in the memory. This type of loader is called absolute because no relocation information is needed; rather it is obtained from the programmer or assembler. The starting address of every module is known to the programmer, this corresponding starting address is stored in the object file, then task of loader becomes very simple and that is to simply place the executable form of the machine instructions at the locations mentioned in the object file. In this scheme, the programmer or assembler should have knowledge of memory management. The resolution of external references or linking of different subroutines are the issues which need to be handled by the

programmer. The programmer should take care of two things: first thing is: specification of starting address of each module to be used. If some modification is done in some module then the length of that module may vary. This causes a change in the starting address of immediate next modules, its then the programmer's duty to make necessary changes in the starting addresses of respective modules. Second thing is, while branching from one segment to another the absolute starting address of respective module is to be known by the programmer so that such address can be specified at respective JMP instruction.

Advantages

1. It is simple to implement
2. This scheme allows multiple programs or the source programs written different languages. If there are multiple programs written in different languages then the respective language assembler will convert it to the language and a common object file can be prepared with all the ad resolution.
3. The task of loader becomes simpler as it simply obeys the instruction regarding where to place the object code in the main memory.
4. The process of execution is efficient.

Disadvantages

1. In this scheme it is the programmer's duty to adjust all the inter segment addresses and manually do the linking activity. For that, it is necessary for a programmer to know the memory management.

If at all any modification is done the some segments, the starting addresses of immediate next segments may get changed, the programmer has to take care of this issue and he needs to update the corresponding starting addresses on any modification in the source.

6.2 LOADER SCHEMES

As illustrated in the previous chapters, the user's source program is being converted to object program in machine language by assemblers and compilers. The loader is a program which accepts the object program, prepares it for execution by the computer, and thus initiates the execution.

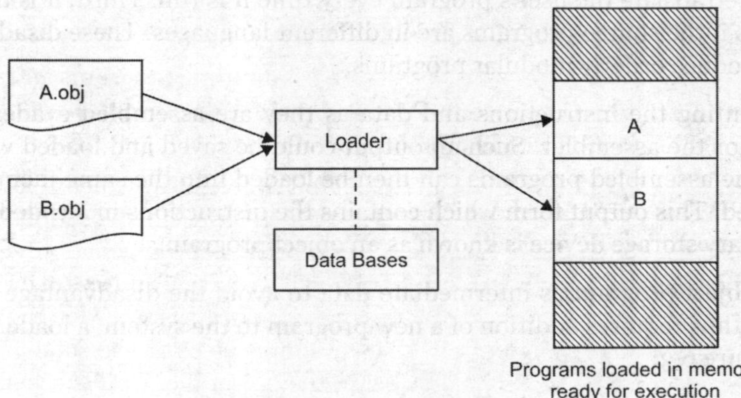

Figure 6.1: General Loading Scheme

One method of performing the loader functions is to have the assembler run in one part of the memory and places the assembled instructions and data, as they are assembled, directly into their assigned memory locations. When the assembly is completed, the assembler causes a transfer to the starting instruction of the program. This is the simplest solution involving no extra procedures. Such a loading scheme is commonly called compile-and-go or assemble-and-go. The assembler simply places the code into the memory, and the typical "loader" consists of a single instruction that transfers to control to the starting instruction of the assembled program. This scheme is illustrated in the figure 6.2:

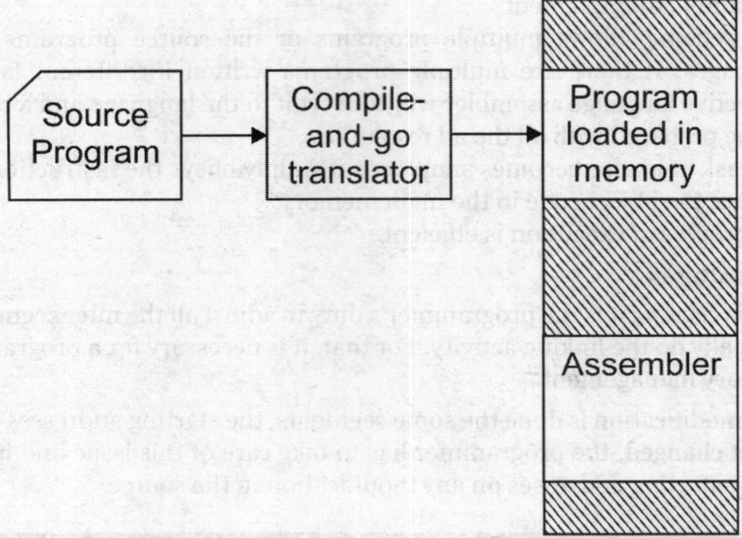

Figure 6.2: Compile-and-go loader scheme

However, this scheme has several disadvantages. First, a portion of memory is wasted because the memory occupied by assembler is unavailable for use by the object program. Second, it is necessary to retranslate the user's program every time it is run. Third, it is difficult to handle multiple segments if the source programs are in different languages. These disadvantages make it very difficult to produce orderly modular programs.

Hence outputting the instructions and data as they are assembled evades the problem of wasting memory for the assembler. Such an output could be saved and loaded whenever it needs to be executed. The assembled programs can then be loaded into the same memory area that the assembler occupied. This output form which contains the instructions in a coded form and can be saved on a secondary storage device is known as an object program.

The use of object program as intermediate data to avoid the disadvantage of the **compile-and-go scheme** thus requires addition of a new program to the system, a loader. This scenario is depicted in the figure 6.3:

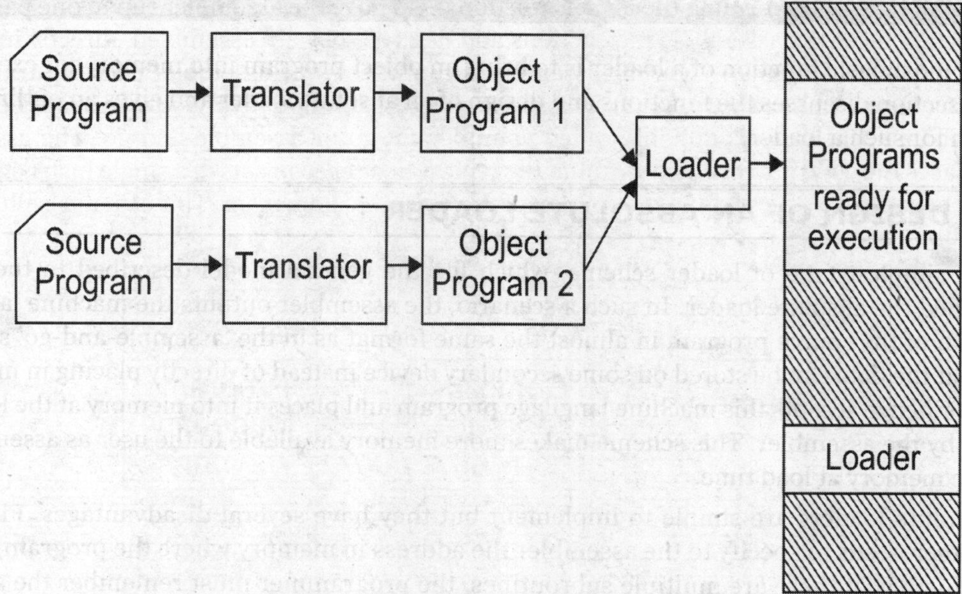

Figure 6.3: General Loader Scheme

The loader accepts the assembled machine instructions, data and other information in an executable computer form. The loader assumes to be smaller than the assembler, so that more memory is available to the user. Another advantage of this scheme is that reassembly is no longer necessary to run the program at a later interval.

A loader is hence a program that performs the loading function. Many loaders also perform relocation and linking. Some systems have linker (or linkage editor) to perform the linking operation and a separate loader to perform relocation and loading. In most cases, a language translator (assembler or compiler) on a particular system produces object programs in the same format as needed. Thus one system loader/linker can be used regardless of the source programming language used.

The loader performs the following tasks:

1. **Allocation:** Programs are allocated space in memory.
2. **Linking:** Symbolic references between object programs are resolved.
3. **Relocation:** The address dependent locations are adjusted to correspond to the allocated space.
4. **Loading:** The machine instructions and data are physically placed into memory for execution.

This chapter presents the design concepts of loader and/or linker. For simplicity, the term loader is used in place of loader and/or linker.

6.3 BASIC LOADER FUNCTIONS

The most basic function of a loader is to bring an object program into memory for execution. The next section discusses the functions and design of an absolute loader and gives an outline of an algorithm for such a loader.

6.3.1 DESIGN OF AN ABSOLUTE LOADER

The simplest type of loader scheme, which fits the general model described in the figure 6.3, is called the absolute loader. In such a scenario, the assembler outputs the machine language translation of the source program in almost the same format as in the 'assemble-and-go' scheme, except that the data can be stored on some secondary device instead of directly placing in memory. The loader hence accepts this machine language program and places it into memory at the location specified by the assembler. This scheme makes more memory available to the user as assembler is not in the memory at load time.

Absolute loaders are simple to implement but they have several disadvantages. First, the programmer needs to specify to the assembler the address in memory where the program is to be loaded. Further, if there are multiple subroutines, the programmer must remember the address of each and use that absolute address explicitly in his other subroutine to perform subroutine linkage.

Here we consider the design of an absolute loader that can be used with any assembler or compiler which produces the desired object code for machine. Following is an example of a sample object program that is output by an assembler or a compiler:

```
HCOPY   00100000107A
T0010001E1410334820390010362810303010154826 1C100300102A0C103900102D
T00101E150C10364820610810334C0000454F46000003000000
T0020391E041030001030E0205D30203FD8205D2810303020575490392C205E38203F
T0020571C1010364C0000F1001000041030E02079302064509039DC20792C1036
T002073073820644C000005
E001000
```

Figure 6.4: Example Object Program

The absolute loader is a simple loader program and does not need to perform such functions as linking and program relocation, hence performing only simple operations. The basic functions of such a loader program can be accomplished in a single pass. The Header Record is checked for verification if the correct program is being presented for loading. When reading a Text Record, the instructions in object code are moved to the indicated address in the memory. When an End Record is encountered, the loader jumps to the specified address for the purpose of executing the currently loaded program. The figure 6.5 shows representation of the above program in memory after loading it into memory:

Memory Address	Contents			
0000	xxxxxxxx	xxxxxxxx	xxxxxxxx	xxxxxxxx
0010	xxxxxxxx	xxxxxxxx	xxxxxxxx	xxxxxxxx
:	:	:	:	:
:	:	:	:	:
0FF0	xxxxxxxx	xxxxxxxx	xxxxxxxx	xxxxxxxx
1000	14103348	20390010	36281030	30101548
1010	20613C10	0300102A	0C103900	102D0C10
1020	36482061	0810334C	0000454F	46000003
1030	000000xx	xxxxxxxx	xxxxxxxx	xxxxxxxx
:	:	:	:	:
:	:	:	:	:
2030	xxxxxxxx	xxxxxxxx	xx0410130	001030E0
2040	205D3020	3FD8205D	28103030	20575490
2050	392C205E	38203F10	10364C00	00F10010
2060	00041030	E0207930	20645090	39DC2079
2070	00041030	20644C00	0005xxxx	xxxxxxxx
2080	2C103638	xxxxxxxx	xxxxxxxx	xxxxxxxx
:	:	:	:	:
:	:	:	:	:

Figure 6.5: Loading of an object program in memory

The memory locations with no instructions are specified with xxxx. This is also an indication that the previous contents of these locations are unchanged. Here we present a simple algorithm for the absolute loader just described:

```
begin
        read Header Record
        verify program name and length
        read first Text Record
        while record type != 'E' do
                begin
                (if object code is in character form, convert it into internal representation)
                move object code to specified location in memory
                read next object program record
                end
        jump to the address specified in End Record
end
```

Figure 6.6: Algorithm for an Absolute Loader

The object program is represented using hexadecimal representation in character form. For example, the machine operation code for STL instruction is represented by the pair of characters '1' and '4'. When these characters are read by the loader, they occupy two bytes of memory. But this operation code must be stored in a single byte with hexadecimal value 14 at the time of execution. Thus each pair of bytes from the object program record must be packed together into one byte during loading. It is hence noted that each printed character in the actual object program represents one byte of the object program record. While on the other hand, each printed character when loaded into memory represents one hexadecimal digit in memory i.e. half byte.

The above method for storage of object programs is inefficient in terms of both space and execution time. Hence, most machine store object programs in binary format, with each byte being stored as a single byte in the object program. In such a representation, a byte may contain a binary value. The bytes in such a convention cannot be interpreted as control characters. For example, the convention indicating the end of record containing hexadecimal 00 would not be suitable while using binary object program.

The object programs in binary format cannot be read and printed in human beings. Therefore, we will continue using the hexadecimal conventions for the rest of the text.

The four loader functions are accomplished as follows in an absolute loading scheme:

1. **Allocation:** by programmer
2. **Linking:** by programmer
3. **Relocation:** by assembler
4. **Loading:** by loader

6.3.2 A SIMPLE BOOTSTRAP LOADER

Bootstrap loader is an absolute loader that is executed when the computer is first turned on or restarted. This bootstrap loader loads the first program to be executed by the computer system, usually an operating system. Here we present a very simple bootstrap loader for SIC/XE. In spite of being a simple program, it illustrates almost all of the logic and coding techniques that are used in any absolute loader. The following is the source code for such a loader:

This bootstrap loader begins at the address 0 of the memory as it is the first program being loaded on a bare machine. It loads the operating system starting at the address 80. As this loader is used for a basic task of loading the initial program, hence it can be represented in a very simple format. A single byte of object code to be loaded can be represented on any device F1 as two hexadecimal digits. However, there is no Header Record, End Record, or control information in the program being loaded. The object code is thus always loaded into consecutive memory locations starting at address 80. After all of the data has been loaded from the device F1, the bootstrap jumps to the address 80 to start execution of the program that was just loaded.

Most of the tasks of the bootstrap loader are performed by the subroutine GETC, which reads a character from device F1 and converts it from ASCII character code to the value of hexadecimal digit that is represented by that character. For example, the ASCII code '0' (hexadecimal 30) is converted to numeric 0, codes '1' through '9' (hexadecimal 31 through 39) are converted to numeric values 1 through 9, and the codes 'A' through 'F' (hexadecimal 41 through 46) are converted to numeric values 10 through 15. This is done by subtracting 48 from the character codes '0' through '9', and subtracting 55 from the codes 'A' through 'F'. The subroutine ignores all the other input characters that have ASCII codes less than hexadecimal 30, hence ignoring any control information even if present in the object program. The subroutine jumps to the address 80 whenever an end-of-file is read from the device.

```
BOOT      START     0         BOOTSTRAP LOADER FOR SIC/XE
.
. THIS BOOTSTRAP LOADER READS AN OBJECT PROGRAM FROM DEVICE F1 AND ENTERS IT INTO
. MEMORY LOCATION STARTING AT ADDRESS 80 (HEXADECIMAL). AFTER ALL OF THE CODE
FROM
. DEVF1 HAS BEEN ENTERED INTO MEMORY, THE BOOTSTRAP EXECUTES A JUMP TO ADDRESS
80 TO
. BEGIN EXECUTION OF THE PROGRAM JUST LOADED. REGISTER X CONTAINS THE NEXT
ADDRESS TO BE
. LOADED.
.
          CLEAR     A         CLEAR REGISTER A TO 0.
          LDX       #128      INITIALIZE REGISTER X TO HEX 80.
LOOP      JSUB      GETC      READ HEX DIGIT FROM PROGRAM BEING LOADED.
          RMO       A, S      SAVE IN REGISTER S.
          SHIFTL    S, 4      MOVE TO HIGH-ORDER 4 BITS OF BYTE.
          JSUB      GETC      GET NEXT HEX DIGIT.
          ADDR      S, A      COMBINE DIGITS TO FORM ONE BYTE.
          STCH      0, X      STORE AT ADDRESS IN REGISTER X.
          TIXR      X, X      ADD 1 TO MEMORY ADDRESS BEING LOADED.
          J         LOOP      LOOP UNTIL END OF INPUT IS REACHED.
.
. SUBROUTINE TO READ ONE CHARACTER FROM INPUT DEVICE AND CONVERT IT FROM ASCII
CODE TO
. HEXADECIMAL DIGIT VALUE. THE CONVERTED DIGIT VALUE IS RETURNED IN REGISTER A.
WHEN AN
. END-OF-FILE IS READ, CONTROL IS TRANSFERRED TO THE STARTING ADDRESS (HEX 80).
.
GETC      TD        INPUT     TEST INPUT DEVICE.
          JEQ       GETC      LOOP UNTIL READY.
          RD        INPUT     READ CHARACTER.
          COMP      #4        IF CHARACTER IS HEX 04 (END OF FILE),
          JEQ       80        JUMP TO START OF PROGRAM JUST LOADED.
          COMP      #48       COMPARE TO HEX 30 (CHARACTER '0').
          JLT       GETC      SKIP CHARACTERS LESS THAN '0'.
          SUB       #48       SUBTRACT HEX 30 FROM ASCII CODE.
          COMP      #10       IF RESULT IS LESS THAN 10, CONVERSION IS COMPLETE.
          JLT       RETURN    OTHERWISE, SUBTRACT 7 MORE
          SUB       #7        (FOR HEX DIGITS 'A' THROUGH 'F').
RETURN    RSUB                RETURN TO CALLER.
INPUT     BYTE      X'F1'     CODE FOR INPUT DEVICE.
          END       LOOP
```

Figure 6.7: Bootstrap Loader for SIC/XE

The loop in bootstrap keeps the register X loaded with the address of next memory location to be loaded. GETC reads and converts a pair of characters from device F1, and combines these two bytes by shifting the first one left 4 bit positions and adding the second to it. The resulting byte is stored at the address currently in register X, by using a STCH instruction which refers to location 0 using indexed addressing. The TIXR instruction is then used to add 1 to the value in register X. For the reason of simplicity, this bootstrap loader does not perform any error checking and assumes for the input to be correct as such. A loader can be made to check for various error conditions that can occur during loading, and the ways to handle them.

6.3.3 MACHINE DEPENDENT LOADER FEATURES

The absolute loader defined in the previous section is fairly simple and efficient, but it has several potential disadvantages. One of them being that the programmer needs to specify every time the exact location where it will be loaded in the memory. If the computer in use is a simple one with a small memory, which can run a single program at a time, this is fairly simple task without creating any difficulty. But with advanced machines and larger memory, this situation is not quite easy as the user may want to run several independent programs together by sharing memory between them. This means the user does not know in advance where the program will be loaded. Efficient sharing of the memory thus requires that relocatable programs be written instead of absolute ones.

Absolute programs also make the use of subroutine libraries difficult. Most such libraries contain many more subroutines than will be used by any one program. To make efficient use of memory, it is efficient thus to locate and load only those routines that are needed by the program. This could only be done if the subroutines have pre-assigned absolute addresses.

The next section discusses the design of a more complex loader that can be used with SIC/XE, and is common with almost all modern computers. This loader provides for program relocation and linking, as well as for the simple loading functions described in the preceding section. The effect of machine architecture on the design of the loader is also studied.

There is a great need for program relocation as an indirect consequence of the change to larger and more powerful computers. The characteristics of the machine are a major concern to how the relocation is implemented. The next section discusses these dependencies by examining various implementation techniques and circumstances in which they might be used.

The section on Program Linking examines the concept from the loader's point of view. Linking is however not a machine dependent function in the sense that relocation is; however, same implementation techniques are often used for both the functions. Moreover, the process of linking usually involves relocation of some of the routines being linked together. For these reasons, linking is discussed together with relocation in this section. Further the data structures used by a linking loader are also presented and a description of the processing logic involved is also provided. This section is thus the starting point for more advanced loader functions.

6.4 RELOCATION

Relocation is the process of updating the addresses used in the address sensitive instructions of a program. It is necessary that such a modification should help to execute the program from designated area of the memory.

The assembler generates the object code. This object code gets executed after loading at storage locations. The addresses of such object code will get specified only after the assembly process is over. Therefore, after loading,

Address of object code = Here address of object code + relocation constant.

There are two types of addresses being generated: Absolute address and, relative address. The absolute address can be directly used to map the object code in the main memory. Whereas the relative address is only after the addition of relocation constant to the object code address. This kind of adjustment needs to be done in case of relative address before actual execution of the code. The typical example of relative reference is: addresses of the symbols defined in the Label field, addresses of the data which is defined by the assembler directive, literals, redefinable symbols. Similarly, the typical example of absolute address is the constants which are generated by assembler are absolute.

The assembler calculates which addresses are absolute and which addresses are relative during the assembly process. During the assembly process the assembler calculates the address with the help of simple expressions.

6.4.1 DIRECT LINKING LOADERS

The direct linking loader is the most common type of loader. This type of loader is a relocatable loader. The loader can not have the direct access to the source code. And to place the object code in the memory there are two situations: either the address of the object code could be absolute which then can be directly placed at the specified location or the address can be relative. If at all the address is relative then it is the assembler who informs the loader about the relative addresses.

The assembler should give the following information to the loader:

1) The length of the object code segment
2) The list of all the symbols which are not defined 111 the current segment but can be used in the current segment.
3) The list of all the symbols which are defined in the current segment but can be referred by the other segments.

The lists of symbols which are not defined in the current segment but can be used in the current segment are stored in a data structure called USE table. The USE table holds the information such as name of the symbol, address, and address relativity.

The lists of symbols which are defined in the current segment and can be referred by the other segments are stored in a data structure called DEFINITION table. The definition table holds the information such as symbol, address.

6.4.2 RELOCATING LOADERS

To avoid reassembling of all subroutines when a single subroutine is changed, and to perform the task of allocation and linking for the programmer, the general class of relocating loaders was introduced.

Loaders which allow for program relocation are known as relocating loaders or relative loaders. In modern computers, it is often desirable to have more than one program at a time sharing the memory and other resources of the machine. The assembler assembles each procedure segment independently and passes on to the loader the text and information as to relocation and intersegment references.

If the programmer knew in advance exactly which programs were to be executed concurrently in this way, one could assign addresses when the programs were assembled so that they would fit together without overlapping or wasting space. Most of the time, however, it is not practical to plan program execution this closely. Because of this reason, it is desirable to be able to load a program into the memory whenever there is room for it. In such situations, the actual starting address of the program is not known until load time.

The absolute loaders discussed in previous section hence perform absolute assembly. Consider the instruction:

LDA THREE 00102D

This statement is translated as 00102D, specifying tegister A be loaded from the memory address 102D. Suppose we attempt to load the program and execute it from some other address 2000 instead of 1000. If this is done, the address 102D would not contain the expected value, as it would be a part of some other user program now.

Some changes need to be done in the address part of this instruction to make it executable when the program is loaded at location 2000. On the other hand, there will be parts of program that should remain same regardless of where the program is loaded. Looking at the object code, it is generally not possible to tell for the values which represent addresses and which represent data items.

Since the assembler does not know the actual location where the program will be loaded, it cannot make the necessary changes in the addresses used by the program. However, the assembler can identify those parts of the object program for the loader which need modification. An object program that contains the information necessary to perform such modifications is called a relocatable program.

Looking in more detail let us take an example program. The figure 6.8 shows three scenarios for the same program.

In the first case when the program is loaded beginning at the address 0000, the JSUB instruction from line 15 is loaded at address 0006. The address field of this instruction contains 01036, which is the address of the instruction labeled RDREC. These addresses are same in this case as assigned by the assembler.

Now if the same program has to be loaded beginning at the address 5000 as shown in the next scenario. The address of the instruction labeled RDREC is in this case 6036. Thus the JSUB instruction should be modified as shown to contain the new address. Similarly if the program is loaded at the location starting from 7420, the JSUB instruction would need to be changed to 4B108456 to correspond to the new address of RDREC.

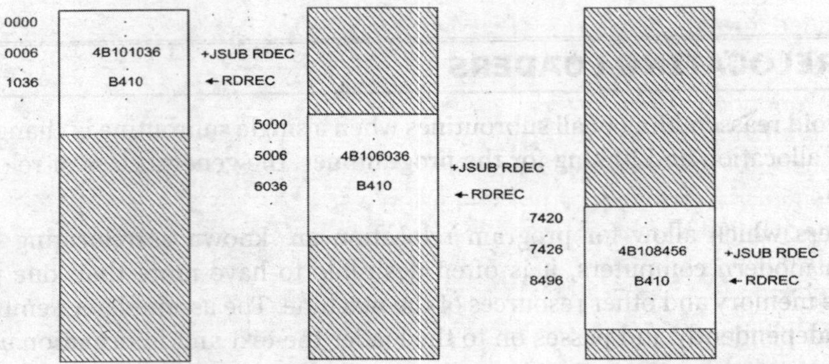

Figure 6.8: Example of Program Relocation

Hence no matter where the program is loaded, RDREC is always 1036 bytes past the starting address of the program. This means one can solve the relocation problem in the following way:

1. When the assembler generates the object code for the JSUB instruction, it inserts the address of RDREC relative to the start of the program. That was the reason behind initializing the counter to 0 for the assembly process.
2. The assembler will also produce a command for loader, instructing it to add the beginning address of the program to the address field in the JSUB instruction at load time.

The command for the loader must be a part of the object program. This can be accomplished by the use of Modification Record, having the following format:

Modification record:	
Col. 1	M
Col.2-7	Starting location of the address field to be modified, relative to the beginning of the program.
Col 8-9	Length of the address filed to be modified, in half bytes.

The length is stored in half-bytes rather than bytes because the address filed to be modified may not occupy an integral number of bytes. The starting location is the location of the byte containing the leftmost bits of the address field to be modified. If this field occupies an odd number of half-bytes, it is assumed to begin in the middle of the first byte at the starting location.

For the JSUB instruction we are using as an example, the Modification Record would be:

M00000705

This record specifies that the beginning address of the program is to be added to a field that begins at the address 000007 relative to the start of the program, and is 5 half-bytes in length. Thus in the assembled instruction 4B101036, the first 12 bits will remain unchanged. The program load address will be added to the last 20 bits (01036) to produce the correct operand address.

The same kind of relocation must be performed for other instructions having addresses specified in them. The rest of the instructions in the program, however, need not be modified when the program is loaded. In some cases, this is because the instruction operand is not a memory address at all. In other cases, no modification is needed because the operand is specified using program-counter relative or base relative addressing.

By now it is clear that that the only parts of the program that require modification at the load time are those that specify direct addresses. For SIC/XE program, the only such direct addresses are found in extended format (4-byte) instructions. This is an advantage of relative addressing that if an attempt is made to relocate the program, it is found that almost every instruction needs modification.

```
HCOPY 000000001077
T0000001D17202D69202D4B1010360320262900003320074B10105D3F2FEC032010
T00001D130F20160100030F200D4B10105D3E2003454F46
T0010360DB410B400B44075101000E32019332FFADB2013A00433200857C003B850
T0010531D3B2FEA1340004F0000F1B410774000E32011332FFA53C003DF2008B850
T001070073B2FEF4F000005
M00000705
M00001405
M00002705
E000000
```

Figure 6.9: A Sample Object Program

The figure 6.9 shows sample object program after being processed by an assembler or a compiler. It is notes that the Text Records are exactly the same as those that would be produced by an absolute loader assembler (program with starting address 0). However, the load addresses in the Text Records are interpreted as relative, rather than absolute locations. The same is true for Modification as well as End Records. There is one Modification Record for each address filed that needs to be changed when the program is relocated.

This is the first method used for relocating programs, by adding a Modification record along with each object program that needs relocation. It is used to describe each part of the object code that must be changed when the program is relocated. The figure 6.10 shows an object program that contains Modification records:

```
HCOPY 000000001077
T0000001D17202D69202D4B1010360320262900003320074B10105D3F2FEC032010
T00001D130F20160100030F200D4B10105D3E2003454F46
T0010360DB410B400B44075101000E32019332FFADB2013A00433200857C003B850
T0010531D3B2FEA1340004F0000F1B410774000E32011332FFA53C003DF2008B850
T001070073B2FEF4F000005
M00000705+COPY
M00001405+COPY
M00002705+COPY
E000000
```

Figure 6.10: Object Program with relocation by Modification Records

Notice that there is one Modification for each value that must be changed during relocation. Each modification Record specifies the starting address and length of the field whose value is to be altered. It then describes the modification to be performed. In this example, all modifications add the value of the symbol COPY, which represents the starting address of the program.

The Modification Record scheme is a convenient means for specifying program relocation. However, it is not well suited for use with all the machine architectures. Consider a relocatable program written for the standard version of SIC. The standard SIC machine does not use relative addressing. In such programs, the instructions needing modifications need to be changed during relocation. This would thus result in object programs more than twice as large as the source program.

On such a machine that uses primarily direct addressing and has a fixed instruction format, it is often more efficient to specify relocation using a different technique. The figure 6.11 shows this method as applied to the SIC machine:

```
HCOPY 000000001077A
T0000001EFFC1400334810390000362800303000154810613C000300002A0C003900002D
T00001E15E000C00364810610800334C0000454F46000003000000
T0010391EFFC040030000030E0105D30103FD8105D2800303010575480392C105E38103F
T0010570A8001000364C0000F1001000
T00106119FE0040030E01079301064508039DC10792C00363810644C000005
E000000
```

Figure 6.11: Object Program with relocation by bit mask

There are no Modification Records in this object program, and the Text Records are same as before except that there is a relocation bit associated with each word of the object code. Since all SIC instructions occupy one word, this means that there is one relocation nit for each possible instruction. The relocation bits are gathered together into a bit mask following the length indicator in each Text Record. In the figure 6.11, this mask is represented as three hexadecimal digits and is underlined for easier identification in the figure 6.11.

If the relocation bit corresponding to a word of object code is set to 1, the program's starting address is to be added to this word whenever the program is relocated. A bit value of 0 indicates that no modification is necessary. If a Text Record contains fewer than 12 words of object code, the bits corresponding to unused words are set to 0. Thus the bit mask FFC (representing the bit string 111111111100) in the Text Record specifies that all 10 words of the object code are to be modified during relocation. The mask E00 in the second Text Record specifies that the first three words are to be modified. The remainder of the object code in this record represents data constants and thus do not require modification.

The other Text Records follow the same pattern. Note that the object code generated from the LDX instruction begins a new Text Record even though there is room for it in the preceding record. This occurs because each relocation bit is associated with a 3-byte segment of object code in the Text Record. Any value that is to be modified during relocation must coincide with one of these 3-byte segments so that is corresponds to a relocation bit. The assembled LDX instruction does require modification because of the direct address. However, if it were placed in the preceding Text Record, it would not be properly aligned to a relocation bit because of the 1-byte data value thus generated. Therefore this instruction must begin a new Text Record in the object program.

Some machines also provide a hardware relocation facility that eliminates some of the need for the loader to perform program relocation. For example, some such machines consider all the memory references to be relative to the beginning of the user's assigned area of memory. The conversion of these relative addresses is performed as the program is executed. However, the loader must still handle relocation of subprograms in connection with linking.

6.5 LINKING

Linking is the process of collecting and combining various pieces of code and data into a single file that can be *loaded* (copied) into memory and executed. Linking can be performed at *compile time*, when the source code is translated into machine code, at *load time*, when the program is loaded into memory and executed by the *loader*, and even at *run time*, by application programs. On early computer systems, linking was performed manually. On modern systems, linking is performed automatically by programs called *linkers*.

Linkers play a crucial role in software development because they enable *separate compilation*. Instead of organizing a large application as one monolithic source file, we can decompose it into smaller, more manageable modules that can be modified and compiled separately. When we change one of these modules, we simply recompile it and relink the application, without having to recompile the other files.

As we have discussed earlier, the execution of program can be done with the help of following steps:

1. Translation of the program (done by assembler or compiler)
2. Linking of the program with all other programs which are needed for execution. This also involves preparation of a program called load module.
3. Loading of the load module prepared by linker to some specified memory location.

The output of translator is a program called object module. The linker processes these object modules binds with necessary library routines and prepares a ready to execute program. Such a program is called binary program. The "binary program also contains some necessary information about allocation and relocation. The loader then load s this program into memory for execution purpose.

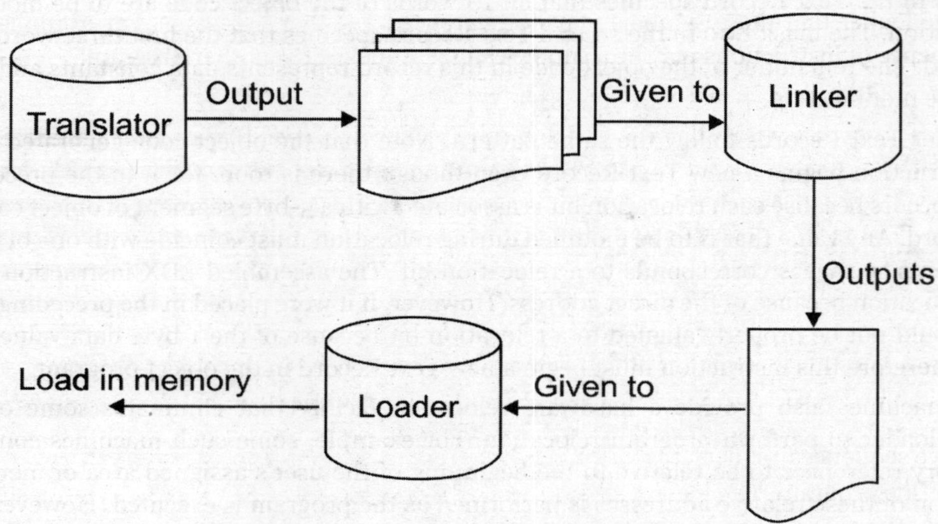

Figure 6.12: Process of linking a program

Various tasks of linker are:

1. Prepare a single load module and adjust all the addresses and subroutine references with respect to the offset location.
2. To prepare a load module concatenate all the object modules and adjust all the operand address references as well as external references to the offset location.
3. At correct locations in the load module, copy the binary machine instructions and constant data in order to prepare ready to execute module.

The linking process is performed in two passes. Two passes are necessary because the linker may encounter a forward reference before knowing its address. So it is necessary to scan all the DEFINITION and USE table at least once. Linker then builds the Global symbol table with the help of USE and DEFINITION table. In Global symbol table name of each externally referenced symbol is included along with its address relative to beginning of the load module. And during pass 2, the addresses of external references are replaced by obtaining the addresses from global symbol table.

6.5.1 PROGRAM LINKING

The problem of subroutine linkage is somewhat as this: a main program A wishes to transfer to subprogram B. The programmer, in program A, could write a transfer instruction to subprogram B. However, the assembler does not know the value of this symbol reference and will declare an error unless a special mechanism has been provided.

This mechanism is typically implemented with a direct-linking loader. The assembler pseudo-op EXTRN followed by a list of symbols indicates that these symbols are defined in other programs but referenced in the present program. Correspondingly if a symbol is defined in one program and referenced in another, we insert it into a symbol list following the pseudo-op ENTRY. In turn, assembler will inform the loader that these symbols may be referenced by other programs. For example, the following sequence of instructions may be a simple calling sequence to another program:

```
MAIN    START
        EXTRN      SUBRT
          .
          .
          L        15, =A(SUBRT)
        BALR         14, 15
          .
          .
        END
```

The above sequence first declares SUBRT as an external variable, i.e. a variable referenced but not defined in this program. The load instruction loads the address of that variable into register 15. The BALR instruction branches to the contents in register 15, which is the address of SUBRT, and leaves the value of the next instruction in register 14.

Here we discuss the handling of programs that consist of multiple control sections. A control section is a part of the program that maintains its identity after assembly; each such control section can be loaded and relocated independently of the others. Different control sections are most often used for subroutines or other logical subdivisions of a program. The programmer can assemble, load, and manipulate each of these control sections separately. The resulting flexibility is a major benefit of using control sections.

When control sections form logically related parts of a program, it becomes necessary to provide some means for linking them together. For example, instructions in one control section might need to refer to the instructions or data located in some another section. Because control sections are independently loaded and relocated, the assembler is unable to process these references in the usual way. The assembler has in fact no idea where any other control sections will be loaded at the execution time. Such references between control sections are called external references. The assembler generates information for each external reference that will allow the loader to perform the required linking.

The figure 6.13 shows a program made up of three control sections:

```
Source Statement
COPY      START     0                            COPY FILE FROM INPUT TO
          EXTDEF    BUFFER,        BUFEND,       OUTPUT
          EXTREF    LENGTH
FIRST     STL       RDREC, WRREC
CLOOP     +JSUB     RETADR                       SAVE RETURN ADDRESS
          LDA       RDREC                        READ INPUT RECORD
          COMP      LEGTH                        TEST FOR EOF (LENGTH = 0)
          JEQ       #0
          +JSUB     ENDFIL                       EXIT IF EOF FOUND
          J         WRREC                        WRITE OUTPUT RECORD
ENDFIL    LDA       CLOOP                        LOOP
          STA       =C 'EOF'                     INSERT END OF FILE MARKER
          LDA       BUFFER
          STA       #3                           SET LENGTH = 3
          +JSUB     LENGTH
          J         WRREC                        WRITE EOF
RETADR    RESW      @RETADR                      RETURN TO CALLER
LENGTH    RESW      1
          LTORG     1                            LENGTH OF RECORD
BUFFER    RESB
BUFEND    EQU       4096                         4096-BYTE BUFFER AREA
MAXLEN    EQU       *
RDREC     CSECT     BUFFEND-BUFFER

.
.         SUBROUTINE TO READ A RECORD INTO BUFFER
.
          EXTREF    BUFFER,        LENGTH,
          CLEAR     BUFEND                       CLEAR LOOP COUNTER
          CLEAR     X                            CLEAR A TO ZERO
          CLEAR     A                            CLEAR S TO ZERO
          LDT       S
RLOOP     TD        MAXLEN                       TEST INPUT DEVICE
          JEQ       INPUT                        LOOP UNTIL READY
          RD        RLOOP                        READ CHARACTER INTO
          COMPR     INPUT                        REGISTER A
          JEQ       A, S                         TEST FOR END OF RECORD (X
          +STCH     EXIT                         '00')
          TIXR      BUFFER, X                    EXIT LOOP IF EOR
          JLT       T                            STORE CHARACTER IN BUFFER
EXIT      +STX      RLOOP                        LOOP UNLESS MAXLEN
          RSUB      LENGTH                       HAS BEEN REACHED
INPUT     BYTE                                   SAVE RECORD LENGTH
MAXLEN    WORD      X 'F1'                       RETURN TO CALLER
WRREC     CSECT     BUFEND-BUFFER                CODE FOR INPUT DEVICE
.
          SUBROUTINE TO WRITE RECORD FROM BUFFER
.
```

```
                EXTR     LENGTH, BUFFER
                CLEAR    X                 CLEAR LOOP COUNTER
                +LDT     LENGTH
       WLOOP    TD       =X '05'           TEST OUTPUT DEVICE
                JEQ      WLOOP             LOOP UNTIL READY
                +LDCH    BUFFER, X         GET CHARACTER FROM BUFFER
                WD       =X '05'           WRITE CHARACTER
                TIXR     T                 LOOP UNTIL ALL CHARACTERS
                JLT      WLOOP              HAVE BEEN WRITTEN
                RSUB                       RETURN TO CALLER
                END      FIRST
```

Figure 6.13: Illustration of Control Sections and Program Linking

These control sections could be assembled together, or they could be assembled independently of one another. In either case, they would appear as separate segments of object code after assembly as shown below:

```
HCOPY 000000001033
DBUFFER000033BUFEND001033LENGTH00002D
RDREC WRREC
T0000001D1720274B1000000320232900003320074B1000003FEC0320160F2016
T00001D0D0100030F200A4B1000003E2000
T00003003454F46
M00000405+RDREC
M00001105+WRREC
M00002405+WRREC

HRDREC 00000000002B
RBUFFERLENGTHBUFEND
T0000001DB410B400B44077201FE3201B332FFADB2015A00433200957900000B850
T00001D0E3B2FE9131000004F0000F1000000
M00001805+BUFFER
MOOOO2105+LENGTH
M00002806+BUFEND
M00002806-BUFFER
E

HWRREC 00000000001C
RLENGTHBUFFER
T0000001CB41077100000E32012332FFA53900000DF2008B8503B2FEE4F000005
M00000305+LENGTH
M00000D05+BUFFER
E
```

Figure 6.14: Corresponding Object Program

The programmer has a natural inclination to think of a program as a logical entity that combines all of the related control sections. From the loader's point of view, however, there is no such thing as a program in this sense, there are only control sections that are to be linked, relocated and loaded. The loader has no way of knowing which control sections were assembled at the same time.

Consider the three separately assembled programs in the figure 6.15, each of which consists of a single control section:

Loc	Source Statement			Object Code
0000	PROGA	START	0	
		EXTDEF	LISTA, ENDA	
		EXTREF	LISTB, ENDB, LISTC, ENDC	
		.		
		.		
0020	REF1	LDA	LISTA	03201D
0023	REF2	+LDT	LISTB+4	77100004
0027	REF3	LDX	#ENDA-LISTA	050014
		.		
		.		
0040	LISTA	EQU	*	
		.		
		.		
0054	ENDA	EQU	*	
0054	REF4	WORD	ENDA-LISTA+LISTC	000014
0057	REF5	WORD	ENDC-LISTC-10	FFFFF6
005A	REF6	WORD	ENDC-LISTC+LISTA-1	00003F
005D	REF7	WORD	ENDA-LISTA-(ENDB-LISTB)	000014
0060	REF8	WORD	LISTB-LISTA	FFFFC0
		END	REF1	

Loc	Source Statement			Object Code
0000	PROGB	START	0	
		EXTDEF	LISTB, ENDB	
		EXTREF	LISTA, ENDA, LISTC, ENDC	
		.		
		.		
0036	REF1	LDA	LISTA	03100000
003A	REF2	+LDT	LISTB+4	772027
003D	REF3	LDX	#ENDA-LISTA	05100000
		.		
		.		
0060	LISTB	EQU	*	
		.		
		.		
0070	ENDB	EQU	*	
0070	REF4	WORD	ENDA-LISTA+LISTC	000000
0073	REF5	WORD	ENDC-LISTC-10	FFFFF6
0076	REF6	WORD	ENDC-LISTC+LISTA-1	FFFFFF
0079	REF7	WORD	ENDA-LISTA-(ENDB-LISTB)	FFFFF0
007C	REF8	WORD	LISTB-LISTA	000060
		END		

Loc	Source Statement			Object Code

```
0000    PROGC    START    0
                 EXTDEF   LISTC, ENDC
                 EXTREF   LISTA, ENDA, LISTB, ENDB
                 .
                 .
0018    REF1     LDA      LISTA                     03100000
001C    REF2     +LDT     LISTB+4                   77100004
0020    REF3     LDX      #ENDA-LISTA               05100000
                 .
                 .
0030    LISTC    EQU      *
                 .
                 .
0042    ENDC     EQU      *
0042    REF4     WORD     ENDA-LISTA+LISTC          000030
0045    REF5     WORD     ENDC-LISTC-10             000008
0048    REF6     WORD     ENDC-LISTC+LISTA-1        000011
004B    REF7     WORD     ENDA-LISTA-(ENDB-LISTB)   000000
004E    REF8     WORD     LISTB-LISTA               000000
                 END
```

Figure 6.15: Sample programs illustrating Linking and Relocation

Each program contains a list of items (LISTA, LISTB, LISTC), and the ends of these lists are marked by the labels ENDA, ENDB, ENDC. The labels on the beginnings and ends of the lists are external symbols and are available for use in linking. Note that each program contains exactly the same set of references to these external symbols. Three of these instruction operands (REF1 through REF3), and the others are the values of the data words (REF4 through REF8).

The corresponding generated object programs are shown in the figure 6.16:

```
HPROGA 000000000063
DLISTA 000040ENDA 000054
RLISTB ENDB LISTC ENDC
:
T000020OA03201D77100004050014
:
T0000540F000014FFFFF600003F000014FFFC0
M00002405+LISTB
M00005406+LISTC
M00005706+ENDC
M00005706-LISTC
M00005A06+ENDC
M00005A06-LISTC
M00005A06+PROGA
M00005D06-ENDB
M00005D06+LISTB
M00006006+LISTB
M00006006-PROGA
E000020
```

```
HPROGB 00000000007F
DLISTB 000060ENDB 000070
RLISTA ENDA LISTC ENDC
:
T000036OB0310000077202705100000
:
T000070OF000000FFFFF6FFFFFFFFFF000060
M00003705+LISTA
M00003E05+ENDA
M00003E05+LISTA
M00007006+ENDA
M00007006-LISTA
M00007006+LISTC
M00007306+ENDC
M00007306-LISTC
M00007606+ENDC
M00007606-LISTC
M00007606+LISTA
M00007906+ENDA•
MOOO07906-LISTA
MOOO07C06+PROGB
M00007C06-LISTA
E

HPROGC 000000000051
DLISTC 000030ENDC 000042
RLISTA ENDA LISTB ENDB
:
T000018OC0310000077100004051000000
:
T000042OF000030000008000011000000000000
M00001905+LISTA
M00001D05+LISTB
M00002105+ENDA
M00002105-LISTA
M00004206+ENDA
M00004206-LISTA
M00004206+PROGC
M00004806+LISTA
M00004B06+ENDA
M00004B06-LISTA
M00004B06-ENDB
M00004B06+LISTB
M00004E06+LISTB
M00004E06-LISTA
E
```

Figure 6.16: Corresponding Object Programs

Consider the first reference marked as REF1. For the first program PROGA, REF1 is simply a reference to a label within the program. It is assembled in the usual way as a program-counter relative instruction. No modification for relocation or linking is necessary. In PROGB, on the other hand, the same operand refers to an external symbol. The assembler uses an extended-format instruction with the address field 00000. The object program for PROGB contains a Modification Record instructing the loader to add the value of the symbol LISTA to this address field when the program is linked. This reference is handled in exactly the same way for PROGC.

The reference marked REF2 is processed in a similar manner. For PROGA, the operand expression consists of an external reference plus a constant. The assembler stores the value of the constant in the address field of the instruction and a Modification Record directs the loader to add to this field the value of LISTB. In PROGB, the same expression is simply a local reference and is assembled using a program-counter relative instruction with no relocation or required linking.

REF3 is an immediate operand whose value is to be the difference between ENDA and LISTA. In PROGA, the assembler has all the information necessary to compute this value. During the assembly of PROGB and PROGC, however, the values of the labels are unknown. In these programs, the expression must be assembled as an external reference even though the final result will be an absolute value independent of the locations at which the programs are loaded.

The remaining references illustrate a variety of other possibilities. The general approach taken is for the assembler to evaluate as much of the expression as it can. The remaining terms are passed on to the loader via a Modification Record. To see this, consider REF4. The assembler for PROGA can evaluate all of the expression in REF4 except for the value of LISTC. This results in an initial value of 000014 and one Modification Record. However, the same expression of PROGB contains no terms that can be evaluated by the assembler. The object code therefore contains an initial value 000000 and three Modification Records. For PROGC, the assembler can supply the value of LISTC relative to the beginning of the program but not the actual address which is unknown till the loading of the program. The initial value of this data word contains the relative address of LISTC. Modification records instruct the loader to add the beginning address of the program, to add the value of ENDA, and to subtract the value of LISTA. Thus the expression in REF4 represents a simple external reference for PROGB, and a combination of relocation and external references for PROGC.

PROGA has been loaded starting at address 4000, with PROGB and PROGC immediately following. Note that each of REF4 through REF8 has resulted in the same value in each of the three programs. This is as it should be, since the same source expression appeared in each program.

For example, the value for reference REF4 in PROGA plus 0054, the relative address 4054. For the values that are instruction operands, the calculated values after loading do not always appear to be equal. This is because there is an additional address calculation step involved for program-counter relative instructions. In these cases it is the target addresses that are the same. For example, in PROGA the reference REF1 is a program-counter relative instruction with displacement 01d. When this instruction is executed, the program counter contains the value 4023. The resulting target address is 4040. No relocation is necessary for this instruction since the program counter will always contain the actual not relative address of the instruction. One could also think of this process as automatically providing the needed relocation at execution time through the target address calculation. In PROGB, on the other hand, reference REF1 is an extended format instruction that contains a direct address. This address after linking is 4040, which is the same as the target address for the same reference in PROGA.

The figure 6.17 shows these three programs as they might appear in memory after loading and linking.

Memory Adderss	*Contents*				
0000	xxxxxxxx	xxxxxxxx	xxxxxxxx	xxxxxxxx	
-	-	-	-	-	
-	-	-	-	-	
3FF0	xxxxxxxx	xxxxxxxx	xxxxxxxx	xxxxxxxx	
4000					
4010					
4020	03201D77	1040C705	0014	....	
4030	....	....	....	....	←PROGA
4040	....	....	....	....	
4050	....	00412600	0080040	51000004	
4060	000083	....	....	....	
4070	....	....	....	....	
4080	....	....	....	....	
4090	....	....	031040	40772027	
40A0	05100014	....	....	....	←PROGB
40B0	....	....	....	....	
40C0	....	....	....	....	
40D0	00	41260000	08004051	00000400	
40E0	0083				
40F0	....	....	0310	40407710	
4100	40C70510	0014			
4110					← PROGC
4120	....	00412600	00080040	51000004	
4130	000083xx	xxxxxxxx	xxxxxxxx	xxxxxxxx	
4140	xxxxxxxx	xxxxxxxx	xxxxxxxx	xxxxxxxx	
-	-	-	-	-	
-	-	-	-	-	

Figure 6.17: Program after Linking and Loading

6.5.2 ALGORITHM FOR A LINKING LOADER

Here we use Modification Records for relocation so that the linking and relocation functions are performed using the same mechanism. As mentioned in the previous section, this type of loader is often found on machines whose relative addressing makes relocation unnecessary for most instructions.

The algorithm for a linking loader is more complicated than the absolute loader algorithm. The input to such a loader consists of a set of object programs, i.e. control sections that are to be linked together. It is possible for a control section to make an external reference to a symbol whose definition does not appear until later in this input stream. In such a case, the required linking operation cannot be performed until an address is assigned to the external symbol involved. Thus a linking loader usually makes two passes over its input, just as an assembler does. In terms of general function, the two passes of a linking loader are quite similar to the two passes of an assembler. Pass I assigns addresses to all external symbols and Pass II performs the actual loading, relocation and linking.

The algorithm for Pass I of the Linking Loader is described in the figure 6.18:

```
begin
get PROGADDR from operating system
set CSADDR to PROGADDR (for the first control section)
while not end of input do
        begin
        read next input record (Header Record for control section)
        set CSLTH to control section length
        search ESTAB for control section name
        if found then
                set error flag (duplicate external symbol)
        else
                enter control section name into ESTAB with value CSADDR
        while record type != 'E' do
                begin
                        read next input record
                        if record type = 'D' then
                                for each symbol in the record do
                                begin
                                        search ESTAB for symbol name
                                        if found then
                                                set error flag (duplicate external symbol)
                                        else
                                                enter symbol into ESTAB with value
                                                (CSADDR + indicated address)
                                end {for}
        end {while != 'E'}
        add CSLTH to CSADDR (starting address for next control section)
end {while not EOF}
end {Pass I}
```

Figure 6.18: Algorithm for Pass I of a Linking Loader

During the first pass, the loader is concerned only with Header and Define record types in the control sections. The beginning load address for the linked program (PROGADDR) is obtained from the operating system. This becomes the starting address (CSADDR) for the first control section in the input sequence. The control section name from the Header record is entered into ESTAB, with the given value by CSADDR. All the external symbols appearing in the Define record for the control section are also entered into ESTAB. Their addresses are obtained by adding their value specified in the Define Record to CSADDR. When the End record is read the control section length CSLTH is added to CSADDR. This calculation gives the starting address for the next control section in sequence.

At the end of Pass I, ESTAB contains all the external symbols defined in the set of control sections together with the address assigned to each of them. Many loaders include as an option the ability to print a load map that shows these symbols and their addresses. Their information is often useful in program debugging.

```
begin
set CSADDR to PROGADDR
set EXECADDR to PROGADDR
while not end of input do
        begin
        read next input record {Header Record}
        set CSLTH to control section length
        while record type != 'E' do
                begin
                read next input record
                if record type = 'T' then
                        begin
                        (if object code in character form,
                        convert into internal representation)
                        move object code from record to location
                        (CSADDR + specified location)
                end (if 'T')
        else if record type = 'M' then
                begin
                        search ESTAB for modifying symbol name
                        if found then
                                add or subtract symbol value at location
                                (CSADDR + specified location)
                        else
                                set error flag (undefined external symbol)
                        end {if 'M'}
                end {while != 'E'}
                if an address is specified {in End Record} then
                        set EXECADDR to (CSADDR + specified address)
                add CSLTH to CSADDR
        end {while not EOF}
jump to location given by EXECADDR {to start execution of loaded program}
end {Pass II}
```

Figure 6.19: Algorithm for Pass II of a Linking Loader

Pass II of our loader performs the actual loading, relocation and linking of the program. CSADDR is used in the same way as it was in Pass I. It always contains the actual starting address of the control section currently being loaded. As each Text record is read, the object code is moved to the specified address. When a Modification record is encountered, the symbol whose value is to be used for modification is looked up in ESTAB. This value is then added to or subtracted from the indicated location in memory.

The last step performed by the loader is usually the transferring of control to the loaded program to begin execution. The End record for each control section may contain the address of the first instruction in that control section to be executed. Our loader takes this as the transfer point to begin execution. If more than one control section specifies a transfer address, the loader arbitrarily uses the last one encountered. If no control section contains a transfer address, the loader uses the beginning of the linked program as the transfer point. This convention is typical of those found in most linking loaders. Normally a transfer address would be placed in the End record for a Main program, but not for a subroutine. Thus the correct execution address would be specified regardless of the order in which the control sections were presented for loading.

6.6 LINKAGE EDITORS

Linkage editor processing is a necessary step that follows the source program assembly or compilation of any problem program. The linkage editor is a processing program and a service program used in association with the language translators.

Every problem program is designed to fulfill a particular purpose. To achieve that purpose, the program can generally be divided into logical units that perform specific functions. A logical unit of coding that performs a function, or several related functions, is a module. Ordinarily, separate functions should be programmed into separate-modules, a process called modular programming. Each module can be written in the symbolic language that best suits the function to be performed. (The symbolic languages are assembler, ALGOL, COBOL, FORTRAN, PL/I, and RPG.)

Each module is separately assembled or compiled by one of the language translators. The input to a language translator is a source module; the output from a language translator is an object module. Before an object module can be executed, it must be processed by the linkage editor. The output of the linkage editor is a load module (Figure 6.20).

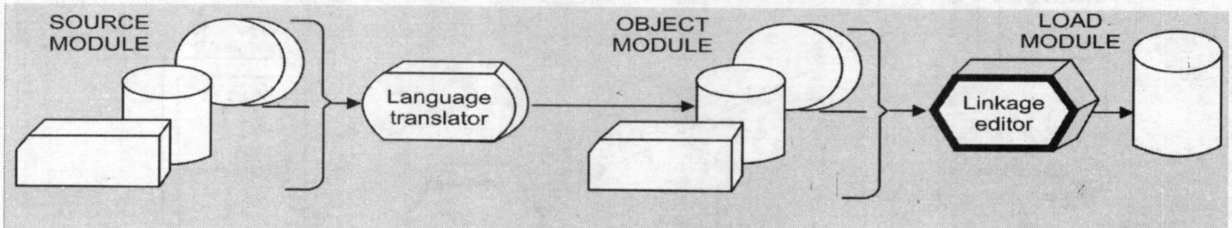

Figure 6.20: Preparing a Source Module for Execution

An object module is in relocatable format with unexecutable machine code. A load module is also relocatable, but with executable machine code. A load module is in a format that can be loaded into virtual storage and relocated by program fetch (Figure 6.21).

Any module is composed of one or more control sections. A control section is a unit of coding (instructions and data) that is, in itself, an entity. All elements of a control section are loaded and executed in a constant relationship to one another. A control section is, therefore, the smallest separately relocatable unit of a program. Each module in the input to the linkage editor may contain symbolic references to control sections in other modules; such references are called external references. These references are made by means of address constants (adcons). The symbol referred to by an external reference must be either the name of a control section or the name of an entry point in a control section. Control section names and entry names are called external names. By matching an external reference with an external name, the linkage editor resolves references between modules. External references and external names are called external symbols (Figure 6.22). An external symbol is one that is defined in one module and can be referred to in another.

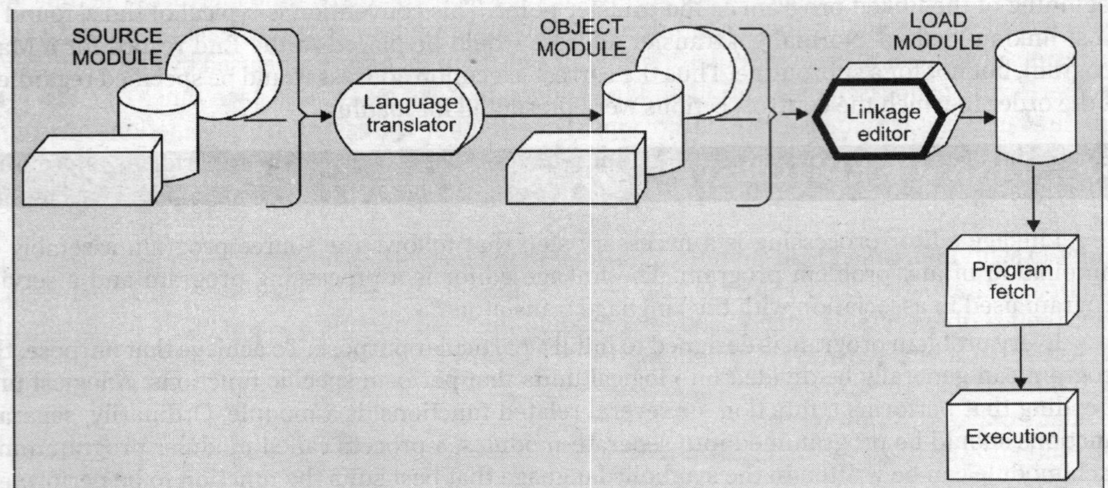

Figure 6.21: Preparing a Source Module for Execution and Executing the Load Module

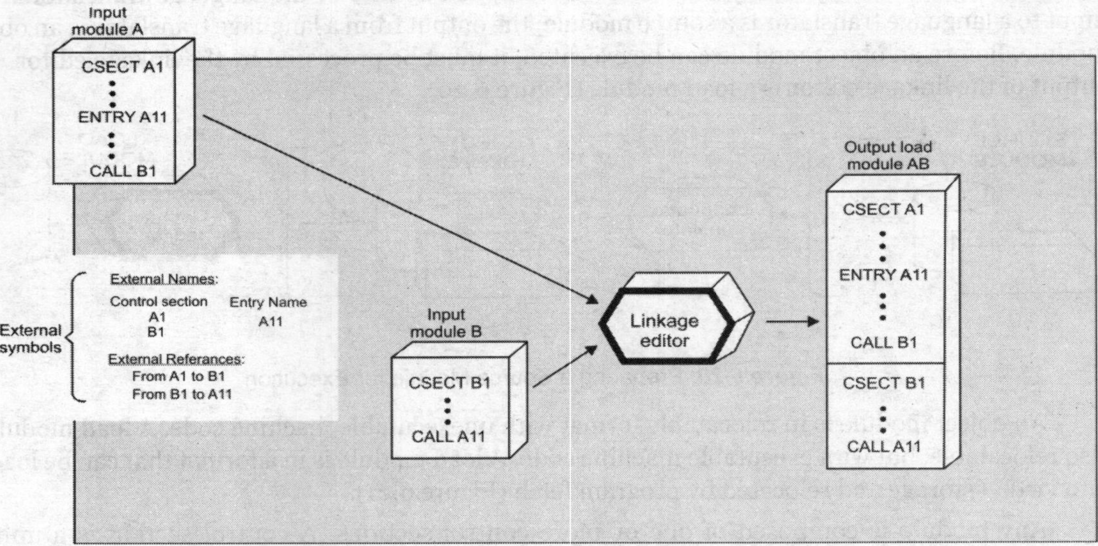

Figure 6.22: External Names and External References

6.6.1 WORKING OF LINKAGE EDITORS

The execution of any program needs four basic functionalities and those are allocation, relocation, linking and loading. As we have also seen in direct linking loader for execution of any program each time these four functionalities need to be performed. But performing all these functionalities each time is time and space consuming task. Moreover if the program contains many subroutines or functions and the program needs to be executed repeatedly then this activity becomes annoyingly complex .Each time for execution of a program, the allocation, relocation linking and -loading needs to be done. Now doing these activities each time increases the time and space complexity. Actually, there is no need to redo all these four activities each time. Instead, if the results of some of these activities are stored in a file then that file can be used by other activities. And performing allocation, relocation, linking and loading can be avoided each time. The idea is to separate out these activities in separate groups. Thus dividing the essential four functions in groups reduces the overall time complexity of loading process. The program which performs allocation, relocation and linking is called binder. The binder performs relocation, creates linked executable text and stores this text in a file in some systematic manner. Such kind of module prepared by the binder execution is called load module. This load module can then be actually loaded in the main memory by the loader. This loader is also called as module loader. If the binder can produce the exact replica of executable code in the load module then the module loader simply loads this file into the main memory which ultimately reduces the overall time complexity. But in this process the binder should knew the current positions of the main memory. Even though the binder knew the main memory locations this is not the only thing which is sufficient. In multiprogramming environment, the region of main memory available for loading the program is decided by the host operating system. The binder should also know which memory area is allocated to the loading program and it should modify the relocation information accordingly. The binder which performs the linking function and produces adequate information about allocation and relocation and writes this information along with the program code in the file is called linkage editor. The module loader then accepts this rile as input, reads the information stored in and based on this information about allocation and relocation it performs the task of loading in the main memory. Even though the program is repeatedly executed the linking is done only once. Moreover, the flexibility of allocation and relocation helps efficient utilization of the main memory. The main difference between a linkage editor and a linking loader is illustrated in the figure 6.23:

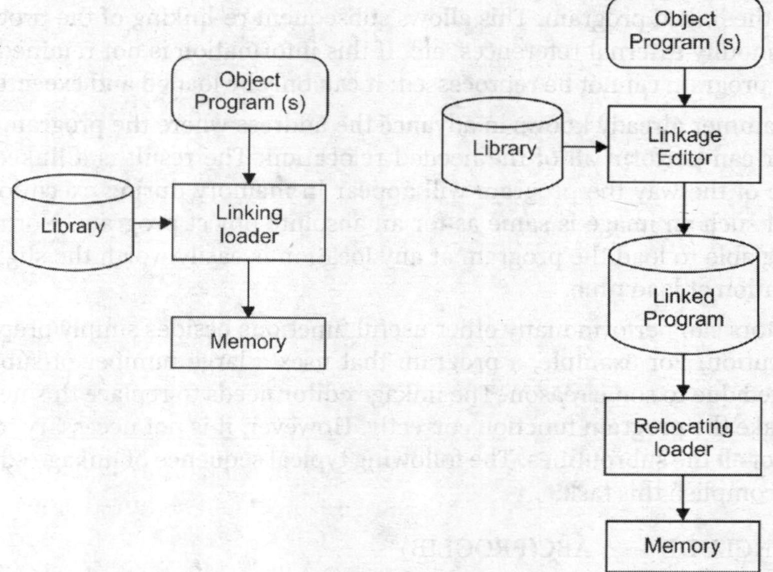

Figure 6.23: Processing of an Object Program using Linking Loader and Linkage Editor

The source program is first assembled or compiled, producing an object program, which may contain several different control sections. A linking loader performs all linking and relocation operations, including library search if specified, and loads the linked program directly into the memory for execution. A linkage editor, on the other hand produces a linked version of the program, known as load module or executable image, which is written to a file or library for later execution.

When the user is ready to run the linked program, a simple relocating loader as described in the previous section, can be used to load the program into memory. The only object code modification necessary is the addition of an actual load address to the relative values within the program. The linkage editor performs relocation of all control sections relative to the start of the linked program. Thus, all items that need to be modified at the load time have values that are relative to the start of the linked program. This means that the loading can be accomplished in one pass without the requirement of any external symbol table. This involves much less overhead than using a linking loader.

If a program is to be executed many times without being reassembled, the use of a linkage editor substantially reduces the overhead required. Resolution of external references and library searching are only performed once when the program is link edited. In contrast, a linking loader searches libraries and resolves external references every time the program is executed.

In some situations, the program is reassembled for nearly every execution. Such situation might occur in a program development and testing environment, or in a program which is used so infrequently that it is not necessary to store the assembled version of the program in a library. In such cases, it is much more efficient to use a linking loader, which avoids the steps of writing and reading the linked program.

The linked program that is produced by the linkage editor is generally in a form that is suitable for processing by a relocating loader. All external references are resolved, and relocation is indicated by some technique such as Modification Records or bit mask, as specified in the previous sections. Even though all the linking has been performed, information concerning the external references is often retained in the linked program. This allows subsequent re-linking of the program to replace control sections, modify external references, etc. If this information is not retained by the linkage editor, the linked program cannot be reprocessed; it can only be loaded and executed.

If the programmer already knows in advance the address where the program will be loaded, the linkage editor can perform all of the needed relocation. The result is a linked program that is an exact image of the way the program will appear in memory during execution. The content and processing of such an image is same as for an absolute object program. Normally the added flexibility of being able to load the program at any location is easily worth the slight overhead for performing relocation at load time.

Linkage editors can perform many other useful functions besides simply preparing an object program for execution. For example, a program that uses a large number of subroutines gets a subroutine changed due to some reason. The linkage editor needs to replace this newer version for the old one, to make the program function correctly. However, it is not necessary to go back to the original versions of all the subroutines. The following typical sequence of linkage editor commands can be used to accomplish this task:

```
INCLUDE    ABC(PROGLIB)
DELETE     PROJECT
```

```
INCLUDE     PROJECT (NEWLIB)
REPLACE     ABC(PROGLIB)
```

Linkage editors can also be used to build packages of subroutines or control sections that are normally used together. This is useful with the subroutine libraries that support high-level programming languages. In languages, there are routines which have a large number of cross-references between themselves because of their closely related functions. However, it is desirable for the reasons of program modularity and maintainability that they remain as separate control sections. If programs having calls to these routines are to be executed, all the cross-references need to be resolved individually. Exactly the same set of cross-references will need to be resolved for some other program which uses them. This represents a substantial amount of overhead. The linkage editor could be used to combine the appropriate subroutines into a package with a command sequence like the following:

```
INCLUDE READR(FTNLIB)
INCLUDE WRITR(FTNLIB)
INCLUDE BLOCK(FTNLIB)
:
:
SAVE FTNIO(SUBLIB)
```

The linked module named FTNIO could be indexed in the directory of SUBLIB under the same names as the original subroutine. Thus a search of SUBLIB before FTNLIB would retrieve FTNIO instead of all the separate routines which need to be linked together for execution. But as FTNIO has all the cross-references already resolved, they need not be resolved individually for each program. This process results in much more efficient linkage editing operation for each program and a considerable overall savings for the system.

Linkage editors allow the user to specify that external references are not to be resolved by automatic library search. For example some 50 programs in a language are using a similar routine; then resolving all these external references means that a total of 50 copies of the routine would be stored. If the library space is an important resource, such a solution might be undesirable. Hence using some commands, the user could specify that no library search be performed during linkage editing. Thus only the external references between the user-written routines would be resolved. A linking loader could then be used to combine the user routines with library routines at execution time. This process involves two separate linking operations, and hence requires a little overhead, but saves large library spaces.

Linkage editors often include a variety of other options and commands like those discussed for linking loaders. When compared to linking loaders, linkage editors offer more flexibility and control, with a slight increase in complexity and overhead.

6.6.2 FUNCTIONS OF THE LINKAGE EDITOR

Linkage editor input may consist of a combination of object modules, load modules, and control statements. The primary function of the linkage editor is to combine these modules, in accordance with the requirements stated on control statements, into a single output load module. Although this linking or combining of modules is its primary function, the linkage editor also:

- Edits modules by replacing, deleting, rearranging, and ordering control sections as directed by control statements.
- Aligns control sections and named common areas on 2K or 4K page boundaries as directed by control statements.
- Accepts additional input modules from data sets other than the primary input data set, either automatically, or upon request.
- Reserves storage for the common control sections generated by assembler and FORTRAN language translators, and static external areas generated by PL/I.
- Computes total length and assigns displacements for all pseudo registers (external dummy sections).
- Creates overlay programs in a structure defined by control statements.
- Creates mUltiple output load modules as directed by control statements.
- Provides special processing and diagnostic output options.
- Assigns module attributes that describe the structure, content, and logical format of the output load module.
- Allocates storage areas for linkage editor processing as specified by the programmer.
- Stores system status index information in the directory of the output module library (systems personnel only).
- Traces the processing history of a program.
- Allows the user to lengthen a control section or named common section without changing source code, reassembling, or recompiling.
- Allows the user to assign an authorization code to a load module that (a) makes it a restricted resource and (b) enables it to pass control to other restricted resources.

6.7 OVERVIEW OF DYNAMIC LINKING

As we have seen in overlay structure certain selective subroutines can be resident in the memory. That means it is not necessary to resident all the subroutines in the memory for all the time. Only necessary routines can be present in the main memory and during execution the required subroutines can be loaded in the memory. This process of postponing linking and loading of external reference until execution is called dynamic linking. For example suppose the subroutine main calls A, B, C, D then it is not desirable to load A, B, C and D along with the main in the memory. Whether A, B, C or D is called by the main or not will be known only at the time of execution. Hence keeping these routines already before are really not needed. As the subroutines get executed when the program runs. Also the linking of all the subroutines has to be performed. And the code of all the subroutines remains resident in the main memory. As a result of all this is that memory gets occupied unnecessarily. Typically "error routines" are such routines which can be invoked rarely. Then one can postpone the loading of these routines during the execution. If linking and loading of such rarely invoked external references could be postponed until the execution time when it was found to be absolutely necessary, then it increases the efficiency of overhead of the loader. In dynamic linking, the binder first prepares a load module in which along with program code the allocation and relocation information is stored. The loader simply loads the main module in the main memory. If any external ·reference to a subroutine comes, then the execution is suspended for a while, the loader brings the required subroutine in the main memory and then the execution process is resumed. Thus dynamic linking both the loading and linking is done dynamically.

6.7.1 DYNAMIC LINKING

A major disadvantage of all the previous schemes is that if a subroutine is referenced but never executed, the loader would still incur the overhead of linking the subroutine. Furthermore, all of these schemes require the programmer to explicitly name all procedures that might be called. It is not possible to write programs as follows:

```
..
READ        SUBNAME, ARGUMENT
ANSWER      = SUBNAME (ARGUMENT)
PRINT       ANSWER
.
```

where the name of the subroutine is an input parameter, SUBNAME, just like other data. Here we discuss a very general type of loading scheme called dynamic linking, in which loading and linking of external references is postponed until execution time. That is, the assembler produces text, binding, and relocation information from a source program. If the main program should execute a transfer instruction to an external address, or should reference an external variable, the loader is called. Only then is the segment containing the external reference is loaded.

An advantage here is that no overhead is incurred unless the procedure to be called or referenced is actually used. A further advantage is that the system can be dynamically reconfigured. But the major drawback of using this type of loading scheme is the considerable overhead and complexity incurred, due to the fact that we have postponed most of the binding process until execution time.

Linkage editors perform the task of linking before the program is loaded for execution. Linking loaders perform the same operations during load time. There can be a scenario when this operation is postponed until execution time. Hence, a subroutine is loaded and linked to the rest of the program when it is first called. Such linking scheme is known as dynamic linking, dynamic loading or load on call.

It is often used to allow several executing programs to share a single copy of subroutine or library. All programs in execution will be using a single copy of the shared subroutine, instead of loading their separate copies in memory. In object-oriented systems, dynamic linking is often used for references to software objects. This allows the implementation of an object and its methods to be determined at the time the program is executed. The implementation can be changed at any time without affecting the program that makes use of the object. Dynamic linking also makes it possible for one object to be shared by several programs.

It also provides some other advantages over the previous linking schemes. Suppose some program contains subroutines that are rarely used. Such routines need to be loaded and linked every time a program runs, even if the program is not using them for the entire execution time. Hence wasting memory and increasing the load time. Dynamic linking provides the ability of loading the routines only when they are needed. If the subroutines involved are fairly large, this can result in substantial saving of time and memory space.

Similarly, there can be programs which use a large number of subroutines, but cannot decide the exact subroutines to be used until the input from the user is examined. This situation could occur, for example, with programs that allow the users to interactively call any of the subroutines of a large mathematical or statistical library. Input data could be supplied by the user, and results could be displayed at the terminal. In such cases, the whole library needs to be loaded at the execution time, but only a few subroutines would be actually used from it. Dynamic linking avoids the necessity to load the entire library for each execution. The subroutine name can be treated as another input item, after the possible set is identified for loading.

There are a number of various mechanisms that can be used to accomplish dynamic loading and linking of subroutines. The figure 6.24 shows a method in which routines that are to be dynamically loaded must be called via an operating system service request. This method could be thought of as a request to a part of loader that is kept in memory during the execution of the program.

Whenever a user program makes a load-and-call service request to the operating system (dynamic loader residing in operating system) with the name of the routine as parameter, the dynamic loader examines its internal tables to determine if the routine is already loaded into memory. If not yet loaded, the routine is loaded from the specified user or system library as shown in the figure 6.24. Control is then passed from the dynamic loader to the routine just loaded.

When the processing of the routine finishes, the control is returned to the dynamic loader which then returns the control to the user program, which was responsible for calling of the routine. After the routine completes execution and the control returns to the user program, the memory allocated to the routine can be freed for later use by other processes. However, this is not done immediately. Sometimes it is desirable to retain this routine in memory for later use by the same or some other program. If a subroutine is still in memory, a second call to it may not require another load operation and the control is directly transferred to the routine by the dynamic loader.

While using dynamic linking, the association of an actual address with the symbolic name of the called routine is not made until the call statement is executed. Another way of describing the same scenario can be that the binding of the name to an actual address is delayed from load time until execution time. This delayed binding results in greater flexibility but requires more overhead since the operating system must intervene in the calling process. Hence, delayed binding gives more capabilities at a higher cost.

Advantages

1. The overhead on the loader is reduced. The required subroutine will be load in the main memory only at the time of execution.
2. The system can be dynamically reconfigured.

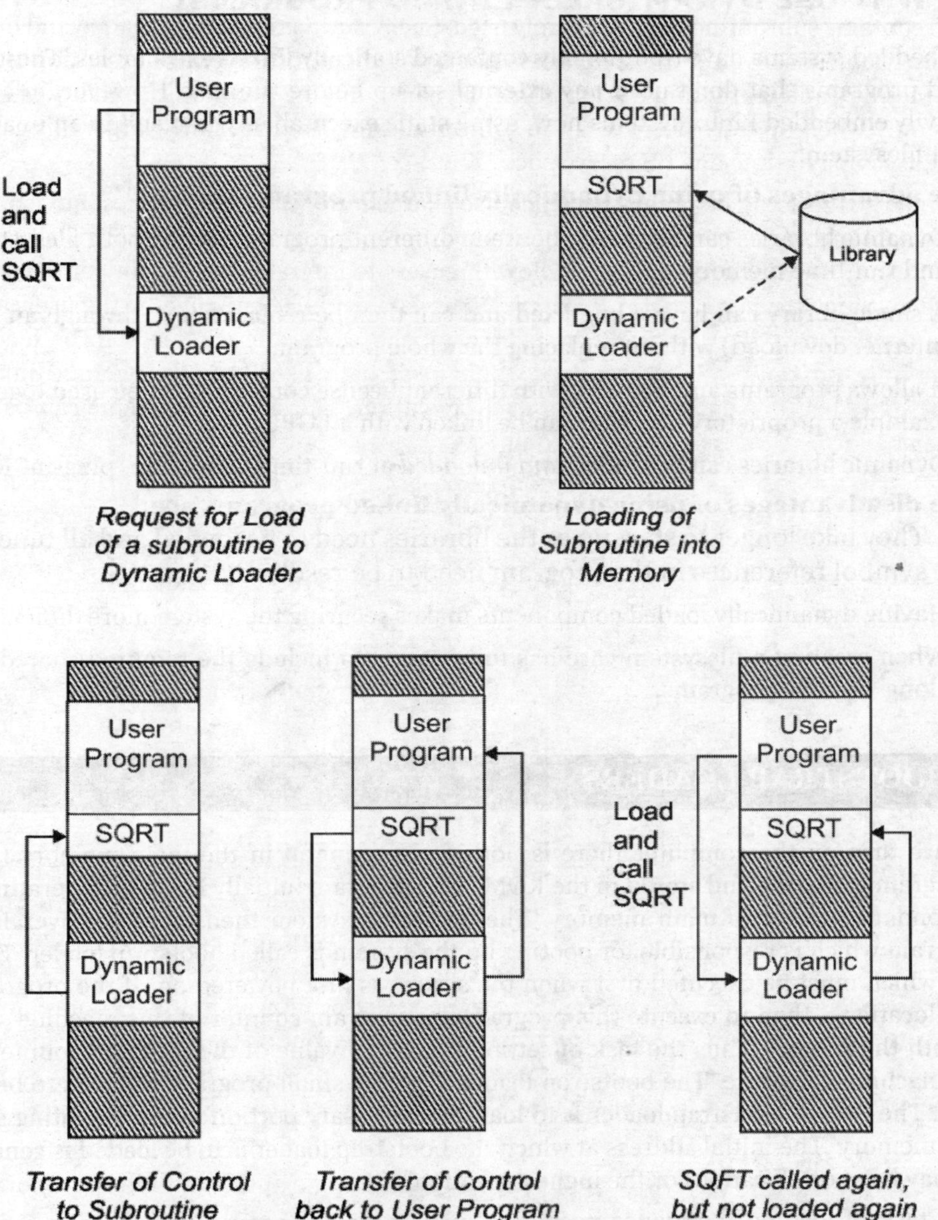

Figure 6.24: Loading and calling of a subroutine using Dynamic Linking

Disadvantages

1. The linking and loading need to be postponed until the execution. During the execution if at all any subroutine is needed then the process of execution needs to be suspended until the required subroutine gets loaded in the main memory.

6.7.2 WHY USE DYNAMICALLY LINKED PROGRAMS?

Embedded systems have traditionally contained statically linked executables. These are self-contained programs that don't need any external set-up before running. However, in all but the most heavily embedded Linux systems now, using static executables will result in an unacceptably large root filesystem.

The advantages of using dynamically linked programs are:

- Dynamic libraries can be shared between different programs saving both filesystem space and run-time memory;
- A single library can have a bug fixed and can then be replaced (e.g. through an over-the-internet download) without replacing the whole program;
- It allows programs and libraries with different license constraints to be used together. For example a proprietary program can be linked with a LGPL library;
- Dynamic libraries can be loaded *and unloaded* at run-time to provide "plug-in" features.

The disadvantages of using dynamically linked programs are:

- They take longer to start up as the libraries need to be loaded and all function and symbol references in the program need to be resolved;
- Having dynamically loaded components makes securing the system more difficult;
- When creating a filesystem care has to be taken to include the required shared libraries along with the programs.

6.8 BOOTSTRAP LOADERS

As we turn on the computer there is nothing meaningful in the main memory (RAM). A small program is written and stored in the ROM. This program initially loads the operating system from secondary storage to main memory. The operating system then takes the overall control. This program which is responsible for booting up the system is called bootstrap loader. This is the program which must be executed first when the system is first powered on. If the program starts from the location x then to execute this program the program counter of this machine should be loaded with the value x. Thus the task of setting the initial value of the program counter is to be done by machine hardware. The bootstrap loader is a very small program which is to be fitted in the ROM. The task of bootstrap loader is to load the necessary portion of the operating system in the main memory .The initial address at which the bootstrap loader is to be loaded is generally the lowest (may be at 0th location) or the highest location.

The task of loading the loader itself into memory is performed by operating system. But the operating system also needs some loader as a system program, so that the computer with no program currently in memory can get things started. For the empty and idle machine, there is no need for program relocation. The address can be specified as an absolute address for any program that needs to be loaded into memory. Most often, this would be operating system and will occupy some predefined location in memory. Hence, some means is required for accomplishing the functions of an absolute loader.

Early computers required an operator to enter the object code for an absolute loader into the memory, by using switches on the console of the computer. However, the process is too expensive and error-prone. Some computers have an absolute loader program resident in the read-only memory (ROM) of system. Whenever the system is rebooted, the machine begins to execute this program from ROM. Some computers execute the loader directly from the ROM while some transfer the program into main memory and then execute it. However, some machines do not have such a read-only memory available. Moreover, if any modifications are required in the loader program, it is inconvenient to change it.

An intermediate solution has to be designed in the form of a built-in hardware function that reads a fixed-length record from some device at a fixed memory location. The particular device to be used can be selected with the use of some console switches. After the record is read, control is automatically transferred to the address where the record is stored in memory. The record is a bunch of machine instructions that further load the absolute program. If the loading process needs more instructions than those present in this record, the first record can help the loading of other records, and these in turn can help loading others. Hence the term bootstrap is used. The first record that is loaded into memory is known as bootstrap loader. This loader facilitates the loading of all those object programs which are loaded into a bare and idle machine. They can be operating system, or any other such program that is to be executed without an operating system.

Hence bootstrap loader is an absolute loader that loads the first program in the memory to be executed, i.e. operating system.

6.8.1 HOW BOOT LOADERS WORKS?

The BIOS is the firmware in the ROM of a PC. When the PC is powered up, the BIOS is the first program that runs. All other programs must be loaded into RAM first. The BIOS contains the following parts:

- POST (Power On Self Test). The running counter that counts the kilobytes of main memory is the most visible part of the POST.
- The Setup Menu, that lets you set some parameters and lets you adjust the real time clock. Most modern BIOS versions let you set the boot order, the devices that BIOS checks for booting. These can be A (the first floppy disk), C (the first hard disk), CD-ROM and possibly other disks as well. The first device in the list will be tried first. Older BIOS-es have only one boot order: A, C. So the BIOS will try to boot from A first and if there is no diskette in the drive it tries to boot from C.
- The boot sector loader. This loads the first 512-byte sector from the boot disk into RAM and jumps to it. This is where the boot loaders described in this paper start.
- The BIOS interrupts. These are simple device drivers that programs can use to access the screen, the keyboard and disks. Boot loaders rely on them, most operating systems do not (the Linux kernel does not use BIOS interrupts once it has been started). MSDOS does use BIOS interrupts.

Apart from the main BIOS there are extension ROMs, which are started by the main BIOS. Every VGA card has one. Also SCSI host adapters and Ethernet cards can have an extension ROM.

It is even possible to put an EPROM on an Ethernet card to boot a machine over the network without any disks.

As far as boot loading facilities are concerned, the PC BIOS is very primitive compared to that of other computer systems. The only thing it knows about disks is how to load the first 512-byte sector.

- The first sector of a diskette can be loaded at address 0000:7C00. The last two bytes of the sector are checked for the values 0x55 and 0xAA, this as a rough sanity check. If these are OK, the BIOS jump to the address 0000:7C00.
- Booting from a hard disk is very similar to booting from a diskette. The first sector of a hard disk (often called the Master Boot Record) is loaded at 0000:7C00 and next the BIOS jump to it. The MBR program must move itself to an address that is different from 0000:7C00 as it is supposed to load a different boot sector from a partition to address 0000:7C00 and jump to that. Modern BIOS versions can treat a certain file on a CD-ROM as a diskette image. They pretend to boot from a diskette by loading the first 512 bytes of the file to 0000:7C00 and jumping to it. Every attempt to access the same diskette using the BIOS routines will be redirected to the image file on CD-ROM. Some other ways to boot a CD-ROM may also be supported (with an emulated hard disk or with no disk emulation at all).

When the boot sector is loaded, the CPU is in real mode. For those who are unfamiliar with 80x86 architecture: real mode is very limited compared to 32-bit protected mode (in which Linux runs). For example: data outside a 64K segment can only be accessed if you change a segment register and data outside the first 1MB of address space (which contains 640kB of main memory) cannot be accessed at all. As GCC does not know about real mode, programs compiled with it can only be run in real mode with some tricks and with severe memory size restrictions. This is the reason why most boot loaders (except GRUB) are written in assembly. All boot sector programs, even that of GRUB are written in assembly[1].

In theory a boot loader could do its job by directly accessing the bare metal, but 512 bytes would be a very small space for that. The boot loader has access to BIOS interrupts, which are subroutines that can be invoked by the INT instruction (software interrupts). These work in real mode only. The following routines are used by most boot loaders.

- INT 0x10 for screen output.
- INT 0x16 for keyboard input.
- INT 0x13 for disk I/O. The parameters to specify sectors on disk used to have a very limited range. Originally it was only possible to specify 1024 cylinders on a hard disk, while hard disks can have more cylinders. This imposed limitations on where it was allowed to put the boot loader and any files accessed by it. You were forced to create a small partition near the start of the hard disk and put the boot loader there. There are three categories of BIOS:
    - o BIOS versions earlier than 1995 could only access IDE disks of around 500MB, as the BIOS sector and head numbers corresponded directly to the register values on the IDE interface.
    - o BIOS versions between 1995 and 1998 can access IDE disks up to about 8GB. They translate the cylinder, head and sector numbers from the INT 0x13 call to different values that better utilize the allowable ranges on the IDE interface.

- o BIOS versions of 1998 or later have a new calling interface using linear block addresses.

  In any of the three categories you have BIOS-es that have bugs that cause them to stop at a lower disk size limit (a category 2 BIOS that should work up to 8GB, but stops at 2GB). In those cases it makes sense to upgrade to a new BIOS version.

- INT 0x15 is a catch-all for many BIOS functions, one of which is moving data to extended memory (the BIOS is required to switch to protected mode temporarily to do that). Other functions are for disabling the A20 gate and for determining the memory size.

6.8.2 PARTS OF A BOOT LOADER

A boot loader typically consists of three programs:

- The **boot sector program** is directly loaded by the BIOS at boot time and is only 512 bytes in size.
- The **second stage program** is loaded by the boot sector program and it does everything you expect the boot loader to do.
- The **boot loader installer** is not run when the system is booted, but it is used to install the boot loader and the second stage program onto the boot disk. These have to be stored in special locations, so they cannot be copied with cp.

6.8.2.1 BOOT SECTOR PROGRAM

The boot sector program can only be 512 bytes in size and not all 512 bytes are even available in all cases. The last two bytes must be 0x55 and 0xAA for the BIOS. The Master Boot Record on a hard disk contains the partition table of 64 bytes, so only the first 446 bytes can be used. If the boot sector program must exist on a DOS partition or on a DOS diskette, there must be a parameter block at the start of the boot sector.

Because of these size restrictions, boot sector programs are just about the only remaining examples of programs on the PC platform that are truly optimized for size and have to be written in assembly for this reason. Further, a boot sector program cannot do everything you want a boot loader to do. Usually a boot sector program does one of the following things (not all three in one program):

- Load another boot sector. This is typical for a boot sector program that lives in the master boot record of a hard disk. It can find the first sector of the selected *active* partition and *chain load* that. The MBR program that came traditionally with MS-DOS has no ability to change the active partition at boot time. There are other boot sector programs that let you select a partition by pressing a key, such as the MBR program of LILO.
- Load a second stage boot loader. It is generally not possible for a boot sector program to look into the directory for a file with a specific name and load that into memory, but exceptions exist, at least for DOS file systems[2]. Most boot sector programs find the second stage by sector number rather than by name. The sector numbers have to be put into the boot sector by the boot loader installer.
- Load the kernel directly. A kernel is typically much larger than a second stage boot loader.

  The boot sector program in the Linux kernel loads the kernel directly into memory without the need for a second stage boot loader. As the kernel is located in contiguous sectors on a diskette, there is no need to traverse file system data structures. However, for bZimage kernels the boot sector program cheats; it invokes a subroutine in the setup part of the kernel for loading the rest of the kernel into high memory.

The boot loader e2boot fits into the first 1kB block of an ext2 partition (it is twice as big as a boot sector program), but with some tricks it finds both the kernel and the RAM disk by name on an ext2 partition and loads them into memory.

Also the boot sector on a DOS disk does not utilize a second stage boot loader to load the MS-DOS kernel files IO.SYS and MSDOS.SYS. The structure of an MSDOS file system is simple enough to find a file with a specific name in the root directory and load it into memory, at least part of it.

6.8.2.2 SECOND STAGE OF BOOT LOADER

This is the real boot program. It contains the user interface and the kernel loader. It can be anywhere from 6.5 kilobytes (LILO) to over 100 kilobytes (GRUB) in size. It contains the following functions:

- User interface. It is a simple command line (old versions of LILO), a menu or both. It allows you to select any number of operating systems and to specify additional parameters to the operating system. The available options are specified by a configuration file. Modern versions of boot loaders can show their menu in a bitmap picture.
- Operating system loader. loads the operating system into memory and runs it. Alternatively we can load another boot loader specific to another operating system and let it run. This is called chain loading.

LOADLIN is not a complete boot loader, but it has only the second stage (without the user interface). It is run from DOS, and it can make use of DOS system calls to read files from disk. What makes its task harder than that of a normal boot loader, it that it must be able to work its way out of some types of memory managers.

6.8.2.3 BOOT LOADER INSTALLER

The third part of the boot loader is only run when the boot loader is installed on a disk. As opposed to the boot sector program and second stage, this is a normal Linux program. In the case of LILO the installer must be rerun each time the configuration is changed or any file has been updated. It performs the following tasks:

- Install the boot sector. If the boot sector will be installed in the MBR of a hard disk or on a DOS file system, not all 512 bytes may be overwritten, but the partition table or the DOS parameter block must be preserved.
- Tell the boot sector where the second stage boot loader is. Usually it writes one or more sector addresses into the boot loader.
- Tell the second stage boot loader where all relevant information is (configuration, kernels). This is the case with LILO. LILO creates a map file that contains all relevant sector addresses and puts pointers to the map file in the boot sector and/or second stage boot loader.

EXERCISES

1. What do you mean by loader?
2. Explain the various types of loaders?
3. What do you mean by absolute loader?
4. Explain the various schemes of loader?
5. Explain the compile-and-go loader scheme?
6. Explain the design of absolute loader?
7. Explain the simple bootstrap loader?
8. Explain the features of machine dependent loader?
9. What do you mean by relocation?
10. Explain the concept of relocating loader?
11. What do you mean by linking?
12. Describe the concept of program linking?
13. What do you mean by linkage editors?
14. Explain the working of linkage editors?
15. What are the functions of linkage editors?
16. What do you mean by dynamic linking?
17. Describe the concept of bootstrap loaders?
18. Explain the various parts of boot loader?

Chapter 7

Operating System

7.1 INTRODUCTION

Operating system (OS) is a program or set of programs, which acts as an interface between a user of the computer and the computer hardware. The main purpose of an OS is to provide an environment in which we can execute programs. The main goals of the OS are (i) To make the computer system convenient to use, (ii) To make the use of computer hardware in efficient way.

Operating System is system software, which may be viewed as collection of software consisting of procedures for operating the computer and providing an environment for execution of programs. It's an interface between user and computer. So an OS makes everything in the computer to work together smoothly and efficiently.

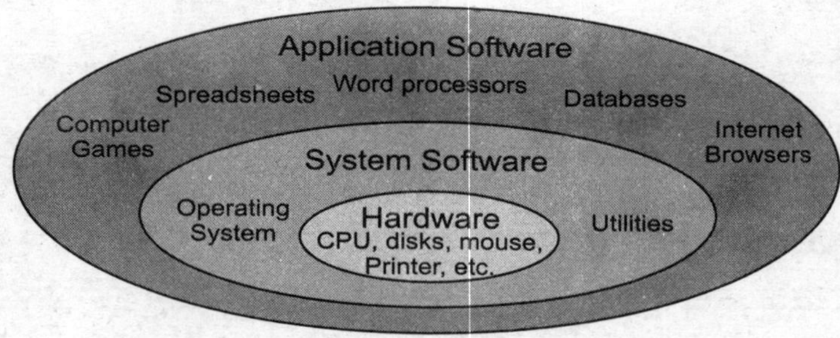

Figure 7.1: The relationship between application and system software

Basically, an OS has three main responsibilities: (a) Perform basic tasks such as recognizing input from the keyboard, sending output to the display screen, keeping track of files and directories on the disk, and controlling peripheral devices such as disk drives and printers (b) Ensure that different programs and users running at the same time do not interfere with each other; and (c) Provide a software platform on top of which other programs can run. The OS is also responsible for security, ensuring that unauthorized users do not access the system. Figure 7.1 illustrates the relationship between application software and system software. The first two responsibilities address the need for managing the computer hardware and the application programs that use the hardware. The third responsibility focuses on providing an interface between application software and hardware so that application software can be efficiently developed. Since the OS is already responsible for managing the hardware, it should provide a programming interface for application developers. As a user, we normally interact with the OS through a set of commands. The commands are accepted and executed by a part of the OS called the command processor or command line interpreter.

In order to understand operating systems we must understand the computer hardware and the development of OS from beginning. Hardware means the physical machine and its electronic components including memory chips, input/output devices, storage devices and the central processing unit. Software is the programs written for these computer systems. Main memory is where the data and instructions are stored to be processed. Input/Output devices are the peripherals attached to the system, such as keyboard, printers, disk drives, CD drives, magnetic tape drives, modem, monitor, etc. The central processing unit is the brain of the computer system; it has circuitry to control the interpretation and execution of instructions. It controls the operation of entire computer system. All of the storage references, data manipulations and I/O operations are performed by the CPU. The entire computer systems can be divided into four parts or components (1) The hardware (2) The OS (3) The application programs and system programs (4) The users. The hardware provides the basic computing power. The system programs the way in which these resources are used to solve the computing problems of the users. There may be many different users trying to solve different problems. The OS controls and coordinates the use of the hardware among the various users and the application programs.

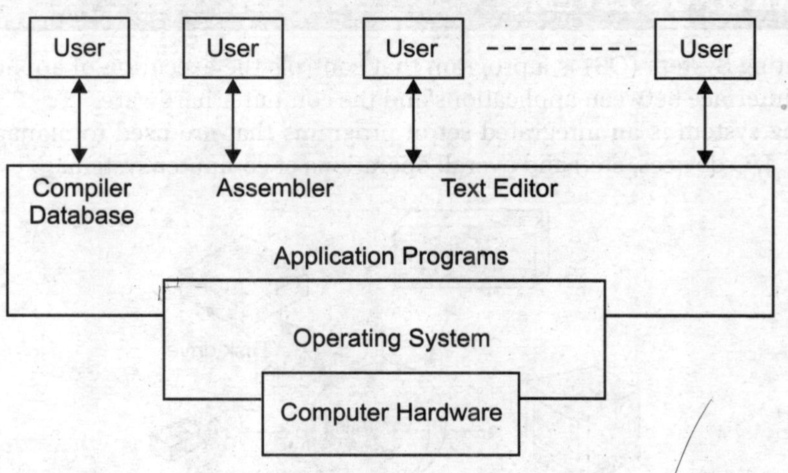

Figure 7.2: Basic components of a computer system

We can view an OS as a resource allocator. A computer system has many resources, which are to be required to solve a computing problem. These resources are the CPU time, memory space, files storage space, input/output devices and so on. The OS acts as a manager of all of these resources and allocates them to the specific programs and users as needed by their tasks. Since there can be many conflicting requests for the resources, the OS must decide which requests are to be allocated resources to operate the computer system fairly and efficiently.

An OS can also be viewed as a control program, used to control the various I/O devices and the users programs. A control program controls the execution of the user programs to prevent errors and improper use of the computer resources. It is especially concerned with the operation and control of I/O devices. As stated above the fundamental goal of computer system is to execute user programs and solve user problems. For this goal computer hardware is constructed. But the bare hardware is not easy to use and for this purpose application/system programs are developed. These various programs require some common operations, such as controlling/use of some input/output devices and the use of CPU time for execution. The common functions of controlling and allocation of resources between different users and application programs is brought together into one piece of software called operating system. It is easy to define operating systems by what they do rather than what they are. The primary goal of the operating systems is convenience for the user to use the computer. Operating systems makes it easier to compute. A secondary goal is efficient operation of the computer system. The large computer systems are very expensive, and so it is desirable to make them as efficient as possible. Operating systems thus makes the optimal use of computer resources. In order to understand what operating systems are and what they do, we have to study how they are developed. Operating systems and the computer architecture have a great influence on each other. To facilitate the use of the hardware operating systems were developed.

An Operating system is concerned with the allocation of resources and services, such as memory, processors, devices and information. The Operating System correspondingly includes programs to manage these resources, such as a traffic controller, a scheduler, memory management module, I/O programs, and a file system.

7.2 OPERATING SYSTEMS

An Operating System (OS) is a program that controls the execution of application programs and acts as an interface between applications and the computer hardware.

"Operating system is an integrated set of programs that are used to manage the resources (CPU, memory, I/O devices, etc.) and overall operations of computer systems."

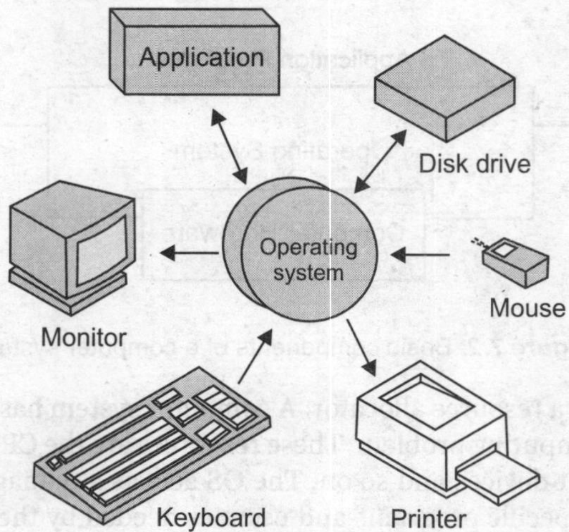

Figure 7.3: Operating System

Operating System is a set of master programs, which is designed to control entire operation of the computer. This is the software that is required in order to run other application software. The operating system can be regarded as a track on which the train runs. As the track acts as a strong link between earth and the train, operating system also acts as a strong link between the hardware and the user of the computer. To run the train, track has to be installed first; similarly the operating system is required in the system to make it operational. It is loaded automatically into the computer whenever we start the computer. Operating system is general-purpose software which is involved in each and every activity of the computer. The operating system decides when and how to process which data, where to store the processed data and from where to supply the data when user requests.

According to this definition, here are the three objectives of operating system:

- **Convenience:** An OS makes a computer more convenient to use.
- **Efficiency:** An OS allows the computer system resources to be used in an efficient manner.
- **Ability to evolve:** An OS should be constructed in such a way as to permit the effective development, testing, and introduction of new system functions without interfering with service.

7.3 WHY WE NEED OPERATING SYSTEM?

For a computer to be able to operate a **computer program** (sometimes known as application or software), the machine must be able to perform a certain number of preparatory operations to ensure exchange between the processor, the memory and the physical resources (peripherals).

The **operating system** (sometimes referred to by its abbreviation OS), is responsible for creating the link between the material resources, the user and the applications (word processor, video game, etc.). When a program wants to access a material resource, it does not need to send specific information to the peripheral device but it simply sends the information to the operating system, which conveys it to the relevant peripheral via its driver. If there are no drivers, each program has to recognize and take into account the communication with each type of peripheral.

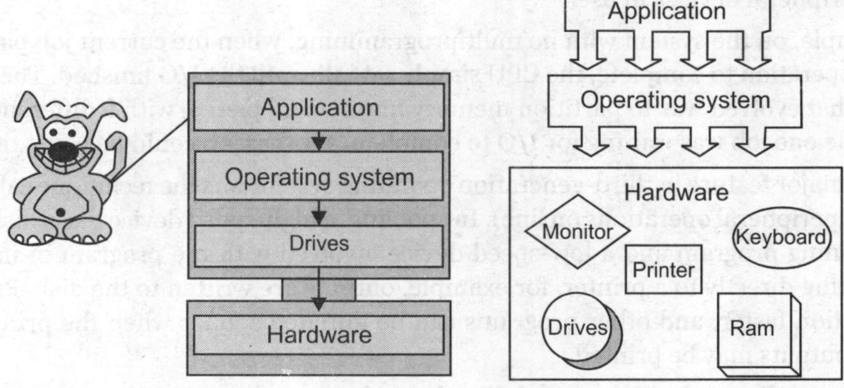

Figure 7.4: The Operating System in a Hierarchy

The operating system thus allows the "dissociation" of programmes and hardware, mainly to simplify resource management and offer the user a simplified Man-machine interface (MMI) to overcome the complexity of the actual machine.

7.4 EVOLUTION OF OPERATING SYSTEMS

Historically operating systems have been tightly related to the computer architecture, it is good idea to study the history of operating systems from the architecture of the computers on which they run.

Operating systems have evolved through a number of distinct phases or generations which corresponds roughly to the decades.

The 1940's - First Generations

The earliest electronic digital computers had no operating systems. Machines of the time were so primitive that programs were often entered one bit at time on rows of mechanical switches (plug boards). Programming languages were unknown (not even assembly languages). Operating systems were unheard of.

The 1950's - Second Generation

By the early 1950's, the routine had improved somewhat with the introduction of punch cards. The General Motors Research Laboratories implemented the first operating systems in early 1950's for their IBM 701. The system of the 50's generally ran one job at a time. These were called single-stream batch processing systems because programs and data were submitted in groups or batches.

The 1960's - Third Generation

The systems of the 1960's were also batch processing systems, but they were able to take better advantage of the computer's resources by running several jobs at once. So operating systems designers developed the concept of multiprogramming in which several jobs are in main memory at once; a processor is switched from job to job as needed to keep several jobs advancing while keeping the peripheral devices in use.

For example, on the system with no multiprogramming, when the current job paused to wait for other I/O operation to complete, the CPU simply sat idle until the I/O finished. The solution for this problem that evolved was to partition memory into several pieces, with a different job in each partition. While one job was waiting for I/O to complete, another job could be using the CPU.

Another major feature in third-generation operating system was the technique called spooling (simultaneous peripheral operations on line). In spooling, a high-speed device like a disk interposed between a running program and a low-speed device involved with the program in input/output. Instead of writing directly to a printer, for example, outputs are written to the disk. Programs can run to completion faster, and other programs can be initiated sooner when the printer becomes available, the outputs may be printed.

Note that spooling technique is much like thread being spun to a spool so that it may be later be unwound as needed.

Another feature present in this generation was time-sharing technique, a variant of multiprogramming technique, in which each user has an on-line (i.e., directly connected) terminal. Because the user is present and interacting with the computer, the computer system must respond quickly to user requests, otherwise user productivity could suffer. Timesharing systems were developed to multiprogram large number of simultaneous interactive users.

Fourth Generation

With the development of LSI (Large Scale Integration) circuits, chips, operating system entered in the system entered in the personal computer and the workstation age. Microprocessor technology evolved to the point that it becomes possible to build desktop computers as powerful as the mainframes of the 1970s. Two operating systems have dominated the personal computer scene: MS-DOS, written by Microsoft, Inc. for the IBM PC and other machines using the Intel 8088 CPU and its successors, and UNIX, which is dominant on the large personal computers using the Motorola 6899 CPU family.

Although many UNIX users, especially experienced programmers, prefer a command-based interface to a GUI, nearly all UNIX systems support a windowing system called the **X Windows** system produced at M.I.T. This system handles the basic window management, allowing users to create, delete, move, and resize windows using a mouse. Often a complete GUI, such as **Motif,** is available to run on top of the X Windows system giving UNIX a look and feel something like the Macintosh or Microsoft Windows, for those UNIX users who want such a thing.

An interesting development that began taking place during the mid-1980s is the growth of networks of personal computers running **network operating systems** and **distributed operating** systems (Tanenbaum and Van Steen, 2002). In a network operating system, the users are aware of the existence of multiple computers and can log in to remote machines and copy files from one machine to another. Each machine runs its own local operating system and has its own local user (or users).

Network operating systems are not fundamentally different from single-processor operating systems. They obviously need a network interface controller and some low-level software to drive it, as well as programs to achieve remote login and remote file access, but these additions do not change the essential structure of the operating system.

A distributed operating system, in contrast, is one that appears to its users as a traditional uniprocessor system, even though it is actually composed of multiple processors. The users should not be aware of where their programs are being run or where their files are located; that should all be handled automatically and efficiently by the operating system.

True distributed operating systems require more than just adding a little code to a uniprocessor operating system, because distributed and centralized systems differ in critical ways. Distributed systems, for example, often allow applications to run on several processors at the same time, thus requiring more complex processor scheduling algorithms in order to optimize the amount of parallelism.

Communication delays within the network often mean that these (and other) algorithms must run with incomplete, outdated, or even incorrect information. This situation is radically different from a single processor system in which the operating system has complete information about the system state.

7.5 OPERATING SYSTEM INTERFACES

The operating system is the core software component of your computer. It performs many functions and is, in very basic terms, an interface between your computer and the outside world. In the section about hardware, a computer is described as consisting of several component parts including your monitor, keyboard, mouse, and other parts. The operating system provides an interface to these parts using what is referred to as "drivers". This is why sometimes when you install a new printer or other piece of hardware, your system will ask you to install more software called a driver.

7.5.1 WHAT DOES A DRIVER DO?

A driver is a specially written program which understands the operation of the device it interfaces to, such as a printer, video card, sound card or CD ROM drive. It translates commands from the operating system or user into commands understood by the component computer part it interfaces with. It also translates responses from the component computer part back to responses that can be understood by the operating system, application program, or user. The figure 7.5 gives a graphical depiction of the interfaces between the operating system and the computer component.

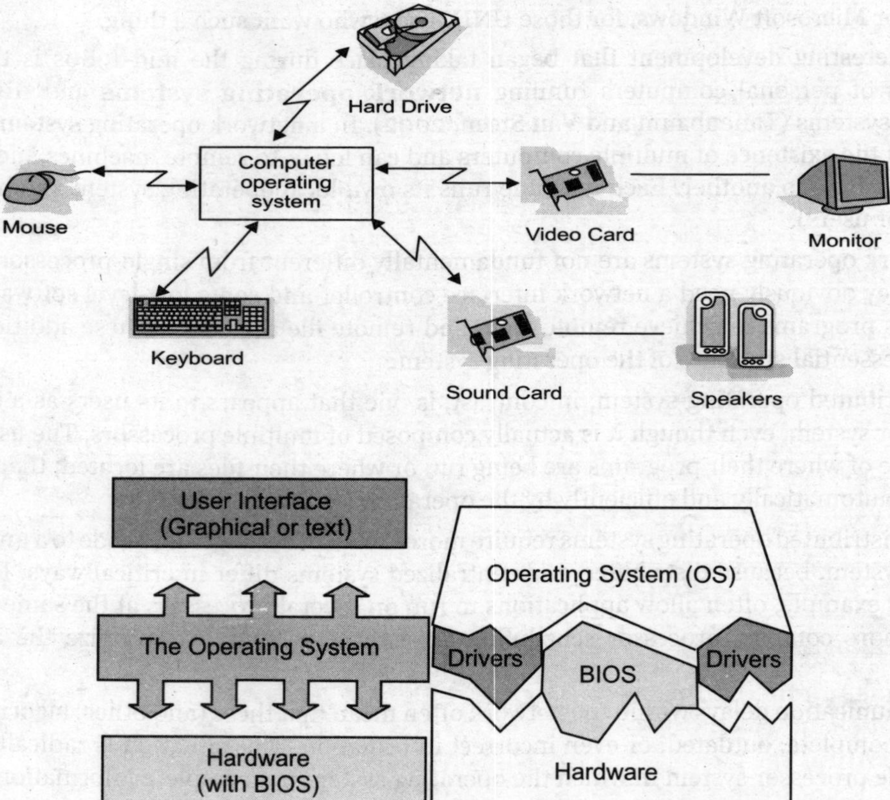

Figure 7.5: System Software

Operating Systems are resource managers. The main resource is computer hardware in the form of processors, storage, input/output devices, communication devices, and data. Some of the operating system functions are: implementing the user interface, sharing hardware among users, allowing users to share data among themselves, preventing users from interfering with one another, scheduling resources among users, facilitating input/output, recovering from errors, accounting for resource usage, facilitating parallel operations, organizing data for secure and rapid access, and handling network communications.

7.5.2 SYSTEM PERFORMANCE

Efficiency of an operating system and overall performance of a computer system are measured usually in terms of the following parameters.

1. Throughput: The amount of work that system can take to do per unit time is called Throughput. It is measured as the number of processes completed by the system per unit time.

For example: Suppose a system is able to complete N number of processes in time T seconds, its throughput is N/T processes per seconds during that interval. Throughput is measured normally in processes/hour.

Note: Throughput of a system does not depend on its jobs processing efficiency only, but also on the nature of jobs processed. For long processes, throughput of a system may be one process per hour, whereas for short processes, it may be 100 processes per hour for the same system.

2. Turnaround time: Turnaround time is the interval between the time of submission of a join to the system for processing to the time of completion of the job. How long it takes a system to complete a job submitted by user.

Higher throughput is desirable form the point of view of overall system performance; individual users are more interested in better turnarounds time for their jobs.

3. Response time: It is the interval between the time of submission of a job to the system for processing to the time of the system producing the first response for the job back to the user.

Response time is used when the turnaround time is not suitable.

For example: In case of interactive systems, a process can produce some output early during its execution and can continue executing while previous results are being output to the user.

In any computer system, it is desirable to maximize and minimize turnaround time and response time.

7.5.3 ROLES OF THE OPERATING SYSTEM

The operating system has various roles:

- **Management of the processor:** the operating system is responsible for managing allocation of the processor between the different programmes using a **scheduling algorithm**. The type of scheduler is totally dependent on the operating system, according to the desired objective.
- **Management of the random access memory:** the operating system is responsible

for managing the memory space allocated to each application and, where relevant, to each user. If there is insufficient physical memory, the operating system can create a memory zone on the hard drive, known as "**virtual memory**". The virtual memory lets you run applications requiring more memory than there is available RAM on the system. However, this memory is a great deal slower.

- **Management of input/output:** the operating system allows unification and control of access of programmes to material resources via drivers (also known as peripheral administrators or input/output administrators).
- **Management of execution of applications:** the operating system is responsible for smooth execution of applications by allocating the resources required for them to operate. This means an application that is not responding correctly can be "killed". **Management of authorisations:** the operating system is responsible for security relating to execution of programmes by guaranteeing that the resources are used only by programmes and users with the relevant authorisations.
- **File management:** the operating system manages reading and writing in the file system and the user and application file access authorisations.
- **Information management:** the operating system provides a certain number of indicators that can be used to diagnose the correct operation of the machine.

7.6 INTERRUPTS

An **interrupt** is a hardware-generated change-of-flow within the system. An interrupt handler deals with the cause of the interrupt. The control is then returned to the interrupted context and instruction.

7.6.1 FUNCTIONS OF INTERRUPTS

Each computer architecture has its own interrupt mechanism but they all have several functions in common.

Below is a brief list of the common functions of interrupts:

- When an interrupt occurs, the control is transferred to the interrupt service routine. The interrupt service routine is generally accessed through an interrupt vector. Interrupt vector knows where to find the appropriate interrupt service routine for the current interrupt.
- The interrupt architecture must save the address of the instruction that has been interrupted (the program counter).
- Incoming interrupts must be disabled if there is an interrupt currently being processed. This is to prevent interrupts from being lost or overwritten by newly arriving interrupts.
- An interrupt is generally caused by a hardware device such as a device driver letting the CPU know that some data has been read from the device and is waiting in the local device buffer.
- A trap is a software-generated interrupt that is either caused by an error or by a user request for an I/O operation.

- An operating system is interrupt driven. This means that if there are no interrupts, then the system will be idle.
- The operating system must preserve the state of the CPU by storing the contents of the registers and the program counter.
- The operating system must determine which type of interrupt has occurred. This can be done either by polling or by using a vectored interrupt system. Polling is the systematic checking of each device to see if it was the device responsible for generating the interrupt. If the operating system has a vectored interrupt system, then the identity of the device and the type of interrupt will be easily identifiable without checking each device.
- The operating system must provide a segment of code that specifies what action is to be taken in the event of an interrupt. There must be a code segment that is specific to each type of interrupt.

7.6.2 CLASSIFICATION OF INTERRUPTS

Different **classes of interrupts** are as follows:

1. Supervisor Call Interrupts (SVC): These interrupts are initiated by a running process that executes SVC instruction. It is a user request for a particular system service such as performing I/O or obtaining more storage etc.
2. I/O Interrupts: These are initiated by I/O. hardware. These interrupts send signal to CPU to indicate that the status of a channel or device has changed. I/O interrupts occur when I/O operation completes, I/O error occurs or a device gets ready etc.
3. External Interrupts: These are caused by different events. These events can the" expiration of a quantum on interrupting clock, pressing of interrupt key or receipt of a signal from another processor in a multiprocessor system etc.
4. Restart Interrupts: These interrupts occur when the restart button of console is pressed or restart signal is received from another processor in multiprocessor system.
5. Program Check Interrupt: These are caused by different problems during the execution of machine language instructions. Some problems include division by zero, arithmetic overflow or underflow, wrong format of data etc.
6. Machine Check Interrupts: These are caused by the hardware that does not function, properly.

7.7 SYSTEM CALLS

System calls provide an interface between a running program and operating system. System calls are generally available as assembly language instructions. Several higher level languages such as C also allow making system calls directly.

The system call interface layer contains entry point in kernel code. All system resources are managed, by the kernel. Any request from user or application that involves access to any system resource must be handled by kernel code. The user process must not be given open access to kernel code for security reason. Many opening into kernel code called system calls are provided to user so that the user processes can invoke the execution of kernel code. System calls allow processes and users to manipulate system resources.

There are three general methods that are used to pass information (parameters) between a running program and the operating system.

- One method is to store parameters in registers.
- Another is to store parameters in a table in memory and pass the address of table.
- The third method is to push parameters on stack and allow operating system to pop the parameters off the stack.

7.7.1 TYPES OF SYSTEM CALLS

The main **types of system calls** are as follows:

1. **Process Control:** These types of system calls are used to control the processes. Some examples are end, abort, load, execute, create process, terminate process etc.
2. **File Management:** These types of system calls are used to manage files. Some examples are Create file, delete file, open, close, read, write etc.
3. **Device Management:** These types of system calls are used to manage devices. Some examples are Request device, release device, read, write, get device attributes etc.
4. **Information Maintenance:** These types of system calls are used to maintain information. Some examples are Get time or date, set time or date, get system data, set system data etc.
5. **Communications:** These types of system calls are used to for communication. Some examples are Create, delete communication connection, send, receive messages etc.

7.8 SINGLE USER OPERATING SYSTEM

A single user OS as the name suggests is designed for one user to effectively use a computer at a time. A single-user operating system is a type of operating system (OS) that is developed and intended for use on a computer or similar machine that will only have a single user at any given time. This is the most common type of OS used on a home computer, as well as on computers in offices and other work environments. There are two general types of single-user operating system: single task and multitasking systems. Though a single-user operating system can be connected to other systems through a network, it is still truly only used by a single person and is different than a multi-user OS.

The operating system installed onto a computer is responsible for handling a number of different tasks and is typically one of the most important programs used on a computer. An operating system manages memory usage and other resources, as well as hardware connectivity and the proper execution of other applications. There are several different types of operating systems, but the single-user operating system is typically the most common.

A single-user operating system that is a single task system is developed for use with a computer or electronic device that will only run one application at a time. This type of OS is typically used on devices such as wireless phones and two-way messaging devices. A single task, single-user operating system can only run one program or application at a time, and so is not as useful for a computer or other device intended to run multiple programs at once.

This is where a multitasking single-user operating system is used instead. A multitasking OS can run multiple applications and programs at once. This is often used on computers where someone may wish to navigate the Internet, run a graphics editing program, play music through a media playing program, and type in notes in a simple word processing program all simultaneously.

A single task OS could not do this, but the multitasking systems are able to handle all of these processes.

Even though a single-user operating system can connect to other computers and systems through a network, it is still only being used by a single user. As long as the computer only has one monitor, keyboard and other input devices, then it is a single-user system. Other computers may be able to access data on the computer, but unless the users of those computers can also run applications on the computer that they see on monitors on their own end, it is still a single-user system.

- **Single-user, single task:** As the name implies, this operating system is designed to manage the computer so that one user can effectively do one thing at a time. The Palm OS for Palm handheld computers is a good example of a modern single-user, single-task operating system.
- **Single-user, multi-tasking:** This is the type of operating system most people use on their desktop and laptop computers today. Microsoft's Windows and Apple's MacOS platforms are both examples of operating systems that will let a single user have several programs in operation at the same time. For example, it's entirely possible for a Windows user to be writing a note in a word processor while downloading a file from the Internet while printing the text of an e-mail message.

7.9 MULTI-USER OPERATING SYSTEM

This type of OS allows multiple users to simultaneously use the system, while here as well, the processor splits its resources and handles one user at a time, the speed and efficiency at which it does this makes it apparent that users are simultaneously using the system, some network systems utilize this kind of operating system.

Multi-user is a term that defines an operating system or application software that allows concurrent access by multiple users of a computer. Time-sharing systems are multi-user systems. Most batch processing systems for mainframe computers may also be considered "multi-user", to avoid leaving the CPU idle while it waits for I/O operations to complete. However, the term "multitasking" is more common in this context.

An example is a UNIX server where multiple remote users have access (such as via Secure Shell) to the UNIX shell prompt at the same time. Another example uses multiple X Window sessions spread across multiple terminals powered by a single machine - this is an example of the use of thin client. Management systems are implicitly designed to be used by multiple users, typically one system administrator or more and an end-user community.

The complementary term, **single-user**, is most commonly used when talking about an operating system being usable only by one person at a time, or in reference to a single-user software license agreement. Multi-user operating systems such as UNIX sometimes have a single user state or run level available for emergency maintenance.

A multi-user operating system is a computer operating system (OS) that allows multiple users on different computers or terminals to access a single system with one OS on it. These programs are often quite complicated and must be able to properly manage the necessary tasks required by the different users connected to it. The users will typically be at terminals or computers that give them access to the system through a network, as well as other machines on the system such as printers. A multi-user operating system differs from a single-user system on a network in that each user is accessing the same OS at different machines.

The operating system on a computer is one of the most important programs used. It is typically responsible for managing memory and processing for other applications and programs being run, as well as recognizing and using hardware connected to the system, and properly handling user interaction and data requests. On a system using a multi-user operating system this can be even more important, since multiple people require the system to be functioning properly simultaneously. This type of system is often used on mainframes and similar machines, and if the system fails it can affect dozens or even hundreds of people.

A multi-user operating system allows multiple users to access the data and processes of a single machine from different computers or terminals. These were previously often connected to the larger system through a wired network, though now wireless networking for this type of system is more common. A multi-user operating system is often used in businesses and offices where different users need to access the same resources, but these resources cannot be installed on every system. In a multi-user operating system, the OS must be able to handle the various needs and requests of all of the users effectively.

This means keeping the usage of resources appropriate for each user and keeping these resource allocations separate. By doing this, the multi-user operating system is able to better ensure that each user does not hinder the efforts of another, and that if the system fails or has an error for one user, it might not affect all of the other users. This makes a multi-user operating system typically quite a bit more complicated than a single-user system that only needs to handle the requests and operations of one person.

In a multi-user system, for example, the OS may need to handle numerous people attempting to use a single printer simultaneously. The system processes the requests and places the print jobs in a queue that keeps them organized and allows each job to print out one at a time. Without a multi-user OS, the jobs could become intermingled and the resulting printed pages would be virtually incomprehensible.

7.10 TYPES OF OPERATING SYSTEMS

In this section are introduced some terms commonly used to describe operating systems. One way of classifying the operating systems is concerned with the number of users the system can support at one time:

1. Uni-programming Systems: These are single job systems which can run one user job at a time. Such type of an operating system would probably be found on a standard SIC

machine. Because of the limited size and lack of data channels and other resources, it would be difficult to support more than one user on such a machine.

2. **Multiprogramming Systems:** A multiprogramming system permits several user jobs to be executed concurrently. The operating system takes care of switching the CPU among the various user jobs. It also provides a suitable run-time environment and other support functions so that the jobs do not interfere with each other.
3. **Multiprocessor Systems:** A multiprocessor system is similar to a multiprogramming system, except that there is more than one CPU available. In most multiprocessor systems, the processors share a common memory. Thus the user can view the system as if it were a powerful single processor.
4. **Network Operating Systems:** A network of computers may be organized in a number of different ways. Each computer may have its own independent operating system, which provides an interface to allow communication via the network. The users can login on remote machines and copy files from one machine to another, etc. This kind of system is known as a network operating system.
5. **Distributed Operating Systems:** A distributed operating system allows a more complex type of network organization. This kind of operating system manages hardware and software resources so that a user views the entire network as a single system. The user is unaware of which machine on the network is actually running a program or storing data.

Operating systems have also been classified by the type of access provided to the user:

1. **Batch Processing Operating Systems:** In batch processing systems, a job is described by a sequence of control statements stored in a machine readable form. The operating system can read and execute a series of such jobs without human intervention. The order in which the jobs are executed can be selected in a number of different ways.
2. **Time Sharing Operating Systems:** A time sharing system provides interactive or controversial access to a number of users. The operating system executes commands as they are entered, attempting to provide each user with a reasonably short response time to each command.
3. **Real Time Operating Systems:** A real time system is designed to respond quickly to external signals such as those generated by data sensors. Real time systems are used, for example, on computers that monitor and control time-critical processes such as nuclear reactor operation or spacecraft flight.

7.11 USER INTERFACE

The user interface provided by an operating system is designed to serve the needs of various groups of people who must deal with the computer. In a simple operating system, such as one designed for a personal computer, the user interface is also relatively simple. The typical user os such a system is primarily concerned with running programs and managing files. The interface is generally designed to be easy to use. It may include a simple command language, a menu from which the user selects options, or a graphical representation of programs and data.

For more complex systems, there may be a number of different user interface languages. Menus and graphical interfaces are sometimes provided for occasional users of the system. There may also be a more complex and more powerful command language that is intended for use by professional programmers and system managers. In addition, there is usually a special language that is used to communicate with the operators of the computer. This operator interface provides facilities for starting and stopping the execution of jobs, inquiring about the status of jobs or system resources, and handling external operations such as the monitoring of tapes and disks.

The user interface of an operating system does not usually present major technical problems. However, the design of this interface is extremely important because it is the part of the system that is experienced by most users. Ideally the user interface should be designed to match the needs of all the various types of users, and be compatible with the goals and purposes of the computing system.

An operating system must also contain service routines to support the user interface. For a personal computer, these might be simple routines to handle input from the keyboard and output to a display. In more complicated systems, there may be interfaces to other computers that are linked into a network with the local system. As a part of the operator interface, many operating systems maintain logs of system activity that can be used for performance analysis and for error recovery.

Machine Dependent Operating System Features

- Interrupt Processing
- Process Scheduling
- I/O Supervision
- Management of Main Memory
- Management of Virtual Memory

Machine Independent Operating System Features

- File Processing
- Job Scheduling
- Resource Allocation
- Protection

7.12 USER OPERATING SYSTEM INTERFACE

A user interface allows for humans to interact with a computer. If a system is not designed to be interacted with directly, the interface may be nonexistent, or perhaps only have a simple interface for debugging. The two major tasks of a user interface are to provide access to core functions, and to organize them into as seamless and intuitive a system as possible.

There exist two fundamental approaches through which a user can interact with the operating system. First technique is command line interface or command interpreter with the help of which a user can directly enter commands and further these commands are executed by operating system. The second approach is GUI (Graphical User Interface) in which user gets graphical interface to interact with the operating system.

7.12.1 COMMAND LINE INTERFACE (CLI)

A CLI (command line interface) is a user interface to a computer's operating system in which the user responds to a visual prompt by typing in a command on a specified line, receives a response back from the system, and then enters another command, and so forth. The MS-DOS Prompt application in a Windows operating system is an example of the provision of a command line interface. Today, most users prefer the graphical user interface (GUI) offered by Windows, Mac OS, BeOS, and others. Typically, most of today's UNIX-based systems offer both a command line interface and a graphical user interface.CLI allows direct command entry. It is sometimes implemented in kernel, sometimes by systems programs. It primarily fetches a command from user and executes it. Sometimes commands are built-in, sometimes commands are just names of programs. If the latter, adding new features doesn't require shell modification

The main function of the command interpreter is to get and execute the next user-specified command. Many of the commands given at this level manipulate files: create, delete, list, print, copy and so on. The MS-DOS and UNIX shell operate in this way. Now here also exists two ways in which these commands can be implemented.

```
Command Prompt
C:\>dir /?
Displays a list of files and subdirectories in a directory.

DIR [drive:][path][filename] [/A[[:]attributes]] [/B] [/C] [/D] [/
  [/O[[:]sortorder]] [/P] [/Q] [/S] [/T[[:]timefield]] [/W] [/X] [

  [drive:][path][filename]
                Specifies drive, directory, and/or files to list.

  /A            Displays files with specified attributes.
  attributes     D  Directories                R  Read-only files
                 H  Hidden files               A  Files ready for ar
                 S  System files               -  Prefix meaning not
  /B            Uses bare format (no heading information or summary)
  /C            Display the thousand separator in file sizes.  This
                default.  Use /-C to disable display of separator.
  /D            Same as wide but files are list sorted by column.
  /L            Uses lowercase.
  /N            New long list format where filenames are on the far
  /O            List by files in sorted order.
  sortorder      N  By name (alphabetic)       S  By size (smallest
                 E  By extension (alphabetic)  D  By date/time (olde
                 G  Group directories first    -  Prefix to reverse
  /P            Pauses after each screenful of information.
  /Q            Display the owner of the file.
  /S            Displays files in specified directory and all subdir
  /T            Controls which time field displayed or used for sort
  timefield   C  Creation
              A  Last Access
              W  Last Written
  /W            Uses wide list format.
Press any key to continue . . .
```

Figure 7.6: MS-DOS CLI

The first approach implies that, the command interpreter itself contains the code to execute command. For example, suppose we entered the command 'delete' to delete a file, then in this case the command interpreter jumps to a section of code that sets up the appropriate parameter and sets the appropriate system call. The summary of this method is that command interpreter has itself its code for executing the command.

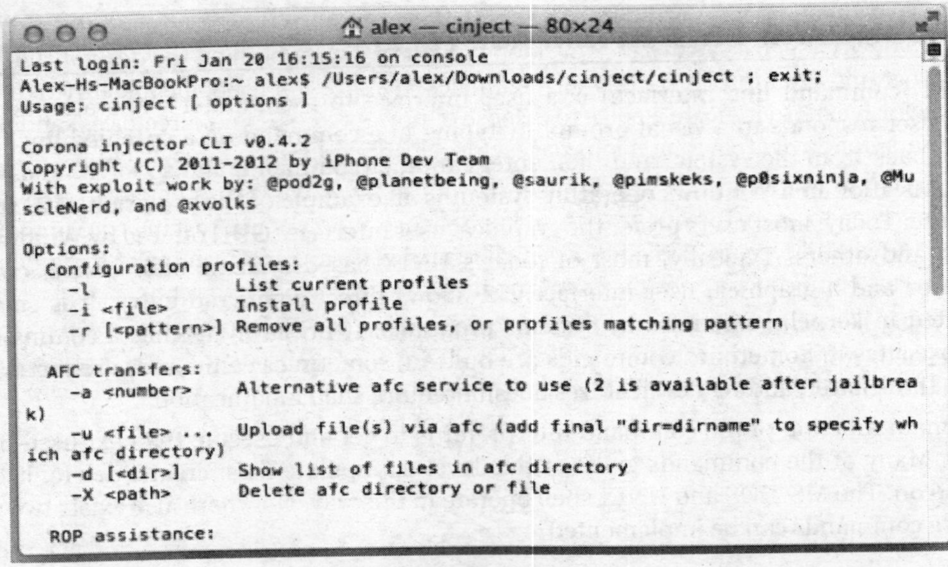

```
alex — cinject — 80×24
Last login: Fri Jan 20 16:15:16 on console
Alex-Hs-MacBookPro:~ alex$ /Users/alex/Downloads/cinject/cinject ; exit;
Usage: cinject [ options ]

Corona injector CLI v0.4.2
Copyright (C) 2011-2012 by iPhone Dev Team
With exploit work by: @pod2g, @planetbeing, @saurik, @pimskeks, @p0sixninja, @Mu
scleNerd, and @xvolks

Options:
  Configuration profiles:
    -l                List current profiles
    -i <file>         Install profile
    -r [<pattern>] Remove all profiles, or profiles matching pattern

  AFC transfers:
    -a <number>       Alternative afc service to use (2 is available after jailbrea
k)
    -u <file> ...     Upload file(s) via afc (add final "dir=dirname" to specify wh
ich afc directory)
    -d [<dir>]        Show list of files in afc directory
    -X <path>         Delete afc directory or file

  ROP assistance:
```

Figure 7.7: UNIX CLI

In the second approach whenever users enter any command the command interpreter does not understand the command in any way, what it does, it merely uses the command to identify a file to be loaded into memory and executed. This approach is used in UNIX operating system. Thus the UNIX command to create a file is 'create file.txt'. Now the UNIX operating system searches for the file create, load the file into memory, and execute it with the parameter file.txt. The function that is associated with the create command would be defined completely by the code in the file create. With the help of this approach a user can add new commands to the system by creating new files with the proper names.

A CLI works by parsing and executing text commands. Although a majority of computer users never need to type commands into a console window, programmers and system administrators still use them quite a bit; their low memory requirements make them useful for highly specialized purposes, such as computer repair, accessing a computer over a network or performing a large number of tasks in a sequential order very quickly.

7.12.2 GRAPHICAL USER INTERFACE (GUI)

A graphical user interface (GUI) are usually similar to the window capabilities provided by the Microsoft Windows series, with control panels to handle access system functions, icons, mouse-controlled pointers, context menus on a right click, multiple windows for multiple windows, and some analogue for the Start button.

A *window* is a (usually) rectangular portion of the monitor screen that can display its contents (e.g., a program, icons, a text file or an image) seemingly independently of the rest of the display screen. A major feature is the ability for multiple windows to be open simultaneously. Each window can display a different application, or each can display different files (e.g., text, image or spreadsheet files) that have been opened or created with a single application.

An *icon* is a small picture or symbol in a GUI that represents a program (or command), a file, a directory or a device (such as a hard disk or floppy). Icons are used both on the *desktop* and within application programs. Examples include small rectangles (to represent files), file folders (to represent directories), a trash can (to indicate a place to dispose of unwanted files and directories) and buttons on web browsers (for navigating to previous pages, for reloading the current page, etc.).

Commands are issued in the GUI by using a mouse, trackball or touchpad to first move a pointer on the screen to, or on top of, the icon, menu item or window of interest in order to *select* that object. Then, for example, icons and windows can be moved by *dragging* (moving the mouse with the held down) and objects or programs can be opened by clicking on their icons.

Many systems now include both CLI and GUI interfaces. Microsoft Windows is GUI with CLI "command" shell. Apple Mac OS X as "Aqua" GUI interfaces with UNIX kernel underneath and shells available. Solaris is CLI with optional GUI interfaces (Java Desktop, KDE).

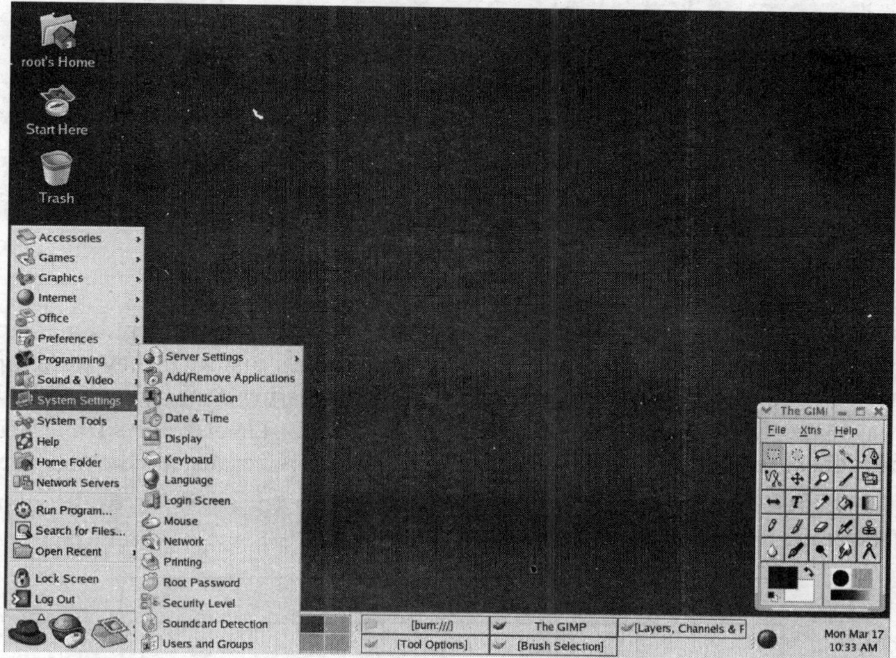

Figure 7.8: Red Hat's Linux GUI

In the last decade262 almost all development in user interfaces has been in the area of the GUI, with two models, Apple's Macintosh and Microsoft's Windows, receiving most of the attention and gaining most of the market share. The popular open-source Linux operating system also supports a graphical user interface.

7.13 OPERATING SYSTEM DESIGN OPTIONS

This section introduces some important concepts related to the design and structure of an operating system.

7.13.1 HIERARCHICAL STRUCTURE

Many real operating systems are designed and implemented using a hierarchical structure. The figure 7.9 shows an example of such operating system structure:

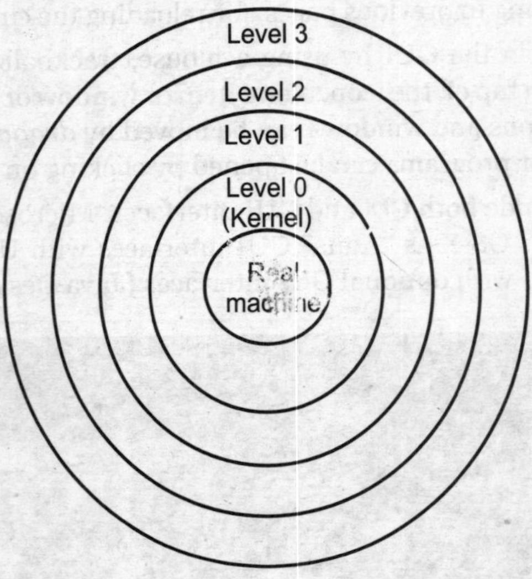

Figure 7.9: Example of a Hierarchical Operating System Structure

The basic principle is a generalization of the extended-machine concept. Each layer or level of the structure can use the functions provided by lower levels just as if they were a part of the real machine. Thus Level 0, often called the kernel of the operating system, deals directly with the underlying hardware. Level 1 deals with the interface provided by Level 0, and so on. User programs deal with the highest-level interface (in this case, Level 3), which represents the user interface.

Following are the functions that are assigned to each level in our sample operating system:

Level	Functions
3	File Management
2	Memory Management
1	I/O Supervision
0	Dispatching, Resource Management

The placement of functions is governed by the relationships between the operations that must be performed. The placement of the functions is done in such a manner that the functions at one level are allowed to refer only to functions provided by the same or lower levels, i.e. there are no outward calls.

There are many advantages to such a hierarchical structure. Operating system routines at a given level can use the relatively simple functions and interfaces provided by lower levels. It is not necessary for the programmer to understand how these lower level functions are actually implemented. The operating system can be implemented and tested one level at a time, beginning with Level 0. This greatly reduces the complexity of each part of the system and makes the tasks of implementation and debugging much simpler.

Hierarchical systems also differ in the rules for passing control from one level to another. In a strict hierarchy, each level may refer only to the level immediately beneath it. Thus Level 2 could communicate directly only with Level 1. This approach has an advantage of simplicity of use as each level has only one interface with which it must be concerned. However, such a restriction can lead to inefficiency because it increases the number of calls that must be performed to reach the inner level. In a transparent hierarchy, each level may communicate directly with the interface of any lower level.

7.13.2 VIRTUAL MACHINES

The hierarchical structure concepts can be extended to provide the users, including the operating systems, with an illusion of running on separate virtual machines. This virtual machine approach makes it possible to run different operating systems concurrently on the same real machine. Thus virtual machines can be thought of as an extension of the concept of multiprogramming down to the lowest level of the operating system.

For example, consider the figure 7.10:

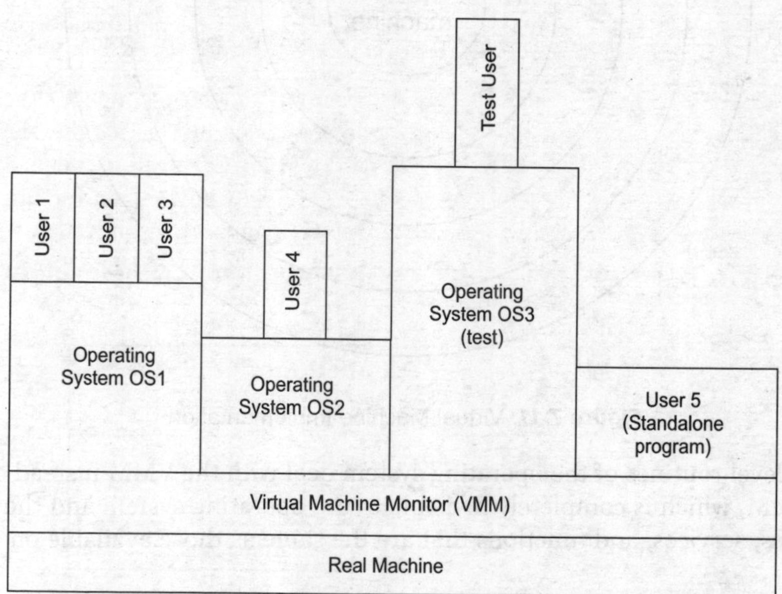

Figure 7.10: Multiple users of a virtual machine operating system

Here operating system OS1 is a multiprogramming system supporting three concurrent users. Operating system OS2 is a single job system. OS3 is an operating system that is currently being tested. There is also a user program that is designed to run in supervisor mode as a stand-alone program, not under the control of any operating system.

All the three operating systems, including the stand-alone system are actually running on the same real machine. However, they do not directly deal with the real machine. Instead, they deal with the virtual machine monitor (VMM), which provides each user with the illusion of running on a separate machine. Thus it is possible to test new operating systems and to allow users with special needs to run in supervisor mode, while at the same time continuing to serve ordinary users in the usual way. If the operating system being tested, or the stand-alone user, causes a system to crash, this crash affects only its own virtual machine. The other users of the real machine can continue their operation without being disturbed.

The figure 7.11 illustrates how this illusion can be accomplished:

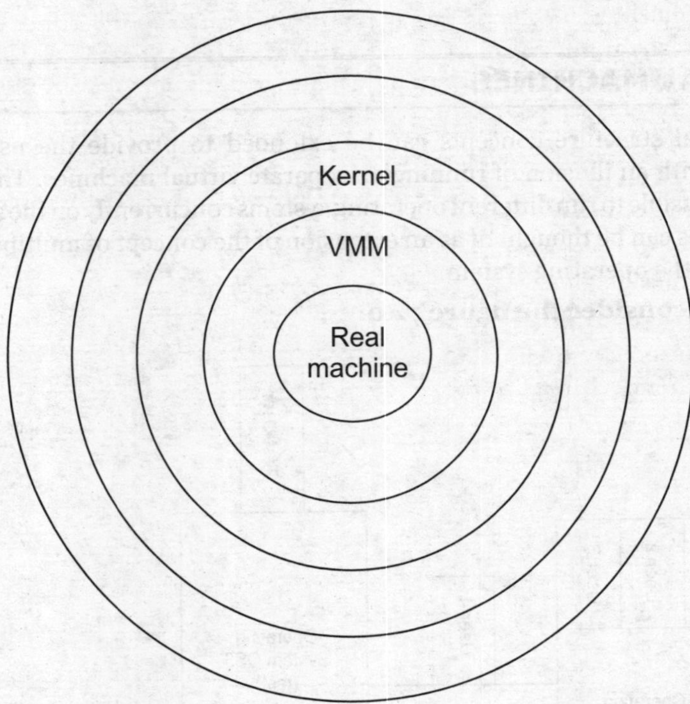

Figure 7.11: Virtual Machine Implementation

The lowest level routines of the operating system deal with the VMM instead of with the real machine. The VMM, which is completely invisible to the operating system and the user program, provides resources, services, and functions that are the same as those available on the underlying real machine.

Each direct user of a virtual machine such as OS1 or User5, actually runs in user mode, not supervisor mode, on the real machine. When such a user attempts to execute a privileged instruction, a program interrupt occurs. This interrupt transfers control to VMM. The VMM simulates the effect of the privileged operation that was being attempted, and then returns control to the user of the virtual machine. Similarly, an interrupt on the real machine also activates the VMM. The VMM determines which virtual machine should be affected by the interrupt and makes the appropriate changes in the status of that virtual machine.

The VMM is a complete but simple, operating system for the real machine. The other operating systems and stand-alone users of the virtual machines are the 'users' of the real operating system. Thus the VMM must provide all of the essential machine-dependent functions. The VMM saves the status information for each virtual machine and switches the real CPU between the various virtual machines. It also provides a separate virtual memory and a set of virtual I/O channels for each virtual machine.

The advantages of the virtual machine approach are flexibility and convenience. Different operating systems can be run concurrently to serve the needs of different types of users. Operating systems and stand-alone programs can be tested while still making the machine available to ordinary users. The use of separate virtual machines can also provide a higher degree of protection since each virtual machine has no access to the resources of each other. The disadvantage is the higher system overhead required to simulate virtual-machine operation. The efficiency of virtual machine operating system depends upon how many operations must be simulated by the VMM, and how many can be performed directly on the real machine.

7.13.3 MULTIPROCESSOR OPERATING SYSTEMS

The previous operating systems were concerned with one central processing unit (CPU). This section describes a design alternative for multiprocessor systems.

An operating system for a machine with multiple processors must perform the same basic tasks that are performed by single processor systems. The figure 7.12 illustrates two possible types of multiprocessor architecture:

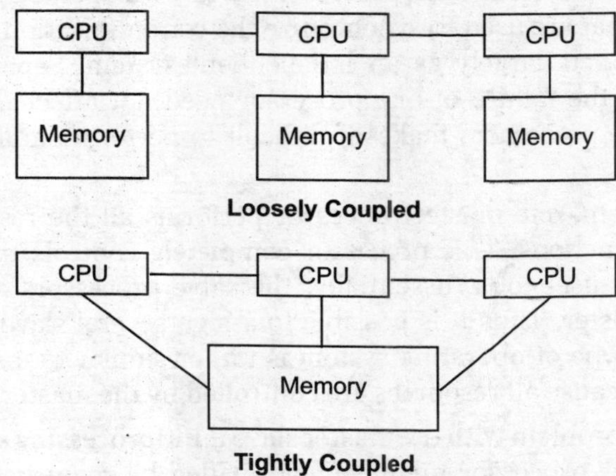

Figure 7.12: Types of Multiprocessor Architecture

In a loosely coupled system, each processor has its own logical address space and its own memory. The processors can communicate with each other, but each can directly access only its own local memory. In a tightly coupled system, all processors share the same logical address space, and there is a common memory that can be accessed by all processors. These types of multiprocessor organization are sometimes referred to as distributed memory systems, and shared memory systems.

The figure 7.13 illustrates the three basic types of multiprocessor operating systems:

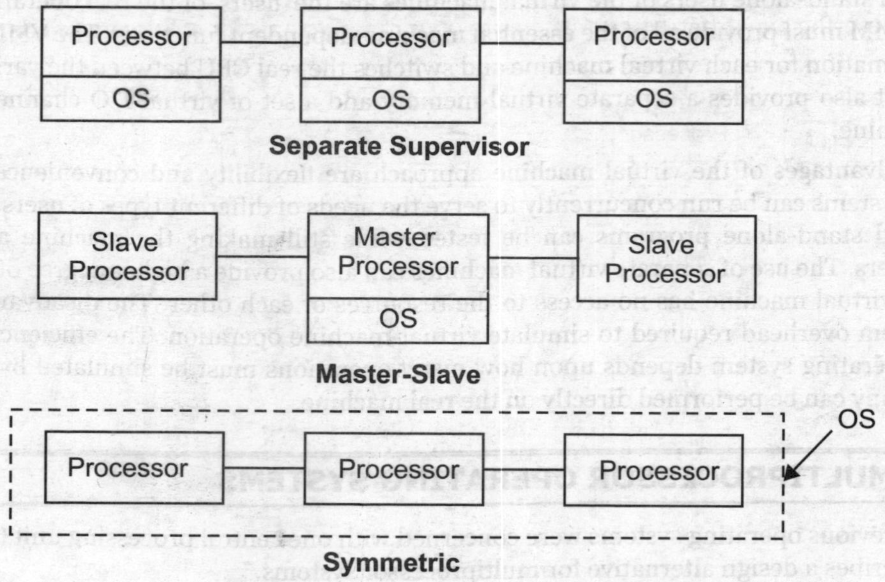

Figure 7.13: Types of Multiprocessor Operating Systems

In a separate supervisor system, each processor has its own operating system. There are some common data structures that are used to synchronize the communication between the processors. However, each processor acts largely as an independent system. Separate supervisor systems are relatively simple, and the failure of one processor need not affect the others. However, the independence between the processors makes it difficult to perform parallel execution of a single user job.

In master slave system, one master processor performs all the resource management and other operating system functions. This processor completely controls the activities of the salve processors, which execute user jobs. Essentially, the salve processors are treated as resources to be scheduled by the master. Thus it is possible to assign several slave processors to execute a user job in parallel. This type of operating system is rather similar to a single processor system. Synchronization is easy because all resources are controlled by the master processor.

The most significant problem with the master slave multiprocessing system is the unbalanced use of resources. A master processor might be overloaded by requests from operating system services, which could cause the salve processors to remain idle much of the time. In addition, any hardware failure in the master slave processor causes the entire system to stop functioning. Such problems can be avoided by allowing any processor to perform any function required by the operating system or by a user program. This approach is called symmetric processing, since all processors have the ability to perform the same set of functions. Hence the potential bottlenecks of the master slave system are avoided. In addition, the failure of any one processor will not necessarily cause the entire system failure and the other processors can continue to perform all the required operations.

7.13.4 DISTRIBUTED OPERATING SYSTEMS

Here we describe two different approaches to operating systems for a network of computers.

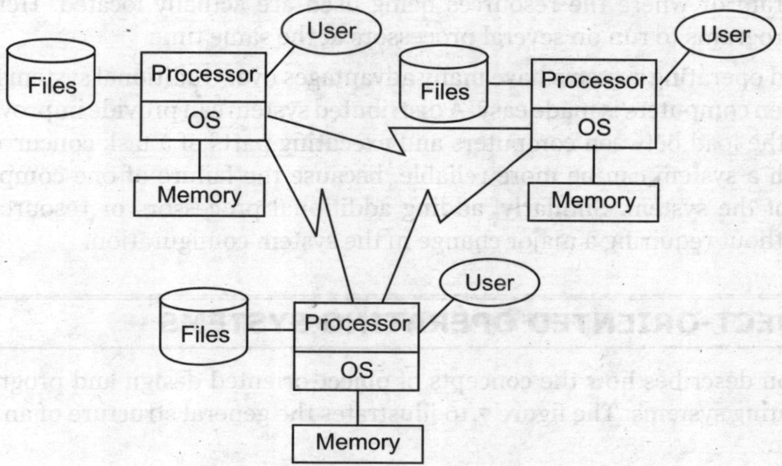

Figure 7.14: Network Operating Systems

In the figure 7.14, each machine on the network has its own independent operating system. These operating systems provide a communication interface that allows various types of interaction via the network. A user of such a system is aware of the existence of the network. The user may login to remote machines, copy files from one machine to another, etc. This approach is often called a network operating system. Except for the network interface, such an operating system is quite similar to those found on the single computer system.

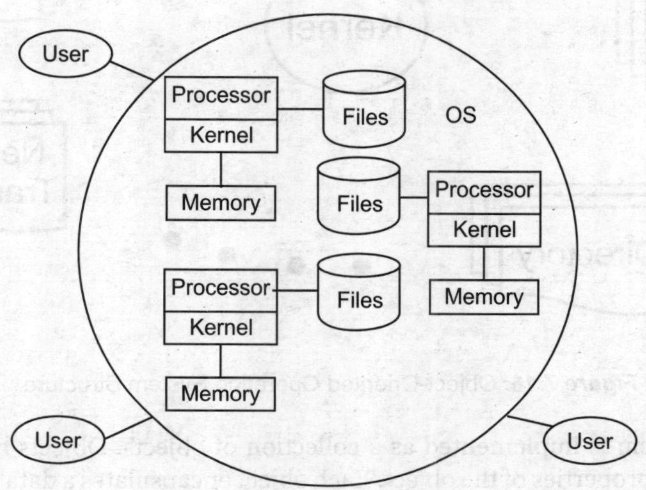

Figure 7.15: Distributed Operating Systems

A distributed operating system represents a more complex type of network organization. This kind of operating system manages hardware and software resources so that a user views the entire network as a single system. The user is not aware of which machine on the network is actually running a program or where the resources being used are actually located. Hence, many such systems allow programs to run on several processors at the same time.

Distributed operating systems have many advantages over traditional systems. The sharing of resources between computers is made easy. A distributed system can provide improved performance by distributing the load between computers and executing parts of a task concurrently on several processors. Such a system can be more reliable, because the failure of one component need not affect the rest of the system. Similarly, adding additional processors or resources can improve performance without requiring a major change in the system configuration.

7.13.5 OBJECT-ORIENTED OPERATING SYSTEMS

This section describes how the concepts of object-oriented design and programming can be applied to operating systems. The figure 7.16 illustrates the general structure of an object-oriented operating system:

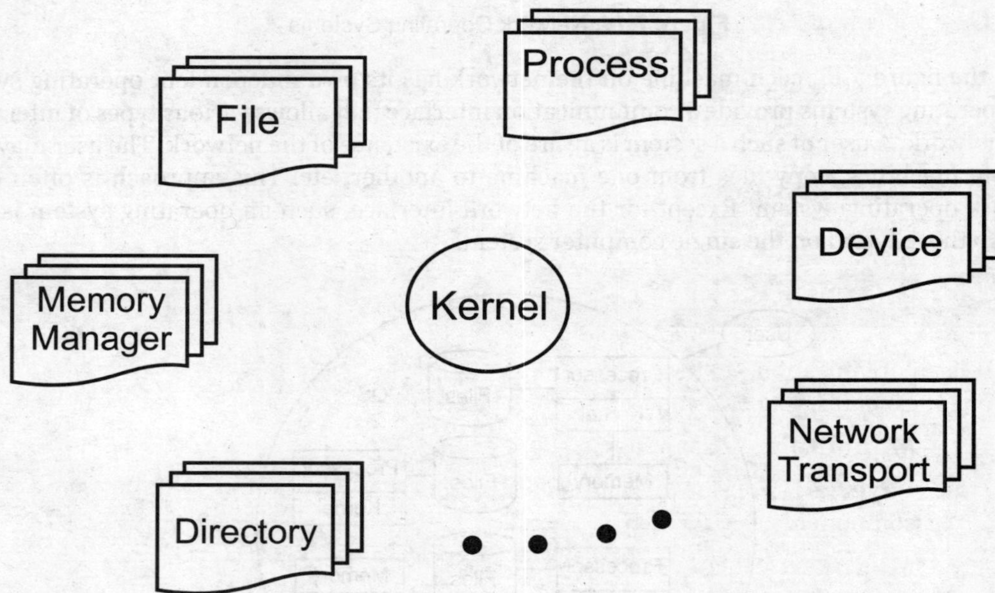

Figure 7.16: Object-Oriented Operating System Structure

Most of the system is implemented as a collection of objects. Objects belong to classes that designate some of the properties of the object. Each object encapsulates a data structure and defines a set of operations on that data structure. The operations defined for objects are called methods. When a user program needs to perform some operation, it does so by invoking one of the methods defined for that subject.

This object-based model is implemented using processes called servers or object managers. When a process wants to invoke a method of an object, it sends a message to the server that manages that object. Servers are also responsible for creating new objects and deleting objects that are no longer needed. The kernel of the operating system is relatively small and simple. This kernel mediates communication, provides some simple process scheduling functions, etc. Most of the functions such as memory management, and network interfaces are also performed by objects.

The object oriented approach to operating system design has several advantages. The fundamental operations performed by all user processes and most operating system routines consist of invoking methods on objects. By invoking methods, processes can request operating system services, send messages to other processes, and perform remote procedure calls.

Object oriented design provides a simple and natural approach to constructing distributed operating systems. From the user's point of view, invoking a method on an object at a remote machine on the network is exactly the same as invoking a method on local object. Thus, distributed applications require no special handling. The implementation of the method may be different on different machines. However, the details of the implementation are hidden from the invoking process. Thus a distributed system that includes a variety of machines presents no special problems.

The problem of providing security is also simplified. The actions that can be performed by a user process can be controlled by a system of capabilities. A capability gives a process the right to invoke a particular method on a specified object. These capabilities are validated by the kernel when it is involved in an invocation request. Since all access to objects is via invoking methods, this means that the part of the system that must be 'trusted' is very small.

Object oriented systems are a relatively new development. However, many computer scientists believe that such systems will be widely used in the near future.

7.14 OPERATING SYSTEM STRUCTURE

It is an organization of operating system component to specify the privilege with which each component executes. The basic operating system structures are

1. **Monolithic:** All components contained in the kernel
2. **Layered:** Top-down approach to separate the functionality and features into components.
3. **Microkernel:** Only essential components included in the kernel
4. **Object-oriented structure:** Collection of interacting objects
5. **Virtual Machines:** Run on the top of any OS
6. **Hybrid kernels:** Both Monolithic and Microkernel designs

7.14.1 MONOLITHIC STRUCTURE

Originally, operating systems were designed as monolithic units. The entire system was just a collection of procedures that implemented the various operations that were required, and any procedure might call any other procedure. For example, MS-DOS, and early UNIX, start with small, simple structure, limited hardware to provide most functionality in least space. It was not divided into modules. The interfaces and levels of functionality are not well separated.

- **MS-DOS** - written to provide the most functionality in the least space; and was not divided into modules. MS-DOS has some structure, but its interfaces and levels of functionality are not well separated.

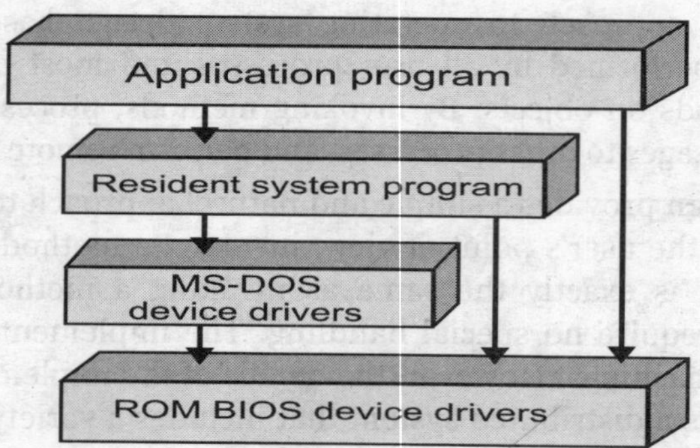

Figure 7.17: MS-DOS layer structure

- **UNIX** - limited by hardware functionality, the original UNIX operating system had limited structuring. The UNIX operating system consists of two separable parts:
    - **The systems programs.** System calls (services) provided by OS are requested by putting the parameters in a well-defined places such as registers or stacks.
    - **The kernel,** which consists of everything below the system-call interface and above the physical hardware. It Provides the file system, CPU scheduling, memory management, and other operating-system functions; a large number of functions for one level. kernel call (supervisor call), switch from user mode to kernel mode (supervisor mode) and transfer control to OS

Some structure can be added to monolithic operating systems. The services, system calls, provided by the operating system are requested by putting the parameters in well-defined places, such as registers, or on the stack and then executing a special TRAP instruction known as the kernel call or supervisor call. This TRAP instruction switches the computer from user mode to kernel mode, and transfers control to the operating system.

Often this is called a **Monolithic Kernel**. This approach leads to maintenance problems. Since any procedure can be called by any other, keeping track of where each procedure is called from is extremely difficult, as is keeping track of what expectations the caller has for the behavior of the procedure being called. As the system evolves, the problem becomes worse. Operating systems are perhaps the worst case of software maintenance. As with other software systems, users and developers are continually requesting new features, and these demands are hard to resist if they are sensible and viable. And as with other software systems, they have bugs which must be fixed. They are usually subtle bugs, but thanks to the Internet they can be exploited by malicious individuals on millions of machines within hours. However, they also need to be able to run on machines whose underlying **hardware** is different. Different machines will have different disk controllers, different video controllers, and different network adapters and so on. A single monolithic operating system will have difficulty dealing with this sort of variation.

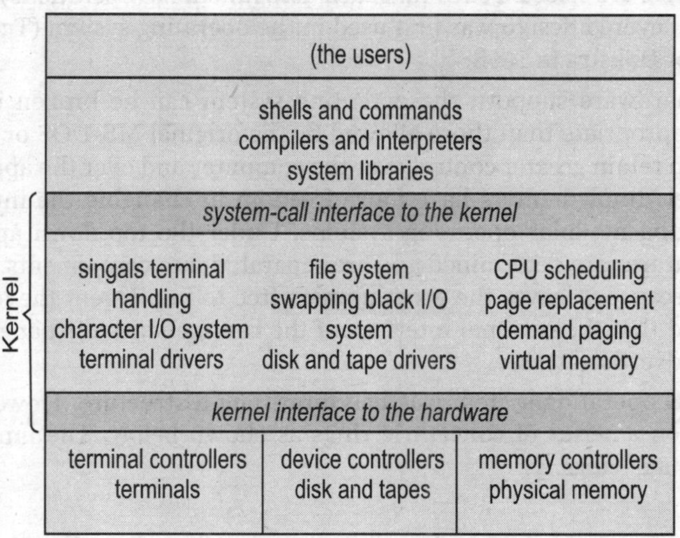

Figure 7.18: UNIX system structure

UNIX operating system consists of two separate parts: the kernel and the system programs. The kernel is further separated into a series of interfaces and device drivers, which has been added and expanded over the years as UNIX has evolved. The traditional UNIX operating system can be viewed in the layered format as shown in the figure 7.18. Everything below the system call interface and above the physical hardware is the kernel. The kernel provides the file system, CPU scheduling, memory management, and other operating system functions through system calls. Taken in sum, that is an enormous amount of functionality to be combined into one level. This monolithic structure was difficult to implement and maintain.

7.14.2 LAYERED STRUCTURES

By the late 1960s, many of problems of monolithic design had been recognized and new programming paradigms were being developed to cope with ever-increasing software complexity. As operating systems are among the largest software systems in existence, they were among the first to be subjected to the new paradigms. The 'structured programming' movement of the late 1960s and early 1970s is reflected in the design of many modern operating systems. A typical operating system can be visualized as being made up of a number of layers, with the innermost layer of software (the kernel) being the only one which has access to the full hardware resources of the underlying machine. Device drivers are implemented as separate 'plug-in' modules which provide a standard interface to particular pieces of hardware. Each layer's services are implemented in terms of a restricted set of hardware operations in combination with the services provided by the more privileged layers below.

Layered Approach introduces a hierarchy of layers, where each layer is constructed above the one below. The operating system is divided into a number of layers (levels), each built on top of lower layers. The bottom layer (layer 0) is the hardware; the highest (layer N) is the user interface. With modularity, layers are selected such that each uses functions (operations) and services of only lower-level layers. A layered design was first used in the operating system (Technische Hogeshool Eindhoven (THE)) of Dijkstra in 1968.

With proper hardware support, the operating system can be broken into pieces that are smaller and more appropriate than those allowed by the original MS-DOS or UNIX systems. The operating system can retain greater control over the computer and over the applications that make use of that computer. Implementers have more freedom in changing the inner workings of the system and in creating modular operating systems. Under the top-down approach, the overall functionality and features are determined and are separated into components. Information hiding is also important, because it leaves the programmers free to implement the low-level routines as they see fit, provided that the external interface of the routine stays unchanged and that routine itself performs the advertised task.

The **MULTICS** operating system was based on such a structure. However, MULTICS was conceptually based on a series of concentric rings as shown below. The inner-rings have more privileges than the outer-rings.

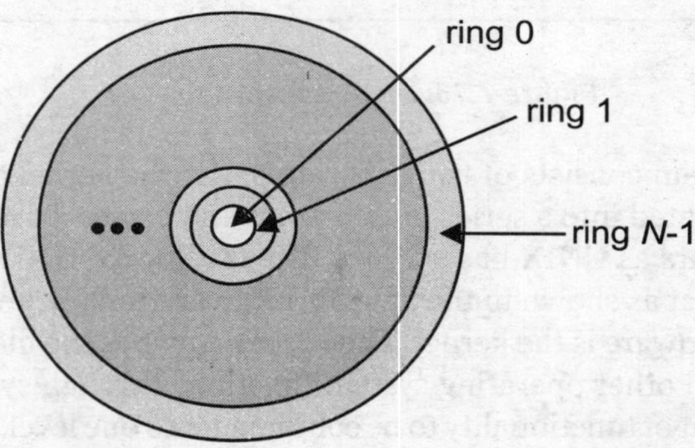

Figure 7.19: MULTICS system structure

7.14.3 MICROKERNEL STRUCTURE

Some systems (notably Mach) are based around a 'microkernel' which adopts a client–server design approach. In a microkernel operating system, a small kernel provides basic scheduling, memory management and communications services. All other services are provided by server processes which have no special privileges. Any other process can act as a client by sending a message requesting a particular service from a server; for example, a message asking a file system server to open a particular file. The file system server sends back a reply indicating the outcome of the operation, including a file descriptor if the file was opened successfully.

The file system server can be designed in such a way that it requires no special privileges. In particular, the disk subsystem on which the file system is implemented will be managed by another server process and the file system server will access the disk server by sending it messages in exactly the same way as any other process would. This obviously requires some further restrictions to prevent programs accessing low-level disk services whenever they feel like bypassing the file system to read someone else's confidential files.

In a microkernel system, the only true 'operating system' components are those in the kernel, and other subsystems such as the filesystem server are just application programs, with no more privileges than a word processing package (or a shell).

In a Microkernel design, the Kernel only provides basic functionality needed for user mode system services. A Microkernel is a kernel design that provides no OS services at all, only the mechanisms needed to implement those services. Because of this, the Kernel itself is usually quite small compared to Monolithic kernels. For example, a microkernel may implement low level memory management and thread management, and Inter Process Communication (IPC).

The kernel thus provides only the following minimal services:

- Interprocess communication.
- Memory management.
- Low level process management.
- Low Level I/O

All other services are provided by user level processes.

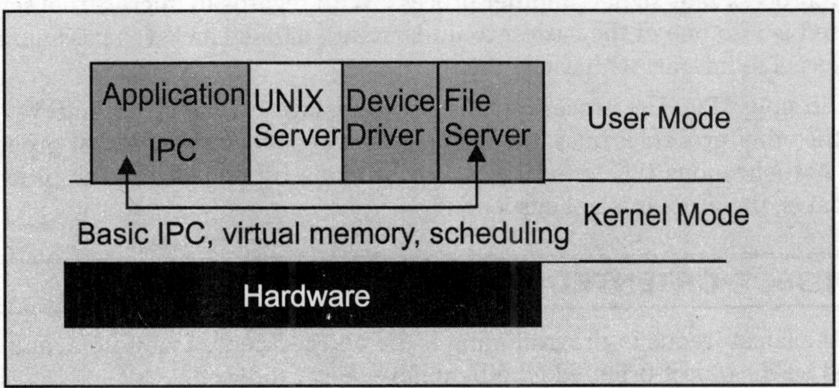

Figure 7.20: A Microkernel

The above image displays a microkernel. Notice the kernel only implements the very basics of basics. In this case, it implements basic process management and scheduling, Inter Process Communication (IPC), and basic virtual memory management.

The Kernel would use external user mode services, such as Device Drivers and File systems, rather then everything implemented as part of the kernel. (As with Monolithic kernels.) Because of this, if an external service crashes, the system may still be functional, and the system will not crash. Inter Process Communication (IPC) and understanding Servers and Device Drivers is important in understanding how Microkernel works.

7.14.3.1 MICROKERNEL SERVERS

Microkernel "Servers" are an external program that is granted special privileges by the kernel that normal programs do not have. These "privileges" may be direct access to hardware, or even physical memory. This allows server programs to interact directly with the hardware devices they are controlling. Remember that microkernels are very minimal. They rely on external programs - servers - to help out.

Servers needed by the kernel itself are normally loaded into memory before the kernel is executed. An example that will be needed is a file system server that will contain the code for parsing the filesystem. Because the Kernel has no filesystem code, it has no way of loading the filesystem server. Because of this, it needs to be loaded before the kernel is executed.

There are several ways. One method is loading a complete RAM image containing both the kernel and supported severs in it. Another method is simply loading the necessary servers at startup within the bootloader, and in someway giving the server information to the kernel upon executing. In both cases, the bootloader can determine what file system loading code to use, however the code can interact with the filesystem server without ever needing to load it in the first place.

7.14.3.2 INTER PROCESS COMMUNICATION (IPC)

IPC is very important in microkernels. It allows separate processes to communicate with each other, usually by sending messages, but it can also be invoked by using shared memory. There are a lot of ways a process can "signal" another process. With regards to microkernel servers, the most commonly used is also one of the easiest to understand, namely message passing. IPC allows the servers and kernel to interact with each other.

In synchronous IPC, The process sending the message is suspended until the other process responds. If the other process is busy, the message is stored in a queue for that process to act upon when ready. Asynchronous IPC is similar to synchronous IPC, however both processes continue executing. That is, the process is not suspended.

7.14.4 OBJECT-ORIENTED STRUCTURE

One of the latest trends in programming is the object-oriented paradigm, and several recent systems based on the object-oriented paradigm have been produced.

Windows NT and its successors (Windows 2000 and Windows XP) adopt a largely object-oriented approach in their designs. An object-oriented design structures the operating system as a collection of interacting objects, each of which belongs to some specific class which defines some specific behavior. New classes can be derived from existing classes which can provide additional behavior or specialized implementations of existing behavior. For example, all classes of object that are derived from a base 'file' class will provide a file system-compatible set of operations such as open, read and close. Each derived class will provide this same interface but will implement it differently. This means that the connection to a local disk appears the same as the connection to a remote disk on another machine, despite the underlying differences in implementation. In the case of file systems, existing operating systems (which are not necessarily designed in an object-oriented manner) do this anyway, but object-oriented operating system designs generalize the idea to other areas than the file system and make it a more explicit part of the design.

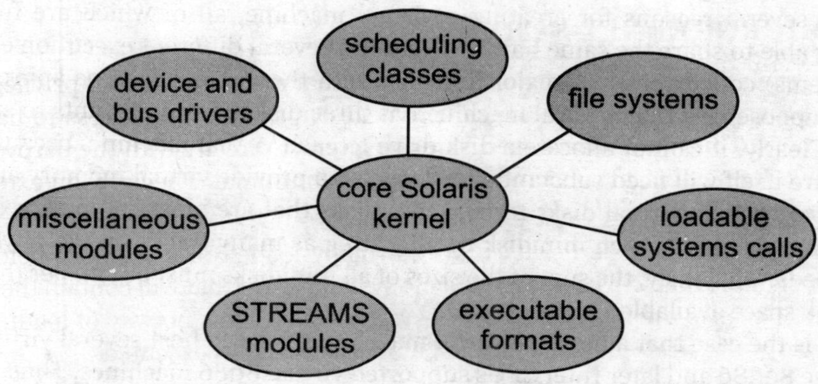

Figure 7.21: Solaris Loadable Modules

For example, the Solaris operating system structure, shown in the figure 7.21, is organized around a core kernel with seven types of loadable kernel modules:

1. Scheduling Classes
2. File Systems
3. Loadable System Calls
4. Executable Formats
5. STREAMS modules
6. Miscellaneous
7. Device and Bus Drivers

Such a design allows the kernel to provide core services yet also allows certain features to be implemented dynamically. For example, device and bus drivers for specific hardware can be added as loadable modules. The overall result resembles a layered system in that each kernel section has defined, protected interfaces; but it is more flexible than a layered system in that any module can call any other module. Furthermore, the approach is like the microkernel approach in that the primary module has only core functions and knowledge of how to load and communicate with other modules; but it is more efficient, because modules do not need to invoke message passing in order to communicate.

7.14.5 VIRTUAL MACHINES

A virtual machine takes the layered approach to its logical conclusion. It treats hardware and the operating system kernel as though they were all hardware. A virtual machine provides an interface identical to the underlying bare hardware. The operating system creates the illusion of multiple processes, each executing on its own processor with its own (virtual) memory. The resources of the physical computer are shared to create the virtual machines. CPU scheduling can create the appearance that users have their own processor. Spooling and a file system can provide virtual I/O. A terminal serves as the virtual machine console. The concept of virtual machines is closely related to layering.

In a typical multi-user system, users are expected to know that the machine is shared by other users, and that resources such as devices are shared between all the users. In virtual machine operating systems an additional layer of abstraction is placed between the users and the system so that it appears to the user that they are using a machine dedicated to them.

There are several reasons for creating a virtual machine, all of which are fundamentally related to being able to share the same hardware yet run several different execution environments (operating systems) concurrently. A major difficulty with the virtual machine approach involves disk systems. Suppose that the physical machine has three disk drives but wants to support seven virtual drives. Clearly, it cannot allocate a disk drive to each virtual machine, because the virtual machine software itself will need substantial disk space to provide virtual memory and spooling/. The solution is to provide virtual disks termed minidisks that are identical in all respects except size. The system implements each minidisk by allocating as many tracks on the physical disks as the minidisk needs. Obviously, the sum of the sizes of all minidisks must be smaller than the size of the physical disk space available.

Usually it is the case that a more powerful machine is used to host several virtual machines. For example, the 80386 and later Intel CPUs supported virtual 8086 machines. Thus, an operating system designed for the 80386 could actually run several copies of MS-DOS and appear to the user to be several different PCs at the same time.

Another example of a virtual machine system is the IBM 370 running the VM operating system. This allowed users to work as if they had a dedicated (but smaller, less powerful) 370 completely at their disposal.

7.14.5.1 ADVANTAGES AND DISADVANTAGES OF VIRTUAL MACHINES

Following are the advantages and disadvantages of Virtual Machines:

1. The virtual-machine concept provides complete protection of system resources since each virtual machine is isolated from all other virtual machines. This isolation, however, permits no direct sharing of resources.
2. A virtual-machine system is a perfect vehicle for operating-systems research and development. System development is done on the virtual machine, instead of on a physical machine and so does not disrupt normal system operation.
3. The virtual machine concept is difficult to implement due to the effort required to provide an exact duplicate of the underlying machine. E.g. machine has 3 disks but wants to support 7 virtual machines resolve by providing virtual disks which are identical in all respects except size. Later, the idea was used in Windows to run MS-DOS .Virtual PC (by MS) can run MS Windows in Mac OS X; Apple has Boot Camp Dual Boot .Virtualization Programs allow users to run Linux, MS Windows, along side with MAC OS X

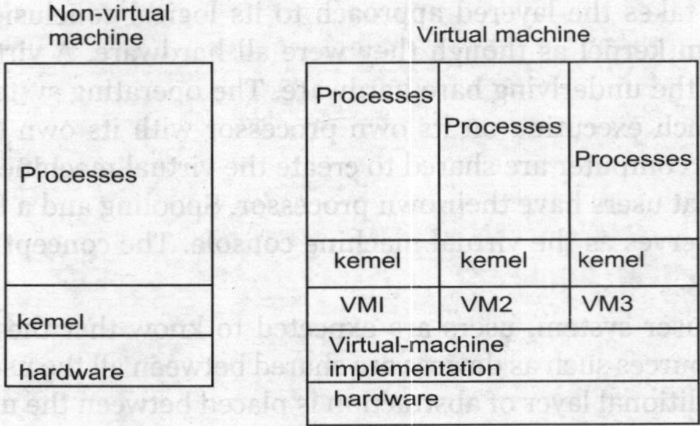

Figure 7.22: Non-Virtual and Virtual Machine Structure

7.14.6 HYBRID KERNELS

There are countless of ways that kernels may be designed. The following are common design models that are based off of the primary design models (Monolithic and Microkernels).

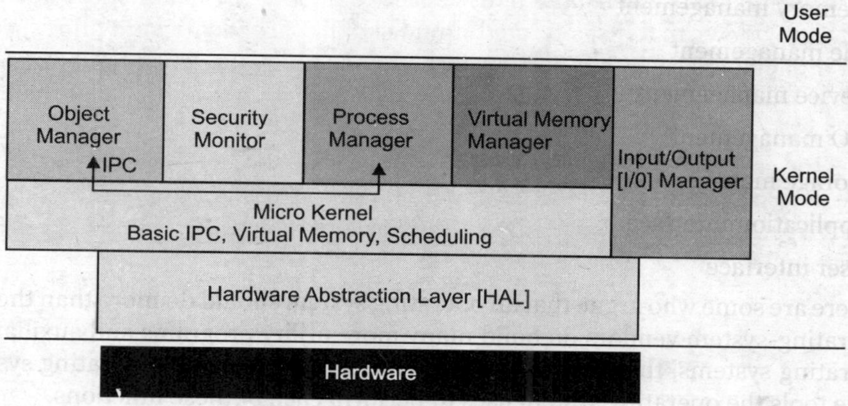

Figure 7.23: Hybrid kernels are Microkernels with aspects from Monolithic kernels

A Hybrid kernel is a kernel combining aspects from both Monolithic and Microkernel designs. Hybrid kernels usually has a structure similar to microkernels, but implemented as a monolithic kernel. Hybrid Kernels, similar to microkernels, use separate sever programs for file systems, device drivers, etc. However, like Monolithic Kernels, these severs execute as part of the Kernel, instead of user space. Hybrid kernels are not in their own design; they are just modified Microkernels with some aspects from monolithic kernels. Microsoft's NT Architecture uses a hybrid approach to their kernel design model. Microsoft describes their kernel as a "Modified microkernel". Several large scale operating systems use a hybrid kernel e.g. Windows (NT, 2000, 2003, XP, Vista)

7.15 DIFFERENT TASKS OF OPERATING SYSTEM

When you turn on the power to a computer, the first program that runs is usually a set of instructions kept in the computer's read-only memory (ROM). This code examines the system hardware to make sure everything is functioning properly. This **power-on self test** (POST) checks the CPU, memory, and basic input-output systems (BIOS) for errors and stores the result in a special memory location. Once the POST has successfully completed, the software loaded in ROM (sometimes called the BIOS or **firmware**) will begin to activate the computer's disk drives. In most modern computers, when the computer activates the hard disk drive, it finds the first piece of the operating system: the **bootstrap loader**.

The bootstrap loader is a small program that has a single function: It loads the operating system into memory and allows it to begin operation. In the most basic form, the bootstrap loader sets up the small driver programs that interface with and control the various hardware subsystems of the computer. It sets up the divisions of memory that hold the operating system, user information and applications. It establishes the data structures that will hold the myriad signals, flags and semaphores that are used to communicate within and between the subsystems and applications of the computer. Then it turns control of the computer over to the operating system.

The operating system's tasks, in the most general sense, fall into six categories:

- Processor management
- Memory management
- File management
- Device management
- I/O management
- Storage management
- Application interface
- User interface

While there are some who argue that an operating system should do more than these six tasks, and some operating-system vendors do build many more utility programs and auxiliary functions into their operating systems, these six tasks define the core of nearly all operating systems. Next, let's look at the tools the operating system uses to perform each of these functions.

7.16 PROCESS MANAGEMENT

The design of an operating system (OS) reflects certain general requirements. All multiprogramming operating systems, from single-user systems such as Windows 98 to mainframe systems such as IBM's mainframe operating system, z/OS, which can support thousands of users, are built around the concept of the process. A process can be thought of as a program in execution. A process will need certain resources, such as CPU time, memory, files, and I/O devices, to accomplish its task. These resources are allocated to the process either when it is created or while it is executing. Early computer systems allowed only one program to be executed at a time. This program had complete control of the system and had access to all the system's resources. In contrast, current-day computer systems allow multiple programs to be loaded into memory and executed concurrently. This evolution required firmer control and more compartmentalization of the various programs; and these needs resulted in the notion of a process, which is a program in execution. A process is the unit of work in a modern time-sharing system.

The more complex the operating system is, the more it is expected to do on behalf of its users. Although its main concern is the execution of user programs, it also needs to take care of various system tasks that are better left outside the kernel itself. A system therefore consists of a collection of processes: operating- system processes executing system code and user processes executing user code. Potentially, all these processes can execute concurrently, with the CPU (or CPUs) multiplexed among them. By switching the CPU between processes, the operating system can make the computer more productive.

Most requirements that the OS must meet can be expressed with reference to processes:

- The OS must interleave the execution of multiple processes, to maximize processor utilization while providing reasonable response time.

- The OS must allocate resources to processes in conformance with a specific policy (e.g., certain functions or applications are of higher priority) while at the same time avoiding deadlock.
- The OS may be required to support interprocess communication and user creation of processes, both of which may aid in the structuring of applications.

We begin our detailed study of operating systems with an examination of the way in which they represent and control processes. After an introduction to the concept of a process, the section discusses process states, which characterize the behavior of processes. Then we look at the data structures that the OS uses to manage processes. These include data structures to represent the state of each process and data structures that record other characteristics of processes that the OS needs to achieve its objectives. Next, we look at the ways in which the OS uses these data structures to control process execution.

7.16.1 PROCESS CONCEPT

A process in operating system terminology is **"a program in execution"**. Unlike a program which is passive entity (resident on secondary storage), the process is an active entity. The process utilizes the resources of the system. A program becomes a process when an executable file is loaded into the memory. Two common techniques for loading executable files are double-clicking an icon representing the executable file and entering the name of the executable file on the command line. Although two processes may be associated with the same program, they are still considered two separate execution sequences. For example, several users may be running different copies of the mail program, or the same user may invoke many copies of the web browser program. Each of these is a separate process; and although text sections are equivalent, the data, heap, and stack sections vary. It is also common to have a process that spawns many processes as it runs.

A process is the unit of work in most systems. Systems consist of a collection of processes: Operating-system processes execute system code, and user processes execute user code. All these processes may execute concurrently.

A process is thus, more than the program code, which is sometimes known as the text section. It also includes the current activity, as represented by the value of the program counter and the contents of the processor registers. A process generally also includes the process stack, which contains temporary data, and a data section, which contains global variables. A process may also include a heap, which is memory that is dynamically allocated during process run time.

Although traditionally a process contained only a single thread of control as it ran, most modern operating systems now support processes that have multiple threads. The operating system is responsible for the following activities in connection with process and thread management: the creation and deletion of both user and system processes; the scheduling of processes; and the provision of mechanisms for synchronization, communication, and deadlock handling for processes.

Modern computer systems allow multiple processes to be loaded into memory at the same time and, through time-sharing (or multitasking), give an appearance that they are being executed at the same time even if there is just one processor. In actual only one is using the CPU at any given moment, while the remaining processes are performing I/O or are waiting. In reality, the

CPU switches back and forth among processes. (The rapid switching back and forth is called multiprogramming).

Each process that runs in an operating system is assigned a process control block that holds information about the process, such as a unique process ID (a number used to identify the process), the saved state of the process, the process priority and where it is located in memory.

The process priority is used to determine how often the process receives processor time. The operating system may run all processes with the same priority, or it may run some processes more often that others. Processes that have been waiting a long time for execution by the processor may have their priority increased so that they will be more likely to be executed in the future.

The details of what constitutes a "process" differ from system to system. The main difference is the amount of *private state* associated with each process. Each process has its own *program counter*, the register that tells it where it is in the program. It also needs a place to store the return address when it calls a subroutine, so that two processes executing the same subroutine called from different places can return to the correct calling points. Since subroutines can call other subroutines, each process needs its own *stack* of return addresses.

7.16.2 PROCESS STATES

In a multitasking environment, a process is not allowed to use the CPU all the time. At intervals (maybe signaled by a timer interrupt) it will be stopped by the operating system so that another process can run. In this state it is not running, but is runnable.

Thus each process has a state, which indicates what it is currently doing. During the lifespan of a process, its execution status may be in one of five states (associated with each state is usually a queue on which the process resides). The various process states are displayed in a state transition diagram, with arrows indicating possible transitions between states. There are two basic process models that are followed for the characterization of process states as follows:

7.16.2.1 TWO STATE PROCESS MODEL

The main responsibility of the operating system is controlling the execution of processes, which includes determining the pattern for execution and allocating resources to processes. The first step is designing an operating system to control processes is to describe the behavior that we would like the process to inhibit.

The simplest possible model can be constructed by observing that at any time, a process is either being executed by the processor or not. In this model, a process may be in one of the two states: Running or Not Running as shown in the figure 7.24:

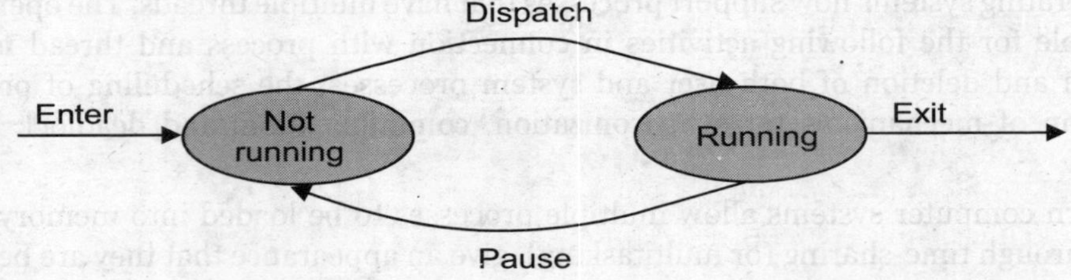

Figure 7.24: Two State Process Model State Transition Diagram

When a new process is created by the operating system, a process control block is created for the process and that process is entered into the system in the Not Running state. The process exists, is known to the OS, and is waiting for an opportunity to execute. From time to time, the currently running process will be interrupted and the dispatcher portion of the operating system will select some other process to run. The former process moves from the Running state to the Not Running state, and one of the other processes moves to the Running state.

In this simple model, each process must be represented in some way so that the operating system can keep track of it. That is, there must be some information relating to each process, including current state and location in memory; this is the process control block. Processes that are not running must be kept in some sort of queue, waiting their turn to execute. The figure 7.25 suggests a structure.

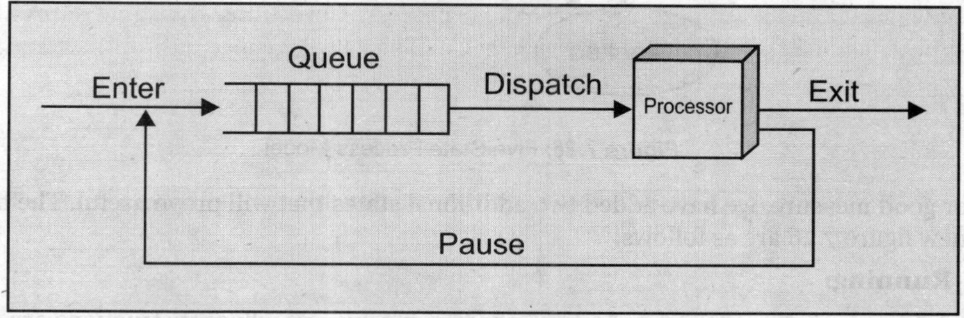

Figure 7.25: Two State Process Model Queuing Diagram

There is a single queue in which each entry is a pointer to the process control block of a particular process. Alternatively, the queue may consist of a linked list of data blocks, in which each block represents one process; we will explore this latter implementation subsequently. The behavior of the dispatcher can be explained in terms of this queuing diagram.

A process that is interrupted is transferred to the queue of waiting processes. Alternatively, if the process has completed or aborted, it is discarded (exits the system). In either case, the dispatcher takes another process from the queue to execute.

7.16.2.2 FIVE-STATE PROCESS MODEL

If all processes were always ready to execute, then the queuing discipline suggested by the two state process model would be effective. The queue is a first-in-first-out list and the processor operates in round-robin fashion on the available processes (each process in the queue is given a certain amount of time, in turn, to execute and then returned to the queue, unless blocked).

However, even with the simple processes, this implementation is inadequate: some processes in the Not Running state are ready to execute, while others are blocked, waiting for an I/O operation to complete. Thus, using a single queue, the dispatcher could not just select the process at the oldest end of the queue. Rather, the dispatcher would have to scan the list looking for the process that is not blocked and that has been in the queue the longest. A more natural way to handle this situation is to split the Not Running state into two states: Ready and Blocked. This is shown in the figure 7.26.

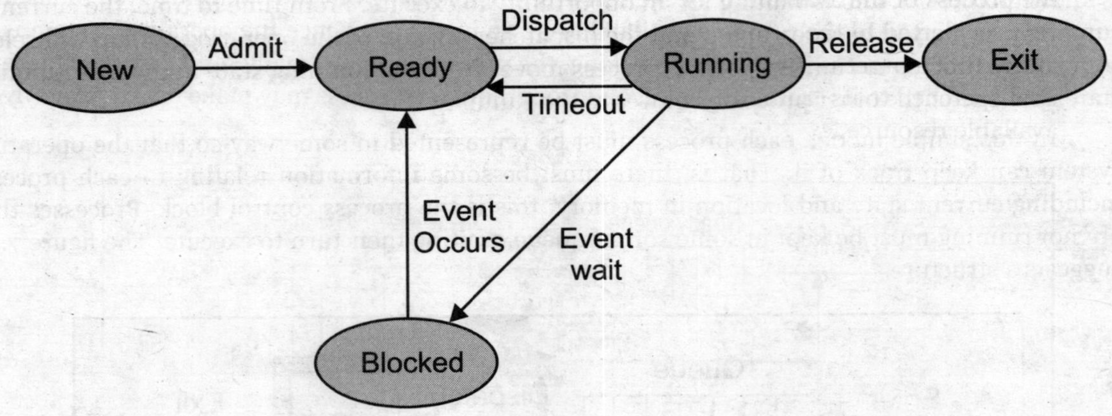

Figure 7.26: Five State Process Model

For good measure, we have added two additional states that will prove useful. The five states in this new figure 7.26 are as follows:

- **Running:**

  A "running", "executing" or "active" process is a process whose instructions are currently executing on a CPU. Hence, it is the process that currently controls the CPU. From this state the process may exceed its allocated time slice and be context switched out and bought back to "ready" state by the operating system, it may indicate that it has finished and be terminated or it may block on some needed resource (such as an input / output resource) and be moved to a "blocked" state.

- **Ready:**

  This state specifies that the process is ready to be assigned to CPU. It could run, but another process has the CPU at the instant. A "ready" or "waiting" process has been loaded into main memory and is awaiting execution on a CPU (to be context switched onto the CPU by the dispatcher, or short-term scheduler). There may be many "ready" processes at any one point of the systems execution. For example, in a one processor system, only one process can be executing at any one time, and all other "concurrently executing" processes will be waiting for execution.

  A ready queue is used in computer scheduling. Modern computers are capable of running many different programs or processes at the same time. However, the CPU is only capable of handling one process at a time. Processes that are ready for the CPU are kept in a queue for "ready" processes. Other processes that are waiting for an event to occur, such as loading information from a hard drive or waiting on an internet connection, are not in the ready queue.

- **Blocked/Waiting:**

  When the process needs to wait for the I/O, either for input to arrive or output to be sent, it is in "block" state and is removed from the CPU (as a blocked process cannot continue execution). The process will remain "blocked" until its resource becomes available, which can unfortunately lead to deadlock. From the blocked state, the operating system may notify the process of the availability of the resource it is blocking on (the operating system itself may be alerted to the resource availability by an interrupt). Once the operating system is aware that a process is no longer blocking, the process is again "ready" and can from there be dispatched to its "running" state, and from there the process may make use of its newly available resource.

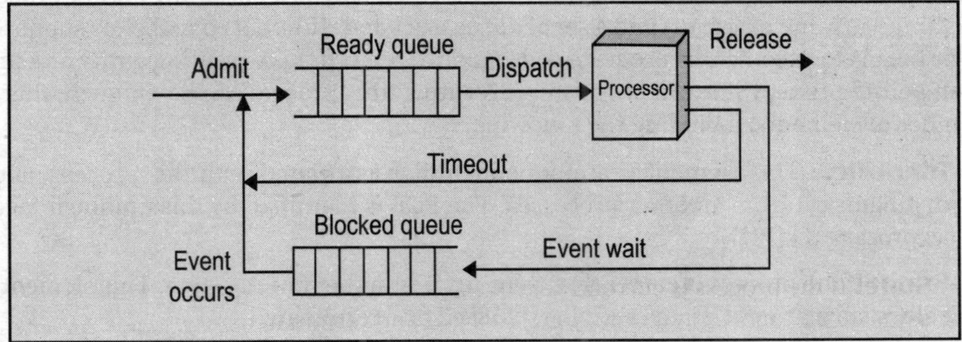

Figure 7.27: Blocked Queue

- **New/Created:**

  A process that has just been created but has not yet been admitted to the pool of executable processes by the operating system acquires this state. Typically, a new process has not yet been loaded into main memory, although its process control block has been created.

  When a process is first created, it occupies the "created" or "new" state. In this state, the process awaits admission to the "ready" state. This admission will be approved or delayed by a long-term, or admission scheduler. Typically in most desktop computer systems, this admission will be approved automatically, however for real time operating systems this admission may be delayed. In a real time system, admitting too many processes to the "ready" state may lead to over-saturation and over-contention for the systems resources, leading to an inability to meet process deadlines

- **Exit/Terminated:**

  A process that has been released from the pool of executable processes by the OS, either because it halted or because it aborted for some reason is known to be terminated or having state exit. A process may be terminated, either from the "running" state by completing its execution or by explicitly being killed. In either of these cases, the process moves to the "terminated" state which states that it has finished execution.

7.16.3 PROCESS CONTROL BLOCK

Recall from previous section that we suggested several definitions of the term process, including

- A program in execution.
- An instance of a program running on a computer.
- The entity that can be assigned to and executed on a processor.
- A unit of activity characterized by the execution of a sequence of instructions, a current state, and an associated set of system resources.

We can also think of a process as an entity that consists of a number of elements. Two essential elements of a process are program code (which may be shared with other processes that are executing the same program) and a set of data associated with that code. Let us suppose that the processor begins to execute this program code, and we refer to this executing entity as a process. At any given point in time, while the program is executing, this process can be uniquely characterized by a number of elements, including the following:

- **Identifier:** This element is a unique identifier associated with this process, and used to distinguish it from all other processes. The PCB is identified by this unique integer known as process ID (PID).
- **State:** If the process is currently executing, it is in the running state. This element contains values such as new, ready, running, blocked and terminated.
- **Priority:** This element stores the priority level information of the current process relative to other processes. The process priority is used to determine how often the process receives processor time. The operating system may run all processes with the same priority, or it may run some processes more often than others. Processes that have been waiting a long time for execution by the processor may have their priority increased so that they will be more likely to be executed in the future.
- **Program counter:** This element holds the address of the next instruction in the program to be executed.
- **Memory pointers:** This element includes pointers to the program code and data associated with this process, plus any memory blocks shared with other processes.
- **Context data:** These are data that are present in registers in the processor while the process is executing.
- **I/O status information:** Includes outstanding I/O requests, I/O devices (e.g., tape drives) assigned to this process, a list of files in use by the process, and so on.
- **Accounting information:** May include the amount of processor time and clock time used, time limits, account numbers, job or process numbers and so on.
- **CPU scheduling information:** This element contains information such as process priority, pointers to scheduling queues and other scheduling parameters.

The information in the preceding list is stored in a data structure, typically called a **process control block** that is created and managed by the operating system which has the structure similar to as shown in the figure 7.28:

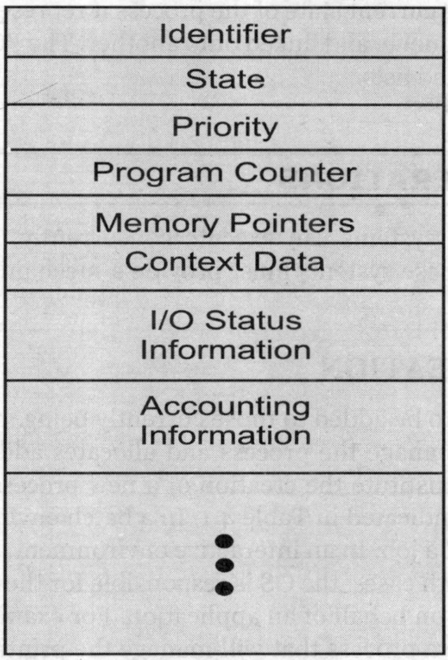

Figure 7.28: A Simplified Process Control Block

The significant point about the process control block is that it contains sufficient information so that it is possible to interrupt a running process and later resume execution as if the interruption had not occurred. The process control block is the key tool that enables the operating system to support multiple processes and to provide for multiprocessing. When a process is interrupted, the current values of the program counter and the processor registers (context data) are saved in the appropriate fields of the corresponding process control block, and the state of the process is changed to some other value, such as blocked or ready (described subsequently).The operating system is now free to put some other process in the running state. The program counter and context data for this process are loaded into the processor registers and this process now begins to execute. Thus, we can say that a process consists of program code and associated data plus a process control block. For a single-processor computer, at any given time, at most one process is executing and that process is in the running state.

PCBs are data structures which are dynamically allocated inside operating system memory. When a process is created operating system allocates a PCB for it, initializes PCB and operating system puts PCB on the correct queue. As a process computes, operating system moves its PCB from queue to queue .When a process is terminated operating system deallocates its PCB.

Operating system keeps all of a process's hardware execution state in the PCB when the process isn't running.

The machine registers contain the hardware context of currently running process. When a context switch occurs, these registers are saved in a special part of the areas (called PCB) of the current process. The Kernel selects a new process to run and loads the hardware context from its PCB. The operating system maintains a collection of queues that represent the state of all processes in the system, typically one queue for each state e.g., ready, waiting, etc. Each PCB is queued onto a state queue according to the current state of the process it represents. As a process changes state, its PCB is unlinked from one queue, and linked onto another. The PCBs are moved between queues, which are represented as linked lists.

7.16.4 PROCESS OPERATIONS

The processes in most systems can execute concurrently, and they may be created and deleted dynamically. Thus, these systems must provide a mechanism for process creation as well as termination.

7.16.4.1 PROCESS CREATION

When a new process is to be added to those currently being managed, the OS builds the data structures that are used to manage the process and allocates address space in main memory to the process. These actions constitute the creation of a new process. Four common events lead to the creation of a process, as indicated in Table 4.1. In a batch environment, a process is created in response to the submission of a job. In an interactive environment, a process is created when a new user attempts to log on. In both cases, the OS is responsible for the creation of the new process. An OS may also create a process on behalf of an application. For example, if a user requests that a file be printed, the OS can create a process that will manage the printing. The requesting process can thus proceed independently of the time required to complete the printing task.

Traditionally, the OS created all processes in a way that was transparent to the user or application program, and this is still commonly found with many contemporary operating systems. However, it can be useful to allow one process to cause the creation of another. For example, an application process may generate another process to receive data that the application is generating and to organize those data into a form suitable for later analysis. The new process runs in parallel to the original process and is activated from time to time when new data are available. This arrangement can be very useful in structuring the application. As another example, a server process (e.g., print server, file server) may generate a new process for each request that it handles. When the OS creates a process at the explicit request of another process, the action is referred to as **process spawning**.

When one process spawns another, the former is referred to as the **parent process**, and the spawned process is referred to as the **child process**. Typically, the "related" processes need to communicate and cooperate with each other. Achieving this cooperation is a difficult task for the programmer.

In general-purpose systems, some way is needed to create processes as needed during operation. There are four principal events led to processes creation.

- System initialization.
- Execution of a process Creation System calls by a running process.
- A user request to create a new process.
- Initialization of a batch job.

Foreground processes interact with users. Background processes that stay in background sleeping but suddenly springing to life to handle activity such as email, webpage, printing, and so on. Background processes are called daemons. This call creates an exact clone of the calling process.

A process may create a new process by some create process such as 'fork'. It chooses to does so, creating process is called parent process and the created one is called the child processes. Only one parent is needed to create a child process. A process has only one parent. This creation of process (processes) yields a hierarchical structure of processes like one in the figure 7.29.

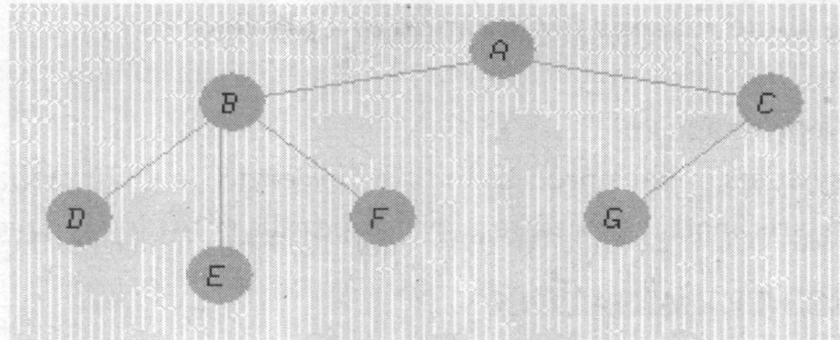

Figure 7.29: Hierarchical Structure of Processes

Notice that each child has only one parent but each parent may have many children. After the fork, the two processes, the parent and the child, have the same memory image, the same environment strings and the same open files. After a process is created, both the parent and child have their own distinct address space. If either process changes a word in its address space, the change is not visible to the other process.

A process may thus create several new processes, via a create-process system call, during the course of execution. The creating process is called a parent process, and the new processes are called the children of that process. Each of these new processes may in turn create other processes, forming a tree of processes. Most operating systems identify processes according to a unique process identifier, which is an integer number.

In general a process will need certain resources to accomplish its task. When a process creates a subprocess, that subprocess may be able to obtain its resources directly from the operating system, or it may be constrained to a subset of the resources of the parent process. The parent may have to partition its resources among its children, or it may be able to share some resources among several of its children. Restricting a child process to a subset of the parent's resources prevents any process from overloading the system by creating too many subprocesses.

Along with the various physical and logical resources that a process obtains when it is created, initialization data may be passed along by the parent process to the child process. When a process creates a new process, two possibilities exist in terms of execution:

- The parent continues to execute concurrently with its children
- The parent waits until some or all of its children have terminated

There are two possibilities in terms of the address space of the new process:

- The child process is a duplicate of the parent process.
- The child process has a new program loaded into it.

In Unix, a new process is started with the fork() command. It starts a new process running in the same program, starting at the statement immediately following the fork() call. After the call, both the parent (the process that called fork()) and the child are both executing at the same point in the program. The child is given its own memory space, which is initialized with *an exactly copy* of the memory space (globals, stack, heap objects) of the parent. Thus the child looks like an exact clone of the parent, and indeed, it's hard to tell them apart. The only difference is that fork() returns 0 in the child, but a non-zero value in the parent.

Following are some reasons for creation of a process:

- User logs on.
- User starts a program.
- Operating systems creates process to provide service, e.g., to manage printer.

Some program starts another process, e.g., Netscape calls xv to display a pictur

7.16.4.2 PROCESS TERMINATION

After a process has been created, it starts running and does whatever it`s job is. However, nothing lasts forever, not even processes. A process terminates when it finishes executing its last statement. Its resources are returned to the system, it is purged from any system lists or tables, and its process control block (PCB) is erased i.e., the PCB's memory space is returned to a free memory pool. In both UNIX and WINDOWS, after a process is created, both the parent and child have their own distinct address spaces. If either process changes a word in its address space, the change is not visible to the other running process.

Any computer system must provide a means for a process to indicate its completion. A batch job should include a Halt instruction or an explicit OS service calls for termination. In the former case, the Halt instruction will generate an interrupt to alert the OS that a process has completed. For an interactive application, the action of the user will indicate when the process is completed. For example, in a time-sharing system, the process for a particular user is to be terminated when the user logs off or turns off his or her terminal. On a personal computer or workstation, a user may quit an application (e.g., word processing or spreadsheet). All of these actions ultimately result in a service request to the OS to terminate the requesting process.

Additionally, a number of error and fault conditions can lead to the termination of a process. Finally, in some operating systems, a process may be terminated by the process that created it or when the parent process is itself terminated.

The new process gets terminated by using any of the following conditions. They are normal exit, error exit, and fatal error, killed by another process. Normal exit and error exit are voluntary whereas fatal error and termination by another process are involuntary.

- **Normal Exit:** Most processes terminates because they have done their job. Most process terminate because they have done their work and get exited. When a compiler has complied the program given to it, the complier executes a system call to tell the operating system that it has finished. This call is exit in UNIX and Exit process in windows. Screen-oriented programs also support voluntary termination. Word processors, internet browsers and similar programs always have an icon or menu item that the user can click to tell the process to remove any temporary files it has open and then terminate.

- **Error Exit:** The second reason for termination is that the process discovers a fatal error. If a user types a certain command to compile the program and no such file exists, the complier simply exists. Screen oriented interactive process generally do not exit when given bad parameters. Instead they pop up a dialog box and ask the user to try again.
- **Fatal Error:** The third reason for termination is an error caused by the process, often due to a program bug. Examples include executing an illegal instruction, referencing nonexistent memory, or dividing by zero. In some systems, a process can tell the operating system that it wishes to handle certain errors itself, in which case the process is signaled instead of terminated when one of the errors occurs.
- **Killed by another:** The fourth reason a process might terminate is that a process executes a system call telling the operating system to kill some other process. In UNIX this call is kill. The corresponding win32 function is Terminate Process. In both cases, the killer must have the necessary authorization to do in the kill.

In some system when a process terminates, either voluntarily or otherwise, all process it created are killed immediately as well. Neither UNIX nor Windows works this way. Termination is very important.

7.17 THREADS

A thread of execution results from a fork of a computer program into two or more concurrently running tasks. The implementation of threads and processes differs from one operating system to another, but in most cases, a thread is contained inside a process. Multiple threads can exist within the same process and share resources such as memory, while different processes do not share these resources.

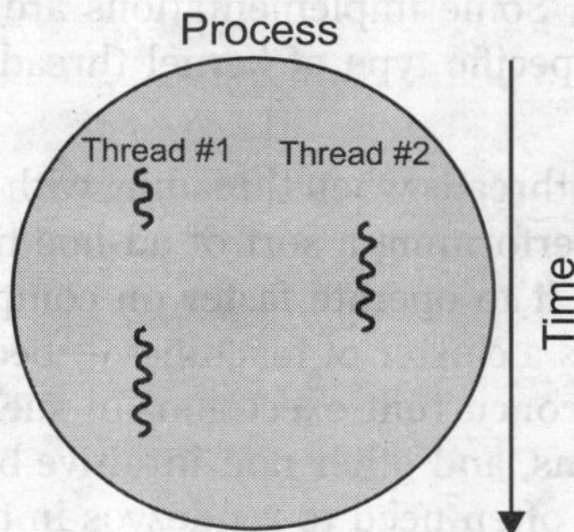

Figure 7.30: A process with two threads of execution.

Despite of the fact that a thread must execute in process, the process and its associated threads are different concept. Processes are used to group resources together and threads are the entities scheduled for execution on the CPU.

A thread is a single sequence stream within in a process. Because threads have some of the properties of processes, they are sometimes called lightweight processes. In a process, threads allow multiple executions of streams. In many respect, threads are popular way to improve application through parallelism. The CPU switches rapidly back and forth among the threads giving illusion that the threads are running in parallel. Like a traditional process i.e., process with one thread, a thread can be in any of several states (Running, Blocked, Ready or Terminated). Each thread has its own stack. Since thread will generally call different procedures and thus a different execution history. This is why thread needs its own stack. An operating system that has thread facility, the basic unit of CPU utilization is a thread. A thread has or consists of a program counter (PC), a register set, and a stack space. Threads are not independent of one other like processes as a result threads shares with other threads their code section, data section, OS resources also known as task, such as open files and signals.

7.17.1 MULTITHREADING

Multithreading as a widespread programming and execution model allows multiple threads to exist within the context of a single process. These threads share the process' resources but are able to execute independently. The threaded programming model provides developers with a useful abstraction of concurrent execution. However, perhaps the most interesting application of the technology is when it is applied to a single process to enable parallel execution on a multiprocessor system.

On a single processor, **multithreading** generally occurs by time-division multiplexing (as in multitasking): the processor switches between different threads. This context switching generally happens frequently enough that the user perceives the threads or tasks as running at the same time. On a multiprocessor or multi-core system, the threads or tasks will generally run at the same time, with each processor or core running a particular thread or task.

Many modern operating systems directly support both time-sliced and multiprocessor threading with a process scheduler. The kernel of an operating system allows programmers to manipulate threads via the system. Some implementations are called a kernel thread, whereas a lightweight process (LWP) is a specific type of kernel thread that shares the same state and information.

Programs can have user-space threads when threading with timers, signals, or other methods to interrupt their own execution, performing a sort of ad-hoc time time slicing. This advantage of a multithreaded program allows it to operate faster on computer systems that have multiple CPUs, with multiple cores, or across a cluster of machines — because the threads of the program naturally lend themselves to truly concurrent execution. In such a case, the programmer needs to be careful to avoid race conditions, and other non-intuitive behaviors. In order for data to be correctly manipulated, threads will often need to rendezvos in time in order to process the data in the correct order. Threads may also require mutually-exclusive operations (often implemented using semaphores) in order to prevent common data from being simultaneously modified, or read while in the process of being modified. Careless use of such primitives can lead to deadlocks.

Another advantage of multithreading, even for single-CPU systems, is the ability for an application to remain responsive to input. In a single threaded program, if the main execution threads blocks on a long running task, the entire application can appear to freeze. By moving such long running tasks to a worker thread that runs concurrently with the main execution thread, it is possible for the application to remain responsive to user input while executing tasks in the background.

Operating systems schedule threads in one of two ways:

- **Preemptive multithreading** is generally considered the superior approach, as it allows the operating system to determine when a context switch should occur. The disadvantage to preemptive multithreading is that the system may make a context switch at an inappropriate time, causing priority inversion or other negative effects which may be avoided by cooperative multithreading.
- **Cooperative multithreading**, on the other hand, relies on the threads themselves to relinquish control once they are at a stopping point. This can create problems if a thread is waiting for a resource to become available.

Traditional mainstream computing hardware did not have much support for multithreading, because switching between threads was generally already quicker than full process context switches. [clarification needed] Processors in embedded systems, which have higher requirements for real-time behaviors, might support multithreading by decreasing the thread-switch time, perhaps by allocating a dedicated register file for each thread instead of saving/restoring a common register file. In the late 1990s, the idea of executing instructions from multiple threads simultaneously has become known as simultaneous multithreading. This feature was introduced in Intel's Pentium 4 Processor, with the name hyper threading.

7.17.1.1 ADVANTAGES OF MULTITHREADING

Multithreading your code can have many benefits:

1. Improve application responsiveness: Any program in which many activities are not dependent upon each other can be redesigned so that each activity is defined as a thread. For example, the user of a multithreaded GUI does not have to wait for one activity to complete before starting another.
2. **Use multiprocessors more efficiently:** Typically, applications that express concurrency requirements with threads need not take into account the number of available processors. The performance of the application improves transparently with additional processors. Numerical algorithms and applications with a high degree of parallelism, such as matrix multiplications, can run much faster when implemented with threads on a multiprocessor.
3. **Improve program structure:** Many programs are more efficiently structured as multiple independent or semi-independent units of execution instead of as a single, monolithic thread. Multithreaded programs can be more adaptive to variations in user demands than single threaded programs.
4. **Use fewer system resources:** Programs that use two or more processes that access common data through shared memory are applying more than one thread of control. However, each process has a full address space and operating systems state. The cost of creating and maintaining this large amount of state information makes each process much more expensive than a thread in both time and space. In addition, the inherent separation between processes can require a major effort by the programmer to communicate between the threads in different processes, or to synchronize their actions.

7.17.2 USER-LEVEL THREADS

Threads are sometimes implemented in userspace libraries, thus called user level threads. The kernel is not aware of them, so they are managed and scheduled in userspace. Some implementations base their user threads on top of several kernel threads to benefit from multi-processor machines (N:M model). User threads are generally fast to create and manage, but cannot take advantage of multithreading or multiprocessing and get blocked if all of their associated kernel threads get blocked even if there are some user threads that are ready to run.

User-level threads are implemented in user-level libraries, rather than via systems calls, so thread switching does not need to call operating system and to cause interrupt to the kernel. In fact, the kernel knows nothing about user-level threads and manages them as if they were single-threaded processes.

The advantages of user level threads are:

The most obvious advantage of this technique is that a user-level threads package can be implemented on an Operating System that does not support threads. Some other advantages are

- A user-level thread does not require modification to operating systems.
- **Simple Representation:**

  Each thread is represented simply by a PC, registers, stack and a small control block, all stored in the user process address space.
- **Simple Management:**

  This simply means that creating a thread, switching between threads and synchronization between threads can all be done without intervention of the kernel.
- **Fast and Efficient:**

  Thread switching is not much more expensive than a procedure call.

Some of the disadvantages of user-level threads are:

- There is a lack of coordination between threads and operating system kernel. Therefore, process as whole gets one time slice irrespective of whether process has one thread or 1000 threads within. It is up to each thread to relinquish control to other threads.
- User-level threads require non-blocking systems call i.e., a multithreaded kernel. Otherwise, entire process will blocked in the kernel, even if there are runnable threads left in the processes. For example, if one thread causes a page fault, the process blocks.

7.17.3 KERNEL-LEVEL THREADS

In this method, the kernel knows about and manages the threads. No runtime system is needed in this case. Instead of thread table in each process, the kernel has a thread table that keeps track of all threads in the system. In addition, the kernel also maintains the traditional process table to keep track of processes. Operating Systems kernel provides system call to create and manage threads.

The advantages of kernel level threads are:

- Because kernel has full knowledge of all threads, Scheduler may decide to give more time to a process having large number of threads than process having small number of threads.
- Kernel-level threads are especially good for applications that frequently block.

Some of the disadvantages of kernel level threads are as follows:

- The kernel-level threads are slow and inefficient. For instance, threads operations are hundreds of times slower than that of user-level threads.
- Since kernel must manage and schedule threads as well as processes. It requires a full thread control block (TCB) for each thread to maintain information about threads. As a result there is significant overhead and increased in kernel complexity.

7.17.4 MULTITHREADING MODELS

Many systems provide support for both user and kernel threads, resulting in different multithreaded models. We look at three common types of threading implementation.

1. **One to One Model (1:1) (Kernel-level threading)**
2. **Many-to-One Model (N:1) (User-level threading)**
3. **Many-to-Many Model (N:M) (Hybrid threading)**

1. One to One Model

In this model each user-level thread maps to kernel thread. Common examples include Windows NT/XP/2000, Linux, Solaris 9 and later.

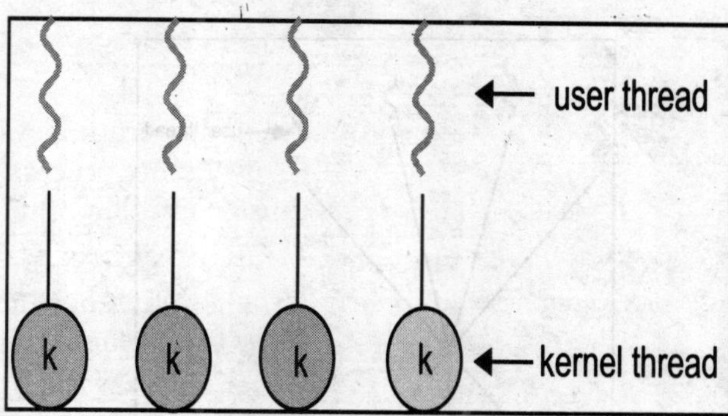

Figure 7.31: Kernel Level Thread Model

One to One threads created by the user are in **One to One** correspondence with schedulable entities in the kernel. This is the simplest possible threading implementation. On Linux, the usual C library implements this approach (via the NPTL or older LinuxThreads). The same approach is used by Solaris, NetBSD and FreeBSD.

2. Many-to-One Model

A **Many-to-One** model implies that all application-level threads map to a single kernel-level scheduled entity; the kernel has no knowledge of the application threads. With this approach, context switching can be done very fast and, in addition, it can be implemented even on simple kernels which do not support threading.

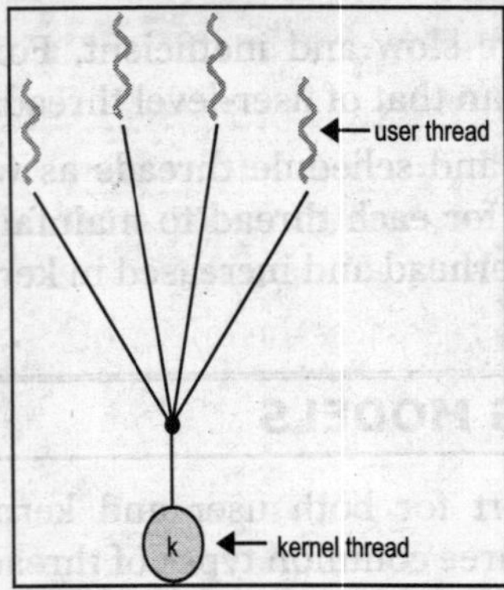

Figure 7.32: User Level Thread Model

One of the major drawbacks however is that it cannot benefit from the hardware acceleration on multi-threaded processors or multi-processor computers: there is never more than one thread being scheduled at the same time.

3. Many-to-Many Model

It allows many user level threads to be mapped to many kernel threads. It allows the operating system to create a sufficient number of kernel threads. Common example includes Solaris prior to version 9.

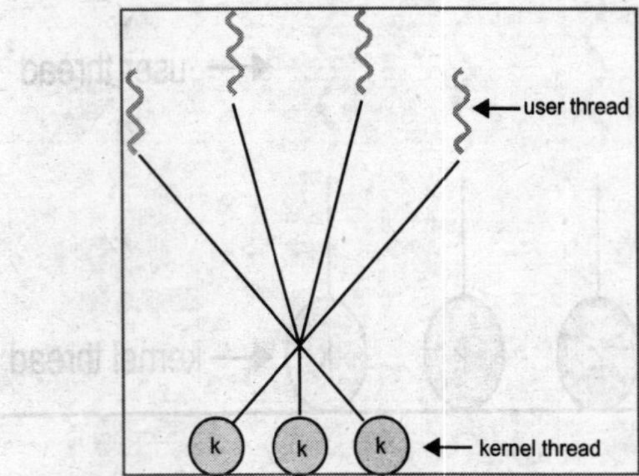

Figure 7.33: Hybrid Thread Model

Many-to-Many maps some N number of application threads onto some M number of kernel entities, or "virtual processors". This is a compromise between kernel-level (**"One to One "**) and user-level (**"Many-to-One"**) threading. In general, "Many-**to-Many**" threading systems are more complex to implement than either kernel or user threads, because both changes to kernel and user-space code are required. In the **Many-to-Many** implementation, the threading library is responsible for scheduling user threads on the available schedulable entities; this makes context switching of threads very fast, as it avoids system calls. However, this increases complexity and the likelihood of priority inversion, as well as suboptimal scheduling without extensive (and expensive) coordination between the user land scheduler and the kernel scheduler.

7.18 SCHEDULING

In a multiprogramming system, multiple processes exist concurrently in main memory. Each process alternates between using a processor and waiting for some event to occur, such as the completion of an I/O operation. The processor or processors are kept busy by executing one process while the others wait. The key to multiprogramming is scheduling.

By switching the CPU among processes, the operating system can make the computers more productive. This chapter introduces basic CPU-scheduling concepts and various CPU-scheduling algorithms are presented.

In fact, four types of scheduling are typically involved, which are shown in the table 7.1. One of these, I/O scheduling, is more conveniently addressed in **next Chapter,** where I/O is discussed. The remaining three types of scheduling, which are types of processor scheduling, are addressed in this chapter.

Table 7.1: Types of Scheduling

Long-term scheduling	The decision to add to the pool of process to be executed
Medium-term scheduling	The decision to add to the number of processes that are partially or fully in main memory
Short-term scheduling	The decision as to which available process will be executed by the processor
I/O scheduling	The decision as to which process is pending I/O request shall be handled by an available I/O device

Every program running on a computer, be it background services or applications, is a process. Older operating systems such as MS-DOS allowed only one process per CPU which can be run at a time. Mainframe operating systems have had multitasking capabilities since the early 1960s. Modern operating systems enable concurrent execution of many processes at once via multitasking even with one CPU. Process management is an operating system's way of dealing with running multiple processes. Since most computers contain one processor, multitasking is done by simply switching processes quickly. Depending on the operating system, as more processes run, either each time slice will become smaller or there will be a longer delay before each process is given a chance to run. Process management involves computing and distributing CPU time as well as other resources. Most operating systems allow a process to be assigned a priority which affects its allocation of CPU time. Interactive operating systems also employ some level of feedback in which the task with which the user is working receives higher priority. Interrupt driven processes will normally run at a very high priority. In many systems there is a background process, such as the System Idle Process in Windows, which will run when no other process is waiting for the CPU.

7.18.1 CPU SCHEDULING

Multiprogramming is the technique of running several programs at a time using timesharing. It allows a computer to do several things at the same time. Multiprogramming creates logical parallelism. The concept of multiprogramming is that the operating system keeps several jobs in memory simultaneously. The operating system selects a job from the job pool and starts executing a job, when that job needs to wait for any I/O operations, the CPU is switched to another job. So the main idea here is that the CPU is never idle. So In multiprogramming some process is running all the times. Thus CPU utilization is maximized in case of multiprogramming.

CPU scheduling is the basis of multi-programmed operating systems. By switching the CPU among processes, CPU is better utilized. The idea of multi-programming is to execute a process until it must wait, typically for the completion of some I/O request.

Scheduling of this kind is a fundamental operating system function. Almost all computer resources are scheduled before use. The CPU is, of course, one of the primary computer resources. Thus its scheduling is central to the operating system design.

7.18.2 TYPES OF SCHEDULERS

The aim of processor scheduling is to assign processes to be executed by the processor or processors over time, in a way that meets system objectives, such as response time, throughput, and processor efficiency. In many systems, this scheduling activity is broken down into three separate functions: long-, medium-, and short term scheduling. The names suggest the relative time scales with which these functions are performed.

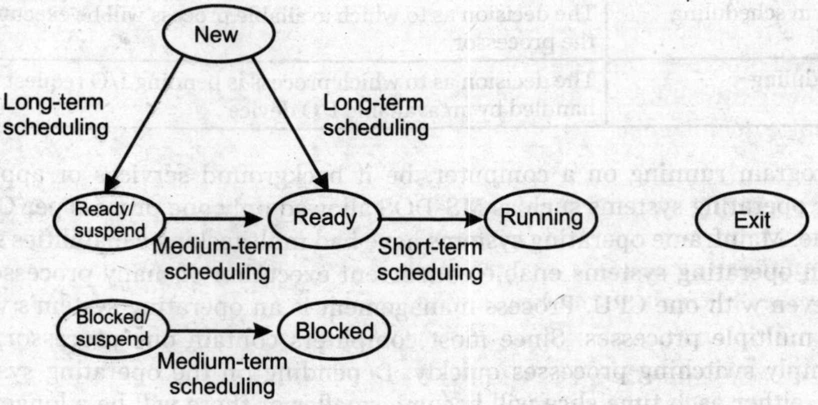

Figure 7.34: Scheduling and Process State Transitions

The figure 7.34 relates the scheduling functions to the process state transition diagram described in the previous chapter. Long-term scheduling is performed when a new process is created. This is a decision whether to add a new process to the set of processes that are currently active. Medium-term scheduling is a part of the swapping function. This is a decision whether to add a process to those that are at least partially in main memory and therefore available for execution. Short-term scheduling is the actual decision of which ready process to execute next. The figure 7.35 reorganizes the state transition diagram of the previous chapter to suggest the nesting of scheduling functions.

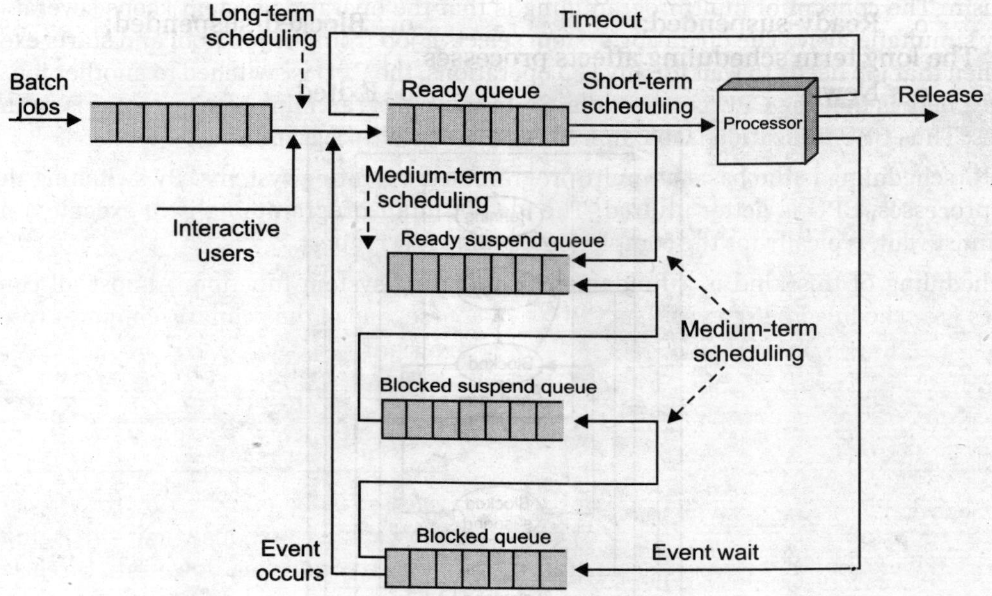

Figure 7.35: Queuing Diagram for Scheduling

Scheduling affects the performance of the system because it determines which processes will wait and which will progress. This point of view is presented in figure 7.35, which shows the queues involved in the state transitions of a process. Fundamentally, scheduling is a matter of managing queues to minimize queuing delay and to optimize performance in a queuing environment.

7.18.3 LEVELS OF SCHEDULING

In many multitasking systems the processor scheduling subsystem operates on three levels, differentiated by the time scale at which they perform their operations. In this sense we differentiate among:

- Long term scheduling: which determines which programs are admitted to the system for execution and when, and which ones should be exited.
- Medium term scheduling: which determines when processes are to be suspended and resumed;
- Short term scheduling (or dispatching): which determines which of the ready processes can have CPU resources, and for how long.

Taking into account the states of a process, and the time scale at which state transition occur, we can immediately recognize that

- Dispatching affects processes
  - o Running;
  - o Ready;
  - o Blocked;
- The medium term scheduling affects processes
  - o Ready-suspended;
  - o Blocked-suspended;
- The long term scheduling affects processes
  - o New;
  - o Exited

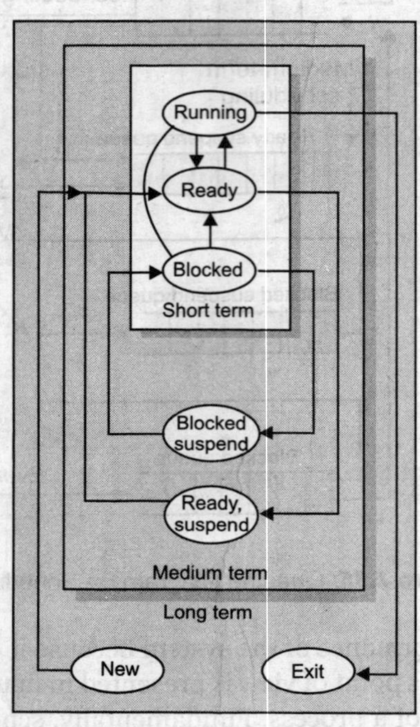

Figure 7.36: Levels of Scheduling

7.18.3.1 LONG-TERM SCHEDULER

Long term scheduling obviously controls the degree of multiprogramming in multitasking systems, following certain policies to decide whether the system can honour a new job submission or, if more than one job is submitted, which of them should be selected. The need for some form of compromise between degree of multiprogramming and throughput seems evident, especially when one considers interactive systems. The higher the number of processes, in fact, the smaller the time each of them may control CPU for, if a fair share of responsiveness is to be given to all processes. Moreover we have already seen that a too high number of processes cause waste of CPU time for system housekeeping chores (trashing in virtual memory systems is a particularly nasty example of this). However, the number of active processes should be high enough to keep the CPU busy servicing the payload (i.e. the user processes) as much as possible, by ensuring that - on average - there always be a sufficient number of processes not waiting for I/O. Simple policies for long term scheduling are

- **Simple First Come First Served (FCFS):** it's essentially a FIFO scheme. All job requests (e.g. a submission of a batch program, or a user trying to log in a time shared system) are honoured up to a fixed system load limit; further requests being refused tout court, or enqueued for later processing.
- **Priority schemes:** Note that in the context of long term scheduling "priority" has a different meaning than in dispatching: here it affects the choice of a program to be entered the system as a process, there the choice of which ready process should be executed.

The long-term, scheduler decides which jobs or processes are to be admitted to the ready queue; that is, when an attempt is made to execute a program, its admission to the set of currently executing processes is either authorized or delayed by the long-term scheduler. Thus, this scheduler dictates what processes are to run on a system, and the degree of concurrency to be supported at any one time - i.e.: whether a high or low amount of processes are to be executed concurrently, and how the split between IO intensive and CPU intensive processes is to be handled. In modern OS's, this is used to make sure that real time processes get enough CPU time to finish their tasks. Long-term scheduling is also important in large-scale systems such as batch processing systems

7.18.3.2 MEDIUM-TERM SCHEDULER

The medium-term scheduler, present in all systems with virtual memory, temporarily removes processes from main memory and places them on secondary memory (such as a disk drive) or vice versa. This is commonly referred to as "swapping out" or "swapping in" The mid-term scheduler may decide to swap out a process which has not been active for some time, or a process which has a low priority, or a process which is page faulting frequently, or a process which is taking up a large amount of memory in order to free up main memory for other processes, swapping the process back in later when more memory is available, or when the process has been unblocked and is no longer waiting for a resource.

In many systems today (those that support mapping virtual address space to secondary storage other than the swap file), the mid-term scheduler may actually perform the role of the long-term scheduler, by treating binaries as "swapped out processes" upon their execution.

Medium term scheduling is essentially concerned with memory management; hence it's very often designed as a part of the memory management subsystem of an OS. Its efficient interaction with the short term scheduler is essential for system performances, especially in virtual memory systems. This is the reason why in paged system the pager process is usually run at a very high (dispatching) priority level.

7.18.3.3 SHORT-TERM SCHEDULER

The short-term scheduler (also known as the dispatcher) executes most frequently. It decides which of the ready, in-memory processes are to be executed (i.e. to be allocated a CPU). Thus the short-term scheduler makes scheduling decisions much more frequently than the long-term or mid-term schedulers - a scheduling decision will at a minimum have to be made after every time slice and these are very short. This scheduler can be preemptive, implying that it is capable of forcibly removing processes from a CPU when it decides to allocate that CPU to another process, or non-preemptive (also known as "voluntary" or "co-operative"), in which case the scheduler is unable to "force" processes off the CPU.

NON-PREEMPTIVE VS PREEMPTIVE SCHEDULING

Non-Preemptive: Non-preemptive algorithms are designed so that once a process enters the running state (is allowed a process), it is not removed from the processor until it has completed its service time (or it explicitly yields the processor). Once a process is in the running state, it will continue until it terminates or blocks itself for I/O .context switch is called only when the process terminates or blocks.

Preemptive: Currently running process may be interrupted and moved to the Ready state by the operating system. It allows for better service since any one process cannot monopolize the processor for very long. Preemptive algorithms are driven by the notion of prioritized computation. The process with the highest priority should always be the one currently using the processor. If a process is currently using the processor and a new process with a higher priority enters, the ready list, the process on the processor should be removed and returned to the ready list until it is once again the highest-priority process in the system.

CPU scheduling decisions may take place when a process:

1. Switches from running to waiting state
2. Switches from running to ready state
3. Switches from waiting to ready
4. Terminates

For cases 1 and 4 CPU scheduling is non-preemptive, while all other scheduling is preemptive.

7.18.4 SCHEDULING ALGORITHMS

The main objective of short-term scheduling is to allocate processor time in such a way as to optimize one or more aspects of system behaviour. Generally, a set of criteria is established against which various scheduling policies may be evaluated. The commonly used criteria can be categorized along two dimensions. First, we can make a distinction between user-oriented and system-oriented criteria. User oriented criteria relate to the behaviour of the system as perceived by the individual user or process.

An example is response time in an interactive system. Response time is the elapsed time between the submissions of a request until the response begins to appear as output. This quantity is visible to the user and is naturally of interest to the user. We would like a scheduling policy that provides "good" service to various users. In the case of response time, a threshold may be defined, say 2 seconds. Then a goal of the scheduling mechanism should be to maximize the number of users who experience an average response time of 2 seconds or less. Other criteria are system oriented. That is, the focus is on effective and efficient utilization of the processor. An example is throughput, which is the rate at which processes are completed. This is certainly a worthwhile measure of system performance and one that we would like to maximize. However, it focuses on system performance rather than service provided to the user. Thus, throughput is of concern to a system administrator but not to the user population. Whereas user-oriented criteria are important on virtually all systems, system oriented criteria are generally of minor importance on single-user systems. On a single-user system, it probably is not important to achieve high processor utilization or high throughput as long as the responsiveness of the system to user applications is acceptable.

Another dimension along which criteria can be classified is those that are performance related and those that are not directly performance related. Performance related criteria are quantitative and generally can be readily measured. Examples include response time and throughput. Criteria that are not performance related are either qualitative in nature or do not lend themselves readily to measurement and analysis. An example of such a criterion is predictability. We would like for the service provided to users to exhibit the same characteristics over time, independent of other work being performed by the system. To some extent, this criterion can be measured, by calculating variances as a function of workload. However, this is not nearly as straightforward as measuring throughput or response time as a function of workload.

The table 7.2 summarizes key scheduling criteria. These are interdependent, and it is impossible to optimize all of them simultaneously. For example, providing good response time may require a scheduling algorithm that switches between processes frequently. This increases the overhead of the system, reducing throughput. Thus, the design of a scheduling policy involves compromising among competing requirements; the relative weights given the various requirements will depend on the nature and intended use of the system.

TABLE 7.2: SCHEDULING CRIT

User Oriented, Performance Related	**Turnaround time** This is the interval of time between the submission of a process and its completion. Includes actual execution time plus time spent waiting for resources, including the processor. This is an appropriate measure for a batch job. **Response time** It is the time from the submission of a request until the response begins to be received. Often a process can begin producing some output to the user while continuing to process the request. Thus, this is a better measure than turnaround time from the user's point of view. The scheduling discipline should attempt to achieve low response time and to maximize the number of interactive users receiving acceptable response time. **Deadlines** When process completion deadlines can be specified, the scheduling discipline should subordinate other goals to that of maximizing the percentage of deadlines met.
User Oriented, Other	**Predictability** A given job should run in about the same amount of time and at about the same cost regardless of the load on the system. A wide variation in response time or turnaround time is distracting to users. It may signal a wide swing in system workloads or the need for system tuning to cure instabilities.
System Oriented, Performance Related	**Throughput** The scheduling policy should attempt to maximize the number of processes completed per unit of time. This is a measure of how much work is being performed. This clearly depends on the average length of a process but is also influenced by the scheduling policy, which may affect utilization. **Processor utilization** This is the percentage of time that the processor is busy. For an expensive shared system, this is a significant criterion. In single-user systems and in some other systems, such as real-time systems, this criterion is less important than some of the others.

System Oriented, Other	**Fairness** In the absence of guidance from the user or other system-supplied guidance, processes should be treated the same, and no process should suffer starvation. **Enforcing priorities** When processes are assigned priorities, the scheduling policy should favour higher-priority processes. **Balancing resources** The scheduling policy should keep the resources of the system busy. Processes that will underutilize stressed resources should be favoured. This criterion also involves medium-term and long-term scheduling.

7.18.5 PROCESS SCHEDULING

The objective of multiprogramming is to have some process running at all times, to maximize CPU utilization. The objective of time sharing is to switch the CPU among processes so frequently that users can interact with each program while it is running. To meet these objectives, the **process** scheduler selects an available process (possibly from a set of several available processes) for program execution on the CPU. For a single-processor system, there will never be more than one running process. If there are more processes, the rest will have to wait until the CPU is free and can be rescheduled.

7.18.5.1 SCHEDULING QUEUES

As processes enter the system, they are put into a job queue, which consists of all processes in the system. The processes that are residing in main memory and are ready and waiting to execute are kept on a list called the ready queue. This queue is generally stored as a linked list. A ready-queue header contains pointers to the first and final PCBs in the list. Each PCB includes a pointer field that points to the next PCB in the ready queue.

The system also includes other queues. When a process is allocated the CPU, it executes for a while and eventually quits, is interrupted, or waits for the occurrence of a particular event, such as the completion of an I/O request.

Suppose the process makes an I/O request to a shared device, such as a disk. Since there are many processes in the system, the disk may be busy with the I/O request of some other process. The process therefore may have to wait for the disk. The list of processes waiting for a particular I/O device is called a device queue. Each device has its own device queue (Figure 7.37).

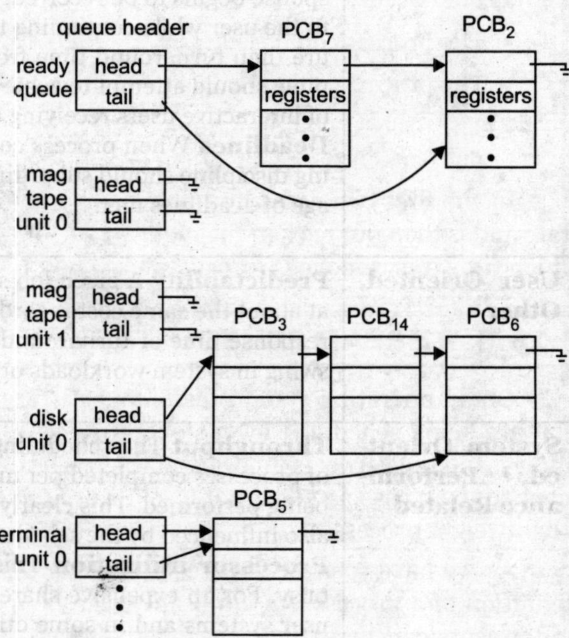

Figure 7.37: The ready queue and various I/O device queues

A common representation for a discussion of process scheduling is a queuing diagram, such as that in Figure 7.38. Each rectangular box represents a queue. Two types of queues are present: the ready queue and a set of device queues. The circles represent the resources that serve the queues, and the arrows indicate the flow of processes in the system.

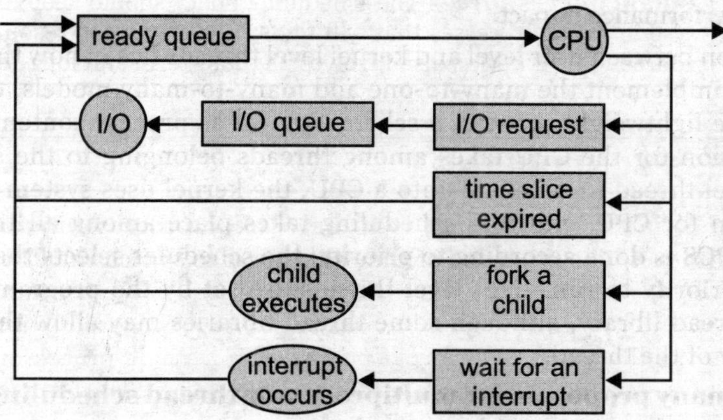

Figure 7.38: Queuing diagram representation of process scheduling

A new process is initially put in the ready queue. It waits there until it is selected for execution, or is dispatched. Once the process is allocated the CPU and is executing, one of several events could occur:

- The process could issue an I/O request and then be placed in an I/O queue.
- The process could create a new subprocess and wait for the subprocess's termination.
- The process could be removed forcibly from the CPU, as a result of an interrupt, and be put back in the ready queue.

In the first two cases, the process eventually switches from the waiting state to the ready state and is then put back in the ready queue. A process continues this cycle until it terminates, at which time it is removed from all queues and has its PCB and resources deallocated.

7.18.6 THREAD SCHEDULING

On an operating system that supports threads, it is the kernel level threads, not processes that are being scheduled by the operating system. User level threads are managed by a thread library, and the kernel is unaware of them. To run on a CPU, user-level threads must ultimately be mapped to an associated kernel-level thread, although this mapping may be indirect and may use a lightweight process.

As we have seen, with threads, the concept of execution is separated from the rest of the definition of a process. An application can be implemented as a set of threads, which cooperate and execute concurrently in the same address space. On a uniprocessor, threads can be used as a program structuring aid and to overlap I/O with processing. Because of the minimal penalty in doing a thread switch compared to a process switch, these benefits are realized with little cost.

However, the full power of threads becomes evident in a multiprocessor system. In this environment, threads can be used to exploit true parallelism in an application. If the various threads of an application are simultaneously run on separate processors, dramatic gains in performance are possible. However, it can be shown that for applications that require significant interaction among threads (medium-grain parallelism), small differences in thread management and scheduling can have a significant performance impact.

One distinction between user level and kernel level threads lies in how they are scheduled. On systems which implement the many-to-one and many-to-many models, the thread library run on an available lightweight process, a scheme known as process contention scope (PCS), since the competition for the CPU takes among threads belonging to the same process. To decide which kernel thread to schedule onto a CPU, the kernel uses system contention scope (SCS). Competition for CPU with SCS scheduling takes place among all the threads in the system. Typically PCS is done according to priority; the scheduler selects the runnable thread with the highest priority to run. User level threads are set by the programmer and are not adjusted by the thread library, although some thread libraries may allow the programmer to change the priority of the thread.

Among the many proposals for multiprocessor thread scheduling and processor assignment, four general approaches stand out:

- **Load sharing:** Processes are not assigned to a particular processor. A global queue of ready threads is maintained, and each processor, when idle, selects a thread from the queue. The term **load sharing** is used to distinguish this strategy from load-balancing schemes in which work is allocated on a more permanent basis.
- **Gang scheduling:** A set of related threads is scheduled to run on a set of processors at the same time, on a one-to-one basis.
- **Dedicated processor assignment:** This is the opposite of the load-sharing approach and provides implicit scheduling defined by the assignment of threads to processors. Each program is allocated a number of processors equal to the number of threads in the program, for the duration of the program execution. When the program terminates, the processors return to the general pool for possible allocation to another program.
- **Dynamic scheduling:** The number of threads in a process can be altered during the course of execution.

7.19 MEMORY MANAGEMENT

In Process Scheduling, it was showed how the CPU can be shared by a set of processes. As a result of CPU scheduling, we can improve both the utilization of the CPU and the speed of the computer's response to its users. To realize this increase in performance, however, we must keep several processes in memory; we must share memory.

Just as processes share the CPU, they also share physical memory. Thus in addition to the responsibility of managing processes, the operating system must efficiently manage the primary memory of the computer. Memory management is needed to enable several processes to share main memory. The part of the operating system which handles this responsibility is called the **memory manager**.

Each process has access to its own personal memory space which appears to be separate from the memory space of any other process. In fact, all processes share a common memory space provided by the hardware of the underlying machine, so one of the things that the operating system has to do is to divide the available memory among the various processes.

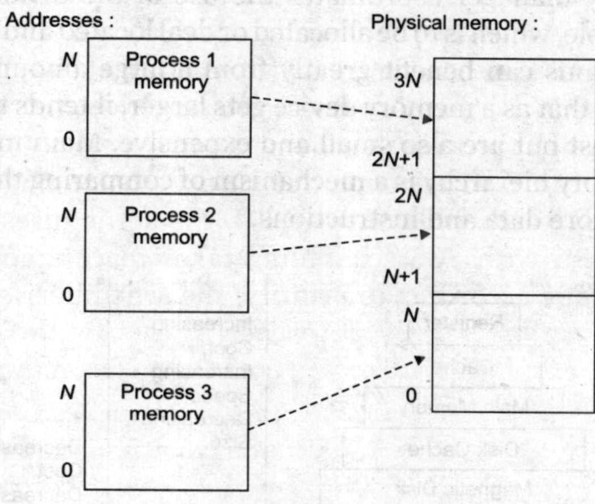

Figure 7.39: Address Translation

Each process has the illusion that it has a range of available memory addresses that it can access from address 0 up to some maximum address. In fact, what a process sees as address 0 might be located at some completely different address in the physical memory of the machine. Address translation is performed by some additional specialized hardware, and the operating system is responsible for managing how this hardware translates the addresses used by processes into the corresponding physical addresses before they are used to access physical memory. Managing the sharing of primary memory and minimizing memory access time are the basic goals of the memory manager.

The main purpose of a computer system is to execute programs. These programs, together with data they access, must be in main memory during execution. To improve both the utilization of CPU and the speed of response to users, the computer must keep several processes in memory. Many memory management schemes exist, reflecting various approaches, and the effectiveness of each algorithm depends on the situation. Selection of memory management scheme for a system depends on many factors, especially on the hardware design of the system. Each algorithm requires its own support.

Memory management is the act of managing computer memory. In its simpler forms, this involves providing ways to allocate portions of memory to programs at their request, and freeing it for reuse when no longer needed. Since every process must have some amount of primary memory in order to execute, the memory manager can allocate a portion of primary memory to each process for its own use. However, the memory manager must keep track of which processes are running in which memory locations, and it must also determine how to allocate and deallocate available memory when new processes are created and when old processes complete execution. The performance of the memory manager is crucial to the performance of the entire system. This chapter is about methods for sharing main memory.

7.19.1 MEMORY HIERARCHY

Current computer architectures arrange the computer's memory in a hierarchical manner, starting from the fastest registers, CPU cache, and random access memory and disk storage. An operating system's memory manager coordinates the use of these various types of memory by tracking which one is available, which is to be allocated or deal located and how to move data between them. Most modern programs can benefit greatly from a large amount of very fast memory. A physical reality, however, is that as a memory device gets larger, it tends to get slower. For example, cache memories are very fast but are also small and expensive. Main memory is inexpensive and large, but is slow. The memory hierarchy is a mechanism of comparing the cost and performance of the various places we can store data and instructions.

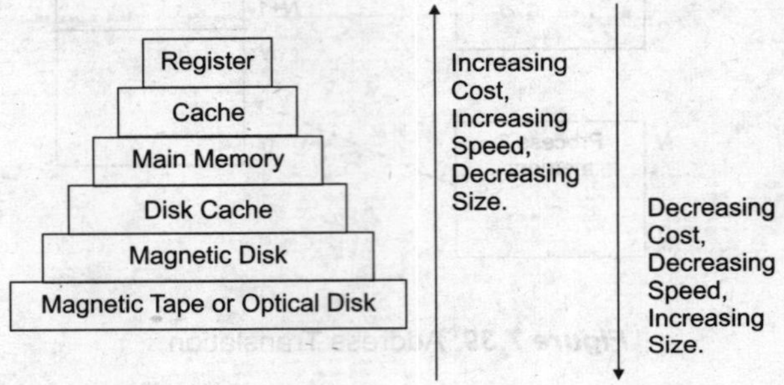

Figure 7.40: Memory Hierarchy

Registers are fastest memory elements. At the top level of the memory hierarchy are the CPU's general purpose registers. The registers provide the fastest access to data. The register file is also the smallest memory object in the memory hierarchy. Registers are also the most expensive memory locations.

Cache is fast and small compared to main memory; acts as a buffer between the CPU and main memory: it contains the most recent used memory locations (address and contents are recorded here). Of course, if the program really accessed main memory on each access, the program would run quite slowly since modern DRAM main memory subsystems are much slower than the CPU. The job of the cache memory subsystems (and the cache controller) is to move data between main memory and the cache so that the CPU can quickly access data in the cache. Every address reference goes first to the cache; if the desired address is not here, then we have a cache miss; The contents are fetched from main memory into the indicated CPU register and the content is also saved into the cache memory .Most software exhibits temporal locality of access, meaning that it is likely that same address will be used again soon, and if so, the address will be found in the cache, when we have a cache hit. Transfers between main memory and cache occur at granularity of cache lines, around 32 or 64 bytes (rather than bytes or processor words). Burst transfers of this kind receive hardware support and exploit spatial locality of access to the cache (future access are often to address near to the previous one)

Since CPUs are only made with instructions for reading and writing to memory, no programs would be able to run without it. There are two types of memory: RAM - random access memory, or read/write memory, which loses its contents when the machine is switched off, and ROM - read only memory, which never loses its contents unless destroyed. ROM is normally used for storing those most fundamental parts of the operating system which are required the instant a computer is switched on, before it knows about disks etc. The **random access memory** *(main memory)* is the most important resource a computer has. It is a large array of bits, organized into words or bytes. Each word or byte is addressable. CPU fetches instructions from memory according to the value (an address) in the PC register. Instructions may invoke the CPU to fetch or store data in memory.

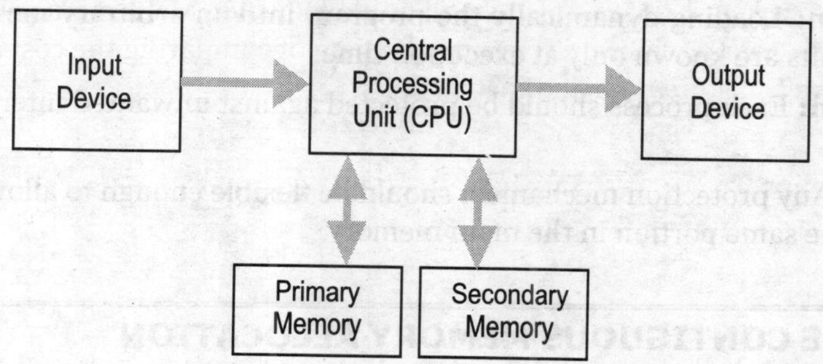

Figure 7.41: A modern computer system

Secondary memory, also known as secondary storage, is the slower and cheaper form of memory. CPU does not access the secondary memory directly. The content in it must first be copied into the primary storage RAM for CPU to process. Secondary memory devices include hard drives, floppy disks, CDs and CDROMs etc.

A program is fetched from hard disk to main memory. – When executed, instructions in the program are fetched from the main memory to CPU.

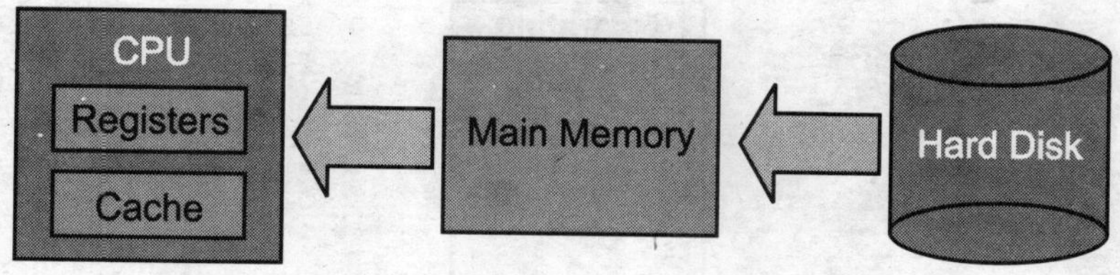

Figure 7.42: Execution of Instructions

Most modern computer systems implement a Virtual Memory scheme that lets them simulate main memory using storage on a disk drive. While disks are significantly slower than main memory, the cost per bit is also significantly lower. Therefore, it is far less expensive (by three orders of magnitude) to keep some data on magnetic storage rather than in main memory. In next chapter we will learn about virtual memory management.

The program is largely unaware of the memory hierarchy. In fact, the program only explicitly controls access to main memory and those components of the memory hierarchy at the file storage level and below (since manipulating files is a program-specific operation). In particular, cache access and virtual memory operation are generally transparent to the program. That is, access to these levels of the memory hierarchy usually takes place without any intervention on the program's part. The program just accesses main memory and the hardware (and operating system) take care of the rest.

7.19.2 MEMORY MANAGEMENT REQUIREMENTS

Following are the memory management requirements:

- **Relocation:** Loading dynamically the program into an arbitrary memory space, whose address limits are known only at execution time.
- **Protection:** Each process should be protected against unwanted interference from other processes.
- **Sharing:** Any protection mechanism should be flexible enough to allow several processes to access the same portion in the main memory.

7.19.3 SINGLE CONTIGUOUS MEMORY ALLOCATION (UNI-PROGRAMMING)

In uni-programming systems a single program can be in memory at a time. Program address is same as real memory address. The main memory is divided into two parts. Resident operating system in low memory and one user process is in high memory. The whole program is in memory for execution. When current program is finished, it is replaced by another program. Program must fit memory. When one program is running, no other program can be executed. It is not efficient especially for I/O waiting, as the CPU needs to wait for the time period when the I/O is performed.

Figure 7.43: Uni-Programming System

When user type command, operating system copies program from disk to memory and execute. It overwrites memory with the new program, thus deleting the previous resident program.

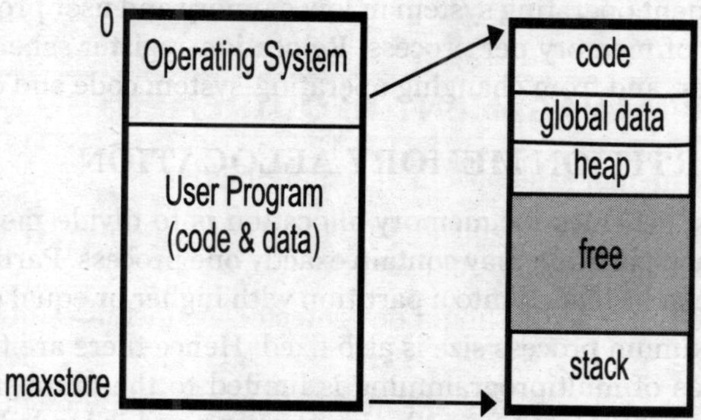

Figure 7.44: Memory Organization for a C Program

Advantages

1. This scheme is simple as no special H/W is required.
2. There is no need for address relocation because program address is equal to physical memory address.

Disadvantages

1. Programs must fit into memory.
2. Unused memory is being wasted.
3. It is Single user. There is no multi-programming.

7.19.4 MULTIPROGRAMMING

This is programming environment when more than one program is resident in memory. These programs are executed concurrently. When one program needs to wait for an I/O to be performed, another program can be allotted the CPU. Hence, the CPU idle time is utilized in an efficient manner.

Memory Allocation in multiprogramming systems can be divided into two categories: Contiguous Memory Allocation and Non-Contiguous Memory Allocation.

1. Contiguous Memory Allocation

(i) Fixed partition memory allocation
(ii) Variable partition memory allocation

2. Non-Contiguous Memory Allocation

(i) Paging (ii) Segmentation

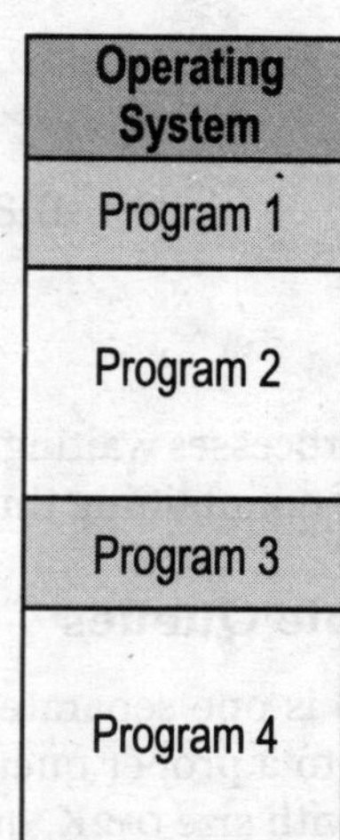

Figure 7.45: Multiprogramming System

7.19.5 CONTIGUOUS MEMORY ALLOCATION

It is straight-forward method to allocate memory to several processes. Memory is divided into two partitions: Resident operating system in low memory and user processes in high memory. It assumes a single area of memory per process. Relocation-register scheme used to protect user processes from each other, and from changing operating-system code and data.

7.19.5.1 FIXED PARTITION MEMORY ALLOCATION

One of the simplest schemes for memory allocation is to divide memory into a number of fixed-sized partitions. Each partition may contain exactly one process. Partitions can be of equal or unequal size. A process can be loaded into a partition with higher or equal size.

In this scheme maximum process size is also fixed. Hence there are fixed maximum number of processes. Thus degree of multiprogramming is limited to the number of partitions. When a partition is free, a process is selected from the input queue and is loaded into the free partition. When the process terminates, the partition is freed and becomes available for another process. This scheme was originally used by the IBM OS/360 operating system (called MFT); it is no longer in use. These partitions could be of different size, but once decided at the time of system generation, they could not be changed.

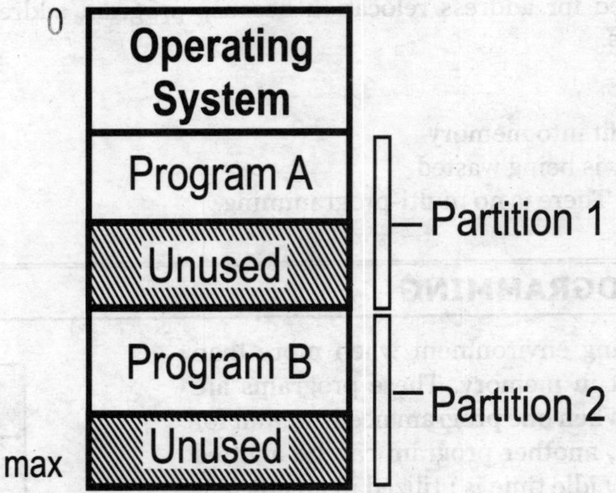

Figure 7.46: Fixed partitions

The processes waiting to be loaded in the memory are held in a queue by the OS. There are two methods of maintaining this queue, multiple queue and single queue.

1) Multiple Queues

There is one separate queue for each partition. Where a process wants to occupy memory, it is added to a proper queue depending upon size of the process. For instance, queue 0 will hold processes with size 0-2K, queue 2 will be processes with size between 3K-5K and queue 1 will take care of processes with size between 6K and 8K etc. as shown in figure 7.47:

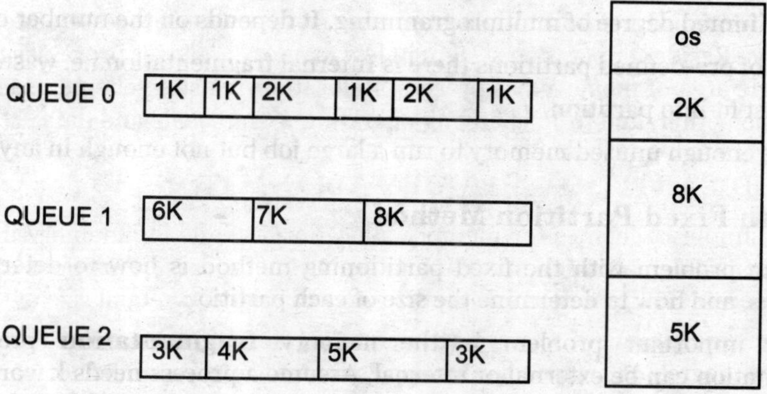

Figure 7.47: Multiple Queues

Advantage of this scheme is that a very small process is not loaded in a very large partition. Thus it avoids memory wastage.

2) Single Queue

In this scheme, whenever a partition becomes free, the job closest to the front of the queue that fits in it could be loaded into the empty partition and run. Since it is undesirable to waste a large partition on a small job, a different strategy is to search the whole input queue whenever a partition becomes free and picks the largest job that fits.

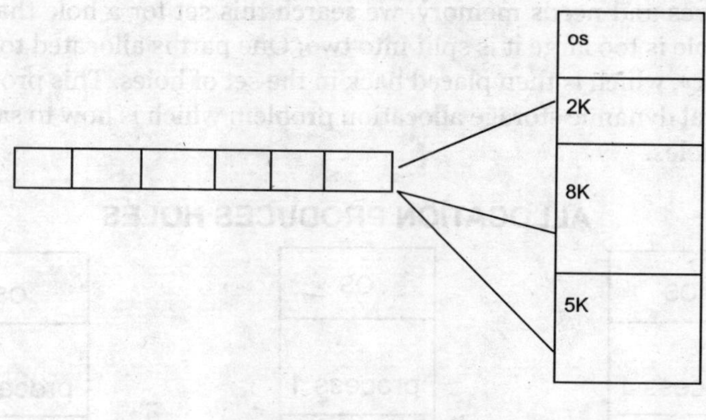

Figure 7.48: Single Queue

Advantages

1. This scheme permits multi-programming.
2. It needs relocating loader.
3. There is usually some H/W protection between partitions. E.g., OS/MFT

Disadvantages

1. There is limited degree of multiprogramming. It depends on the number of partitions.
2. Because of pre-defined partitions there is Internal fragmentation i.e. wasted space.
3. Jobs must fit into partition.
4. Could be enough unused memory to run a large job but not enough in any one partition.

Problems with Fixed Partition Method

1. The main problem with the fixed partitioning method is how to determine the no. of partitions, and how to determine the size of each partition.
2. Another important problem is the memory **fragmentation** problem. Memory fragmentation can be external or internal. Assume a process needs k words. Then, it may be run in a partition of m words where $K \leq m$. If $k = m$, then (m-k) is **internal frag**On the other hand, if one partition is currently not being used at all, then this is **external fragmentation**.

7.19.5.2 DYNAMIC (VARIABLE) PARTITION MEMORY ALLOCATION

Variable partitions come into existence to overcome the problem of fragmentation in fixed partition scheme. When variable partitions are used, the number and size of the processes in the memory vary dynamically.

Memory is divided into variable length partitions. These Variable sized holes in memory are allocated on need of processes. Each partition holds one program. A program occupies contiguous locations. OS keeps track of used and free memory segments. A free memory segment is called a hole. In general, there is at any time a set of holes, of various sizes, scattered throughout memory. When a process arrives and needs memory, we search this set for a hole that is large enough for this process. If the hole is too large it is split into two: One part is allocated to the arriving process, the other is of memory, which is then placed back in the set of holes. This procedure is a particular instance of the general dynamic storage allocation problem which is how to satisfy a request of size n from a list of free holes.

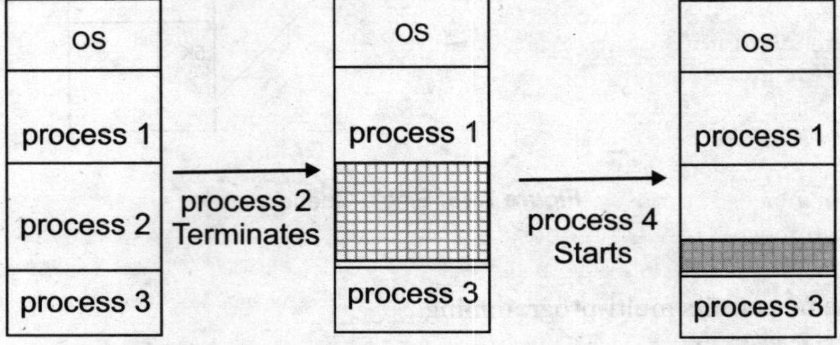

Figure 7.49: Holes during Allocation

Memory organized as before but partition created dynamically at the start of a job. i.e. OS attempts to allocate a contiguous block of memory = process size. E.g. OS MVT

Example

Total memory = 500K

J1 requires 100K

J2 requires 50K

J3 requires 240K

J4 requires 120K

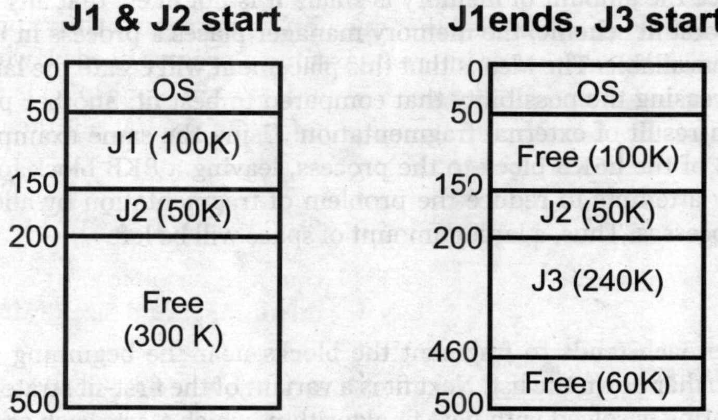

Figure 7.50: An example

160K of memory area is free but we cannot start J4 because there is not a contiguous 120K memory block. That is memory fragmentation is there.

Memory holes appear after programs are replaced. Removing the holes create extra overhead. The fragmentation problem could be solved by moving running programs to close free gaps and create larger ones called compaction.

PARTITION SIZE SELECTION

It is concerned with how to satisfy a request for memory from a given set of free holes. **Most popular strategies are described below:**

(i) Best fit

The allocator places a process in the smallest block of unallocated memory in which it will fit. For example, suppose a process requests 18KB of memory and the memory manager currently has a list of unallocated blocks of 6KB, 16KB, 22KB, 19KB, and 26KB blocks. The best-fit strategy will allocate 18KB of the 19KB block to the process. One problem with scheme is that it requires an expensive search of the entire free list to find the best hole. More importantly, it leads to the creation of lots of little holes that are not big enough to satisfy any requests. This situation is called fragmentation, and is a problem for all memory-management strategies.

(ii) First fit

There may be many holes in the memory, so the operating system, simply scans the free list beginning at the start of primary memory and allocates memory from the first hole it encounters large enough to satisfy the request. Using the same example as above, first fit will allocate 18KB of the 22KB block to the process. First-fit is generally better than best-fit because it leads to less fragmentation. Problem with this scheme is that Small holes tend to accumulate near the beginning of the free list, making the memory allocator search farther and farther each time.

(iii) Worst fit

The best fit and first fit strategies both leave a tiny segment of memory unallocated just beyond the new process. Since the amount of memory is small, it is not likely that any new processes can be loaded here. In worst fit scheme, the memory manager places a process in the largest block of unallocated memory available. The idea is that this placement will create the largest hole after the allocations, thus increasing the possibility that compared to best fit; another process can use the remaining space as a result of external fragmentation. Using the same example as above, worst fit will allocate 18KB of the 26KB block to the process, leaving a 8KB block for future use. Thus the worst fit strategy attempts to reduce the problem of fragmentation by allocating the largest fragments to new processes. Thus, a larger amount of space will be left.

(iv) Next Fit

The first fit approach tends to fragment the blocks near the beginning of the list without considering blocks further down the list. Next fit is a variant of the first-fit strategy. The problem of small holes accumulating is solved with next fit algorithm, which starts each search where the last one left off, wrapping around to the beginning when the end of the list is reached.

7.19.6 FRAGMENTATION

Both the best fit and first fir strategies suffer from the problem of external fragmentation. As the processes are loaded and removed from memory, the free memory space is broken into little pieces. External fragmentation exists when there is enough total memory space to satisfy a request, but the available spaces are contiguous. Storage is fragmented into a large number of small holes. This fragmentation problem can be severe. In the worst case, we could have a block of free memory between every two processes. If all these small pieces of memory were in one big free block instead, we might be able to run several more processes.

Depending upon the total amount of memory storage and the average process size, external fragmentation may be a major or minor problem. Statistical analysis of fist-fir, for instance, reveals that even with some optimization, given the N allocated blocks, another 0.5 N blocks will be lost to fragmentation. That is, one third of the memory may become unusable. This property is known as 50-percent rule. Memory fragmentation can be internal as well as external.

7.19.6.1 INTERNAL FRAGMENTATION

A process is allocated more memory space than it requested because the overhead (to track the small hole that would have remained) is larger than the hole itself .e.g. If a partition of size 100k is allocated to a process of size 60k, then the 40k space of that partition is wasted and cannot be allocated to any other process. This is called internal fragmentation.

7.19.6.2 EXTERNAL FRAGMENTATION

External fragmentation is the phenomenon in which free storage becomes divided into many small pieces over time. It is a weakness of certain storage allocation algorithms, occurring when an application allocates and deallocates ("frees") regions of storage of varying sizes, and the allocation algorithm responds by leaving the allocated and deallocated regions interspersed. The result is that although free storage is available, it is effectively unusable because it is divided into pieces that are too small to satisfy the demands of the application. The term "external" refers to the fact that the unusable storage is outside the allocated regions. For example, in dynamic memory allocation, a block of 1000 bytes might be requested, but the largest contiguous block of free space has only 300 bytes. Even if there are ten blocks of 300 bytes of free space, separated by allocated regions, one still cannot allocate the requested block of 1000 bytes, and the allocation request will fail.

One solution to the problem of external fragmentation is compaction. The goal is to shuffle the memory contents so as to place all free memory together in one large block. Compaction is not always possible.

7.19.7 COMPACTION

Compaction is a solution to external fragmentation that consolidates separate free holes into a contiguous block. It may not work for all processes. It works by moving all the allocated blocks to one end of memory, thus combining all the holes. Aside from the obvious cost of all that copying, there is an important limitation to compaction: Any pointers to a block need to be updated when the block is moved. Unless it is possible to find all such pointers, compaction is not possible. Pointers can stored in the allocated blocks themselves as well as other places in the client of the memory manager. In some situations, pointers can point not only to the start of blocks but also into their bodies. For example, if a block contains executable code, a branch instruction might be a pointer to another location in the same block. Compaction is performed in three phases. First, the new location of each block is calculated to determine the distance the block will be moved. Then each pointer is updated by adding to it the amount that the block it is pointing (in) to will be moved. Finally, the data is actually moved.

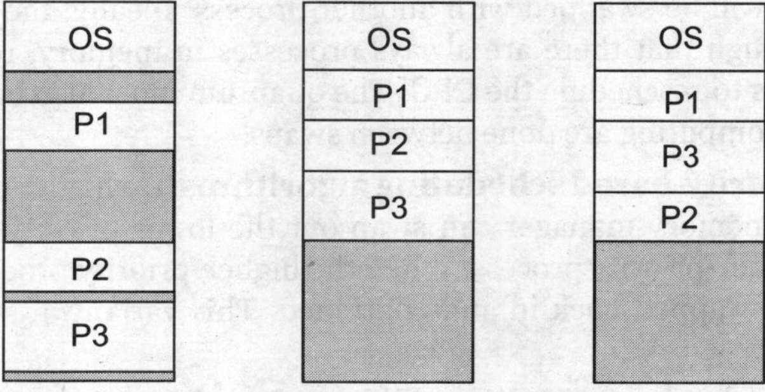

Figure 7.51: Compaction

Drawbacks with variable partitions:

1. External fragmentation is there which can be removed by compaction. As processes are loaded and removed from memory, the free memory space is broken into little pieces; external fragmentation exists when enough total memory space exists to satisfy a request, but it is not contiguous; hence memory is fragmented into a large set of small holes. For example it may happen that two free partitions of size 30k and 40k are available and a process of 50 k has to be accommodated. In this case both the available partitions cannot be allocated to that processes, because it will violate our assumption. For this scheme, viz. that only contiguous memory should be allocated to that process. As a result there is wastage of memory space. This is called 'external fragmentation'.
2. Swapping is difficult, if not impossible.

7.19.8 SWAPPING

The process of organizing memory into fixed partitions on batch system is simple compared to time sharing systems. On batch systems, each job is loaded into a partition when it gets to the head of the queue. It stays in memory until it has finished. As long as enough jobs can be kept in memory to keep the CPU busy all the time, there is no reason to use anything more complicated. On time-sharing machines, sometimes there is not enough main memory to hold all the currently active processes, therefore excess processes must be kept on disk and brought in to run dynamically. To run these processes they must be brought into the main memory. Moving processes from the main memory to disk and back is called **swapping**.

Swapping is an approach to memory management which consists of bringing each process in its entirety, running it for a while, and then putting it back on the disk. When a job finishes, we first swap back jobs from disk before allowing new jobs to start. When a job is blocked we have a choice of leaving it in memory or swapping it out. One way of looking at this scheme is that it increases the multiprogramming level (the number of jobs 'in memory') at the cost of making it (much) more expensive to switch jobs.

For example, in multiprogramming environment with a round-robin CPU-scheduling algorithm, when a quantum expires, the memory manager will start to swap out the process that just finished, and to swap in another process to the memory space that has been freed. In the meantime, the CPU scheduler will allocate a **time slice** to some other process in memory. When each process finishes its quantum, it will be swapped with another process. Ideally, the memory manager can swap processes fast enough that there are always processes in memory, ready to execute, when the CPU scheduler wants to reschedule the CPU. The quantum must also be sufficiently large that reasonable amounts of computing are done between swaps.

For example in **priority-based scheduling algorithms**, if a higher-priority process arrives and wants service, the memory manager can swap out the lower-priority process so that it can load and execute the higher-priority process. When the higher-priority process finishes, the lower-priority process can be swapped back in and continued. This variant of swapping is sometimes called the roll out, roll in.

Normally a process that is swapped out will be swapped back into the same memory space that it occupied previously. This restriction is dictated by the method of address binding. If binding is done at assembly or load time, then the process cannot be moved to different locations. If execution-time binding is being used, then it is possible to swap a process into a different memory space, because the physical addresses are computed during execution time. Swapping out a process involves copying all memory containing data (and program code if it has changed) onto the disk, and releasing the main memory that it was using. The process is then suspended until there is an opportunity to swap it back in again. All data and program code is restored from the copy on disk, allowing the process to continue running in main memory from the point before it was swapped out.

Swapping requires a backing store. The backing store is commonly a fast disk. It must be large enough to accommodate copies of all memory images for all users, and must provide direct access to these memory images. The system maintains a ready queue consisting of all processes whose memory images are on the backing store or in memory and are ready to run. Whenever the CPU scheduler decides to execute a process, it calls the dispatcher. The dispatcher checks to see whether the next process in the queue is in memory. If the process is not, and there is no free memory region, the dispatcher swaps out a process currently in memory and swaps in the desired process. It then reloads registers as normal and transfers control to the selected process.

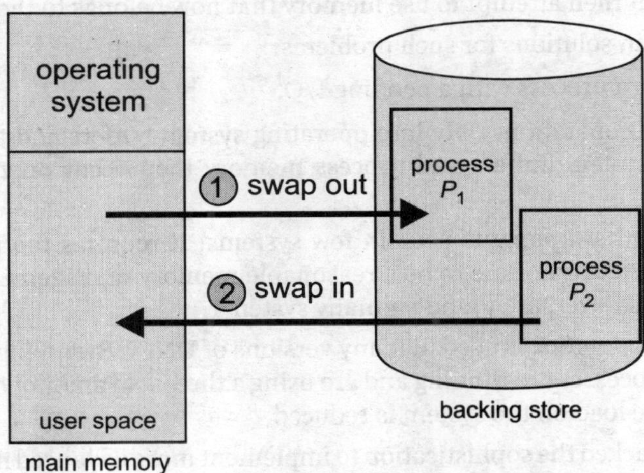

Figure 7.52: Swapping of two processes using disk as a backing store

For efficient CPU utilization, we want our execution time for each process to be long relative to the swap time. The major part of the swap time is transfer time. The total transfer time is directly proportional to the amount of memory swapped.

The mid-term scheduler, present in all systems with virtual memory, temporarily removes processes from main memory and places them on secondary memory (such as a disk drive) or vice versa. This is commonly referred to as "swapping out" or "swapping in" The mid-term scheduler may decide to swap out a process which has not been active for some time, or a process which has a low priority, or a process which is page faulting frequently, or a process which is taking up a large amount of memory in order to free up main memory for other processes, swapping the process back in later when more memory is available, or when the process has been unblocked and is no longer waiting for a resource.

Notice that the major part of the swap time is transfer time. The total transfer time is directly proportional to the amount of memory swapped. If there is a computer system with 512 MB main memory and a resident operating system taking 25 MB, the maximum size of the user process is 487 MB. However, many user processes may be much smaller than this, say 10 MB. A 10 MB process could be swapped out in 258 milliseconds, compared with 6.4 seconds required for swapping 256 MB. Clearly, it would be useful to know exactly how much memory a user process is using, not simply how much it might be using. Then we would need to swap only what is actually used, reducing swap time. For this method to be effective, the user must keep the system informed of any changes in memory requirements. Thus, a process with dynamic memory requirements will need to issue system calls to inform operating system of its changing memory needs.

Swapping is constrained by other factors as well. If we want to swap a process, we must be sure that it is completely idle (inactive). Idle process is one which is not running and not doing any I/O. Generally swap space is allocated as a separate chunk of disk, separate from the file system, so that its use is as fast as possible. However, if the I/O is asynchronously accessing the user memory for I/O buffers, then the process cannot be swapped. Assume that the I/O operation is queued because the device is busy. If we were to swap out a process and swap in another process in its place, the I/O operation might then attempt to use memory that now belongs to the new process.

There are two main solutions for such problems:

- Never swap a process with a pending I/O.
- Execute I/O operations only into operating system buffers and the transfers between operating system buffers and process memory then occur only when the process is swapped in.

Currently, standard swapping is used in few systems. It requires too much swapping time and provides too little execution time to be a reasonable memory management solution. Modified versions of swapping, however, are found on many systems.

A modification of swapping is used in many versions of UNIX. Swapping is normally disabled but will start if many processes are running and are using a threshold amount of memory. Swapping is again halted when the load on the system is reduced.

Early PC's which lacked the sophistication to implement more advanced memory management methods which ran multiple large processes by using a modified version of swapping. A prime example is the Microsoft Windows 3.1 operating system, which supports concurrent execution of processes in memory. If a new process is loaded and there is insufficient main memory, an old process is swapped to disk. This operating system, however, does not provide full swapping, because the user rather than scheduler decides when it is time to preempt one process for another. Any swapped-out process remains swapped out until the user selects that process to run again. Subsequent versions of Microsoft operating systems take advantage of the advanced MMU features now found in personal computers.

7.19.9 PAGING

Paging is a memory-management technique that permits the physical address space of a process to be non-contiguous. Paging avoids the considerable overhead of fitting memory chunks of varying sizes into backing storage. Most memory management schemes used before the introduction of paging suffered this problem. The problem arises because when some code fragments or data residing in main memory need to be swapped out, space must be found on the backing store. The backing store also has fragmentation problems discussed in connection with main memory, except that access is much slower, so compaction is impossible. Because of its advantages over earlier methods, paging in its various forms is commonly used in most operating systems.

In paging, the Logical memory is divided into equal, small pieces, called pages. However, process 'sees' a contiguous, flat address space. Each process is given a page table to define the valid addresses and map them to physical memory. The page table is usually invisible to the process. Page tables make it easy to allocate new memory for a process, as the each new page can be allocated from anywhere in physical memory.

Physical memory is divided into fixed sized frames. Pages and page frames are of same size. Paging allocates physical memory to processes in fixed size chunks called page frames. Pages are stored in page frames. Pages can be *arbitrarily* mapped onto frames i.e. a frame is a place where a (logical) page can be (physically) placed

When process generates an address, dynamically translate to the physical page frame which holds data for that page. Page sizes are typically powers of 2 (Generally 2-4 KB on modern systems).

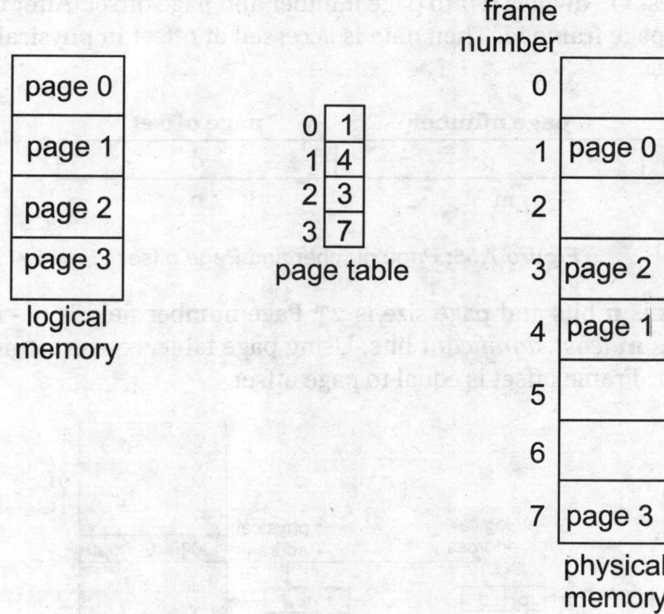

Figure 7.53: Paging model of Logical and Physical Memory

Each Program has its own address space. For example, three processes A, B, C are stored on disk and are about to be loaded in the memory (by the operating system).

Process A has two pages

Process B has three pages

Process C has two pages

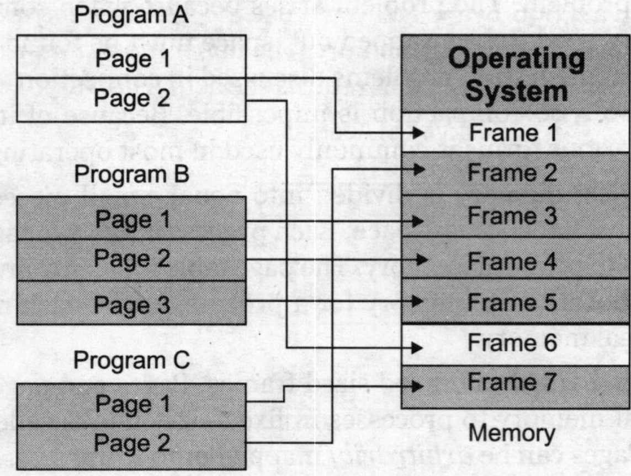

Figure 7.54: An example of paging technique

A logical address now consists of two parts: a page number and an offset within that page. For every logical address OS divides it into page number and page offset. After that page number is translated to physical page frame id. Then data is accessed at offset in physical page frame. MMU splits logical address as:

page number	page offset
p	d
m−n	n

Figure 7.55: Page number and Page offset

If logical address is **n** bits and page size is 2^m. Page number field is **n - m** *most significant* bits. Page offset field is **m** *least significant* bits. Using page table, convert logical page number to physical frame number. Frame offset is equal to page offset

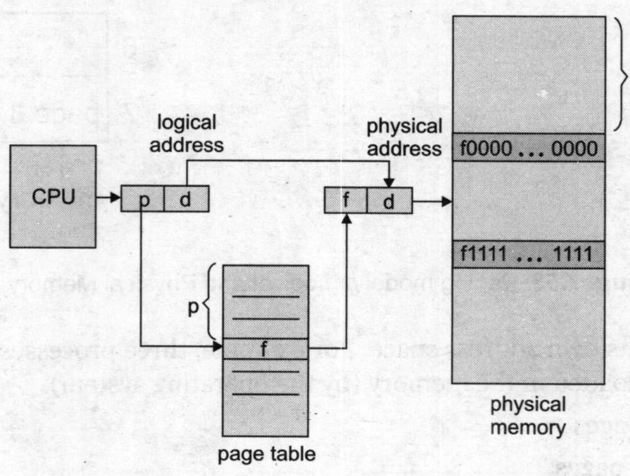

Figure 7.56: Paging hardware

For example, with a 4,096-byte page, you'd use the *least significant* 12 bits of the virtual address as the offset within the page in physical memory. The upper *most significant* 20 bits of the address you would use as an index into a page table that returns the actual upper 20 bits of the physical address.

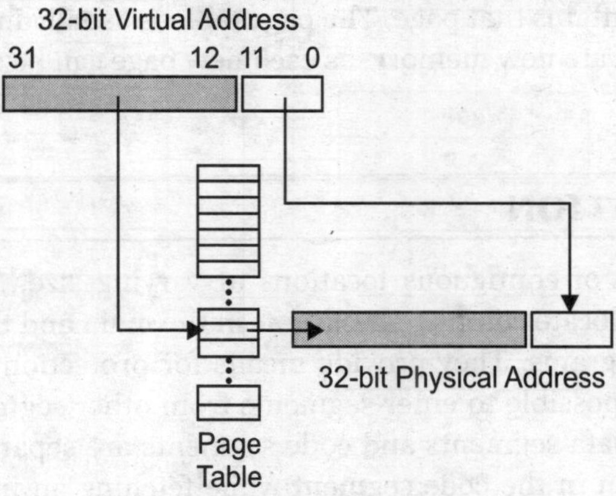

Figure 7.57: Address translation

Steps to access physical Address

- Extract page number and offset from logical address.
- Check that page number is within address space of process.
- Look up page number in page table to find frame number.
- Add offset to resulting physical frame number.

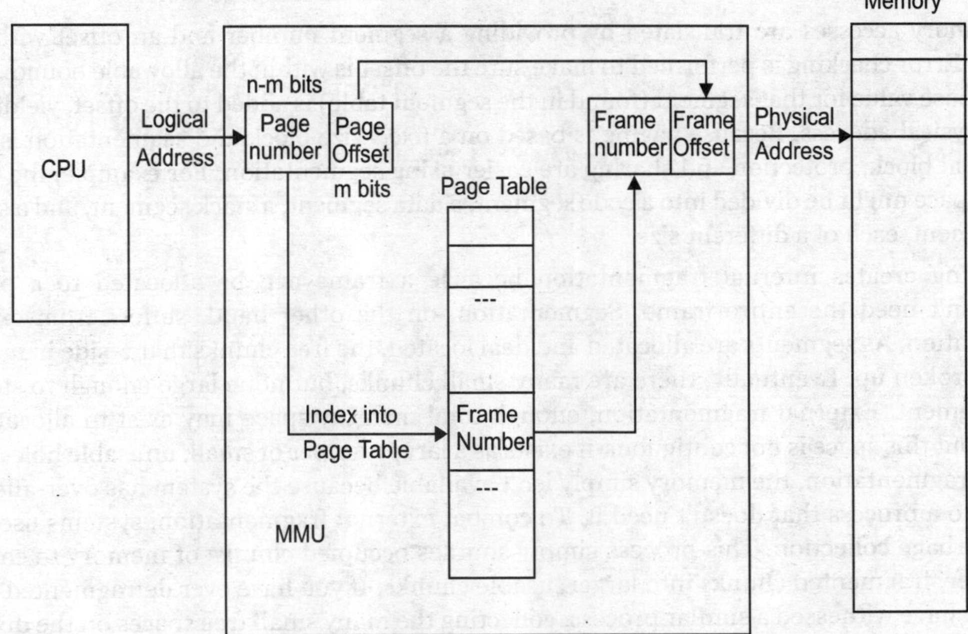

Figure 7.58: Logical-to-Physical Address conversion by MMU

Paging avoids external fragmentation. A page table is used for mapping virtual memory to physical memory. In other words the translation from page number to physical page frame id is done through a page table. Page table is a linear array indexed by virtual page number that gives the physical page frame that contains that page. The page table is usually invisible to the process. Page tables make it easier to allocate new memory, as each new page can be allocated from anywhere in physical memory.

7.19.10 SEGMENTATION

A segment is a block of contiguous locations of varying size. Segments are used by the operating system (OS) to relocate complete programs in the main and the disk memory. Segments can be shared between programs. They provide means for protection from unauthorized access and/or execution. It is not possible to enter segments from other segments unless the access has been specifically allowed. Data segments and code segments are separated. It should also not be possible to alter information in the code segment while fetching an instruction nor should it be possible to execute data in a data segment.

Instead of dividing the virtual address space into equal, fixed-size pages, and the physical address space into equal-size page frames, the virtual address space is divided into logical, variable-length units, or segments. Physical memory isn't really divided or partitioned into anything. When a segment needs to be copied into physical memory, the operating system looks for a chunk of free memory large enough to store the entire segment. Each segment has a base address, indicating were it is located in memory, and a bounds limit, indicating its size. Each program, consisting of multiple segments, now has an associated segment table instead of a page table.

Memory accesses are translated by providing a segment number and an offset within the segment. Error checking is performed to make sure the offset is within the allowable bound. If it is, then the base value for that segment (found in the segment table) is added to the offset, yielding the actual physical address. Because paging is based on a fixed-size block and segmentation is based on a logical block, protection and sharing are easier using segmentation. For example, the virtual address space might be divided into a code segment, a data segment, a stack segment, and a symbol table segment, each of a different size.

Paging creates internal fragmentation because a frame can be allocated to a process that doesn't need the entire frame. Segmentation, on the other hand, suffers from external fragmentation. As segments are allocated and deal located, the free chunks that reside in memory become broken up. Eventually, there are many small chunks, but none large enough to store an entire segment. External fragmentation, enough total memory space may exist to allocate to a process, but this space is not contiguous-it exists as a large number of small, unusable holes. With internal fragmentation, the memory simply isn't available because the system has over-allocated memory to a process that doesn't need it. To combat external fragmentation, systems use some sort of garbage collection. This process simply shuffles occupied chunks of memory to coalesce the smaller, fragmented chunks into larger, usable chunks. If you have ever defragmented a disk drive, you have witnessed a similar process, collecting the many small free spaces on the disk and creating fewer, larger ones.

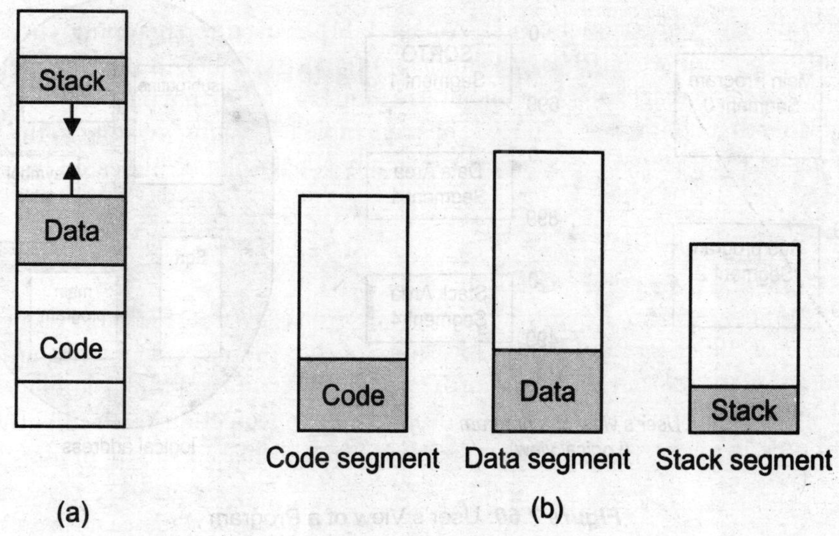

Figure 7.59: Dynamic data structure allocation: (a) in a single address space, boundary problems can lead to a growing data part bumping into the stack area; (b) segmentation avoids such boundary problems by allocating separate segments.

Segmentation is a memory management scheme that supports a user view of memory with modularizations (collection of segments). User views memory as a collection of variable-sized segments, rather than a linear array of bytes. It supports "Object oriented" approach. User views program as a set of objects: like Stack, Routines. , Arrays etc. Each object is stored in a segment. Frames start on 2^m memory boundaries. Segments start anywhere. Therefore, operating system will *add* a segment base and offset. Separate segments for different types of memory content:

main program
program libraries
constants
stack
objects
symbol table
. . .

and each segment can have its own protection, grow independently, etc.

Elements are identified within a segment by their offset from the beginning of the segment. A process is divided into a number of segments that don't need to be equal in size. When a process is brought into the main memory, then all of its segments are usually brought into main memory and a process segment table is setup.

Programmer's view of memory is not usually as a single linear address space. Programmer doesn't know how large these will be, or how they'll grow, and doesn't want to manage where they go in memory. In following example these segments can be stored anywhere in memory.

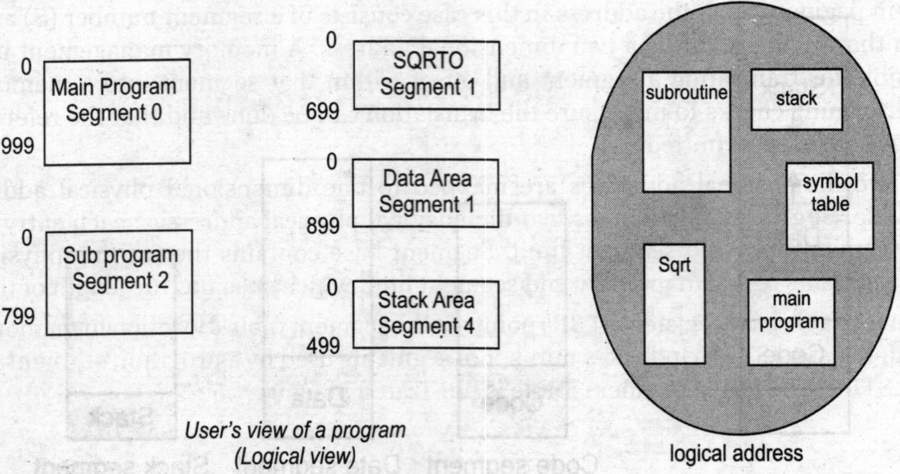

Figure 7.60: User's View of a Program

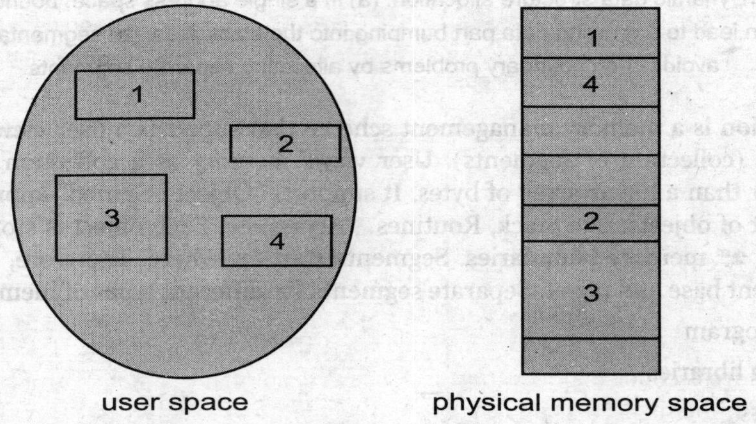

Figure 7.61: User Space and Physical Memory Space

User can now refer to objects in the program by a two-dimensional address. But the actual physical memory is still a one-dimensional sequence of bytes. There must be a mapping from logical to physical address.

Segmentation is a memory management scheme that supports this user view of the memory. A logical address space is a collection of segments. Each segment has a name and a length. The addresses specify both the segment name and the offset within the segment. The user therefore specifies each address by two quantities: a segment name and an offset. For simplicity of implementation, segments are numbered and are referenced by a segment number rather than a segment name. Thus, a logical address consists of a two parts:

`<segment-number, offset>`

Like in paging system the address in this case consists of a segment number (S) and an offset (D) within that segment, forms a two dimensional address. A memory management unit (MMU) is responsible for translating a segment and offset within that segment into a memory address, and for performing checks to make sure the translation can be done and that the reference to that segment and offset is permitted.

The two dimensional addresses are mapped to one dimensional physical addresses by a segment table. **Segment table** maps two-dimensional physical addresses; each entry in segment table has segment base and segment limit. Segment base contains the starting physical address where the segments reside in memory and segment limit which specifies the length of the segment.

Segment-table base register (STBR) points to the segment table's location in memory. Segment table length register (STLR) indicates number of segments used by a program; segment number s is legal if s < STLR. The use of Segment Table is illustrated in figure 7.62.

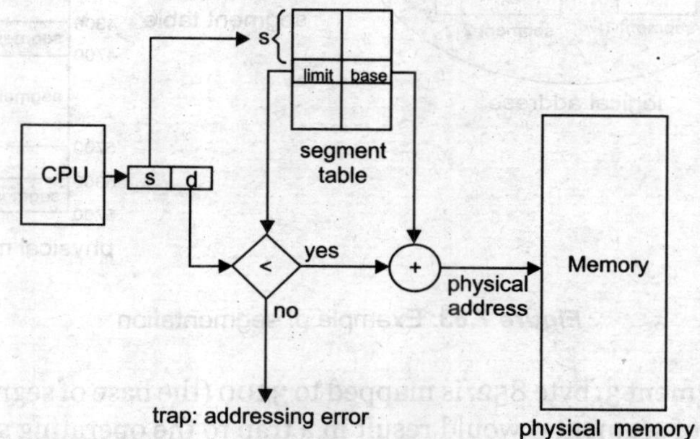

Figure 7.62: Segmentation Hardware

A logical address consists of two parts: a segment number s, and an offset into that segment d. The segment number is used as an index to the segment table. The offset d of the logical address must be between 0 and the segment limit. If it is not, we trap to the operating system. When an offset is legal, it is added to the segment base to produce the address in physical memory of the desired byte. The segment table is thus essentially an array of base-limit register pairs.

Segmentation and paging share lot of common principles of operation, except that pages are physical in nature and hence are of fixed size, whereas segments are logical division of a program and hence are normally of variable sizes.

A segment has a set of permissions, and a length, associated with it. If the currently running process is allowed by the permissions to make the type of reference to memory that it is attempting to make, and the offset within the segment is within the range specified by the length of the segment, the reference is permitted; otherwise, a hardware exception is raised.

As an example, consider the situation shown in figure 7.62. We have five segments numbered 0 through 4. The segments are stored in physical memory as shown. The segment table has a separate entry for each segment, giving the beginning address of the segment in physical memory (or base) and the length of that segment (or limit). For example, segment 2 is 400 bytes long and begins at location 4300. Thus, a reference to byte 53 of segment 2 is mapped onto location 4300 + 53= 4353.

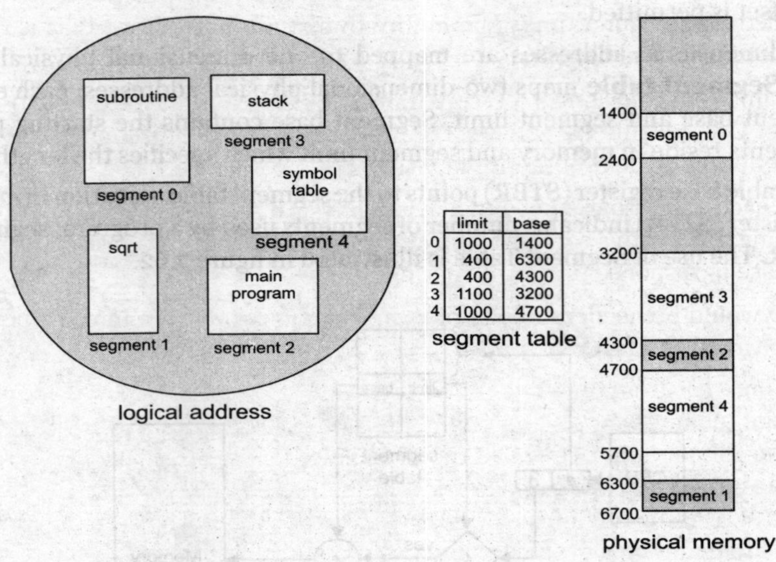

Figure 7.63: Example of segmentation

A reference to segment 3, byte 852, is mapped to 3200 (the base of segment 3) + 852= 4052. A reference to byte 1222 of segment 0 would result in a trap to the operating system, as this segment is only 1,000 bytes long.

7.20 VIRTUAL MEMORY

In previous section used memory management techniques for multiprogramming. However the requirement was that an entire process must be in memory for execution. Another way in which the memory manager enhances the ability of the operating system to support multiple processes running simultaneously is by the use of **virtual memory**. Virtual memory strategies allow a process to use the CPU when only part of its address space is loaded in the primary memory i.e. virtual memory is a technique that allows the execution of processes that may not be completely in memory.

The requirement that instructions must be in physical memory to be executed seems both necessary and reasonable; but it is also unfortunate, since it limits the size of physical memory. In fact, an examination of real programs shows that the entire program is not always needed. For instance, consider the following:

- Programs often have code to handle unusual error conditions. Since these errors seldom occur in practice, this code is almost never executed.
- Arrays, lists and tables are often allocated more memory than they actually need. For example, an array may be declared 100*100 elements, even though it is seldom larger than 10*10 elements.

- Certain options and features of a program may be used rarely. For instance, the routines on U.S. government computers that balance the budget are only rarely used.

In the cases when the whole program is needed, it may never be the case that whole of the program is needed at the same time. The ability to execute a program that is only partially in memory would confer several benefits:

- A program would no longer be constrained by the amount of physical memory that is available. Users would be able to write programs for an extremely large virtual address space, simplifying the programming task.
- Because each user program could take less physical memory, more programs could be run at the same time, with a corresponding increase in CPU utilization and throughput but with no increase in response time or turnaround time.
- Less I/O would be needed to load or swap each user program into memory, so each user program would run faster.

Thus, running a program that is not entirely in memory would benefit both the system and the user. In the virtual memory approach, each process's address space is partitioned into parts that can be loaded into primary memory when they are needed and written back to secondary memory otherwise. **Virtual memory** is a computer system technique which gives an application program the impression that it has contiguous working memory (an address space); while in fact it may be physically fragmented and may even overflow on to disk storage. Benefit of this scheme is that the system can run programs which are actually larger than the primary memory of the system, hence the idea of virtual memory.

Virtual memory is the separation of the user logical memory from physical memory. This separation allows an extremely large virtual memory to be provided for programmers when only smaller physical memory is available. Virtual memory makes the task of programming much easier because the programmer no longer needs to worry about the limited amount of physical memory available.

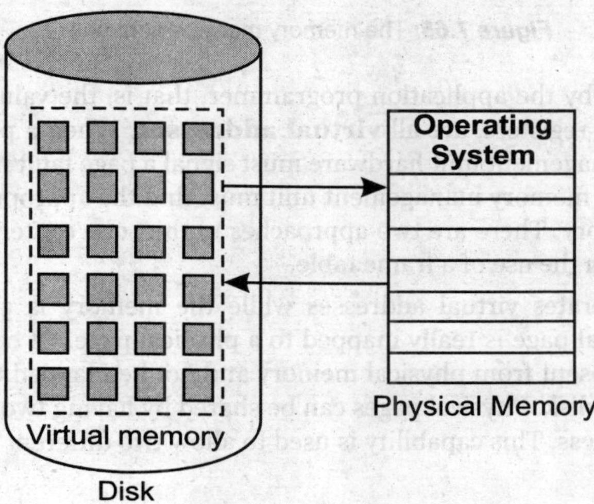

Figure 7.64: Virtual Memory

All modern general-purpose computer operating systems use virtual memory techniques for ordinary applications, such as word processors, spreadsheets, multimedia players, accounting, etc. Older operating systems generally had no virtual memory functionality.

If data is not available in main memory, but is available in slower virtual memory, the virtual memory subsystem is responsible for moving the data from hard disk to main memory (and then the caching subsystem may move the data from main memory to cache for even faster access by the CPU).

7.20.1 VIRTUAL ADDRESSES AND PHYSICAL ADDRESSES

On system that supports virtual memory overlays have almost disappeared. Operating systems that support virtual addressing rely on the services of **memory management unit or MMU.** The memory management unit sits logically between the processor and the main memory. For some computers, the memory management unit is an optional component, while for others, including most modern microprocessors, the memory management unit is an integral part of the processor chip.

However it takes, as input, the virtual addresses issues by the program and produces, as output, the physical addresses used by the memory. This is illustrated in the figure 7.65:

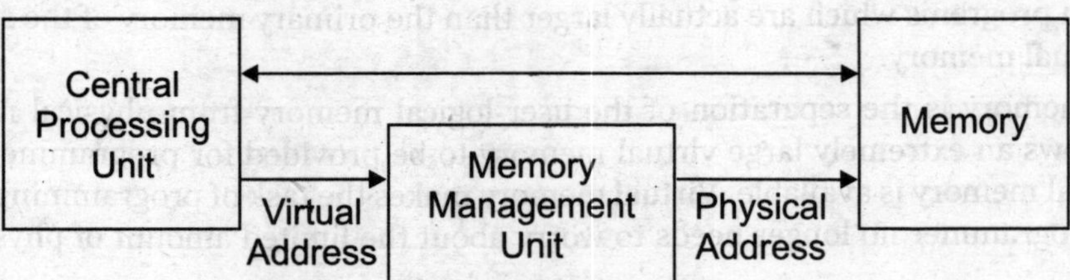

Figure 7.65: The memory management unit

The addresses seen by the application programmer, that is, the values of pointer variables, object handles and index registers, are all **virtual addresses**. When a program issues a virtual address, the memory management unit hardware must signal a page fault if the desired page is not in main memory, and the memory management unit must find the appropriate physical address if the page is in main memory. There are two approaches to this, one centered on the use of a page table, and one centered on the use of a frame table.

The processor generates virtual addresses while the memory is accessed using physical addresses. Both the virtual page is really mapped to a physical page. Of course, it is also possible for a virtual page to be absent from physical memory and not be mapped to a physical address as soon, residing instead on disk. Physical pages can be shared by having two virtual addresses point to the same physical address. This capability is used to allow two different programs to share data and code.

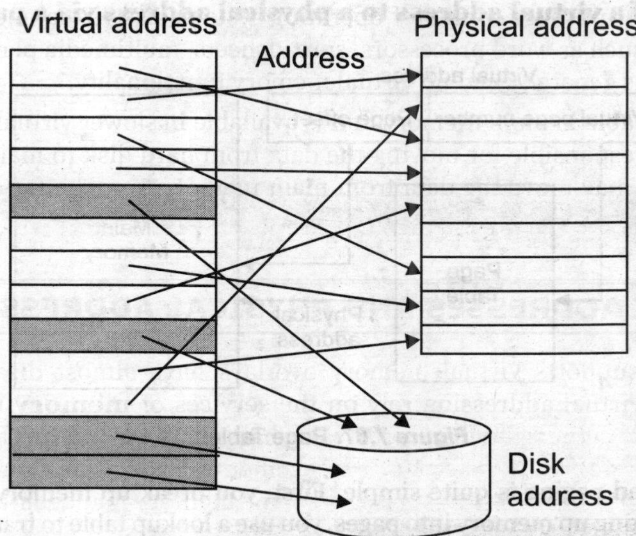

Figure 7.66: Virtual Address mapping

Virtual memory hence involves the separation of logical memory as perceived by users from physical memory. This separation allows an extremely large virtual memory to be provided for the programmers while only a smaller physical memory is available. Virtual memory makes the task of programming much easier as the programmer does not need to worry about the limited size of physical memory available.

The **virtual address space** of a process refers to the logical view of how a process is stored in the memory. Typically, this view is a contiguous memory having addresses normally starting from 0. Though the physically memory may be organized in page frames and that the physical page frames assigned to a process may not be contiguous. It is up to the MMU to map logical pages to the physical pages in the memory.

7.20.2 PAGE TABLES

Almost all implementations use page tables to translate the virtual addresses seen by the application program into physical addresses (also referred to as "real addresses") used by the hardware to process instructions. Each entry in the page table contains a mapping for a virtual page to either the real memory address at which the page is stored, or an indicator that the page is currently held in a disk file. (Although most do, some systems may not support use of a disk file for virtual memory.)

Systems can have one page table for the whole system or a separate page table for each application. If there is only one, different applications which are running at the same time share a single virtual address space, i.e. they use different parts of a single range of virtual addresses. Systems which use multiple page tables provide multiple virtual address spaces - concurrent applications think they are using the same range of virtual addresses, but their separate page tables redirect to different real addresses.

The mapping of a virtual address to a physical address via a page table

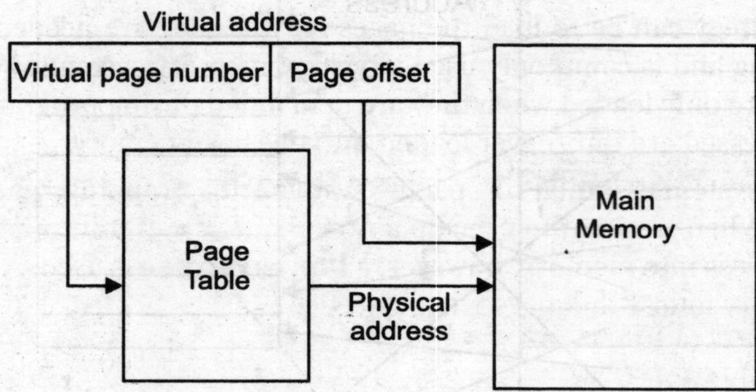

Figure 7.67: Page Tables

The concept behind paging is quite simple. First, you break up memory into blocks of bytes called pages. After breaking up memory into pages, you use a lookup table to translate the H.O. bits of a virtual address to select a page; you use the L.O. bits of the virtual address as an index into the page. For example, with a 4,096-byte page, you'd use the L.O. 12 bits of the virtual address as the offset within the page in physical memory. The upper 20 bits of the address you would use as an index into a lookup table that returns the actual upper 20 bits of the physical address (see Figure 7.68).

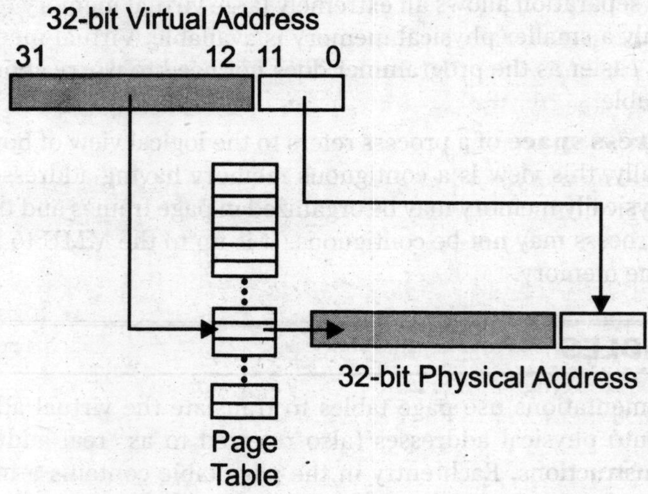

Figure 7.68: Translating a Virtual Address to a Physical Address

Of course, a 20-bit index into the page table would require over one million entries in the page table. If each entry is 32 bits (20 bits for the offset plus 12 bits for other purposes), then the page table would be four megabytes long. This would be larger than most of the programs that would run in memory! However, using what is known as a multi-level page table, it is very easy to create a page table that is only 8 kilobytes long for most small programs. The details are unimportant here; just rest assured that you don't need a four megabyte page table unless your program consumes the entire four gigabyte address space.

7.20.3 DEMAND PAGING

An alternative strategy can be to load the pages only as they are needed. This technique is known as demand paging and is commonly used in virtual memory systems. With demand-paged virtual memory, pages are only loaded when they are demanded during program execution. Hence pages that are never accessed are thus never loaded into physical memory.

A demand-paging system is similar to a paging system with swapping, where processes reside in secondary memory. When we want to execute a process, we swap it into memory. Rather than swapping the entire process into memory, however, a **lazy swapper** is used. A lazy swapper never swaps a page into memory unless that page will be needed.

7.20.3.1 BASIC CONCEPT

If a program has a lot of pages which do not get used, there is no need of loading them in the first place and then swapping them out. One way is that no page should be brought into memory until it was needed. Demand paging follows that pages should only be brought into memory if the executing process demands them. This is often referred to as lazy evaluation as only those pages demanded by the process are swapped from secondary storage to main memory. Contrast this to pure swapping, where all memory for a process is swapped from secondary storage to main memory during the process startuWhen a process is to be swapped into main memory for processing, the pager guesses which pages will be used prior to the process being swapped out again. The pager will only load these pages into memory. This process avoids loading pages that are unlikely to be used and focuses on pages needed during the current process execution period. Therefore, not only is unnecessary page load during swapping avoided but we also try to preempt which pages will be needed and avoid loading pages during execution.

Commonly, to achieve this process a page table implementation is used. The page table maps logical memory to physical memory. The page table uses a bitwise operator to mark if a page is valid or invalid. A **valid page** is one that currently resides in main memory. An **invalid page** is one that currently resides in secondary memory.

Virtual memory is implemented through demand paging. In a system that uses demand paging, the operating system copies a disk page into physical memory only if an attempt is made to access it (i.e., if a page fault occurs). It follows that a process begins execution with none of its pages in physical memory, and many page faults will occur until most of a process's working set of pages is located in physical memory.

7.20.3.2 VALID-INVALID BIT

Hardware support for distinguishing between pages in memory and pages in memory but swapped into secondary memory uses the valid/invalid bit. A valid page is one that currently resides in main memory. An invalid page is one that currently resides in secondary memory.

With each page table entry a valid–invalid bit is associated. Initially valid/invalid bit is set invalid. If valid bit is 1 it means that associated page is both legal and is in memory. If valid bit is set to 0 then reference is either invalid i.e. the page is not in the current process's address space, or page is valid for the process, but currently still on disk.

Pages table entry for the current process is either marked as invalid or it contains the disk address of the page. During address translation, if valid/invalid bit in page table entry is 0 it implies page fault.

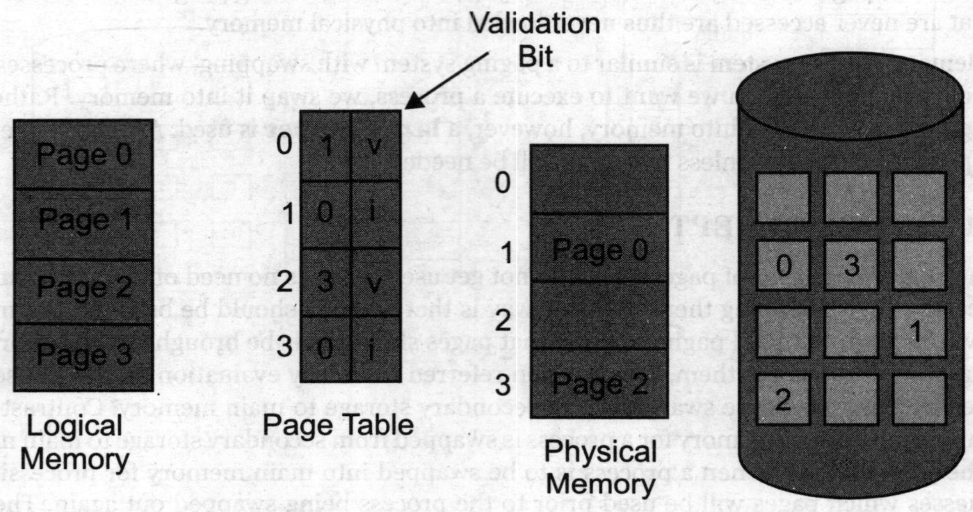

Figure 7.69: Page Table with valid/invalid bits

A Virtual Memory subsystem is responsible for transparently copying data between the disk and main memory as needed by a program.

7.20.3.3 PAGE FAULTS

In order for this system to work, the memory manager must keep track of all the pages that are currently loaded into the primary memory. This information is stored in a page table maintained by the memory manager. A page fault occurs whenever a process requests a page that is not currently loaded into primary memory. It is now easy to see how the paging concept goes hand in hand with the logical memory concept: each time the system pages out a frame of physical memory, it sets a flag in the page table next to the logical page that was removed. If a process attempts to read from that page of logical memory the system first examines the flag to see if the page is available and, if it is not, a page fault occurs.

A page fault is a hardware or software interrupt (depending on implementation) which passes control to the operating system. The operating system proceeds to locate the missing page in the swap area and move it back into a free frame of physical memory. It then binds the addresses by updating the paging table and, when control returns to the waiting process, the missing page is automatically restored, as if it had never been gone.

The location of the physical frame is completely irrelevant to the user process. A frame does not have to be moved back into the same place that it was removed from, because the runtime binding of addresses takes care of its relocation.

When a process tries to access a page, the following steps are generally followed:

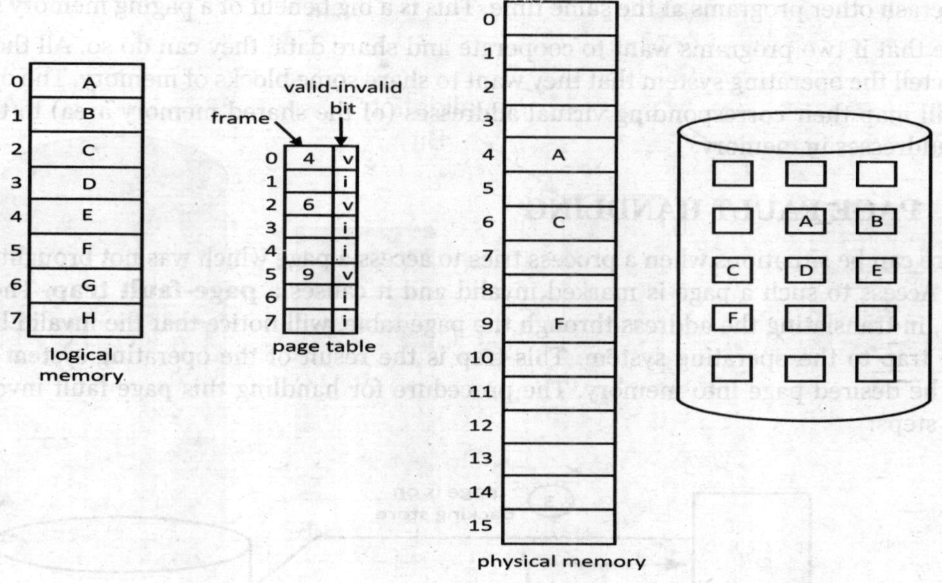

Figure 7.70: Page Table, when some pages are not in memory

Whenever a page fault occurs and all the page frames in primary memory have been loaded with a page from virtual memory, the memory manager must decided which page to swap out of primary memory in order to load the requested page. Various different algorithms known as replacement polices are employed to determine the best page to replace. Several of these polices we will study in this chapter.

When a process attempts to access a virtual address that is not currently in memory the processor cannot find a page table entry for the virtual page referenced. At this point the processor notifies the operating system that a page fault has occurred.

If the faulting virtual address is invalid this means that the process has attempted to access a virtual address that it should not have. Maybe the application has gone wrong in some way, for example writing to random addresses in memory. In this case the operating system will terminate it, protecting the other processes in the system from this rogue process.

If the faulting virtual address was valid but the page that it refers to is not currently in memory, the operating system must bring the appropriate page into memory from the image on disk. Disk access takes a long time, and so the process must wait quite a while until the page has been fetched. If there are other processes that could run then the operating system will select one of them to run. The fetched page is written into a free physical page frame and an entry for the virtual page frame number is added to the processes page table. The process is then restarted at the machine instruction where the memory fault occurred. This time the virtual memory access is made, the processor can make the virtual to physical address translation and so the process continues to run.

One important issue resulting from the fact that each program as a separate page table and the programs themselves don't have access to the page table is that programs cannot interfere with the operation of other programs by overwriting those other program's data (assuming, of course, that the operating system is properly written). Further, if your program crashes by overwriting itself, it cannot crash other programs at the same time. This is a big benefit of a paging memory system.

Note that if two programs want to cooperate and share data, they can do so. All they've got to do is to tell the operating system that they want to share some blocks of memory. The operating system will map their corresponding virtual addresses (of the shared memory area) to the same physical addresses in memory.

7.20.3.4 PAGE FAULT HANDLING

There can be situations when a process tries to access a page which was not brought into the memory. Access to such a page is marked invalid and it causes a **page-fault trap**. The paging hardware, in translating the address through the page table, will notice that the invalid bit is set, causing a trap to the operating system. This trap is the result of the operating system's failure to bring the desired page into memory. The procedure for handling this page fault involves the following steps:

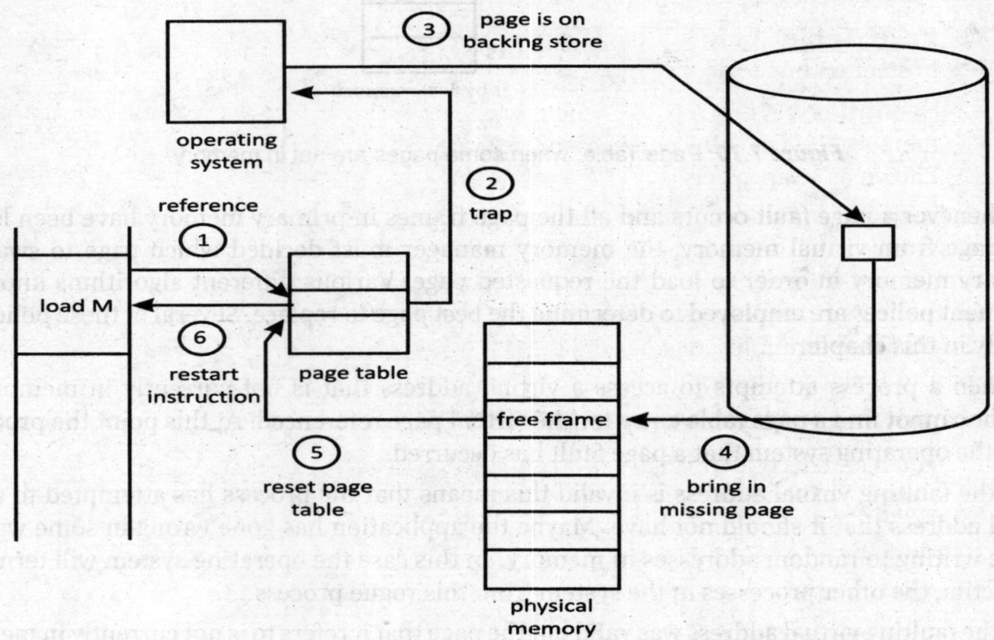

Figure 7.71: Page Fault

1. An internal table is checked for this process to determine whether the reference was a valid or an invalid memory access.
2. If the reference was valid, the process is terminated. If it was valid, but the page has not yet been brought into memory, the following steps are followed for paging it in.
3. A free frame is located.

4. A disk operation to read the desired page into newly allocated frame is scheduled.
5. After the disk read operation is completed, the internal page table kept with the process is modified, to indicate that the page is now in memory.
6. The instruction that was interrupted by the trap is restarted. The process can now access the page as though it had always been in memory.

In the extreme case, one can start executing a process with simply no pages in the memory. When the operating system sets the instruction pointer to the first instruction of the process, which is obviously not in the memory hence causing a page fault to occur. After the page is bought into the memory, the process starts execution faulting for each page that is not present in the memory, until all the pages it needs are present in the memory. At that point it can execute with no further page faults. This scheme is popularly known as **pure demand paging**, which suggests never bringing a page in memory until it is required.

Some programs also have the capability of accessing several new pages of memory with each instruction execution, thereby causing multiple page-faults with each instruction. Such situations arise problems for the effective system performance. However such situations are unlikely to occur in the current scenario of running processes, as programs tend to have the locality of reference. The hardware for demand paging is similar to the hardware for paging and swapping.

1. **Page Table:** This table has the entries for valid-invalid bits or special value of protection bits to signify the entry as invalid.
2. **Secondary Memory:** This memory holds those pages that are not present in main memory. It is usually a high-speed disk and the section of disk used for this purpose is known as swap space.

There is a need for starting of the instruction from same point after the page fault has been processed. As the state of the interrupting process is saved before processing the interrupt, the process can be restarted at the same place it was before the page fault occurred. The difference is just that the page it requests is now present in the memory due to the processing of the page fault. As a worst case example, consider the three-address instruction such as ADD which adds the contents of A to B placing the results in C.

The following steps are executed for this instruction:

1. Fetch and decode the instruction (ADD).
2. Fetch A.
3. Fetch B.
4. Add A and B.
5. Store sum in C.

If the page fault occurs when we try to store C, we will have to get the desired page, bring it in, correct the page table, and restart the instruction. Thus the restart will require fetching the instruction again, decoding it again, fetching the two operands again, and then adding them again. Hence there is not much repeated work unless the page fault occurs.

The major difficulty arises only when one instruction may modify several other instructions. Paging is added between the CPU and the memory in a computer system and it should be entirely transparent to the user.

7.21 I/O MANAGEMENT

So far we have studied how resources like processor and main memory are managed. We shall now examine the I/O management. Humans interact with machines by providing information through IO devices. Ultimately, a computer is useful only if it can access devices and communicate with people and objects. Common I/O devices include keyboards, displays, disks, mice, printers, scanners, and keyboards. They also include devices on the system board such as timers, and graphics chips, and audio chips. Clearly, management of all these devices can affect the throughput of a system. For this reason, input output management also becomes one of the primary responsibilities of an operating system. Each piece of hardware that is connected to a computer requires software to control it. This software is known as a device driver. The device driver allows us to have a consistent interface to the kernel and to hide device-specific details within the driver (for instance, the kernel outside of the device drivers shouldn't care whether your computer has a Microsoft mouse or a Logitech mouse). A device driver accesses the device controller to control the device itself. A device controller is the hardware (and/or firmware) that controls the operation of the device.

Device drivers implement mechanism, not policy. A mechanism specifies the ways of interacting with the device. A policy enforces who can access the device and in what way they can control it. The policy will be handled at higher layers in the operating system and the device driver has only to implement the operations needed to interface with the device.

Very broadly, the device subsystem of an operating system contains three components:

1. **Generic device driver code:** these are abstract interfaces for devices and code for managing instances of and references to devices
2. **Drivers for specific devices:** this is code written for interfacing with specific devices. This group also includes the code for bus drivers, such as discovering components on a USB bus and sending and receiving data on the bus.
3. **The buffer cache:** this manages the caching and I/O to block-oriented devices such as disks.

In this chapter we shall examine the role of operating systems in managing IO devices. In particular, we shall examine how the end use of the devices determines the way they are regulated for communication with either humans or with systems.

7.21.1 APPLICATION I/O INTERFACED

Structuring techniques and interfaces for the operating system enable I/O devices to be treated in a standard, uniform way. For instance, how an application can open a file on a disk without knowing what kind of disk it is, and how new disks and other devices can be added to a computer without the operating system being disrupted.

The actual differences are encapsulated in ken modules called device drivers mat internally are custom tailored to each device but that export one of the standard interfaces.

The purpose of the device-driver layer is to hide the differences among device controllers from the I/O subsystem of the kernel, much as the I/O system calls.

Character-stream or block: A character-stream device transfers bytes one by one, whereas a block device transfers a block of bytes as a unit.

Sequential or random-access: A sequential device transfers data in a fixed order that is determined by the device, whereas the user of a random-access device can instruct the device to seek to any of the available data storage locations.

Synchronous or asynchronous: A synchronous device is one that performs data transfers with predictable response times. An asynchronous device exhibits irregular or unpredictable response times.

Sharable or dedicated: A sharable device can be used concurrently by several processes or threads; a dedicated device cannot.

Speed of operation: Device speeds range from a few bytes per second to a few gigabytes per second.

Read-write, read only, or write only: Some devices perform both input and output, but others support only one data direction. For the purpose of application access, many of these differences are hidden by the operating system, and the devices are grouped into a few conventional types.

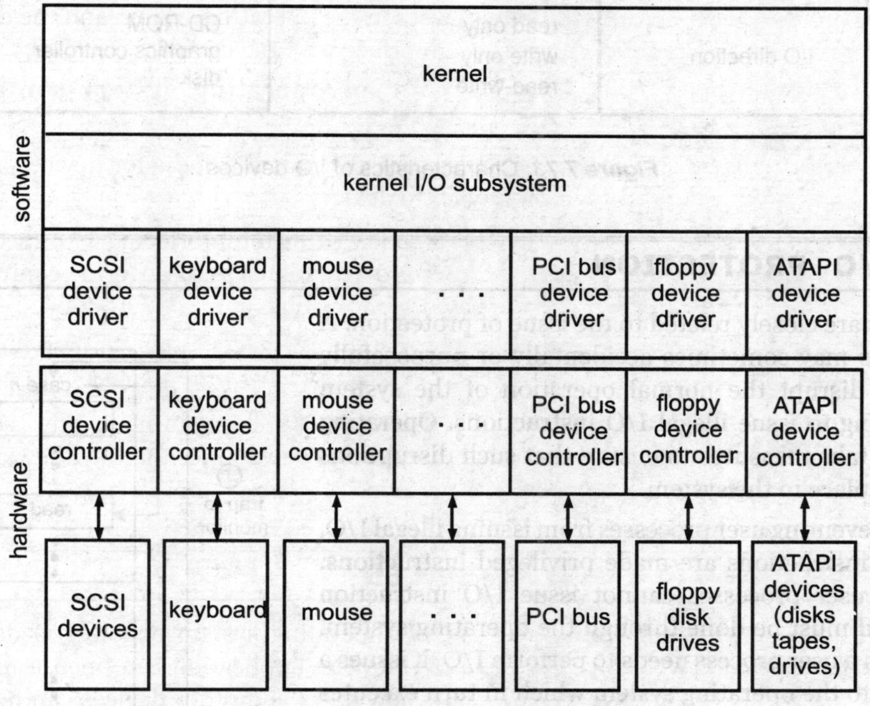

Figure 7.72: A kernel I/O structure

Operating systems also provide special system calls to access a few additional devices, such as a time-of-day clock and a timer. The performance and addressing characteristics of network I/O differ significantly from those of disk I/O; most operating systems provide a network I/O interface that is different from the **read-write-seek** interface used for disks.

aspect	variation	example
data-transfer mode	character block	terminal disk
access method	sequential random	modem CD-ROM
transfer schedule	synchronous asynchronous	tape keyboard
sharing	dedicated sharable	tape keyboard
device speed	latency seek time transfer rate delay between operations	
I/O direction	read only write only read-write	CD-ROM graphics controller disk

Figure 7.73: Characteristics of I/O devices

7.21.2 I/O PROTECTION

Errors are closely related to the issue of protection. A user process may sometimes accidentally or purposefully attempt to disrupt the normal operation of the system by attempting to issue illegal I/O instructions. Operating system can take measures to ensure that such disruptions do not take place in the system.

For preventing user processes from issuing illegal I/O, all the I/O instructions are made privileged instructions. Hence the user processes cannot issue I/O instruction directly, and must be done through the operating system. Hence when a user process needs to perform I/O, it issues a system call to the operating system which in turn executes I/O on its behalf as shown in the figure 7.74.

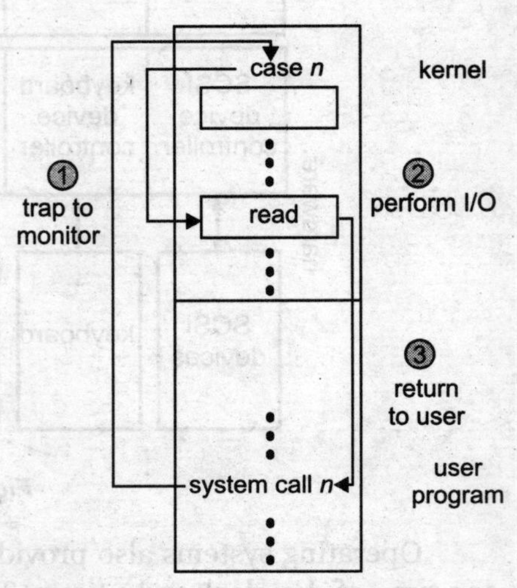

Figure 7.74: Use of system call to perform I/O

The operating system checks for the request to be valid or not before execution. Only if the request is valid it gets executed and the control gets transferred to the user process again. In addition, the memory mapped and I/O port memory locations must be protected from user access by the memory protection system. There may be situations when the user access to I/O cannot be denied. In those cases, the operating system may provide a locking mechanism to allow a user process to access some portion of the I/O subsystem.

7.22 DEVICE MANAGEMENT

Where more than one program or process wants to use a peripheral device such as a printer, the Input / Output system is responsible for controlling and sharing access to the device. A printer can only print one document at a time, but simply locking it as if it were a file could mean other programs waiting a very long time to print.

Instead, the I/O system holds print jobs in a **print queue**, and releases them to the printer when it becomes available. The queued document are held in a special file known as a **spool file** and I/O system process which controls printing is called a **print spooler**.

It is normally possible to control the operation of the print spooler from the user interface or with a utility program, e.g.: to change the order in which queued jobs are printed or remove a job from the queue. In recent versions of Windows this is done via the Printers applet in the Control Panel.

Other devices such as hard disk drives and CD-ROMs are also shared, and the I/O system ensures that requests from the file system to access information stored on different parts of a disk are sorted into the most appropriate order before implementing them.

7.22.1 DEVICE CONTROLLERS

The **controller** is the hardware that controls the communication between the system and the peripheral drive unit. It takes care of low level operations such as error checking, moving disk heads, data transfer, and location of data on the device.

A device is connected to a computer through a **device controller**, which converts between the serial bit stream and a block of bytes and performs error correction if necessary. Each controller has a few device registers that are used for communicating with the CPU, and a data buffer that an OS can read or write. A computer system contains a multitude of I/O devices and their respective controllers:

- Network card
- Disk controller
- Serial port
- Sound card
- Graphics adapter
- DVD-ROM controller
- USB

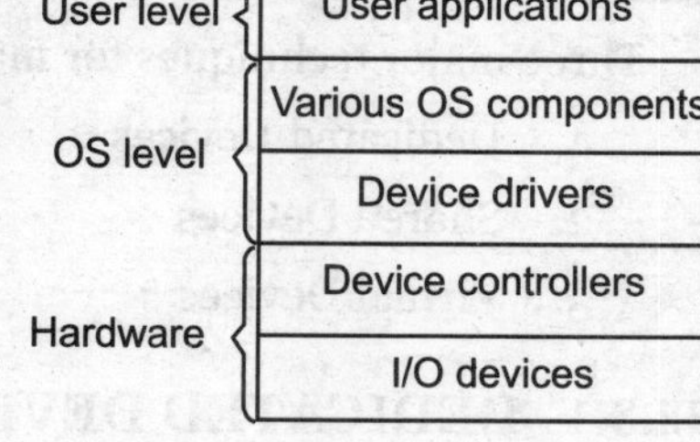

Figure 7.75: Level of I/O devices

7.22.2 DEVICE DRIVERS

A device driver (or device handler) is a program which controls a particular type of device that is attached to a computer. It is effectively the interface between the device and the operating system. There are device drivers for printers, displays, CD-ROM readers, diskette drives, and so on.

Device drivers regulate or control computer hardware downloading and installing the latest device drivers frequently resolves hardware problems.

Since the number of device registers and the natures of device instructions vary from device to device, a **device driver** OS component is responsible hiding the complexity of an I/O device, so that the OS can access various devices in a relatively uniform manner.

The **device driver** is the software that operates the **controller**. This software must be available to the kernel if you wish to use the device. The device drivers must match the device that you wish to use. Drivers perform functions to: probe, attach, open, close, read, write, reset, stop, timeout, select, strategy, dump, psize, ioctl, and process transmit and receive interrupts for a device. When a program attempts to access a device the kernel traps the request, looks up the appropriate information in its tables, and transfers control to the device driver.

Device drivers are often specific to a particular release of an operating system, e.g.: Windows 2000 device drivers may not work with Windows XP. Many device drivers are built into the operating system, but if you buy a device which was produced after the operating system was released, you may have to explicitly install a device driver which converts the general input/output instructions of the operating system to messages that the device type can Some Windows programs use virtual device drivers which interface with the Windows Virtual Machine Manager. There is a virtual device driver for each of the principal hardware devices, including the hard disk drive controller, keyboard and serial and parallel ports. Virtual device drivers handle software interrupts from the system rather than hardware interrupts and are used to maintain the status of a hardware device that has changeable settings.

Device drivers are not held in ROM like the BIOS, but are loaded into RAM from disk every time the computer starts up. Once a device driver has been loaded, the Kernel can call upon device driver processes to deal with any interrupt from the device, and the I/O system can use device driver processes to control it.

A Windows device driver file usually has a file name suffix of DLL or EXE. A virtual device driver usually has the suffix of VXD.

7.22.3 TECHNIQUES FOR DEVICE MANAGEMENT

Three major techniques for managing and allocating devices are as follows:

1. Dedicated Devices
2. Shared Devices
3. Virtual Devices

7.22.3.1 DEDICATED DEVICES

A dedicated device is allocated to a job for the job's entire duration. Some devices lend themselves to this form of allocation. It is difficult, for example, to share some device such as a card reader, tape, or a printer. If several users were to use the printer at the same time, the output would be messed up and will not be of use to any of the users. Hence the dedicated assignment may be inefficient if the job does not fully and continually utilize the device. The other techniques are usually preferred over this technique as they are more beneficial in such cases.

7.22.3.2 SHARED DEVICES

Some devices such as disks, drums, and other Direct Access Storage Devices (DASD) have the ability to be concurrently shared by several processes. Several processes can read from a single disk at the same time. The management of a shared device can become somewhat complicated in some cases. For example, if two processes simultaneously request a read() from disk X, some mechanism must be applied to determine which request should be handled first, and which needs to wait. This may be done partially by the software (the I/O scheduler, the traffic controller, etc.) or entirely by the hardware (computers with very sophisticated channels and control units).

The policies for establishing which process' request is to be satisfied first might be based on:

- a priority list, or
- the objective of achieving improved system output

Shared devices are further discussed in next sections.

7.22.3.3 VIRTUAL DEVICES

Some devices which would normally have to be dedicated (for example, card readers) may be converted into shared devices through the techniques such as spooling. For example, a spooling program can read and copy all card input to a disk at a high speed. Afterwards when a process attempts to read a card, the spooling program attempts to intercept the request and converts it to a read from the disk. Since a disk can be easily shared by several users, we have hence converted a dedicated device to a shared device, by changing one card reader to several 'virtual' card readers. The technique is equally applicable to a large number of peripheral devices, such as printers, and other slow I/O devices.

7.22.4 CHANNELS AND CONTROL UNITS

Device management should also take responsibility for the channels and control units. The channels are the special processors that execute the channel programs (i.e. the CCWs). Due to the high cost of the channels, there are usually fewer channels than the devices. The channels must, therefore, be switched from one device to another. Further costs can be saved by taking advantage of the fact that relatively few I/O devices are in use at one time. Thus, it is beneficial to separate the device's electronics from its mechanical components. The electronics for several devices can be replaced by a single control unit, which can then be switched from one device to another. The figure 7.76 illustrates the relationship between channels, control units, and devices.

Typically, there are up to control units up to eight control units per channel and up to eight devices of the same type per control unit. In order to initiate an I/O operation, a path is required between memory and the device. For example, to access the drum J requires the use of a channel A and drum control unit D. If an I/O operation to drum G were already in progress, it would not be possible to initiate I/O on drum J because channel A would not be available.

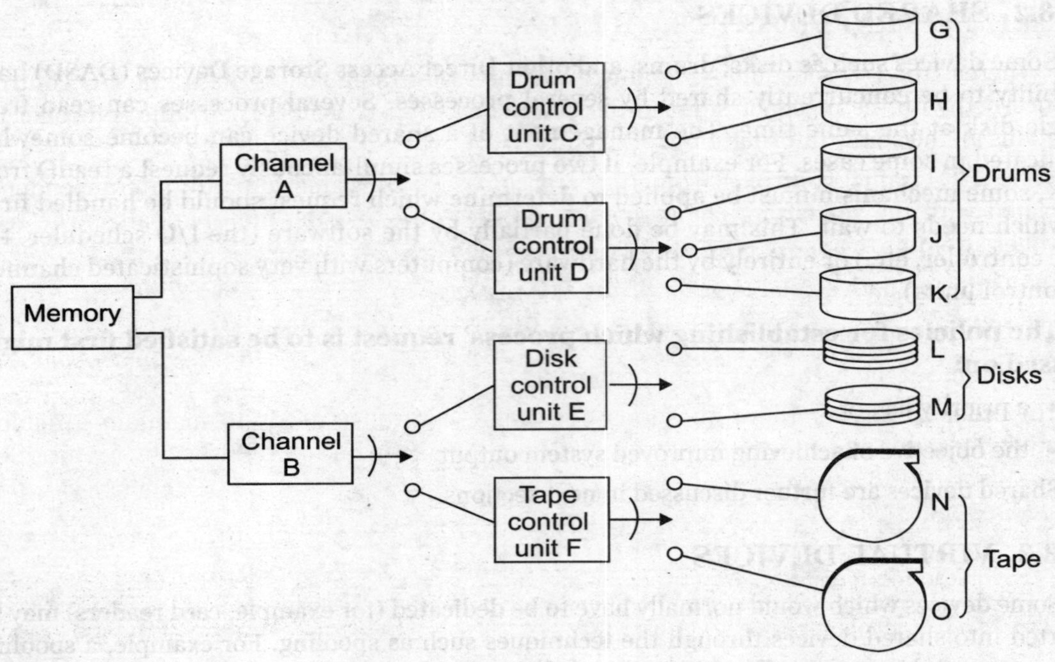

Figure 7.76: I/O configuration of a computer system

The device management routines must keep track of the status of channels, control units, as well as devices. Since the channels and control units are usually scarce, they can create serious bottlenecks. Several hardware techniques can be used to minimize this problem such as independent device operation, device buffering, multiple paths, and block multiplexing.

7.22.5 I/O TRAFFIC CONTROLLER, I/O SCHEDULER, I/O DEVICE HANDLERS

The functions of device management can be divided into the following three parts:

1. **I/O Traffic Controller**

   It keeps track of the status of all devices, control units, and channels.

2. **I/O Scheduler**

   It implements the policy algorithms used to allocate channels, control units, and device access to I/O requests from jobs.

3. **I/O Device Handlers**

   These perform the actual dynamic allocations, once the I/O scheduling has made the decision, by constructing the channel program, issuing the start I/O instruction, and processing the device interrupts. There is usually a separate device handler for each type of device.

7.22.5.1 I/O TRAFFIC CONTROLLER

Whereas the I/O scheduler is mainly concerned with the policies, the traffic I/O controller is concerned with the mechanics of can the device be assigned or not. The traffic controller thus maintains all the status information.

The I/O traffic controller sometimes becomes complicated due to interdependencies associated with the scarcity of channels and control units, and the multiple paths. The traffic controller attempts to answer at least three key questions:

- Is there a path available to service an I/O request?
- If more than one path is available?
- If none of the paths is available, when will one be free?

In order to answer these questions, the traffic controller needs to maintain a database reflecting the status and connections between devices. This can be accomplished by means of Unit Control Blocks (UCB), Control Unit Control Blocks (CUCB), and Channel Control Blocks (CCB) as depicted in the figure 7.77.

Unit Control Block (UCB)
Device unit identification
Status of device
List of control units connected to this device
List of processes waiting for this device

Channel Control Block (CCB)
Channel identification
Status of channel
List of control units connected to this channel
List of processes waiting for this channel

Control Unit Control Block (CUCB)
Control unit identification
Status of control unit
List of devices connected to this control unit
List of channels connected to this control unit
List of processes waiting for this control unit

Figure 7.77: Control Blocks

The first question can be answered by starting at the desired UCB and by working back through the connected control units and channels trying to find a combination that is available. In a similar manner, it is also possible to determine all available paths. The second question may be important especially when the I/O configuration is not symmetric, as shown in the figure 7.78.

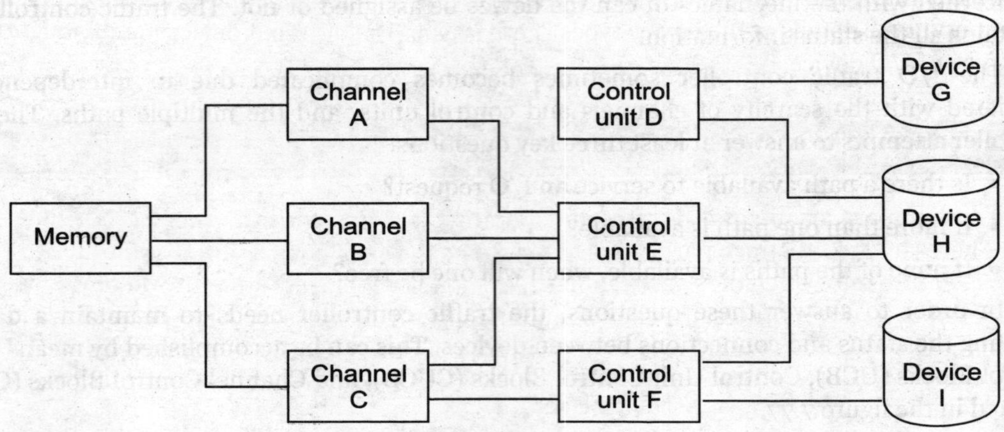

Figure 7.78: Asymmetric I/O configuration

Since choosing one path may block out other I/O requests, thus one path may conflict with fewer I/O requests than another path. In the figure 7.78, there may be up to five different paths to device H, yet only one possible path for either device G or I.

Under heavy I/O loads, it is quite likely that there will not be any path available at the time an I/O request is issued by a process. When an I/O completion interrupt occurs, one or more components, such as device, control units and channels, become available again. The operating system could try all I/O requests that are waiting to see if any can now be satisfied. If however, hundreds of I/O requests were waiting, this could be a rather time consuming approach. A more efficient approach could be to list all I/O requests that are interested in the component in the control block. Only those particular I/O requests would then have to be examined.

7.22.5.2 I/O SCHEDULER

If there are more I/O requests pending than the available paths, it is necessary to choose which I/O requests should be satisfied first. Many of the same concerns discusses in process scheduling are applicable here. One important difference is that the I/O requests are not normally time-sliced, i.e. once the channel program has been started it is not normally interrupted until it has been completed. Most channel programs are quite short and are terminated within 50-100ms. However, it is possible to encounter channel programs that take seconds or even minutes to terminate.

Many different policies may be incorporated into the I/O scheduler. For example, if a process has a higher priority assigned by the process scheduler, it is reasonable also to assign a higher priority to its I/O requests. This would thus help in fast completion of that job.

Once the I.O scheduler has determined the relative orderings of the I/O requests, the I/O traffic controller must determine which of them can be satisfied. The I/O device handlers then provide another level of device independent I/O scheduling and optimization.

7.22.5.3 I/O DEVICE HANDLER

In addition to setting up the channel command words, handling of error conditions, and processing I/O interrupts, the I/O device handlers provide detailed scheduling algorithms that are dependent upon the details of the device type. There is usually a different device handler algorithm for each type of I/O device.

7.23 FILE SYSTEMS

File systems are an integral part of any operating systems with the capacity for long term storage. There are two distinct parts of a file system, the mechanism for storing files and the directory structure into which they are organized. In modern operating systems where it is possible for several users to access the same files simultaneously it has also become necessary for such features as access control and different forms of file protection to be implemented. A file is a collection of binary data. A file could represent a program, a document or in some cases part of the file system itself. In modern computing it is quite common for there to be several different storage devices attached to the same computer. A common data structure such as a file system allows the computer to access many different storage devices in the same way, for example, when you look at the contents of a hard drive or a CD you view it through the same interface even though they are completely different mediums with data mapped on them in completely different ways. Files can have very different data structures within them but can all be accessed by the same methods built into the file system. The arrangement of data within the file is then decided by the program creating it. The file systems also store a number of attributes for the files within it.

The hard disk is, of course, a medium for storing information. Hard disks grow in size every year, and as they get larger, using them in an efficient way becomes more difficult. The file system is the general name given to the logical structures and software routines used to control access to the storage on a hard disk system. Operating systems use different ways of organizing and controlling access to data on the hard disk, and this choice is basically independent of the specific hardware being used--the same hard disk can be arranged in many different ways, and even multiple ways in different areas of the same disk.

On top of storing and managing files on a drive the file system also maintains a system of directories in which the files are referenced. Modern hard drives store hundreds of gigabytes. The file system helps organize this data by dividing it up into directories. A directory can contain files or more directories. Like files there are several basic operations that a file system needs to be able to perform on its directory structure to function properly.

It needs to be able to **create** a file. This is also covered by the overview of operation on a file but as well as creating the file it needs to be added to the directory structure. When a file is **deleted** the space taken up by the file needs to be marked as free space. The file itself also needs to be removed from the directory structure. Files may need to be **renamed**. This requires an alteration to the directory structure but the file itself remains un-changed. In order to use the disk properly the user will require knowing what is in all the directories stored on it. On top of this the user needs to be able to **browse** through the directories on the hard drive.

Since the first directory structures were designed they have gone through several large evolutions. Before directory structures were applied to file systems all files were stored on the same level. This is basically a system with one directory in which all the files are kept. The next advancement on this which would be considered the first directory structure is the two level directories. In this there is a single list of directories which are all on the same level. The files are then stored in these directories. This allows different users and applications to store there files separately. After this came the first directory structures as we know them today, directory trees. Tree structure directories improves on two level directories by allowing directories as well as files to be stored in directories. All modern file systems use tree structure directories, but many have additional features such as security built on top of them.

Protection can be implemented in many ways. Some file systems allow you to have password protected directories. In this system, the file system won't allow you to access a directory before it is given a username and password for it. Others extend this system by given different users or groups access permissions. The operating system requires the user to log in before using the computer and then restrict their access to areas they don't have permission for. The system used by the computer science department for storage space and coursework submission on raptor is a good example of this. In a file system like NTFS all type of storage space, network access and use of device such as printers can be controlled in this way. Other types of access control can also be implemented outside of the file system. For example applications such as win zip allow you to password protect files.

There are many different file systems currently available to us on many different platforms and depending on the type of application and size of drive different situations suit different file system. To design a file system for a tape backup system then a sequential access method would be better suited than a direct access method given the constraints of the hardware. Several file systems are currently available; these include NTFS for the Windows NT and XP operating systems and ext2 which is used in Linux.

The five main major activities of an operating system in regard to file management are:

1. The creation and deletion of files.
2. The creation and deletion of directories.
3. The support of primitives for manipulating files and directories.
4. The mapping of files onto secondary storage.
5. The back up of files on stable storage media.

7.23.1 FILE CONCEPTS

In any computer system but especially in personal computers, a file is an entity of data available to system users (including the system itself and its application programs) that is capable of being manipulated as an entity (for example, moved from one file directory to another). The file must have a unique name within its own directory. Some operating systems and applications describe files with given formats by giving them a particular file name suffix. (The file name suffix is also known as a file name extension.) For example, a program or executable file is sometimes given or required to have an ".exe" suffix. In general, the suffixes tend to be as descriptive of the formats as they can within the limits of the number of characters allowed for suffixes by the operating system.

In a computer, a file system is the way in which files are named and where they are placed logically for storage and retrieval. The DOS, Windows, OS/2, Macintosh, and UNIX-based operating systems all have file systems in which files are placed somewhere in a hierarchical (tree) structure. A file is placed in a directory (folder in Windows) or subdirectory at the desired place in the tree structure. As a whole, the part of the operating system dealing with files is known as the file system.

File systems specify conventions for naming files. These conventions include the maximum number of characters in a name, which characters can be used, and, in some systems, how long the file name suffix can be. A file system also includes a format for specifying the path to a file through the structure of directories. Sometimes the term refers to the part of an operating system or an added-on program that supports a file system. Example of such add-on file systems is the Network File System (NFS).

7.23.2 FILE VIEWS

A file is a named collection of related information, usually a sequence of bytes, with two views:

- **Logical (programmer's) view** defines how the users see the file. Users see it as linear sequence of contiguous bytes.
- **Physical (operating system) view** defines how the file is stored on secondary storage. It has many possibilities, not necessarily contiguous.

These two views can (obviously) be very different from one another. The most visible aspect of a computer is the data that it is storing. This view is generally of files and directories.

The operating system abstracts the hardware details of storing a file, and presents a clean file interface, using which we can access the files and modify them. The users generally do not care how the file is stored on the hardware, how the sectors on the hard drive are arranged, etc. All those low level details are handled by the operating system. File systems are generally arranged in a tree like manner, where root and branches are directories and files are leafs.

7.23.3 FILE TYPES

File is a collection of data or information. Almost all information stored in a computer must be in a file. All files have a name by which they can be accessed by the user. In most modern file systems the name consists of three parts, its unique name, a period and an extension. The file extension allows the operating system to decide what to do with the file if someone tries to open it. The operating system maintains a list of file extension associations. The system also stores the location of a file. File types refer to classifying the content of the file, such as a program, text file, executable program or data file. There are many different types of files: data files, text files, program files, multimedia files, and so on. Different types of files store different types of information. The problem for the users and operating system is to somehow maintain the type of the file. Some operating systems (notably Windows) rely on the file extension to indicate the type of file. Others, like UNIX, rely on a magic number in the file header to indicate the type.

In Windows operating systems, the file type is derived from the filename extension. Typical file types and their extensions are

File Extension	File Type
.bas	basic source program
.c	c source program
.dll	system library
.doc	Word document
.exe ,.com, .bin	executable program
.txt	text file
.obj, o	Object files
.mpeg	Multimedia
.htm, .html	A plain text document with added code that enables it to be read on theWorld Wide Web
.jpg , .gif	An image file
.pdf	Portable Document Format file
.ps	PostScript file

Windows associates applications (programs) with specific file types. For example, the default application that opens to process a file of type .txt is the Notepad editor

7.23.4 FILE ATTRIBUTES

Each file has an associated collection of information, known as its attributes. Various operating systems may store various attributes for files. Some will store the owner of the file, while others won't. Generally, there are a few attributes that are always there: the name of the file, the size, type, location, time when it was created, protection information, etc. The information about files is kept in the directory where these files are residing.

The particular information kept for each file varies from OS to OS. File have some properties like Filename, Type, Size, Owner, Version, Creation date, Last modified date-time, and some special attribute set by owner Read-only, Hidden. The following information maybe kept in a directory entry; not all systems keep all this information:

- **File name:** The symbolic file name is the only information kept in human-read form.
- **File type:** This information is needed for those systems that support different types.
- **Location:** This is a pointer to the device and location on that device of the file.
- **Size:** The current size of the file.
- **Current position:** This is a pointer to the current read or writes position in the file.
- **Protection:** Access-control information controls that can do reading, writing, executing, and so on.
- **Usage count:** This value indicates the number of processes that are currently using (have opened) this file.

- **Time, date, and process identification:** This information may be kept for creation, last modification, and last use. These data can be useful for protection and for usage monitoring.

7.23.5 FILE OPERATIONS

In order for a file system to function properly they need a number of defined operations for creating, opening and editing a file. Almost all file systems provide the same basic set of methods for manipulating files.

7.23.5.1 CREATING A FILE

A file system must be able to create a file. To do this there must be enough space left on the drive to fit the file. There must also be no other file in the directory it is to be placed with the same name. Once the file is created the system will make a record of all the attributes. Two steps are needed in creating a file. First, a space in the file system must be found for the file. Second, an entry for the new file must be made in the directory. The directory entry records the name of the file and the location in the file system.

7.23.5.2 EDITING A FILE

Once a file has been created we may need to edit it. This may be simply appending some data to the end of it or removing or replacing data already stored within it. When doing this the system keeps a write pointer marking where the next write operation to the file should take place.

7.23.5.3 WRITING A FILE

To write a file, a system call is made specifying both the name and the file and the information to be written to the file. Given the name of the file, the system searches the directory to find the location of the file. The directory entry will need to store a pointer to the current block of the file (usually the beginning of the file). Using this pointer, the address of the next block can be computed where the information will be written. The write pointer must be updated - in this way; successive writes can be used to write a sequence of blocks to the file. The operating system must maintain the write pointer in the file.

7.23.5.4 READING A FILE

In order for a file to be useful it must of course be readable. To do this all you need to know the name and path of the file. From this the file system can ascertain where on the drive the file is stored. While reading a file the system keeps a read pointer. This stores which part of the drive is to be read next.

In some cases it is not possible to simply read the entire file into memory. File systems also allow you to reposition the read pointer within a file. To perform this operation the system needs to know how far into the file you want the read pointer to jump. An example of where this would be useful is a database system. When a query is made on the database it is obviously inefficient to read the whole file up to the point where the required data is, instead the application managing the database would determine where in the file the required bit of data is and jump to it. This operation is often known as a file seeks.

To read a file, a system call is made that specifies that specifies the name of the file and where (in memory) the next block of the file should be put. Again, the directory is searched for the associated directory entry, and the directory will need a pointer to the next block to be read. Once the block is read, the pointer is updated.

7.23.5.5 REPOSITIONING A FILE

The directory is searched for the appropriate entry, and the current-file-position pointer is repositioned to a given value. Repositioning within a file need not involve any actual I/O. This file operation is also known as files seek.

7.23.5.6 DELETING A FILE

File systems also allow you to delete files. To do this it needs to know the name and path of the file. To delete a file the directory is searched for the named file .the systems simply removes its entry from the directory structure and adds all the space it previously occupied to the free space list (or whatever other free space management system it uses).

These are the most basic operations required by a file system to function properly. They are present in all modern computer file systems but the way they function may vary. The OS provides systems calls to create, write, read, reset, and delete files.

7.23.5.7 TRUNCATING A FILE

Truncating a file means erasing the contents of the file but keeping the directory entry (i.e. freeing the memory allocated to the file, but not altering the directory entry of the file). The file will effectively be empty.

More commonly, copies of the file can also be created, and since files are named object, renaming an existing file may also be needed. If the file is a binary object format, we may also want to execute it. Also of use are facilities to lock sections of an open file for multiprocess access, to share sections, and even to map sections into memory or virtual-memory systems.

7.23.5.8 OPEN FILES

For open files, the operating system usually maintains several lists. There is a global list, which contains references to open files all across the system (for all processes), there is also a local list that maintains open files per process.

Depending on the setup, these lists and data structures will contain:

- **File Pointer:** The read/write pointer inside the file.
- **File Open Count:** In the global table the system needs to maintain how many instances of this file are currently opened by various processes.
- **Disk location of the file:** The hard drive location of the file is usually kept in memory to avoid having to read the hard drive to save something to a file.
- **Access Rights:** Each file is opened in some access mode (read only, etc.) An operating system can store this in a per-process open file table so that it can deny or allow some file operation on a per-process basis.

7.23.6 FILE STRUCTURE

Four terms are in common use when discussing files:

1. Field
2. Record
3. File
4. Database

1. Field: A **field** is the basic element of data. An individual field contains a single value, such as an employee's last name, a date, or the value of a sensor reading. It is characterized by its length and data type (e.g., ASCII string, decimal). Depending on the file design, fields may be fixed length or variable length. In the latter case, the field often consists of two or three subfields: the actual value to be stored, the name of the field, and, in some cases, the length of the field. In other cases of variable-length fields, the length of the field is indicated by the use of special demarcation symbols between fields.

2. Record: A **record** is a collection of related fields that can be treated as a unit by some application program. For example, an employee record would contain such fields as name, social security number, job classification, date of hire, and so on. Again, depending on design, records may be of fixed length or variable length. A record will be of variable length if some of its fields are of variable length or if the number of fields may vary. In the latter case, each field is usually accompanied by a field name. In either case, the entire record usually includes a length field.

3. File: A **file** is a collection of similar records. The file is treated as a single entity by users and applications and may be referenced by name. Files have file names and may be created and deleted. Access control restrictions usually apply at the file level. That is, in a shared system, users and programs are granted or denied access to entire files. In some more sophisticated systems, such controls are enforced at the record or even the field level. Some file systems are structured only in terms of fields, not records. In that case, a file is a collection of fields.

4. Database: A **database** is a collection of related data. The essential aspects of a database are that the relationships that exist among elements of data are explicit and that the database is designed for use by a number of different applications. A database may contain all of the information related to an organization or project, such as a business or a scientific study. The database itself consists of one or more types of files. Usually, there is a separate database management system that is independent of the operating system, although that system may make use of some file management programs.

File types also can be used to indicate the internal structure of the file. As mentioned in Section file types, source and object files have structures that match the expectations of the programs that read them. Further, certain files must conform to a required structure that is understood by the operating system. For example, the operating system requires that an executable file have a specific structure so that it can determine where in memory to load the file and what the location of the first instruction is. Some operating systems extend this idea into a set of system-supported file structures, with sets of special operations for manipulating files with those structures. For instance, DEC's VMS operating system has a file system that supports three defined file structures.

This point brings us to one of the disadvantages of having the operating system support multiple file structures: The resulting size of the operating system is cumbersome. If the operating system defines five different file structures, it needs to contain the code to support these file structures. In addition, every file may need to be definable as one of the file types supported by the operating system. When new applications require information structured in ways not supported by the operating system, severe problems may result.

For example, assume that a system supports two types of files: text files (composed of ASCII characters separated by a carriage return and line feed) and executable binary files. Now, if we (as users) want to define an encrypted file to protect the contents from being read by unauthorized people, we may find neither file type to be appropriate. The encrypted file is not ASCII text lines but rather is (apparently) random bits. Although it may appear to be a binary file, it is not executable. As a result, we may have to circumvent or misuse the operating system's file-types mechanism or abandon our encryption scheme.

7.23.6.1 INTERNAL FILE STRUCTURE

Internally, locating an offset within a file can be complicated for the operating system. Disk systems typically have a well-defined block size determined by the size of a sector. All disk I/O is performed in units of one block (physical record), and all blocks are the same size. It is unlikely that the physical record size will exactly match the length of the desired logical record. Logical records may even vary in length. Packing a number of logical records into physical blocks is a common solution to this problem. For example, the UNIX operating system defines all files to be simply streams of bytes. Each byte is individually addressable by its offset from the beginning (or end) of the file. In this case, the logical record size is 1 byte. The file system automatically packs and unpacks bytes into physical disk blocks — say, 512 bytes per block—as necessary. The logical record size, physical block size, and packing technique determine how many logical records are in each physical block. The packing can be done either by the user's application program or by the operating system. In either case, the file may be considered to be a sequence of blocks. All the basic I/O functions operate in terms of blocks. The conversion from logical records to physical blocks is a relatively simple software problem. Because disk space is always allocated in blocks, some portion of the last block of each file is generally wasted. If each block were 512 bytes, for example, then a file of 1,949 bytes would be allocated four blocks (2,048 bytes); the last 99 bytes would be wasted.

The waste incurred to keep everything in units of blocks (instead of bytes) is internal fragmentation. All file systems suffer from internal fragmentation; the larger the block size, the greater the internal fragmentation.

7.23.7 FILE MANAGEMENT SYSTEMS

The increased simplicity of the file systems provided by modern operating systems has enabled a concentration on efficiency, security and constrained access, and robustness. Operating systems provide a layer of system-level software, using system-calls to provide services relating to the provision of files. This obviates the need for each application program to manage its own disk allocation and access. As a kernel-level responsibility, the file management system provides a central role in resource (buffer) allocation and process scheduling.

A file management system is that set of system software that provides services to users and applications in the use of files. Typically, the only way that a user or application may access files is through the file management system. This relieves the user or programmer of the necessity of developing special-purpose software for each application and provides the system with a consistent, well-defined means of controlling its most important asset.

Following are the objectives for a file management system:

1. To meet the data management needs and requirements of the user, which include storage of data and the ability to perform the aforementioned operations
2. To guarantee, to the extent possible, that the data in the file are valid
3. To optimize performance, both from the system point of view in terms of overall throughput and from the user's point of view in terms of response time
4. To provide I/O support for a variety of storage device types
5. To minimize or eliminate the potential for lost or destroyed data
6. To provide a standardized set of I/O interface routines to user processes
7. To provide I/O support for multiple users, in the case of multiple-user systems

With respect to the first point, meeting user requirements, the extent of such requirements depends on the variety of applications and the environment in which the computer system will be used. For an interactive, general-purpose system, the following constitute a minimal set of requirements:

1. Each user should be able to create, delete, read, write, and modify files.
2. Each user may have controlled access to other users' files.
3. Each user may control what types of accesses are allowed to the user's files.
4. Each user should be able to restructure the user's files in a form appropriate to the problem.
5. Each user should be able to move data between files.
6. Each user should be able to back up and recover the user's files in case of damage.
7. Each user should be able to access his or her files by name rather than by numeric identifier.

These objectives and requirements should be kept in mind throughout our discussion of file management systems.

7.23.8 FILE SYSTEM ARCHITECTURE

One way of getting a feel for the scope of file management is to look at a depiction of a typical software organization, as suggested in Figure 7.79. Of course, different systems will be organized differently, but this organization is reasonably representative.

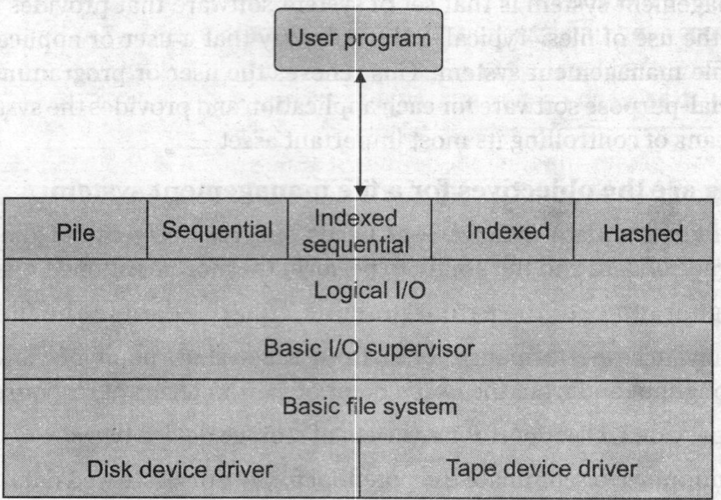

Figure 7.79: File System Software Architecture

There are mainly five levels of file system architecture explain as:

1. **Device drivers:** It is the lowest level of the file system architecture. **Device drivers** communicate directly with peripheral devices or their controllers or channels. A device driver is responsible for starting I/O operations on a device and processing the completion of an I/O request. For file operations, the typical devices controlled are disk and tape drives. Device drivers are usually considered to be part of the operating system.
2. **Basic File System:** The next level is referred to as the **basic file system**, or the **physical I/O** level. This is the primary interface with the environment outside of the computer system. It deals with blocks of data that are exchanged with disk or tape systems. Thus, it is concerned with the placement of those blocks on the secondary storage device and on the buffering of those blocks in main memory. It does not understand the content of the data or the structure of the files involved. The basic file system is often considered part of the operating system.
3. **Basic I/O Supervisor:** The **basic I/O supervisor** is responsible for all file I/O initiation and termination. At this level, control structures are maintained that deal with device I/O, scheduling, and file status. The basic I/O supervisor selects the device on which file I/O is to be performed, based on the particular file selected. It is also concerned with scheduling disk and tape accesses to optimize performance. I/O buffers are assigned and secondary memory is allocated at this level. The basic I/O supervisor is part of the operating system.
4. **Logical I/O: Logical I/O** enables users and applications to access records. Thus, whereas the basic file system deals with blocks of data, the logical I/O module deals with file records. Logical I/O provides a general-purpose record I/O capability and maintains basic data about files.
5. **Access methods:** The level of the file system closest to the user is often termed the **access method (described in next sections)**. It provides a standard interface between applications and the file systems and devices that hold the data. Different

access methods reflect different file structures and different ways of accessing and processing the data. Some of the most common access methods are shown in Fig. 7.79.

7.23.9 FILE MANAGEMENT FUNCTIONS

Another way of viewing the functioning of a file system is shown in Figure 7.80. Let us follow this diagram from left to right. Users and application programs interact with the file system by means of commands for creating and deleting files and for performing operations on files. Before performing any operation, the file system must identify and locate the selected file. This requires the use of some sort of directory that serves to describe the location of all files, plus their attributes. In addition, most shared systems enforce user access control: Only authorized users are allowed to access particular files in particular ways. The basic operations that a user or application may perform on a file are performed at the record level. The user or application views the file as having some structure that organizes the records, such as a sequential structure (e.g., personnel records are stored alphabetically by last name). Thus, to translate user commands into specific file manipulation commands, the access method appropriate to this file structure must be employed.

Whereas users and applications are concerned with records or fields, I/O is done on a block basis. Thus, the records or fields of a file must be organized as a sequence of blocks for output and unblocked after input. To support block I/O of files, several functions are needed. The secondary storage must be managed. This involves allocating files to free blocks on secondary storage and managing free storage so as to know what blocks are available for new files and growth in existing files. Both disk scheduling and file allocation are concerned with optimizing performance. As might be expected, these functions therefore need to be considered together. Furthermore, the optimization will depend on the structure of the files and the access patterns. Accordingly, developing an optimum file management system from the point of view of performance is an exceedingly complicated task.

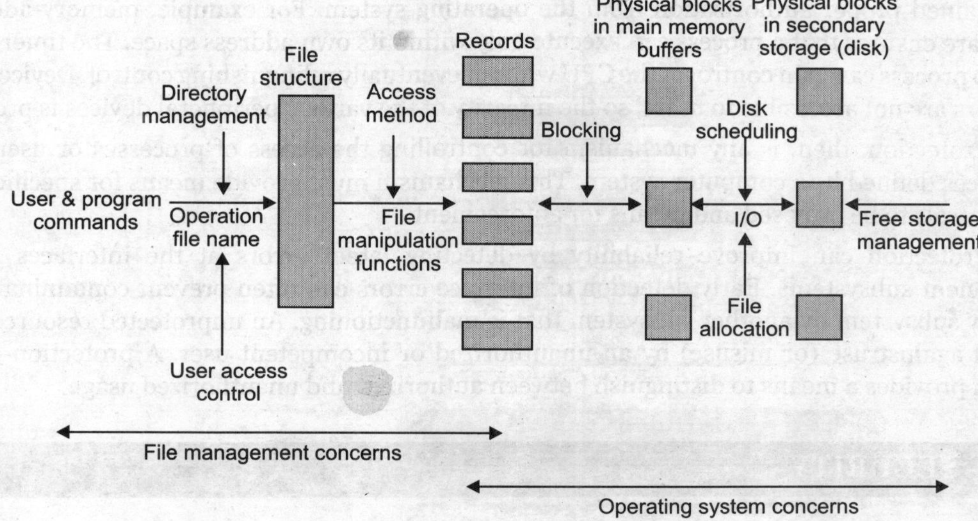

Figure 7.80: Elements of File Management

Figure 7.80 suggests a division between what might be considered the concerns of the file management system as a separate system utility and the concerns of the operating system, with the point of intersection being record processing. This division is arbitrary; various approaches are taken in various systems. In the remainder of this chapter, we look at some of the design issues suggested in Figure 7.80. We begin with a discussion of file organizations and access methods.

Although this topic is beyond the scope of what is usually considered the concerns of the operating system, it is impossible to assess the other file-related design issues without an appreciation of file organization and access. Next, we look at the concept of file directories. These are often managed by the operating system on behalf of the file management system. The remaining topics deal with the physical I/O aspects of file management and are properly treated as aspects of operating system design. One such issue is the way in which logical records are organized into physical blocks. Finally, there are the related issues of file allocation on secondary storage and the management of free secondary storage.

7.24 NETWORKING

A distributed system is a collection of processors that do not share memory, peripheral devices, or a clock. The processors communicate with one another through communication lines called network. The communication-network design must consider routing and connection strategies, and the problems of contention and security.

7.25 PROTECTION SYSTEM

If a computer system has multiple users and allows the concurrent execution of multiple processes, then access to data must be regulated. For that purpose, mechanisms ensure that files, memory segments, CPU, and other resources can be operated on by only those processes that have gained proper authorization from the operating system. For example, memory-addressing hardware ensures that a process can execute only within its own address space. The timer ensures that no process can gain control of the CPU without eventually relinquishing control. Device-control registers are not accessible to users, so the integrity of the various peripheral devices is protected.

Protection, then, is any mechanism for controlling the access of processes or users to the resources defined by a computer system. This mechanism must provide means for specification of the controls to be imposed and means for enforcement.

Protection can improve reliability by detecting latent errors at the interfaces between component subsystems. Early detection of interface errors can often prevent contamination of a healthy subsystem by another subsystem that is malfunctioning. An unprotected resource cannot defend against use (or misuse) by an unauthorized or incompetent user. A protection-oriented system provides a means to distinguish between authorized and unauthorized usage.

7.26 SECURITY

A system can have adequate protection but still be prone to failure and allow inappropriate access. Consider a user whose authentication information (her means of identifying herself to the system) is stolen. Her data could be copied or deleted, even though file and memory protection are working. It is the job of security to defend a system from external and internal attacks. Such attacks spread across a huge range and include viruses and worms, denial-of-service attacks (which use all of a system's resources and so keep legitimate users out of the system), identity theft, and theft of service (unauthorized use of a system). Prevention of some of these attacks is considering operating-system functions on some systems, while others leave the prevention to policy or additional software. Due to the alarming rise in security incidents, operating-system security features represent a fast-growing area of research and of implementation.

There are two generic levels of security, internal and external. Internal security can be thought of as protecting the computer's resources from the programs concurrently running on the system. Most operating systems set programs running natively on the computer's processor, so the problem arises of how to stop these programs doing the same task and having the same privileges as the operating system (which is after all just a program too). Processors used for general purpose operating systems generally have a hardware concept of privilege. Generally less privileged programs are automatically blocked from using certain hardware instructions, such as those to read or write from external devices like disks. Instead, they have to ask the privileged program (operating system kernel) to read or write. The operating system therefore gets the chance to check the program's identity and allow or refuse the request.

Typically an operating system offers (or hosts) various services to other network computers and users. These services are usually provided through ports or numbered access points beyond the operating systems network address. Services include offerings such as file sharing, print services, email, web sites, and file transfer protocols (FTP), most of which can have compromised security. These threats are categorized under external threats and are usually dealt with using add-on software like firewalls and antivirus programs.

7.27 RESOURCE ALLOCATION AND ACCOUNTING

When multiple users or multiple jobs running are concurrently on the operating system, resources must be allocated to each of them. Some (such as CPU cycles, main memory, and file storage) may have special allocation code and rules, while others (such as I/O devices) may have general request and release code. To keep track of which users use how much and what kinds of computer resources, the OS should also implement an Accounting scheme.

7.28 APPLICATION PROGRAM INTERFACES

Just as drivers provide a way for applications to make use of hardware subsystems without having to know every detail of the hardware's operation, **application program interfaces** (APIs) let application programmers use functions of the computer and operating system without having to directly keep track of all the details in the CPU's operation. Let's look at the example of creating a hard disk file for holding data to see why this can be important.

A programmer writing an application to record data from a scientific instrument might want to allow the scientist to specify the name of the file created. The operating system might provide an API function named **MakeFile** for creating files. When writing the program, the programmer would insert a line that looks like this:

MakeFile [1, %Name, 2]

In this example, the instruction tells the operating system to create a file that will allow random access to its data (signified by the 1 -- the other option might be 0 for a serial file), will have a name typed in by the user (%Name) and will be a size that varies depending on how much data is stored in the file (signified by the 2 -- other options might be zero for a fixed size, and 1 for a file that grows as data is added but does not shrink when data is removed). Now, let's look at what the operating system does to turn the instruction into action.

The operating system sends a query to the disk drive to get the location of the first available free storage location.

With that information, the operating system creates an entry in the file system showing the beginning and ending locations of the file, the name of the file, the file type, whether the file has been archived, which users have permission to look at or modify the file, and the date and time of the file's creation.

The operating system writes information at the beginning of the file that identifies the file, sets up the type of access possible and includes other information that ties the file to the application. In all of this information, the queries to the disk drive and addresses of the beginning and ending point of the file are in formats heavily dependent on the manufacturer and model of the disk drive.

Because the programmer has written the program to use the API for disk storage, the programmer doesn't have to keep up with the instruction codes, data types and response codes for every possible hard disk and tape drive. The operating system, connected to drivers for the various hardware subsystems, deals with the changing details of the hardware. The programmer must simply write code for the API and trust the operating system to do the rest.

APIs have become one of the most hotly contested areas of the computer industry in recent years. Companies realize that programmers using their API will ultimately translate this into the ability to control and profit from a particular part of the industry. This is one of the reasons that so many companies have been willing to provide applications like readers or viewers to the public at no charge. They know consumers will request that programs take advantage of the free readers, and application companies will be ready to pay royalties to allow their software to provide the functions requested by the consumers.

EXERCISES

1. What do you mean by operating system?
2. Why we need operating system?
3. Explain the evolution of operating systems?
4. Explain the interfaces of operating system?
5. Explain the role of the operating system?
6. What do you mean by interrupt?
7. Explain the various functions of interrupts?
8. What do you mean by system calls?
9. Explain the types of system calls?
10. Explain the single user and multi user operating system?
11. Explain the types of operating systems?
12. Explain the user interface of an operating system?

13. Explain the various design options of operating system?
14. Explain the various structures of operating system?
15. Explain the different tasks of operating system?
16. Explain the concept of process management?
17. Explain the process control block in detail?
18. Explain the types of process models?
19. Explain the various operations on processes?
20. What do you mean by thread?
21. Want do you mean by multithreading?
22. What are the advantages of multithreading?
23. Explain the user and kernel level threads?
24. Explain the various models of multithreading?
25. What do you mean by scheduling?
26. Explain the concept of CPU scheduling?
27. Explain the various types of scheduler?
28. Explain the different level of scheduling?
29. Explain the scheduling criteria for scheduling?
30. Explain the concept of process and thread scheduling?
31. What do you mean by memory management?
32. Explain the memory hierarchy in detail?
33. Explain the techniques of contiguous memory allocation?
34. What do you mean by fragmentation?
35. What do you mean by compaction?
36. Explain the concept of swapping in detail?
37. Explain the concept of paging in detail?
38. Explain the concept of segmentation in detail?
39. What do you mean by virtual memory?
40. Explain the concept of demand paging in detail?
41. Explain the concept of page faults?
42. How can you handle page faults?
43. Explain the role of I/O management?
44. Explain the various techniques of device management?
45. Explain the I/O configuration of a computer system?
46. Explain the functions of device management?
47. Explain the file management system?
48. Explain the various types of files?
49. Explain the various operations on files?
50. Explain the structure of a file?
51. Explain the architecture of file systems?
52. Explain the functions of file management?
53. Explain the protection and security of operating system?
54. Explain the application program interface in detail?

Chapter

8

System Software Tools

8.1 INTRODUCTION

In the previous unit we discussed several types of system software such as compiler, linker, loader and assembler. We also presented a detailed description of operating system. In this unit, we take up issues related to a DBMS, text editor and a debugging system.

A *Database Management System* (DBMS) is a software program that enables the creation and management of databases. The DBMS is a suite of services (software applications) for managing databases, which involves:

- enabling simple access to data
- allowing multiple users access to the information
- manipulating the data found in the database (inserting, deleting, editing)

A text editor is a program that enables you to create and edit text files. The distinction between editors and word processors is not clear-cut, but in general, word processors provide many more formatting features. Interactive program debugging system provides programmers with facilities that aid in the testing and debugging of programs. Although the desirability of such systems has been recognized for some time, there are relatively few actual debugging systems in practical use.

8.2 FILE PROCESSING SYSTEM

The traditional file-oriented approach to information processing has for each application a separate master file and its own set of personal files. COBOL language supported these file-oriented applications. It was used for developing applications such as of payroll, inventory, and financial accounting. However, in general an organization needs flow of information across these applications also and this requires sharing of data, which is very difficult to implement in the traditional file approach. In addition, a major limitation of file-based approach is that the programs are dependent on the files and the files are dependent upon the programs.

A File can store records and we can extract these records using different applications programs.

- The simplest data retrieval task from file requires extensive programming. Also this is a time consuming and a high skill activity.
- To access the data in file the programmer must aware of the physical structure of the file.
- Security features such as effective password protection, locking parts of file etc are very difficult to program.
- The File system exhibits structural dependence. That is a change in file structure such as addition or deletion of a field requires the modification of all programs using that file.
- Data dependence: A change in file data characteristic such as change in a field data type from integer to decimal requires changes in all programs that access the file.

A typical file processing system is supported by conventional operating systems. The system stores permanent record in various files. It uses various application programs to extract records from, and add records to the appropriate files. Before using DBMS to store and retrieve data, organizations stored information in file processing systems.

But as the number of files in the system expands, system administration becomes difficult too. Each file must have its own file management system, composed of programs that allow user to create the file structure, add data to the file, delete data from the file, modify the data in the file, list the file contents etc.

Even a simple file processing system containing 25 files requires 5 * 25 =125 file management programs. Each department in the organization owns its data by creating its own files. So the number of files can multiply rapidly.

Security features such as effective password protection, locking out part of files or part of system itself and other data confidentiality measures are difficult to program and are usually omitted. The file system's structure and lack of security makes it difficult to pool data. The same basic data is stored in different locations. But it is very unlikely that that data stored in different locations will always be updated consistently, hence maintaining different versions of same data. The file processing system is simply not suitable for modern data management and information requirement.

8.2.1 DISADVANTAGES OF FILE PROCESSING SYSTEM

The conventional file processing system suffers from the following shortcomings.

- Data Redundancy
- Data Inconsistency
- Difficulty in Accessing Data
- Data Isolation
- Integrity Problems
- Atomicity Problem
- Concurrent Access anomalies
- Security Problems

1. **Data Redundancy:** Data Redundancy means same information is duplicated in several files. This makes data redundancy.
2. **Data Inconsistency:** Data Inconsistency means different copies of the same data are not matching. That means different versions of same basic data are existing. This occurs as the result of update operations that are not updating the same data stored at different places. **Example:** Address Information of a customer is recorded differently in different files.
3. **Difficulty in Accessing Data:** It is not easy to retrieve information using a conventional file processing system. Convenient and efficient information retrieval is almost impossible using conventional file processing system.
4. **Data Isolation:** Data are scattered in various files, and the files may be in different format, writing new application program to retrieve data is difficult.
5. **Integrity Problems:** The data values may need to satisfy some integrity constraints. For example the balance field Value must be grater than 5000. We have to handle this through program code in file processing systems. But in database we can declare the integrity constraints along with definition itself.
6. **Atomicity Problem:** It is difficult to ensure atomicity in file processing system. For example transferring $100 from Account A to account B. If a failure occurs during execution there could be situation like $100 is deducted from Account A and not credited in Account B.
7. **Concurrent Access anomalies:** If multiple users are updating the same data simultaneously it will result in inconsistent data state. In file processing system it is very difficult to handle this using program code. This results in concurrent access anomalies.
8. **Security Problems:** Enforcing Security Constraints in file processing system is very difficult as the application programs are added to the system in an ad-hoc manner.

8.3 DATABASE

A database system is basically just a computerized record-keeping system. The database itself can be regarded as a kind of electronic filling cabinet; i.e., it is a repository or container for a collection of computerized data files. Users of the system perform a variety of operations on such files.

A database (abbreviated DB) is an entity in which data can be stored in a structured manner, with as little redundancy as possible. Different programs and different users must be able to use this data. Therefore, the concept of a database is generally linked to that of a network used for sharing this information, hence the term **base**. "Information system" is the general term used for the overarching structure which includes all data-sharing mechanisms that have been installed.

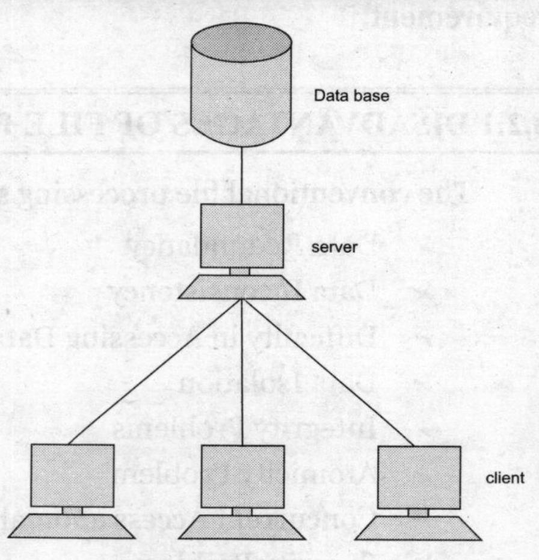

Figure 8.1: Database

Definition: A shared collection of logically related data (and a description of this data), designed to meet the information needs of an organization.

For example:

- Adding new, empty files to the database
- Inserting data into existing files
- Retrieving data from existing files
- Changing data in existing files
- Deleting data from existing files
- Removing existing files from the database

The definition of a database is a structured collection of records or data that is stored in a computer system. In order for a database to be truly functional, it must not only store large amounts of records well, but be accessed easily. In addition, new information and changes should also be fairly easy to input. In order to have a highly efficient database system, you need to incorporate a program that manages the queries and information stored on the system. This is usually referred to as DBMS or a Database Management System.

- A database is a collection of persistent data that is used by the application systems of some given enterprise.

The term "enterprise" here in simply a convenient generic term for any reasonably self-contained commercial, scientific, technical, or other organization. An enterprise might be a single individual (with a small personal database), or a complete corporation or similar large body (with a large shared database), or anything in between.

Some examples:

1. A manufacturing company
2. A bank
3. A hospital
4. A university
5. A government department

Any enterprise must necessarily maintain a lot of data about its operation. Such data is the "persistent data". The enterprises just mentioned would typically include the following among their persistent data:

1. Product data
2. Account data
3. Patient data
4. Student data
5. Planning data

8.4 DATABASE SYSTEM

A database is an organised pool of logically-related data. Data is stored within the data structures of the database. A DBMS is a suite of computer software providing the interface between users and a database or databases. A DBMS is a shell which surrounds a database or series of databases and through which all interactions take place with the database. The interactions catered for by most existing DBMS fall into four main groups:

- **Data Definition:** Defining new data structures for a database, removing data structures from the database, modifying the structure of existing data.
- **Data Maintenance:** Inserting new data into existing data structures, updating data in existing data structures, deleting data from existing data structures.
- **Data Retrieval:** Querying existing data by end-users and extracting data for use by application programs.
- **Data Control:** Creating and monitoring users of the database, restricting access to data in the database and monitoring the performance of databases.

Both a database and its DBMS conform to the principles of a particular data model. Data models include the hierarchical data model, the network data model, the relational data model and the object-oriented data model.

8.5 DATABASE MANAGEMENT SYSTEMS

A *Database Management System* (DBMS) is a software program that enables the creation and management of databases. Generally, these databases will be more complex than the text file/spreadsheet example in the previous lesson. In fact, most of today's database systems are referred to as a *Relational Database Management System (RDBMS)*, because of their ability to store related data across multiple tables.

Early on, the need for a management system in order to control both data and users quickly arose. Database management is done using a system called a **DBMS** (Database management system). The DBMS is a suite of services (software applications) for managing databases, which involves:

- enabling simple access to data
- allowing multiple users access to the information
- manipulating the data found in the database (inserting, deleting, editing)

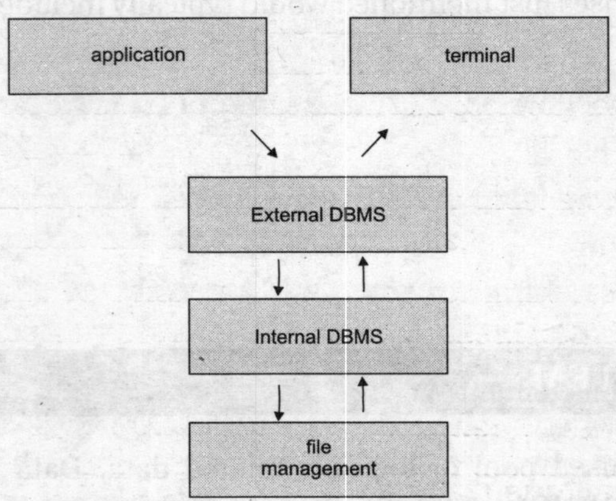

Figure 8.2: DBMS Subsystems

The DBMS can be broken down into three subsystems:

- **The file management system:** for storing information in a physical medium
- **the internal DBMS:** for placing information in order
- **the external DBMS:** represents the user interface

8.5.1 COMPONENTS OF DBMS

Following are the various components of DBMS:

- **DBMS Engine** accepts logical requests from various other DBMS subsystems, converts them into physical equivalents, and actually accesses the database and data dictionary as they exist on a storage device.
- **Data Definition Subsystem** helps the user create and maintain the data dictionary and define the structure of the files in a database.
- **Data Manipulation Subsystem** helps the user to add, change, and delete information in a database and query it for valuable information. Software tools within the data manipulation subsystem are most often the primary interface between user and the information contained in a database. It allows the user to specify its logical information requirements.
- **Application Generation Subsystem** contains facilities to help users develop transaction-intensive applications. It usually requires that the user perform a detailed series of tasks to process a transaction. It facilitates easy-to-use data entry screens, programming languages, and interfaces.
- **Data Administration Subsystem** helps users manage the overall database environment by providing facilities for backup and recovery, security management, query optimization, concurrency control, and change management.

8.5.2 DATABASE MANAGEMENT SYSTEM FUNCTIONS

The Database Management System performs the following functions.

- Data Dictionary Management
- Data Storage Management
- Data Transformation and Presentation
- Security Management
- Multi User Access Control
- Backup and Recovery Management
- Data Integrity Management
- Database Access Languages and Application Interface
- Database Communication Interface

1. Data Dictionary Management

The data dictionary stores the definitions of data elements and their relationships. This information is termed as metadata. The metadata includes definition of data, data types, relationship between data, integrity constraints etc. Any changes made in a database structure are automatically reflected in the data dictionary. In short the DBMS provides data abstraction and it removes structural and data dependency from the system.

2. Data Storage Management

The DBMS creates the complex structures required for data storage. The users are freed from defining, programming and implementing the complex physical data characteristics.

3. Data Transformation and Presentation

DBMS supports data independence. Hence the DBMS translate logical request into commands that physically locate and retrieve the requested data. The DBMS formats the physically retrieved data according to the logical data format specifications.

4. Security Management

The DBMS creates a security system that enforces user security and data privacy within the database. Security rules determine the access rights of the users. Read/write access is given to the user is specified using access rights.

5. Multi-user Access Control

The DBMS ensures that multiple users can access the database concurrently without compromising the integrity of the database. Hence the database ensures data integrity and data consistency.

6. Backup and Recovery Management

The DBMS provide backup and data recovery procedures to ensure data safety and integrity. DBMS system provides special utilities which allow the DBA to perform routine and special backup and restore procedures. Recovery Management deals with the recovery of the database after a failure.

7. Data Integrity Management

The DBMS promotes and enforce integrity rules to eliminate data integrity problems, thus minimizing the data redundancy and maximizing data consistency.

8. Database Access Languages and Application Interface

The DBMS provides data access via query language. A query language is a non-procedural language that is the user only need to specify what must be done without specifying how it is to be done. The DBMS query language contains two components: a data definition language (DDL) and a data manipulation language (DML). The DBMS also provide data access to programmers via programming languages.

9. Database Communication Interfaces

Different users may access the database through a network environment. So the DBMS provide communication functions to access the database through computer network environment.

Features commonly offered by database management systems include:

1. Query ability

Querying is the process of requesting attribute information from various perspectives and combinations of factors. Example: "How many 2-door cars in Texas are green?" A database query language and report writer allow users to interactively interrogate the database, analyze its data and update it according to the users privileges on data.

2. Backup and replication

Copies of attributes need to be made regularly in case primary disks or other equipment fails. A periodic copy of attributes may also be created for a distant organization that cannot readily access the original. DBMS usually provide utilities to facilitate the process of extracting and disseminating attribute sets. When data is replicated between database servers, so that the information remains consistent throughout the database system and users cannot tell or even know which server in the DBMS they are using, the system is said to exhibit replication transparency.

3. Rule enforcement

Often one wants to apply rules to attributes so that the attributes are clean and reliable. For example, we may have a rule that says each car can have only one engine associated with it (identified by Engine Number). If somebody tries to associate a second engine with a given car, we want the DBMS to deny such a request and display an error message. However, with changes in the model specification such as, in this example, hybrid gas-electric cars, rules may need to change. Ideally such rules should be able to be added and removed as needed without significant data layout redesign.

4. Security

For security reasons, it is desirable to limit who can see or change specific attributes or groups of attributes. This may be managed directly on an individual basis, or by the assignment of individuals and privileges to groups, or (in the most elaborate models) through the assignment of individuals and groups to roles which are then granted entitlements.

5. Computation

Common computations requested on attributes are counting, summing, averaging, sorting, grouping, cross-referencing, and so on. Rather than have each computer application implement these from scratch, they can rely on the DBMS to supply such calculations.

6. Change and access logging

This describes who accessed which attributes, what was changed, and when it was changed. Logging services allow this by keeping a record of access occurrences and changes.

7. Automated optimization

For frequently occurring usage patterns or requests, some DBMS can adjust themselves to improve the speed of those interactions. In some cases the DBMS will merely provide tools to monitor performance, allowing a human expert to make the necessary adjustments after reviewing the statistics collected.

8.5.3 CHARACTERISTICS OF A DBMS

The DBMS is the software that interacts with the users, application programs, and the database. Among other things, the DBMS allows users to insert, update, delete, and retrieve data from the database. Having a central repository for all data and data descriptions allows the DBMS to provide a general inquiry facility to this data, called a query language. The provision of a query language (such as SQL) alleviates the problems with earlier systems where the user has to work with a fixed set of queries or where there is a proliferation of programs, giving major software management problems.

The three-level architecture defined by the ANSI/SPARC model keeps data and processing separate.

Generally speaking, a DBMS must have the following characteristics:

- **Physical independence:** The physical level may be modified independently of the conceptual level. This means that the user cannot see all the hardware components of the database, which is simply a transparent structure for representing the stored information.
- **Logical independence:** The conceptual level must be editable without disrupting the physical level. In other words, the database's administrator must be able to make improvements without affecting the users' experience.
- **Ease of use:** People who are not familiar with the database must be able to describe their query without referencing the database's technical components.
- **Speedy access:** The system must be able to reply to queries as quickly as possible. This requires fast search algorithms.
- **Centralized administration:** The DBMS must enable the administrator to manipulate data, add elements, and verify their integrity in a centralized manner**Limiting redundancy:** The DBMS must be able to avoid redundant information whenever possible, both to minimize errors and to prevent wasting memory.
- **Integrity verification:** The data must be internally coherent, and when some elements reference other elements, the latter must be present.
- **Data sharing:** The DBMS must allow for multiple users to simultaneously access to the database.
- **Data security:** The DBMS must be capable of managing each user's data access rights.

Comparison of DBMS with File processing system:

DBMS	File processing system
1. There are numbers of files in this.	1.There are less files in this System.
2. Files are stored in the tables.	2. Data is stored in the files.
3. It has complex structure.	3. It has simple structure.
4. Data can be shared in DBMS.	4. Data can't be shared.

5. There are chances of inconsistency.	5. There are no chances of inconsistency.
6. It deals with multiple users.	6.It mainly deals with the single Users.
7.Data is more secure in this System.	7.Data is less secure in this system
8.DBMS system is costlier than the file processing system	8.This system is cheaper than the DBMS.

8.5.4 ADVANTAGES AND DISADVANTAGES OF DBMSs

Many of the advantages of DBMSs, such as:

1. Control of data redundancy The database approach eliminates redundancy where possible. However, it does not eliminate redundancy entirely, but controls the amount of redundancy inherent in the database. For example, it's normally necessary to duplicate key data items to model relationships between data, and sometimes it's desirable to duplicate some data items to improve performance. The reasons for controlled duplication will become clearer when you read the chapters on database design.

2. Data consistency By eliminating or controlling redundancy, we're reducing the risk of inconsistencies occurring. If data is stored only once in the database, any update to its value has to be performed only once and the new value is immediately available to all users. If data is stored more than once and the system is aware of this, the system can ensure that all copies of the data are kept consistent. Unfortunately, many of today's DBMSs don't automatically ensure this type of consistency.

3. Sharing of data In a file-based approach (the predecessor to the DBMS approach), typically files are owned by the people or departments that use them. On the other hand, the database belongs to the entire organization and can be shared by all authorized users. In this way, more users share more of the data. Furthermore, new applications can build on the existing data in the database and add only data that is not currently stored, rather than having to define all data requirements again. The new applications can also rely on the functions provided by the DBMS, such as data definition and manipulation, and concurrency and recovery control, rather than having to provide these functions themselves.

4. Improved data integrity As we've already stated, database integrity is usually expressed in terms of **constraints**, which are consistency rules that the database is not permitted to violate. Constraints may apply to data within a single record or they may apply to relationships between records. Again, data integration allows users to define, and the DBMS to enforce, integrity constraints.

5. Improved maintenance through data independence Since a DBMS separates the data descriptions from the applications, it helps make applications immune to changes in the data descriptions. This is known as data independence and its provision simplifies database application maintenance.

Other advantages include: improved security, improved data accessibility and responsiveness, increased productivity, increased concurrency, and improved backup and recovery services.

1. Better service to the users A DBMS is often used to provide better services to the users.

In conventional system, availability of information is often poor, since it normally difficult to obtain information that the existing systems were not designed for. Once several conventional systems are combined to form one centralized database, the availability of information and its updateness is likely to improve since the data can now be shared and DBMS makes it easy to respond to anticipated information requests.

Centralizing the data in the database also means that user can obtain new and combined information easily that would have been impossible to obtain otherwise. Also use of DBMS should allow users that don't know programming to interact with the data more easily, unlike file processing system where the programmer may need to write new programs to meet every new demand.

2. Flexibility of the System is Improved Since changes are often necessary to the contents of the data stored in any system; these changes are made more easily in a centralized database than in a conventional system. Applications programs need not to be changed on changing the data in the database.

3. Standards can be enforced Since all access to the database must be through DBMS, so standards are easier to enforce. Standards may relate to the naming of data, format of data, structure of the data etc. Standardizing stored data formats is usually desirable for the purpose of data interchange or migration between systems.

4. Security can be improved In conventional systems, applications are developed in an adhoc/temporary manner. Often different system of an organization would access different components of the operational data, in such an environment enforcing security can be quiet difficult. Setting up of a database makes it easier to enforce security restrictions since data is now centralized. It is easier to control that has access to what parts of the database. Different checks can be established for each type of access (retrieve, modify, delete etc.) to each piece of information in the database.

Consider an **Example** of banking in which the employee at different levels may be given access to different types of data in the database. A clerk may be given the authority to know only the names of all the customers who have a loan in bank but not the details of each loan the customer may have. It can be accomplished by giving the privileges to each employee.

5. Organization's requirement can be identified All organizations have sections and departments and each of these units often consider the work of their unit as the most important and therefore consider their need as the most important. Once a database has been setup with centralized control, it will be necessary to identify organization's requirement and to balance the needs of the competating units. So it may become necessary to ignore some requests for information if they conflict with higher priority need of the organization. It is the responsibility of the DBA (Database Administrator) to structure the database system to provide the overall service that is best for an organization.

For example: - A DBA must choose best file Structure and access method to give fast response for the high critical applications as compared to less critical applications.

6. Overall cost of developing and maintaining systems is lower It is much easier to respond to unanticipated requests when data is centralized in a database than when it is stored in a conventional file system. Although the initial cost of setting up of a database can be large, one normal expects the overall cost of setting up of a database, developing and maintaining application programs to be far lower than for similar service using conventional systems, Since the productivity of programmers can be higher in using non-procedural languages that have been developed with DBMS than using procedural languages.

7. Data Model must be developed Perhaps the most important advantage of setting up of database system is the requirement that an overall data model for an organization be build. In conventional systems, it is more likely that files will be designed as per need of particular applications demand. The overall view is often not considered. Building an overall view of an organization's data is usual cost effective in the long terms.

8. Provides backup and Recovery Centralizing a database provides the schemes such as recovery and backups from the failures including disk crash, power failures, software errors which may help the database to recover from the inconsistent state to the state that existed prior to the occurrence of the failure, though methods are very complex.

8.5.5 DISADVANTAGES OF THE DATABASE APPROACH

A database system generally provides on-line access to the database for many users. In contrast, a conventional system is often designed to meet a specific need and therefore generally provides access to only a small number of users. Because of the larger number of users accessing the data when a database is used, the enterprise may involve additional risks as compared to a conventional data processing system in the following areas.

1. Complexity As we've already mentioned, a DBMS is an extremely complex piece of software, and all users (database designers and developers, DBAs, and end-users) must understand the DBMS's functionality to take full advantage of it.

2. Cost of DBMS The cost of DBMSs varies significantly, depending on the environment and functionality provided. For example, a single-user DBMS for a PC may cost only $100. However, a large mainframe multi-user DBMS servicing hundreds of users can be extremely expensive, perhaps $100,000 to $1,000,000. There is also the recurrent annual maintenance cost, which is typically a percentage of the list price.

3. Cost of conversion In some situations, the cost of the DBMS and any extra hardware may be insignificant compared with the cost of converting existing applications to run on the new DBMS and hardware. This cost also includes the cost of training staff to use these new systems, and possibly the employment of specialist staff to help with the conversion and running of the system. This cost is one of the main reasons why some companies feel tied to their current systems and cannot switch to more modern database technology. The term **legacy system** is sometimes used to refer to an older, and usually inferior, system (such as file-based, hierarchical, or network systems).

4. Performance Typically, a file-based system is written for a specific application, such as invoicing. As a result, performance is generally very good. However, a DBMS is written to be more general, to cater for many applications rather than just one. The effect is that some applications may not run as fast using a DBMS as they did before.

5. Higher impact of a failure The centralization of resources increases the vulnerability of the system. Since all users and applications rely on the availability of the DBMS, the failure of any component can bring operations to a complete halt until the failure is repaired.

6. Confidentiality, Privacy and Security When information is centralised and is made available to users from remote locations, the possibilities of abuse are often more than in a conventional data processing system. To reduce the chances of unauthorised users accessing sensitive information, it is necessary to take technical, administrative and, possibly, legal measures.

Most databases store valuable information that must be protected against deliberate trespass and destruction.

7. Data Quality Since the database is accessible to users remotely; adequate controls are needed to control users updating data and to control data quality. With increased number of users accessing data directly, there are enormous opportunities for users to damage the data. Unless there are suitable controls, the data quality may be compromised.

8. Data Integrity Since a large number of users could be using a database concurrently, technical safeguards are necessary to ensure that the data remain correct during operation. The main threat to data integrity comes from several different users attempting to update the same data at the same time. The database therefore needs to be protected against inadvertent changes by the users.

9. Enterprise Vulnerability Centralising all data of an enterprise in one database may mean that the database becomes an indispensable resource. The survival of the enterprise may depend on reliable information being available from its database. The enterprise therefore becomes vulnerable to the destruction of the database or to unauthorised modification of the database.

8.6 THREE-LEVEL ARCHITECTURE PROPOSAL FOR A DBMS

In this section we describe the generalized architecture of a database system called the ANSI/SPARC model. A large number of commercial systems and research database models fit this framework. The architecture, shown in Figure 8.3, is divided into three levels: the external level, the conceptual level, and the internal level.

The view at each of these levels is described by a scheme. A scheme is an outline or a plan that describes the records and relationships existing in the view. The word scheme, which means a systematic plan for attaining some goal, is used interchangeably in the database literature with the word schema. The word schema is used in the database literature for the plural instead of schemata, the grammatically correct word. The scheme also describes the way in which entities at one level of abstraction can be mapped to the next level.

8.6.1 EXTERNAL OR USER VIEW

The external or user view is at the highest level of database abstraction where only those portions of the database of concern to a user or application program are included. Any number of user views (some of which may be identical) may exist for a given global or conceptual view.

Each external view is described by means of a scheme called an external schema. The external schema consists of the definition of the logical records and the relationships in the external view. The external schema also contains the method of deriving the objects in the external view from the objects in the conceptual view. The objects include entities, attributes, and relationships. (The terms view, scheme, and schema are sometimes used interchangeably when there is no confusion as to what is implied).

8.6.2 CONCEPTUAL OR GLOBAL VIEW

At this level of database abstraction all the database entities and the relationships among them are included. One conceptual view represents the entire database. This conceptual view is defined by the conceptual schema. It describes all the records and relationships included in the conceptual view and, therefore, in the database. There is only one conceptual schema per database. This schema also contains the method of deriving the objects in the conceptual view from the objects in the internal view.

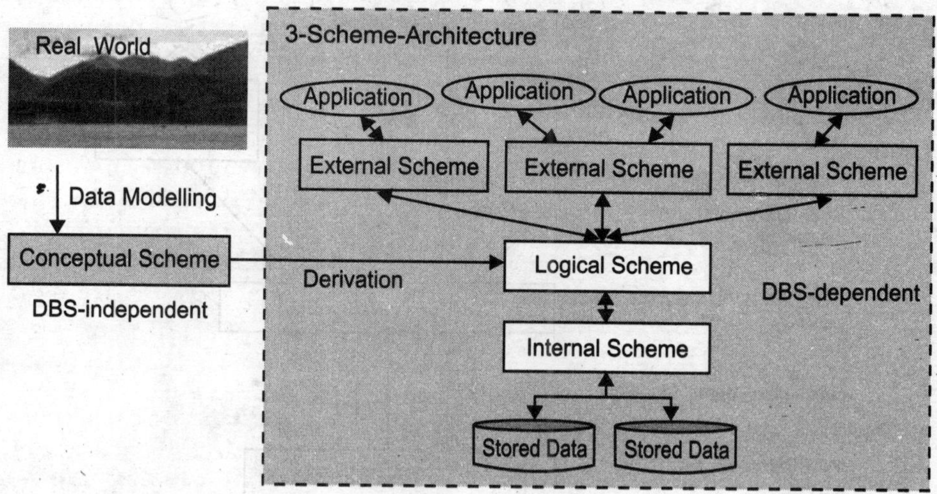

Figure 8.3: Three levels of architecture of a DBMS

The description of data at this level is in a format independent of its physical representation. It also includes features that specify the checks to retain data consistency and integrity.

8.6.3 INTERNAL VIEW

We find this view at the lowest level of abstraction, closest to the physical storage method used. It indicated how the data will be stored and describes the data structures and access methods to be used by the database. The internal view is expressed by the internal schema, which contains the definition of the stored record, the method of representing the data fields, and the access aids used.

8.6.4 MAPPING BETWEEN VIEWS

Two mappings are required in a database system with three different views as shown in Figure 8.3. A mapping between the external and conceptual views gives the correspondence among the records and the relationships of the external and conceptual views. The external view is an abstraction of the conceptual view, which in its turn is an abstraction of the internal view.

It describes the contents of the database as perceived by the user or application program of that view. The user of the external view sees and manipulates a record corresponding to the external view. There is a mapping from a particular logical record in the external view to one (or more) conceptual record(s) in the conceptual view. A number of differences could exist between the two. Names of the fields and record, for instance, may be different. A number of conceptual fields can be combined into a single logical field, for example, Last_Name and First_Name at the conceptual level but Name at logical level. A given logical record could be derived from a number of conceptual records.

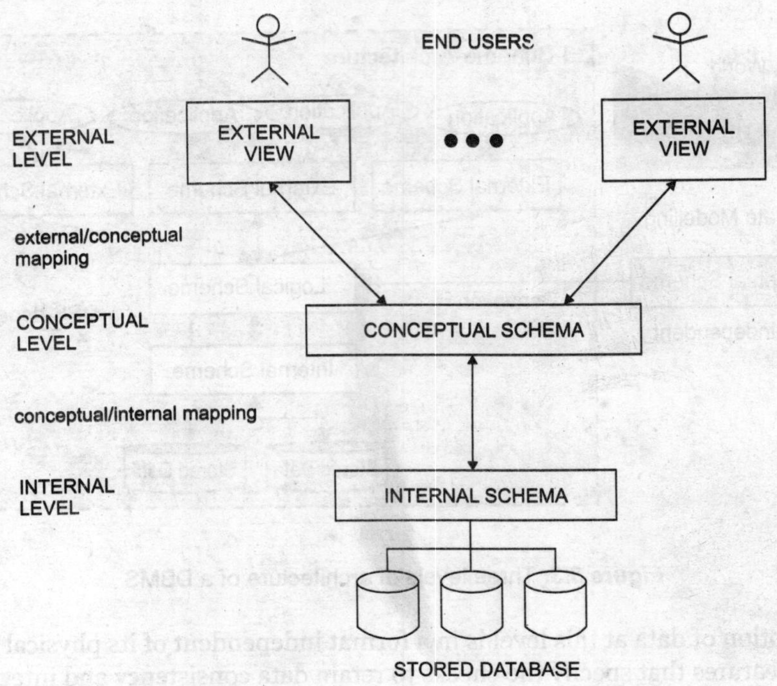

Figure 8.4: Different Schemas

Similarly, there is a mapping from a conceptual record to an internal one. An internal record is a record at the internal level, not necessarily a stored record on a physical storage device. The internal record of Figure 8.4 may be split up into two or more physical records. The physical database is the data that is stored on secondary storage devices. It is made up of records with certain data structures and organized in files. Consequently, there is an additional mapping from the internal record to one or more stored records on secondary storage devices. This may have been implemented using some form of nonlinear addressing. The internal record is assumed to be linearly addressed. However, this complexity is managed by the DBMS and the user need not be aware of its presence nor be concerned with it.

Mapping between the conceptual and the internal levels specifies the method of deriving the conceptual record from the physical database. Again, differences similar to those that exist between external and conceptual views could exist between the conceptual and internal views. Such differences are indicated and resolved in the mapping.

Differences that could exist, besides the difference in names, include the following:

- Representation of numeric values could be difference in the two views. One view could consider a field to be decimal, whereas the other view may regard the field as binary. A two-way transformation between such values can be easily incorporated in the mapping. If, however, the values are stored in a binary format, the range of values may be limited by the underlying hardware.
- Representation of string data can be considered by the two views to be coded differently. One view may perceive the string data to be in ASCII code, the other view may consider the data to be in EBCDIC code. Again, two-way transformation can be provided.
- The value for a field in one view could be computed from the values in one or more fields of the other view. For example, the external view may use a field containing a person's age, whereas the conceptual view contains the date of birth. The age value could be derived from the data of birth by using a date function available from the operating system. Another example of a computed field would be where an external view requires the value of the hours worked during a week in a field, whereas the conceptual view contains fields representing the hours worked each day of the week. The former can be derived from the latter by simple addition. These two examples of transformation between the external and conceptual views are not bidirectional. One cannot uniquely reflect a change in the total hours worked during a week to hours worked during each day of the week. Therefore, a user's attempt to modify the corresponding external fields will not be allowed by the DBMS.

Such mapping between the conceptual and internal levels is a correspondence that indicated how each conceptual record is to be stored and the characteristics and size of each field of the record. Changing the storage structure of the record involves changing the conceptual view to internal view mapping so that the conceptual view does not require any alteration.

The conceptual view can assume that the database contains a sequence of records for each conceptual record type. These records could be accessed sequentially or randomly. The actual storage could have been done to optimize performance. A conceptual record may be split into two records, which the less frequently used record (part of the original record) on a slower storage device and the more frequently used, record on a faster device. The stored record could be in a physical sequence, or one or more indices may be implemented for faster access to record occurrences by the index fields. Pointers may exist in the physical records to access the next record occurrence in various orders. These structures are hidden from the conceptual view by the mapping between the two.

8.7 DATA INDEPENDENCE

Data independence is the type of data transparency that matters for a centralized DBMS. It refers to the immunity of user applications to make changes in the definition and organization of data.

Physical data independence deals with hiding the details of the storage structure from user applications. The application should not be involved with these issues, since there is no difference in the operation carried out against the data.

The data independence and operation independence together gives the feature of data abstraction. There are two levels of data independence.

First level

The logical structure of the data is known as the **schema definition**. In general, if a user application operates on a subset of the attributes of a relation, it should not be affected later when new attributes are added to the same relation. Logical data independence indicates that the conceptual schema can be changed without affecting the existing schemas.

Second level

The physical structure of the data is referred to as "physical data description". Physical data independence deals with hiding the details of the storage structure from user applications. The application should not be involved with these issues since, conceptually; there is no difference in the operations carried out against the data. There are two types of data independence:

1. **Logical data independence:** The ability to change the logical (conceptual) schema without changing the External schema (User View) is called logical data independence. For example, the addition or removal of new entities, attributes, or relationships to the conceptual schema should be possible without having to change existing external schemas or having to rewrite existing application programs.
2. **Physical data independence:** The ability to change the physical schema without changing the logical schema is called physical data independence. For example, a change to the internal schema, such as using different file organization or storage structures, storage devices, or indexing strategy, should be possible without having to change the conceptual or external schemas.

8.7.1 DATA INDEPENDENCE TYPES

Data independence has two types:

1. Physical Independence
2. Logical Independence

With knowledge about the three-scheme architecture the term data independence can be explained as follows: Each higher level of the data architecture is immune to changes of the next lower level of the architecture.

Physical Independence

The logical scheme stays unchanged even though the storage space or type of some data is changed for reasons of optimisation or reorganisation.

[The ability to change the physical schema without changing the logical schema is called as Physical Data Independence.]

Logical Independence

The external scheme may stay unchanged for most changes of the logical scheme. This is especially desirable as the application software does not need to be modified or newly translated. [The ability to change the logical schema without changing the external schema or application programs is called as Logical Data Independence.]

8.8 DBMS FACILITIES

Two main types of facilities are provided by a DBMS.

- The data definition facility or data definition language (DDL)
- The data manipulation facility or data manipulation language (DML)

8.8.1 DATA DEFINITION LANGUAGE

Database management systems provide a facility known as data definition language (DDL), which can be used to define the conceptual scheme and also give some details about how to implement this scheme in the physical devices used to store the data. This definition includes all the entity sets and their associated attributes as well as the relationships among the entity sets. The definition also include any constraints that have to be maintained, including the constraints on the values that can be assigned to different attributes in the same or different record. These definitions, which can be described as metadata about the data in the database, are expressed in the DDL of the DBMS and maintained in a complied form (usually as a set of tables). The complied form of the definitions is known as a data dictionary, directory, or system, catalog. The data dictionary contains information on the data stored in the database and is consulted by the DBMS before any data manipulation operation.

The database management system maintains the information on the file structure, the method used to efficiently access the relevant data (i.e., the access method). It also provides a method whereby the application programs indicate their data requirements. The application program could use a subset of the conceptual data definition language or a separate language. The database system also contains mapping functions that flow it to interpret the stored data for the application program. (Thus, the stored data is transformed into a form compatible with the application program).

The internal schema is specified in a somewhat similar data definition language called data stored definition language. The definition of the internal view is compiled and maintained by the DBMS. The complied internal schema specifies the implementation details of the internal database, including the access method employed. This information is handled by the DBMS; the user need not be aware of these details.

8.8.2 DATA MANIPULATION LANGUAGE

The language used to manipulate data in the database is called data manipulate language (DML). Data manipulation involves retrieval of data from the database insertion of new data into the database, and deletion or modification of existing data. The first of these data manipulation operations is called a query. A query is a statement in the DML that requests the retrieval of data form the database. The subset of the DML used to pose a query is known as a query language; however, we use the terms DML and query language synonymously.

The DML provide commands to select and retrieve data from the database. Commands are also provided to insert, update, and delete records. They could be used in an interactive mode or embedded in conventional programming language such as Assembler, COBOL, FORTRAN, Pascal, or PL/I. The data manipulation functions provided by the DBMS can be invoked in application programs directly by procedure calls or by processor statement. The latter would be replaced by appropriate procedure calls by either a pre-processor or the compiler. An example of a procedure call and a pre-processor statement is given below:

Procedure call: Call Retrieve (EMPLOYEE.Name, EMPLOYEE.Address)

Pre-processor statement: %select EMPLOYEE.Name, EMPLOYEE.Address from

Employee;

These pre-processor statements, indicated by the presence of the leading % symbol, would be replaced by data manipulation language statements in the compiled version of the application program. Commands in the conventional languages allow permissible operations on the database such as data retrieval, addition, modification, or deletion.

The DML can be procedural; the user indicates not only what to retrieve but how to go about retrieving it. If the DML is nonprocedural, the user has to indicate only what is to be retrieved. The DBMS in this tries to optimize the exact order of retrieving the various components to make up the required response.

Data definition of the external view in most current DBMSs is done outside the application program or interactive session. Data manipulation is done by procedure calls to subroutines provided by a DBMS or via pre-processor statements. In an integrated environment, data definition and manipulation are achieved using a uniform set of constructs that forms part of the user's programming environment.

8.9 OVERALL SYSTEM STRUCTURE

For our purposes, we may assume that the database management system is structured and interfaces with various users as shown in Figure 8.5.

1. Database systems are partitioned into modules for different functions. Some functions (e.g. file systems) may be provided by the operating system.
2. Components include:

- **File manager** manages allocation of disk space and data structures used to represent information on disk. Responsibility for the structure of the files and managing the file space rests with the file manager. It is also responsible for locating the block containing the required record, requesting this block from the disk manager, and transmitting the required record to the data manager. The file manager can be implemented using an interface to the existing file subsystem provided by the operating system of the host computer or it can include a file subsystem written especially for the DBMS.
- **Database manager:** The interface between low-level data and application programs and queries. The data manager is the central software component of the DBMS. It is sometimes referred to as the database control system. One of the functions of the data manager is to convert operations in the user's queries coming directly via the query processor or indirectly via an application program from the user's logical view to a physical file system. The data manager is responsible for interfacing with the file system. In addition, the tasks of enforcing constraints to maintain the consistency and integrity of the data, as well as

its security, are also performed by the data manager. Synchronizing the simultaneous operations performed by concurrent users is under the control of the data manager. It is also entrusted with backup and recovery operations.

- **Query processor** translates statements in a query language into low-level instructions the database manager understands. (May also attempt to find an equivalent but more efficient form.) The database user retrieves data by formulating a query in the data manipulation language provided with the database. The query processor is used to interpret the online user's query and convert it into an efficient series of operations in a form capable of being sent to the data manager for execution. The query processor uses the data dictionary to find the structure of the relevant portion of the database and uses this information in modifying the query and preparing an optimal plan to access the database.
- **Disk Manager**
  The disk manager is part of the operating system of the host computer and all physical input and output operations are performed by it. The disk manager transfers the block or page requested by the file manager so that the latter need not be concerned with the physical characteristics of the underlying storage media.
- **DML precompiler** converts DML statements embedded in an application program to normal procedure calls in a host language. The precompiler interacts with the query processor.
- **DDL compiler** converts DDL statements to a set of tables containing metadata stored in a data dictionary.

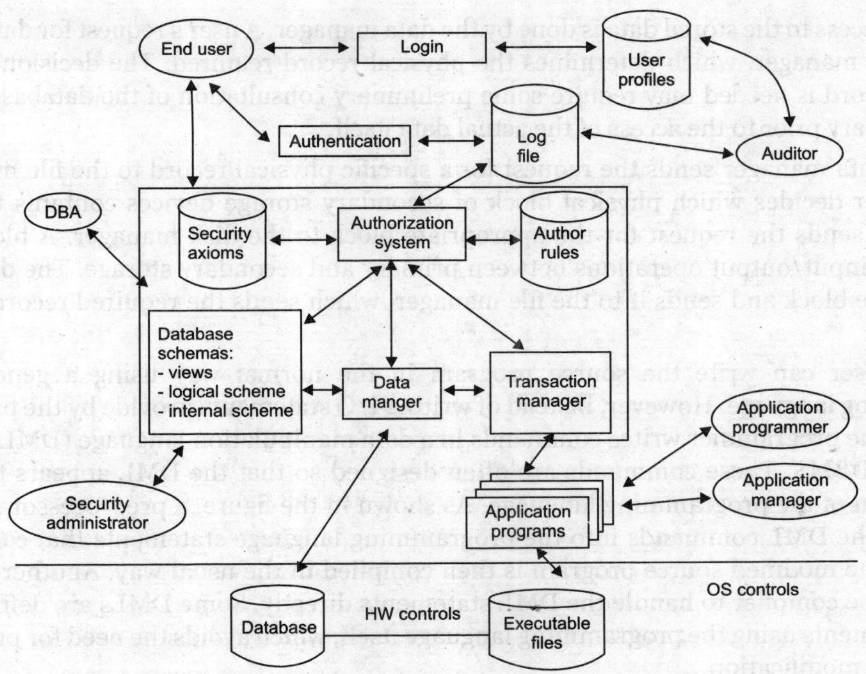

Figure 8.5: Database system structure

In addition, several data structures are required for physical system implementation:

- **Data files:** It stores the database itself.
- **Data dictionary:** it stores information about the structure of the database. It is used heavily. Great emphasis should be placed on developing a good design and efficient implementation of the dictionary. Information pertaining to the structure and usage of data contained in the database, the metadata, is maintained in a data dictionary. The term system catalog also describes this metadata. The data dictionary, which is a database itself, documents the data. Each database user can consult the data dictionary to learn what each piece of data and the various synonyms of the data fields mean. In an integrated system (i.e., in a system where the data dictionary is part of the DBMS) the data dictionary stores information concerning the external, conceptual, and internal levels of the database. It contains the source of each data-field value, the frequency of its use, and an audit trail concerning updates, including who and when of each update. Currently data dictionary systems are available as add-ons to the DBMS. Standards have yet to be evolved for integrating the data dictionary facility with the DBMS so that the two databases, one for metadata and the other for data, can be manipulated using an unified DDL/DML.
- **Indices:** It provides fast access to data items holding particular values.

8.10 DATABASE ACCESS

Any access to the stored data is done by the data manager. A user's request for data is received by the data manager, which determines the physical record required. The decision as to which physical record is needed may require some preliminary consultation of the database and/or the data dictionary prior to the access of the actual data itself.

The data manager sends the request for a specific physical record to the file manager. The file manager decides which physical block of secondary storage devices contains the required record and sends the request for the appropriate block to the disk manager. A block is a unit of physical input/output operations between primary and secondary storage. The disk manager retrieves the block and sends it to the file manager, which sends the required record to the data manager.

The user can write the source program in the normal way using a general-purpose programming language. However, instead of writing I/O statements provide by the programming language, the programmer writes commands in a data manipulation language (DML) defined for use with a DBMS. These commands are often designed so that the DML appears to be merely an extension of the programming language. As shown in the figure, a preprocessor may be used to convert the DML commands into the programming language statements that call the DBMS routines. The modified source program is then compiled in the usual way. Another approach is to modify the compiler to handle the DML statements directly. Some DMLs are defined as set of CALL statements using the programming language itself, which avoids the need for preprocessing or compiler modification.

8.11 USE OF A DBMS

Here we discuss the method by which a DBMS is related to other pieces of system software. The two principle methods of user interaction with a DBMS are illustrated in the figure 8.6:

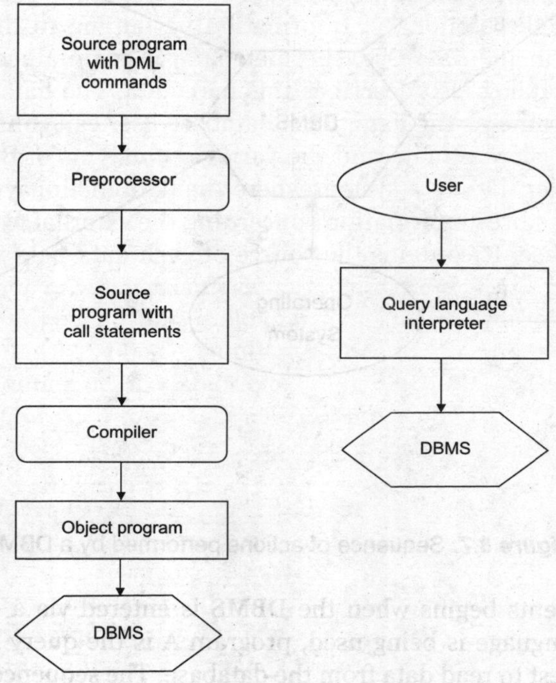

Figure 8.6: Interaction with a DBMS using a data manipulation language and a query language

The other approach to DBMS interaction, as shown in the figure, does not require the user to write programs to access the database. Instead, the users enter commands in a special query language defined by the DBMS. These commands are processed by a query-language interpreter, which calls DBMS routines to perform the requested operations.

Each of these approaches to user interaction has its own advantages. With a query language, it is possible to obtain results much more quickly because there is no need to write and debug programs. Query languages can also be used effectively by non programmers, or by individuals who program only occasionally. Most query languages, however, have built-in limitations. For example, it may be difficult or impossible to perform a function for which the language was not designed. On the other hand, a DML allows the programmer to use all the flexibility and power of a general-purpose programming language. However, this approach requires much more effort from the user. Most modern database management systems provide both a query language and a DML so that a user can choose form of interaction that best meets his or her needs.

The sequence of operations performed by a DBMS in processing a request is essentially the same regardless of whether a DML or a query language is being used. These actions are illustrated in the figure 8.7:

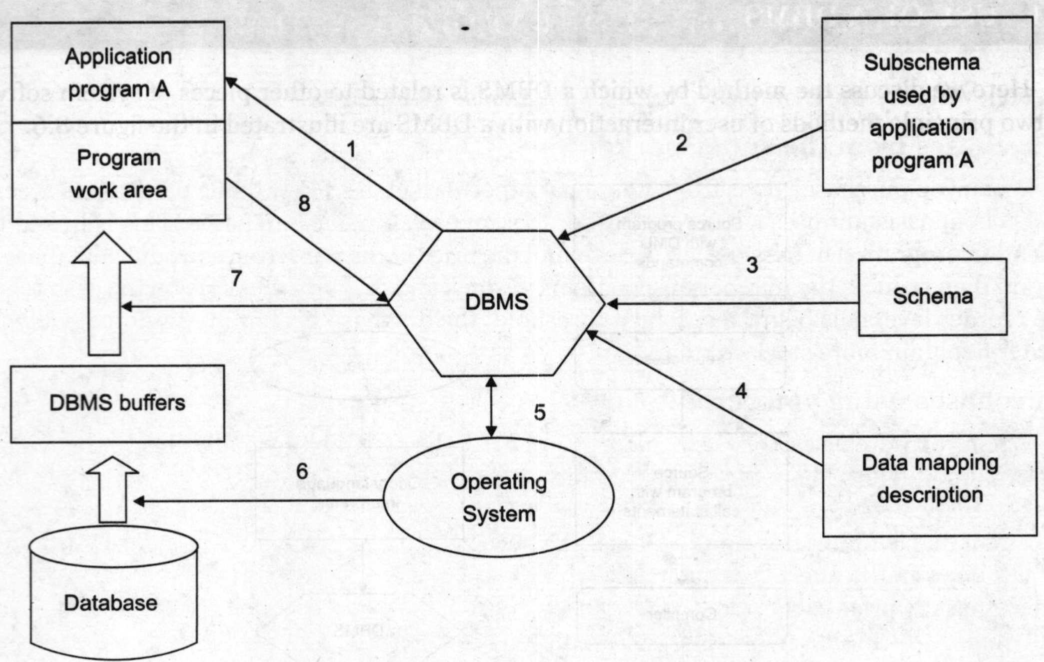

Figure 8.7: Sequence of actions performed by a DBMS

The sequence of events begins when the DBMS is entered via a call from the application program A. If a query language is being used, program A is the query language interpreter. We assume this call is a request to read data from the database. The sequence of events for other types of database operations is similar.

The request from program A is stated in terms of the subschema being used by A. To process a request, the DBMS must first examine the subschema definition being used. The DBMS must also consider the relationship between the subschema and the schema to interpret the request in terms of overall logical database structure. After determining the logical database records that must be read, the DBMS examines the data mapping description. This operation gives the information needed to locate the required records in the files of the database. At this point, the DBMS has converted a logical request for subschema record into physical requests to read data from one or more files. These requests for I/O are passed to the operating system using system calls. The operating system then issues channel and device commands to perform the necessary physical I/O operations. These I/O operations read the required records from the database into a DBMS buffer area.

After the physical I/O operations have been completed, all the data requested by the application program is present in the physical memory. However, this information must still be converted into the form expected by the program. The DBMS accomplishes this conversion by again comparing the schema and the subschema. Finally, the DBMS return control to the application program and makes available to the program a variety of status information, including any possible error indications.

8.12 EXAMPLES OF THE USE OF DATABASE SYSTEMS

Following are the examples of the use of database systems:

1. Purchases from the supermarket

When you purchase goods from your local supermarket, it's likely that a database is accessed. The checkout assistant uses a bar code reader to scan each of your purchases. This is linked to an application program that uses the bar code to find the price of the item from a product database. The program then reduces the number of such items in stock and displays the price on the cash register. If the reorder level falls below a specified threshold, the database system may automatically place an order to obtain more stocks of that item.

2. Purchases using your credit card

When you purchase goods using your credit card, the assistant normally checks that you have sufficient credit left to make the purchase. This check may be carried out by telephone or it may be done automatically by a card reader linked to a computer system. In either case, there is a database somewhere that contains information about the purchases that you've made using your credit card. To check your credit, there is a database application program that uses your credit card number to check that the price of the goods you wish to buy, together with the sum of the purchases you've already made this month, is within your credit limit. When the purchase is confirmed, the details of your purchase are added to this database. The application program also accesses the database to check that the credit card is not on the list of stolen or lost cards before authorizing the purchase. There are other database application programs to send out monthly statements to each cardholder and to credit accounts when payment is received.

3. Booking a holiday at the travel agents

When you make inquiries about a holiday, the travel agent may access several databases containing holiday and flight details. When you book your holiday, the database system has to make all the necessary booking arrangements. In this case, the system has to ensure that two different agents don't book the same holiday or overbook the seats on the flight. For example, if there is only one seat left on the flight from London to New York and two agents try to reserve the last seat at the same time, the system has to recognize this situation, allow one booking to proceed, and inform the other agent that there are now no seats available. The travel agent may have another, usually separate, database for invoicing.

4. Using the local library

Whenever you visit your local library, there is probably a database containing details of the books in the library, details of the readers, reservations, and so on. There will be a computerized index that allows readers to find a book based on its title, or its authors, or its subject area, or its ISBN. The database system handles reservations to allow a reader to reserve a book and to be informed by post when the book is available. The system also sends out reminders to borrowers who have failed to return books on the due date. Typically, the system will have a bar code reader, similar to that used by the supermarket described earlier, which is used to keep track of books coming in and going out of the library.

5. Using the Internet

Many of the sites on the Internet are driven by database applications. For example, you may visit an online bookstore that allows you to browse and buy books, such as Amazon.com. The bookstore allows you to browse books in different categories, such as computing or management, or it may allow you to browse books by author name. In either case, there is a database on the organization's Web server that consists of book details, availability, shipping information, stock levels, and on-order information. Book details include book titles, ISBNs, authors, prices, sales histories, publishers, reviews, and in-depth descriptions. The database allows books to be cross-referenced: for example, a book may be listed under several categories, such as computing, programming languages, bestsellers, and recommended titles. The cross-referencing also allows Amazon to give you information on other books that are typically ordered along with the title you are interested in.

8.13 INTRODUCTION TO A TEXT EDITOR

The interactive text editor has become an important aspect of almost any computing environment. No longer are editors thought of as tools for programmers. It is now increasingly recognized that a text editor should be considered the primary interface to the computer for all types of "knowledge workers" as they compose, organize, study and manipulate computer-based information. An interactive editor is a computer program that allows a user to create and revise a target document. The term document includes objects such as computer programs, text, equation, table's linker, loader and Operating System, diagrams, line art and photographs; anything that one might find on a printed page: A text editor is a program in which the primary elements being edited are character strings of the target text. We also presented a detailed descriptive of UNIX operating system. In this unit, we take up issues related to a Text Editor and a Debugging system.

8.13.1 EDITING PROCESS

The document-editing process is an interactive user-computer dialogue designed to accomplish four tasks:

1) Select the part of the target document to be viewed and manipulated
2) Determine how to format this view on-line and how to display it
3) Specify and execute operations that modify the target document
4) Update the view appropriately.

Editing phase involves how the target document is created or altered with a set of operations such as insert, delete, replace, move and copy. The editing functions are often specialized to operate on elements meaningful to the type of editor.

For example, a manuscript-oriented editor might operate on elements such as single characters, words, lines, sentences and paragraphs.

A program-oriented editor might operate on elements such as identifiers, keywords and statements.

8.14 TEXT EDITORS

A text editor is considered a primary interface to the computer for all types of "knowledge workers" as they compose, organize, study, and manipulate computer-based information. An interactive editor is a computer program that allows a user to create and revise a target document. The term document includes objects such as computer programs, text, equations, tables, diagrams, and almost anything that can appear on a printed page. Our discussion is however limited to the text editors only, in which the primary elements being edited are character strings of the target text.

The document editing process is an interactive user-computer dialogue designed to accomplish the following four tasks:

1. **Select a part of the target document to be viewed and manipulated**

   Selection of the part of the document to be viewed and edited involves first travelling through the document to locate the area of interest. This search is accomplished with operations such as next screenful, bottom, and find pattern. Travelling specifies where an area of interest is; the selection of what is to be viewed and manipulated there is controlled by filtering. Filtering extracts the relevant subset of the target document at the point of interest, such as the next screenful of text or the next statement.

2. **Determine how to format this view on-line and how to display it**

   Formatting then determines how the result of filtering will be seen as a visible representation on a display screen or other device.

3. **Specify and execute operations that modify the target document**

   In the actual editing phase, the target document is created or altered with a set of operations such as insert, delete, replace, move, and copy. The editing functions are often specialized to operate on elements meaningful to the type of editor.

4. **Update the view properly**

   In the simple scenario, the user may then travel to the end of the document. A screenful of text would be filtered, this segment would be formatted, and the view would be displayed on an output device.

8.14.1 TYPES OF TEXT EDITORS

Text editors come in the following forms:

1. **Line Editors**

   The scope of edit operations in line editor is limited to a line of text. The line is designated positionally e.g. by specifying a serial number in the text, or contextually e.g. by specifying a context which uniquely identifies it. The primary advantage of such editors is their simplicity.

2. **Steam Editors**

   A steam editor views the entire text as a steam of characters as a steam of characters. This permits the edit operations to cross line boundaries. They support character, line and context oriented commands based on the current editing context indicated by the position of a text pointer. This pointer can be manipulated by using positioning or search commands.

Both these editors maintain multiple representations of text. One representation (display form) shows the text as a sequence of lines. The editor maintains an internal form which is used to perform the edit operations. This form contains end-of-line characters and other edit characters. The editor ensures that both these representations at compatible with each other at any instant of time.

3. **Screen Editors**

A line or steam editor does not display the text in the manner it would appear if printed. A screen editor uses the what-you-see-is-what-you-get principle in editor design. The editor displays a screenful of text at a single instant of time. The user can move the cursor over the screen, position it at the point where one desires to perform some editing and proceed with the editing directly. Thus it is possible to see the effect of an edit operation on the screen. This is very useful while formatting the text to produce printed documents.

4. **Word Processors**

Word processors are document editors with additional features to produce well formatted hard copy outputs. Essential features of word processors are commands for moving sections of text from one place to another, merging of text, and searching and replacement of text. Many word processors support a spell-check option. These editors are used frequently by authors, office personnel and computer professionals.

5. **Structure Editors**

A structure editor incorporates an awareness of the structure of a document. This is useful in browsing through a document e.g. if a programmer wishes to edit a specific function in a program file. The structure is specified by the user while creating or modifying the document. Editing requirements are specified using the structure. A special class of structure editors, called syntax-directed editors, is used in programming environments.

8.14.2 USER INTERFACE

Following are the various user interfaces:

- **Conceptual Model**

The user of an editor is presented with a conceptual model of the editing system, which is an abstract framework on which the editor and the world on which it operates are based. It provides an easily understood abstraction of the target document and its elements, with a set of guidelines describing the effects of operations on these elements. Besides the conceptual model, the user interface is concerned with the input devices, the output devices, and the interaction language of the system.

- **Input Devices**

Input devices are used to enter elements of the text being edited, to enter commands, and to designate editable elements. These devices, as used with editors, can be divided into three categories: text devices, button devices, and locator devices. Text or string devices are typically typewriter like keyboards on which a user presses and releases keys, sending a unique code for each key. All the current computer keyboards are of the QWERTY variety. Some of the alternative keyboard arrangements have also been proposed, but none of these alternatives seem likely to be widely accepted in the near future because of the retraining effort that would be required.

Button or choice devices generate an interrupt or set a system flag, usually causing invocation of an associated application-program action. Such devices typically include a set of special function keys on an alphanumeric keyboard or on the display itself, or the buttons can be simulated in software by displaying text strings or symbols on the screen.

Locator devices are two dimensional analog-to-digital converters that position a cursor symbol on the screen by observing the user's movement of the device. The most common locator devices used for editing applications are the mouse and the data tablet. The data tablet is a flat, rectangular, electromagnetically sensitive panel, on which a ballpoint-pen-like stylus or a puck is moved. The tablet returns to a system program coordinates of the position on the data tablet at which the stylus or puck is currently located. The program can then map these data-tablet coordinates to the screen coordinates and move the cursor to the corresponding screen position. Locator devices can also incorporate one or more buttons that can be used to specify editing operations.

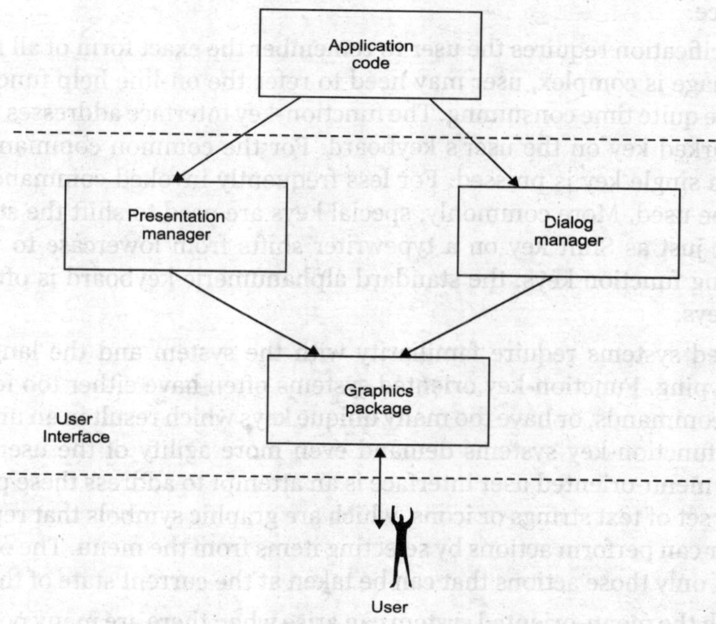

Figure 8.8: User Interface

Text devices with arrow keys can also be used to simulate locator devices. Each of these keys shows an arrow that points up, down, left, or right. Pressing an arrow key typically generates an appropriate character sequence, to whose response the editor moves the cursor in the direction of the arrow on the key pressed.

Voice-input devices can translate the spoken words into their equivalent textual form. These devices may prove to be the text input devices of the future. Voice recognizers are currently available for command input on some systems.

- **Output Devices**

  The output device lets the user view the elements being edited and the results of the editing operations. The first output devices were teletypewriters and other character-printing terminals that generated output on paper. Further introduced were the 'glass teletypes' based on cathode ray tube (CRT) technology which used the CRT screen to simulate the hard-copy teletypewriter. Today's advanced CRT terminals use hardware assistance for such features as moving the cursor, inserting and deleting characters and lines, and scrolling lines and pages. The more modern professional workstations support multiple proportionally spaced character fonts to produce realistic facsimiles of hard-copy documents.

- **Interaction Language**

  The interaction language of a text editor is generally one of the several common types. The typing-oriented or text-command oriented method is the oldest of the major editor interfaces. The user communicates with the editor by typing text strings both for command names and for operands. These strings are sent to the editor and are usually echoed to the output device.

The typed specification requires the user to remember the exact form of all the commands. If the command language is complex, user may need to refer the on-line help function or a manual and the typing can be quite time consuming. The function-key interface addresses these deficiencies by associating a marked key on the user's keyboard. For the common commands in a function-key editor, usually a single key is pressed. For less frequently invoked commands, an alternative textual syntax can be used. More commonly, special keys are used to shift the standard function-key interpretations, just as Shift key on a typewriter shifts from lowercase to uppercase. As an alternative to shifting function keys, the standard alphanumeric keyboard is often overloaded to simulate function keys.

Typing oriented systems require familiarity with the system and the language, as well as some expertise in typing. Function-key oriented systems often have either too few keys requiring multiple keystroke commands, or have too many unique keys which result in an unwieldy keyboard. In either case, the function-key systems demand even more agility of the user than a standard keyboard does. The menu-oriented user interface is an attempt to address these problems. A menu is a multiple-choice set of text strings or icons, which are graphic symbols that represent objects or operations. The user can perform actions by selecting items from the menu. The editor prompts the user with a menu of only those actions that can be taken at the current state of the system.

A problem with the menu-oriented system can arise when there are many possible actions and several choices are requested to complete an action. The display area for the menu is rather limited, therefore the user might be presented with several consecutive menus in a hierarchy before the appropriate command and its options appear. Since this can be annoying, hence the menu oriented systems allow the users to turn off menu control and return to a typing or function-key interface. Other systems have the most used functions on a main command menu and the less frequently used menus are handled by the secondary menus. Interfaces such as this, in which prompting and menu information are provided to the user at a little added cost and a little degradation in response time are becoming increasingly popular.

8.14.3 DESIGN OF AN EDITOR

The main functions of an editor are travelling, editing, viewing and displaying the text. Travelling is the movement of editing context to a new position within the text. This may be explicitly done by the user, or may be implied by a user command. Viewing is the formatting of text in a manner desired by the user. This is an abstract view, independent of the physical characteristics of an input-output device. The display component maps this view into the physical characteristics of the display device in use. This determines where a particular view may appear on the user's screen. This separation of viewing and display functions gives rise to some interesting possibilities like multiple windows on the same screen, concurrent edit operations using the same display terminal, etc. A simple text editor may combine these viewing and display functions.

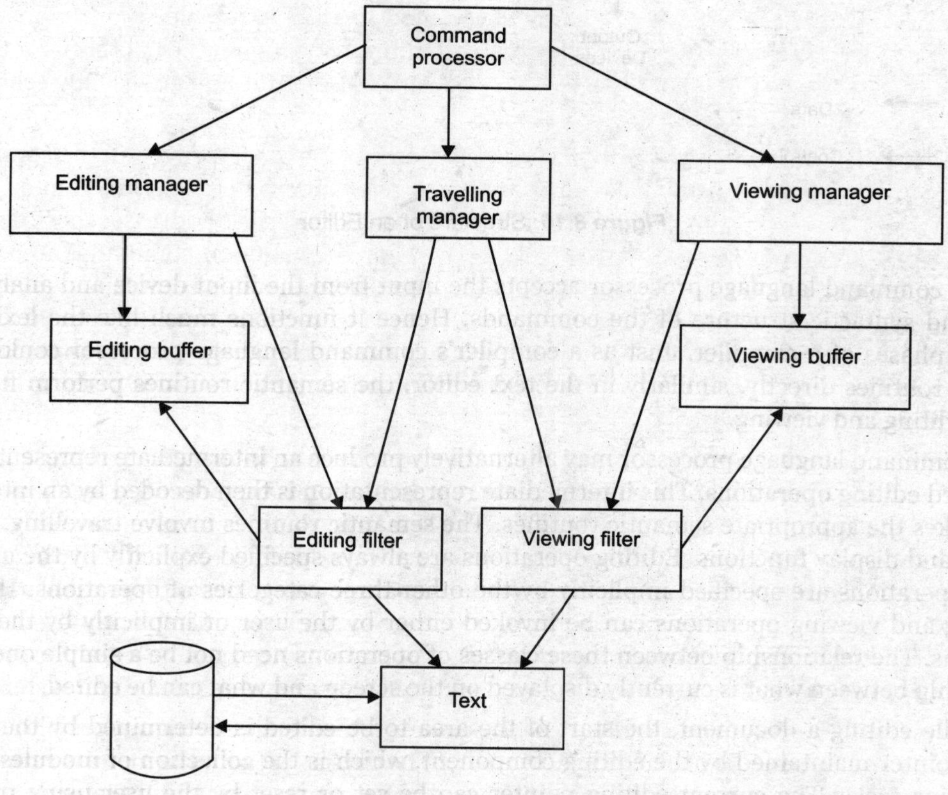

Figure 8.9: Design of an Editor

Most text editors have a structure similar to that shown in the figure 8.10, regardless of the particular features they offer and the computers on which they are implemented:

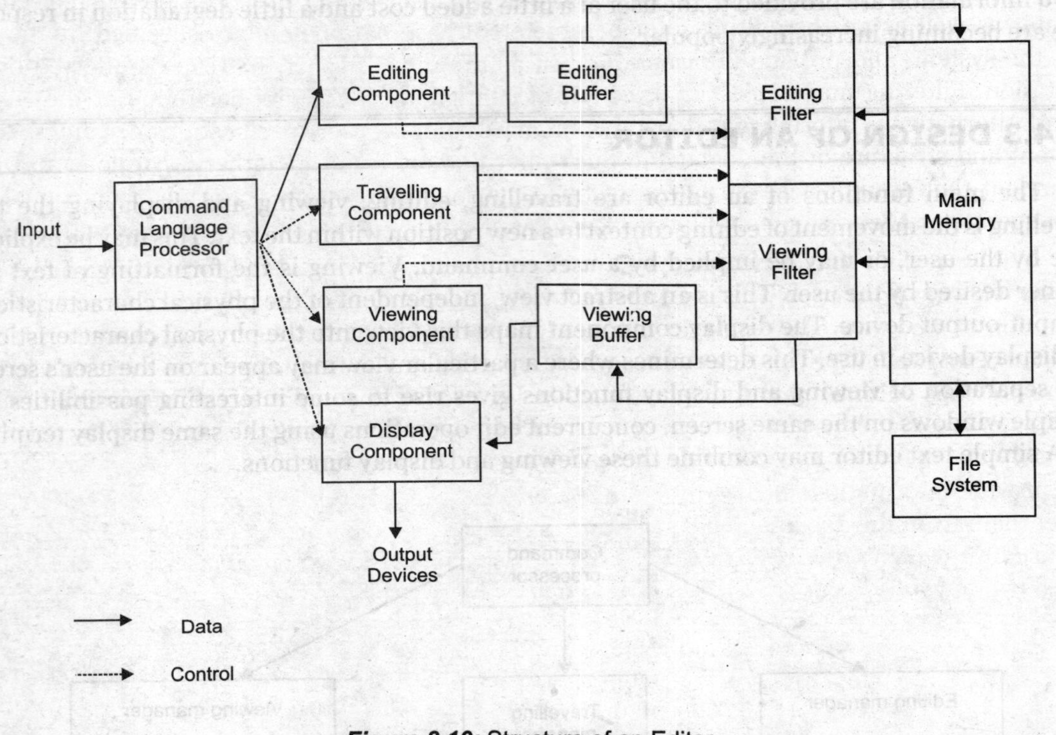

Figure 8.10: Structure of an Editor

The command language processor accepts the input from the input device and analyzes the tokens and syntactic structure of the commands. Hence it functions much like the lexical and syntactic phases of a compiler. Just as a compiler's command language processor could invoke semantic routines directly, similarly in the text editor, the semantic routines perform functions such as editing and viewing.

A command language processor may alternatively produce an intermediate representation of the desired editing operations. This intermediate representation is then decoded by an interpreter that invokes the appropriate semantic routines. The semantic routines involve travelling, editing, viewing, and display functions. Editing operations are always specified explicitly by the user, and display operations are specified implicitly by the other three categories of operations. However, travelling and viewing operations can be invoked either by the user or implicitly by the editing operations. The relationship between these classes of operations need not be a simple one-to-one relationship between what is currently displayed on the screen and what can be edited.

While editing a document, the start of the area to be edited is determined by the current editing pointer maintained by the editing component, which is the collection of modules dealing with editing tasks. The current editing pointer can be set or reset by the user using travelling commands, such as next paragraph and next screen, or implicitly by the system as a side effect of the previous editing operation, such as delete paragraph. The travelling component of the editor performs the setting of current editing and viewing pointers, and thus determines the point at which the viewing or editing filtering begins.

When an editing command is issued by the user, the editing component invokes the editing filter, which filters the document to generate a new editing buffer based on the current editing pointer as well as on the editing filter parameters. These parameters are specified by the user and the system, and provide information such as the range of text that can be affected by the operation. Filtering may consist of selection of contiguous characters beginning at the current point. Alternatively, filtering may depend upon mare complex user specifications pertaining to the content and structure of the document. Such filtering may result in gathering of portions of the document that are not necessarily contiguous. The semantic routines of the editing component then operate on the editing buffer, which is a filtered subset of the document data structure.

While viewing the document, the start of the area to be viewed is again determined by the current viewing pointer, which is maintained by the viewing component of the editor which is a collection of modules responsible for determining the next view. The current viewing pointer can be set or reset explicitly by the user with a travelling command or implicitly by the system as a result of the previous editing operation. When the display needs to be updated, the viewing component invokes the viewing filter, which filters the document to generate a new viewing buffer based on the current viewing filter parameters. These parameters can be issued by both the user and the system, and provide information such as the number of characters needed to fill the display, and how to select them from the document. This viewing buffer can then be passed to the display component of the editor, which produces a display by mapping the buffer to a rectangular subset of the screen called window.

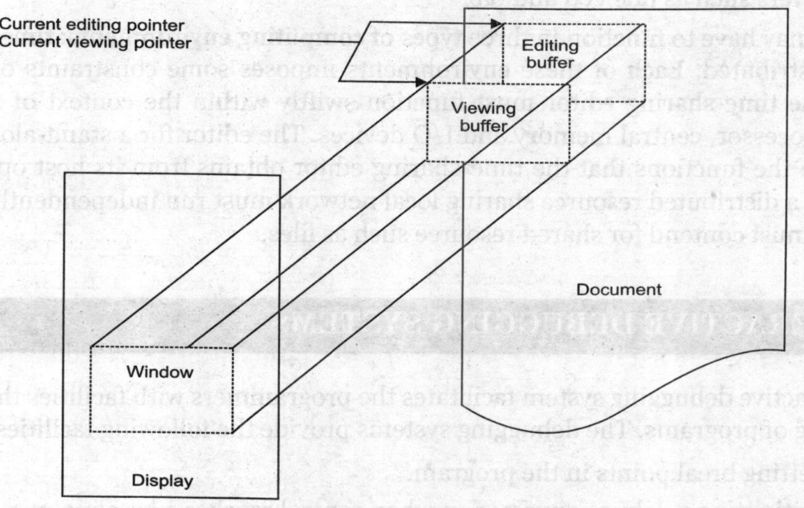

Figure 8.11: Editing and Viewing buffer

The editing and viewing buffers, while independent, can be related in many ways. In the simplest case, they can be identical in the sense that the user edits the text directly on the screen. On the other hand, they can be completely disjoint. The editing and viewing buffers can also partially overlap, or one may be completely contained in the other. In this case the editing filter creates an editing buffer that contains the document from the selected character to the end of the document. The viewing buffer contains the part of the document that is visible on the screen, only the last part of which is in the editing buffer.

Windows typically cover the entire screen or a rectangular portion of it. The mapping of viewing buffer to a window is accomplished by the following two components of the system:

1. The viewing component formulates an ideal view, often expressed in a device-independent intermediate representation. This view can be a very simple one consisting of a window's worth of text arranged so that the lines are not broken in the middle of words. At the other extreme, the idealized view may be a facsimile of a page of fully formatted and typeset text with equations, tables, and figures.
2. The display component takes the idealized view from the viewing component and maps it to a physical output device in the most efficient manner possible.

The components of the editor deal with a user document on two levels: in the main memory and in the disk file system. Loading an entire document into main memory may be infeasible, but if only a part of document is loaded editing might be unacceptably slow. In some systems, this problem is solved by mapping the entire file into virtual memory and letting the operating system perform demand paging. Another scheme can be to provide editor paging routines, which read one or more logical portions of a document into memory as needed.

Documents are often represented internally using an editor data structure which allows addition, deletion, and modification with minimum of input output and character movement. When stored on disk, the document may be represented in terms of this data structure or in an editor-independent general-purpose format, which might consist of character strings with embedded control characters such as linefeed and tab.

Editors may have to function in three types of computing environments: time sharing, stand-alone, and distributed. Each of these environments imposes some constraints on the design of the editor. The time-sharing editor must function swiftly within the context of the load on the computer's processor, central memory and I/O devices. The editor for a stand-alone system must have access to the functions that the time-sharing editor obtains from its host operating system. The editor for a distributed resource sharing local network must run independently on each user's machine and must contend for shared resource such as files.

8.15 INTERACTIVE DEBUGGING SYSTEMS

An interactive debugging system facilitates the programmers with facilities that aid in testing and debugging of programs. The debugging systems provide the following facilities:

1. Setting breakpoints in the program.
2. Initializing a debug conversation when control reaches a breakpoint.
3. Displaying the values of variables.
4. Assigning new values to the variables.
5. Testing user defined assertions and predicates involving program variables.

8.15.1 DEBUGGING FUNCTIONS AND CAPABILITIES

Debugging systems must have the following capabilities:

1. Execution Sequencing

The main requirement of a debugging system is the presence of a set of unit test functions that can be specified by the programmers. Some such functions deal with execution sequencing, i.e. the observation and control of the flow of program execution.

2. Breakpoints

The programmer should be able to define breakpoints which cause execution to be suspended when a specified point in a program is reached. After suspension of execution, various debugging commands can be used to analyze the progress of program and to diagnose the errors detected. Execution of the program can then be resumed.

3. Conditional Expressions

The programmer should also be able to define conditional expressions that are continually evaluated during the debugging session. Program execution gets suspended when any one of these conditions becomes true.

4. Tracing

Tracing can be used to track the flow of execution logic and data modifications. The control flow can be traced at different levels of detail, like procedure, branch, individual instruction, etc. The tracing can also be based on conditional expressions.

5. Traceback

Traceback shows the path by which the current statement was reached. It also shows which statements were responsible for modification of a given variable or parameter.

6. Program Display

A debugging system should also have good program-display capabilities. It must be possible to display the program being debugged, complete with statement numbers. The user should be able to control the level at which this display occurs. It is also useful to modify and incrementally recompile the program during debugging session. The system should save all the debugging specifications, so that the programmer does not need to reissue all of them all over again. It should also be possible to symbolically display or modify the contents of any of the variables and constants in the program, and then resume execution.

For providing these functions, the debugging system needs to consider the language in which the program is being written. Most user environments and application systems provide the use of several different programming languages. There is a need for a debugging tool which works in such multilingual situations. The commands which initiate actions and gather data about a program's execution should thus be common among all languages.

These requirements have a number of consequences for the debugger and other software. When the control is transferred to the debugger, the execution of the program being debugged is temporarily suspended. The debugger must then be able to determine the language in which the program is written and set its context accordingly. It should also be able to switch the context when a program written in some other language is called from the current program. Such changes should be informed to the used to avoid any confusion.

The notations for various functions of the debugger vary according to the language of program being debugged. However, the functions are accomplished in the similar manner for any programming language. For completion of the functions of debugger, it must have access to the information gathered by the language translator. However, the internal symbol dictionary formats vary according to the languages being translated. Future compilers and assemblers tend to work for proving a consistent interface with the debugging system.

Another issue in debugging is related to the display of source code during debugging session. There are two options for solving this issue. The language translator may provide the source code tagged in some standard way so that the debugger has a uniform method of navigation. Alternatively, the translator may supply an interface module that does the navigation and display in response to requests from debugger.

A debugging system should also be able to deal with optimized code. The code from the production environments is normally optimized, and handling of such an optimized code creates some problems for the debugger. Many optimizations involve the rearrangements of segments of code in the program. For example, invariant expressions can be removed from the loops, separate loops can be combined into single loop, a loop can be unrolled into a straight-line code, redundant expressions can be eliminated, blocks of code can be rearranged to eliminate unnecessary branch instructions, etc. All such optimizations create problems for the debugger. The user of the debugging system deals with the source program in its original form, before any optimization is performed. However, the rearrangement of code alters the execution sequence and may affect breakpoints, tracing, and even statement counts if entire statements are involved. In case of errors in the program, it may be difficult to trace the original location of the error.

Storage of variable also creates some problem with the working of the debugger. At the time of translation of a program, the compiler assigns a home location in main memory to each variable. However, the variables may sometimes be held in registers to improve the speed of access. Statements referring to such variables use the value stored in the registers instead of taking the value from the home location. There is no problem with such optimizations, until the user changes the value of the variable at its home location while debugging. This modified value may not be used by the program while the execution resumes.

Such type of optimized code requires much cooperation from the optimizing compiler while debugging. The compiler must retain information about any transformations applied on the program, and this information can be made available to the debugger to modify the request made by the user, and thereby perform the intended operation. For example, the effect of a breakpoint can be simulated on some eliminated statement, and a modified variable can be stored in the appropriate register as well as at the home location. However, some more complex optimizations cannot be handled so easily by the debugger.

8.15.2 RELATIONSHIP WITH OTHER PARTS OF THE SYSTEM

An interactive debugger needs to be related to the other parts of the system in the following ways:

1. Availability

An important requirement for the interactive debugger is that it is always available, and appears as a part of the run-time environment and an integral part of the system. While an error is detected, immediate debugging must be possible because of the difficulty in reproduction of program failure at some other time. Thus the debugger must communicate and cooperate with the other operating system components.

For example, debugger's availability at the production time is even more important than application development time because when an application fails during production run; work dependent on that application stops. Since the production environment is quite different from the test environment, many program failures cannot be repeated for debugging outside the production environment.

2. Consistency

The debugger must exist in a consistent manner with the security and integrity components of the system. It must not be possible for someone to use the debugger to access any code or data that would otherwise be not accessible to that individual. It must also not be possible to use the debugger to interfere with any aspect of system integrity. Use of the debugger must be subject to normal authorization mechanisms and must leave the usual audit trials.

3. Coordination

The debugger must coordinate its activities with the existing and future compilers and interpreters. The debugging facilities in existing languages should also continue to exist and be maintained. The requirements for a cross-language debugger assume that such a facility would be installed as an alternative to the individual language debuggers.

8.15.3 USER-INTERFACE CRITERIA

The debugger must be designed in an interactive manner so that the system gets accepted by its users. The most common complaint about debugging products is that they need to be learnt. The best way to overcome this difficulty is to have a system that is simple in its organization and familiar in its language. This simple organization contributes to ease of training and ease of use.

The full-screen displays and windowing systems should be used as much as possible. The main advantage of such systems is the great deal of information that can be displayed and can be changed easily and quickly. By using menus and full-screen editors, the user has much less information to enter and remember. Hence it contributes the friendliness of the debugging system.

Menus must have titles that clearly identify the task they help to perform. Directions must precede any choices that are available to the user. Indentation should be used to separate portions of the menus. It must be possible for the user to directly choose the menu that needs to be performed without having to retrace a hierarchy of menus.

The use of full-screen menus is desirable, but the debugging system must also support interactive users when a full-screen terminal device is not present. Every action that can be taken at a full-screen terminal must have equivalence with the linear debugging language also.

The commands must be simple, clear and logical. They should be as similar to the underlying programming language as possible. A consistent use of parameters should be possible with the commands. Parameters should be automatically checked for errors in such attributes as type and range of values. Default values should also be provided for most parameters and the users must be able to determine when such default values have been applied.

The command formats should be as flexible as possible. The command language should minimize the use of punctuation such as parenthesis, slashes, quotation marks, etc. Most of the information must be conveyed to the user by use of prompting techniques.

Any interactive system should have an online help facility with a list of commands that can assist the inexperienced and occasional users. For more advanced and professional users, help can provide multi-level and specific functions. If help facility is provided with menus, an explanatory text must be provided for all options available on the screen. Help should be accessible from any state of debugging session. As the situation gets difficult, the users are more likely to require such a facility.

The sequence of steps involved in dynamic debugging of a program as follows:

1. The user compiles the program under the debug option. The compiler produces two files: the compiled code file and the debug information file.
2. The user activates the debugging system and indicates the name of the program to be debugged. The debugging system opens the compiled code file and debug information file for the program.
3. The user specifies his debug requirements, i.e. a list of breakpoints and actions to be performed at those breakpoints. The debugger instruments the program, and builds a debug table containing the pairs (statement number, debug action).
4. The instrumental program gets control and executes up to a breakpoint.
5. A software interrupt is generated when the <SI_instrn> is executed. Control is given to the debugging system which consults the debug table and performs the debug actions specified for the breakpoint. A debug conversation is now opened during which the user may issue some debug commands or modify the breakpoints and debug actions associated with those breakpoints. After that control returns to the instrumented program.
6. Steps 4 and 5 are repeated until the end of debug session is reached.

8.15.4 DEBUG ASSERTIONS

A debug assertion is a relation between the values of program variables. An assertion can be associated with a program statement. The debugging system verifies the assertion when execution reaches that statement. Program execution continues if the assertion is fulfilled, else a debug conversation is opened. The user can now perform actions to locate the cause of the program malfunction. Use of such debug assertions eliminates the need to produce voluminous information for debugging purposes.

EXERCISES

1. What do you mean by file processing system?
2. What are the disadvantages of file processing system?
3. What do you mean by database?
4. What do you mean by database system?
5. What do you mean by database management system?
6. Explain the components of DBMS?
7. Explain the functions of DBMS?
8. Explain the various characteristics of DBMS?

9. Explain the advantages and disadvantages of DBMS?
10. Explain the three level architecture of DBMS?
11. What do you mean by data independence?
12. Explain the facilities of DBMS?
13. Explain the overall system structure of DBMS?
14. Explain the use of DBMS in detail?
15. Explain the examples for use of DBMS?
16. What do you mean by text editor?
17. Explain the concept of editing process?
18. Explain the types of text editors?
19. Explain the various user interfaces?
20. Explain the design of an editor?
21. What do you mean by interactive debugging system?
22. Explain the debugging functions and capabilities?
23. Explain the criteria of user interface?
24. What do you mean by debug assertion?

OTHER USEFUL BOOKS BY THE AUTHOR

INTERNET APPLICATIONS

Salient Features

- Explains the basics of internet and its working, internet service provider (ISP), internet addressing (DNS) and IP addresses).
- Presents the structure and working of an E-mail message.
- Deals with the file transfer protocol (FTP), Gopher, Telnet, newsgroup, WWW.
- Deals with Web designing using HTML and DHTML.
- Describes the components and working of search engines.
- Explains the concept of intranet and extranet.

ISBN : 9789381068397 | **Pages (Approx.) : 700**

COMPUTER FUNDAMENTALS AND PROGRAMMING IN C

Salient Features

- Explains the introduction to computers and operating system.
- Describes the concept of number systems, computer codes and arithmetic, logic gates and Boolean algebra.
- Deals with the building of different logic circuits.
- Introduces the concept of primary/secondary storage and Input/ Output devices.
- Complete introduction to C programming features are given in detail.
- Around 200 solved C programs and 100 objective type questions are included.

ISBN : 9789381068380 | **Pages (Approx.) : 750**

COMPUTER ORGANIZATION AND ARCHITECTURE

Salient Features

- Extensive coverage of electronic basics, architectural advancement of computer systems.
- Presents the analysis and design of sequential and combinational circuits.
- Demonstrates the concept of register transfer language and CPU organization.
- Provide the description for machine and assembly language.
- Covers the concept of control unit and I/O organization.
- Provides the conceptual detail of pipeline and vector processing.
- Covers basic memory concepts and other alternative architectures that have emerged in recent years.

ISBN : 9789381068311 | **Pages (Approx.) : 750**

Fundamentals of COMPUTERS, OPERATING SYSTEMS AND INFORMATION TECHNOLOGY

Salient Features

- Provides a comprehensive coverage of the subject.
- Explains the introduction to computers, computer generations, classification of computers and applications of computer in corporate environment.
- Presents the basic organization of a computer system and its internal working. It also explains different types of processors.
- Describes the concept of number systems, computer codes and arithmetic, logic gates and Boolean algebra.
- Deals with the building of different logic circuits like multiplexer, demultiplexer, encoder, decoder, generators, flip-flops, registers and counters etc.
- Introduces the concept of primary/secondary storage and Input/ Output devices.
- Describes the concept of operating system.

ISBN : 9789381068335 **Pages (Approx.) : 950**

KHANNA BOOK PUBLISHING EDITION

WINDOWS BASED COMPUTER COURSES

A VISUAL APPROACH

Ikvinderpal Singh • Baljinder Singh

COMPUTER FUNDAMENTALS AND IT • MS DOS • WINDOWS VISTA • MICROSOFT OFFICE

WINDOWS BASED COMPUTER COURSES
A Visual Approach

Salient Features

- Computer Fundamentals summarizes the simple concepts of computer technology related to hardware and software advancements and IT gives the close look to data communication, networking and internet.
- MS DOS is single user operating system tell the beginners about the various useful internal and external commands.
- Windows Vista is the latest and greatest in the illustrious line of Windows operating systems from Microsoft.
- Microsoft Office is essential software for the beginners for the creation of documents, spreadsheets, presentation and databases using of Microsoft Word, Microsoft Excel, Microsoft PowerPoint and Microsoft Access.

ISBN : 9789381068359 **Pages (Approx.) : 1000**

ELECTRONICS

ANALOG AND DIGITAL

R Singh • I Singh • B Singh

ELECTRONICS - ANALOG AND DIGITAL

Salient Features

- Extensive coverage of electronic basics, architectural advancement of analog and digital systems.
- Presents analysis of semiconductor diodes and transistors.
- Provides description of Includes various network theorems: Thevenin's and Norton's Theorems.
- Provides various number system and codes, logic gates, flip-flops, registers and counters.
- Gives detailed description of semiconductor memories and AD and DA converters.
- Presents complex topic of logic families includes TTL, CMOS, ECL, RTL, IIL, etc.

ISBN : 9789380016955 **Pages (Approx.) : 639**

SOLVED PROGRAMMING IN C

Salient Features

- Includes 1600 solved programs.
- Includes system-level programming.
- Numerous examples are included to illustrate concepts and techniques.
- Each and every program given in the book is perfectly working.

ISBN : 9789380016191 **Pages (Approx.) : 530**

SOLVED PROGRAMMING IN C++

Salient Features

- Includes 2200 solved programs.
- Includes system-level programming.
- Numerous examples are included to illustrate concepts and techniques.
- Each and every program given in the book is perfectly working.

ISBN : 9789380016184 **Pages (Approx.) : 880**

C++ AND DATA STRUCTURES

Salient Features

- Extensive coverage of C++ and Data structure basics, pictorial representation of each and every Data Structures is given in detail.
- Includes numerous illustrative examples to understand the topic easily.
- Demonstrates the implementation of algorithm in a good programming style.
- Around 300 solved C++ programs are included.
- Around 300 objective type questions are included.
- Around 200 algorithms are included.

ISBN : 9789380016795 **Pages (Approx.) : 1260**

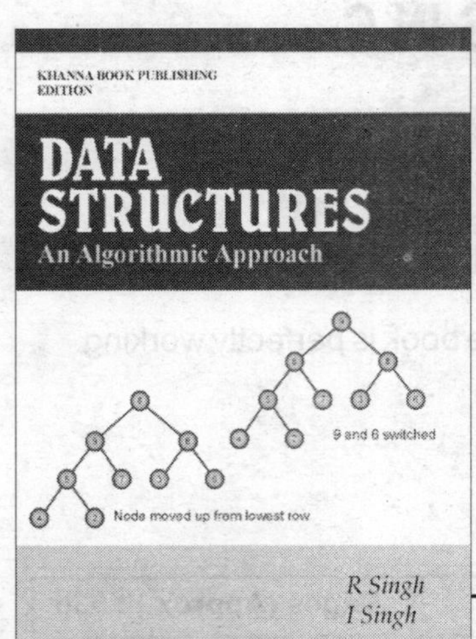

DATA STRUCTURES An Algorithmic Approach

Salient Features

- Extensive coverage of Data structure basics, pictorial representation of each and every Data Structures is given in detail.
- Demonstrates the development of algorithms in a lucid manner.
- Includes numerous illustrative examples to understand the topic easily.
- Demonstrates the implementation of algorithms in a good programming style.
- Objective-type questions have been provided.
- Around 300 algorithms are included.

ISBN : 9789380016702 **Pages (Approx.) : 680**

DATA STRUCTURES An Algorithmic Approach with C

Salient Features

- Extensive coverage of Data structure basics, pictorial representation of each and every Data Structures is given in detail.
- Demonstrates the development of algorithms in a lucid manner.
- Includes numerous illustrative examples to understand the tópic easily.
- Demonstrates the implementation of algorithms in a good programming style.
- Objective-type questions have been provided.
- Around 200 solved C programs and algorithms are included.

ISBN : 9789380016696 **Pages (Approx.) : 960**

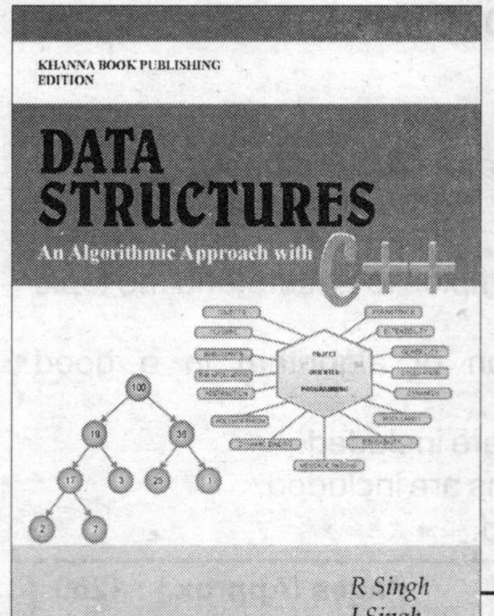

DATA STRUCTURES An Algorithmic Approach with C++

Salient Features

- Extensive coverage of Data structure basics, pictorial representation of each and every Data Structures is given in detail.
- Demonstrates the development of algorithms in a lucid manner.
- Includes numerous illustrative examples to understand the topic easily.
- Demonstrates the implementation of algorithms in a good programming style.
- Objective-type questions have been provided.
- Around 200 solved C++ programs and algorithms are included.

ISBN : 9789380016856 **Pages (Approx.) : 940**

EXPERT C PROGRAMMING

Salient Features

- Complete introduction to C programming features are given in detail.
- Includes numerous illustrative examples to understand the topic easily.
- Demonstrates every program in a good programming style.
- Around 300 solved C programs are included.
- Around 300 objective type questions are included.

ISBN : 9789380016764 **Pages (Approx.) : 718**

R Singh
I Singh

EXPERT C++ PROGRAMMING

Salient Features

- Complete introduction to C++ programming features are given in detail.
- Includes numerous illustrative examples to understand the topic easily.
- Demonstrates every program in a good programming style.
- Around 500 solved C++ programs are included.
- Around 300 objective type questions are included.

ISBN : 9789380016771 **Pages (Approx.) : 1105**

KHANNA BOOK PUBLISHING EDITION

Computer Oriented Numerical and Statistical Techniques

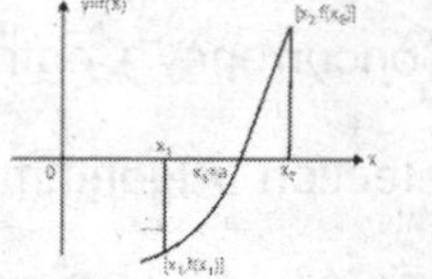

R Singh
I Singh

COMPUTER ORIENTED NUMERICAL AND STATISTICAL TECHNIQUES

Salient Features

- Extensive coverage of computer basics, numerical and error analysis and solution of transcendental and polynomial equations.
- Presents analysis of numerical differentiation, numerical integration, solution of ordinary and partial differential equations in enough detail.
- Provides description of interpolation formulae, and solution of linear equations.
- Detailed analysis of techniques like measures of central tendency and measure of dispersion.
- Covers all statistical techniques moment generating functions, Skewness and Kurtosis.
- Detailed analysis of Correlation, Linear, non-linear and multiple regression analysis.

ISBN : 9789380016788 **Pages (Approx.) : 860**

SOFT COMPUTING

Salient Features

- Detailed explanation of soft computing concepts.
- Extensive coverage of fundamental concepts of artificial neural network.
- Description on fuzzy logic techniques.
- Concepts of neuro-fuzzy and genetic algorithm are included.
- Detailed analysis of each and every type of probability.
- Demonstrates the concept of fuzzy logic and probability.

ISBN : 9789380016979 **Pages (Approx.) : 670**

FUZZY SYSTEMS

Salient Features

- Simple and easy language.
- Description on fuzzy logic techniques.
- Discusses on the introduction to fuzzy sets, fuzzy relations, fuzzy graphs and fuzzy rules.
- Concepts of neuro-fuzzy and genetic algorithm are included.
- Demonstrates the concept of fuzzy logic and probability, fuzzy implications and reasoning.
- Covers concept of fuzzy identification model, fuzzy databases, and fuzzy SQL.
- Fundamental ideas on Artificial intelligence and pattern recognition are discussed.

ISBN : 9789380016498 **Pages (Approx.) : 496**

DISTRIBUTED DATABASE SYSTEMS

Salient Features

- Description on Design and Architecture of Distributed Database Systems.
- Fundamental ideas on Query Processing and Optimization.
- Concepts of Distributed Transaction Management explain in a lucid manner.
- Detailed explanation of Distributed Concurrency Control and Reliability protocols are given.
- Gives the Distributed Deadlock Detection Algorithms and Recovery Schemes.
- Demonstrates the concept of Distributed Database Administration.

ISBN : 9789381068168 **Pages (Approx.) : 510**

MOBILE COMPUTING

Salient Features

- Detailed explanation of Cellular Telephone Systems, Satellite Communication, Wireless LANs and Bluetooth.
- Fundamental ideas on Modern Wireless Communication Systems: 2G/2.5G/3G/4G Wireless Networks and Standards.
- Detailed explanation of Multi Access Technique & Wireless Standards.
- Gives the Wireless LAN standards: IEEE 802.11 Concepts, Spread Spectrum Wireless LAN, Infrared Wireless LANs, Other Physical Layer Protocol (IEEE 802.11b, IEEE 802.11a).
- Extensive coverage of Wireless PAN (Bluetooth), HIPERLAN, Mobile Network Layer (Mobile IP), Mobile Transport Layer (Mobile TCP), Mobile Data network (GPRS).

ISBN : 9788190698236 **Pages (Approx.) : 470**

DIGITAL IMAGE PROCESSING

Salient Features

- Extensive coverage of fundamental concepts of Digital Image Processing.
- Gives mathematical development when it provides a guide to proper implementation of image signal representation.
- Covers all Image processing techniques.
- Presents hardware architecture for image processing.
- Covers all techniques of color image processing.
- Provides examples of simple applications.

ISBN : 9788190744214 **Pages (Approx.) : 530**

NETWORK OPERATING SYSTEMS

Salient Features

- Description of various Network Operating Systems: Windows 2000/2003/XP, Unix/Linux.
- Overview of Network Operating System and Some Special topics.
- Provides a detailed treatment of Disk Management and Servers.
- Covers the concept of User, Group and Computer Accounts
- Detailed explanation of the Managing active directory, Performance Monitoring and Security.

ISBN : 9788190744199 **Pages (Approx.) : 700**

Introduction to MICROPROCESSORS 8085 and 8086

Salient Features

- Extensive coverage of microprocessor basics, architectural advancement of microprocessor and typical microprocessor development schemes.
- Presents analysis of 8085 and 8086 microprocessor and its internal architecture, interfacing and programming in enough detail.
- Gives detailed description of peripheral interfacing devices includes 8237 DMA Controller, 8255 programmable peripheral interface, 8253/8254programmable timer/counter, 8259 programmable interrupt controller, 8251 USART and RS232C
- Covers addressing modes and interrupts of both 8085 and 8086 microprocessor in enough detail.
- Detailed analysis of Assembly language programming based on intel 8085/8086.

ISBN : 9789381068573 **Pages (Approx.) : 465**

NETWORK DESIGN AND PERFORMANCE ANALYSIS

Salient Features

- Discusses on the introduction to Requirements Analysis and Specifications.
- Detailed explanation of the Traffic Engineering & Capacity Planning.
- Covers the concept of Choosing Service Provider, Vendor and Service Levels.
- Design and Architecture of Access Network Design and Security.
- Detailed explanation of Documentation and Network Management.
- Demonstrates the concept of the Network Optimization.

ISBN : 9789381068410 **Pages (Approx.) : 320**

ARTIFICIAL NEURAL NETWORKS

Salient Features

- Extensive coverage of fundamental concepts of Artificial neural network.
- Presents architecture and algorithm of every net in enough detail.
- Provides examples of simple applications.
- Gives mathematical development when it provides a guide to proper implementation of net.
- Covers all supervised and unsupervised learning methods.

ISBN : 9788190698207 **Pages (Approx.) : 300**